Beginning EJB™ 3 Application Development

From Novice to Professional

Raghu R. Kodali and Jonathan Wetherbee
with Peter Zadrozny

Apress®

Beginning EJB™ 3 Application Development: From Novice to Professional

Copyright © 2006 by Raghu R. Kodali and Jonathan Wetherbee with Peter Zadrozny

ISBN-13 (pbk): 978-1-59059-671-5

ISBN-10 (pbk): 1-59059-671-4

ISBN-13 (electronic): 978-1-4302-0238-7

Printed and bound in the United States of America (POD)

Lead Editor: Steve Anglin
Technical Reviewer: Tom Marrs
Editorial Board: Steve Anglin, Ewan Buckingham, Gary Cornell, Jason Gilmore, Jonathan Gennick, Jonathan Hassell, James Huddleston, Chris Mills, Matthew Moodie, Dominic Shakeshaft, Jim Sumser, Keir Thomas, Matt Wade
Senior Project Manager: Sofia Marchant
Copy Edit Manager: Nicole LeClerc
Copy Editor: Damon Larson
Assistant Production Director: Kari Brooks-Copony
Production Editor: Kelly Winquist
Compositors: Dina Quan, Gina Rexrode
Proofreader: Linda Marousek
Indexer: Julie Grady
Artist: April Milne
Cover Designer: Kurt Krames
Manufacturing Director: Tom Debolski

Distributed to the book trade worldwide by Springer-Verlag New York, Inc., 233 Spring Street, 6th Floor, New York, NY 10013. Phone 1-800-SPRINGER, fax 201-348-4505, e-mail orders-ny@springer-sbm.com, or visit http://www.springeronline.com.

For information on translations, please contact Apress directly at 2855 Telegraph Avenue, Suite 600, Berkeley, CA 94705. Phone 510-549-5930, fax 510-549-5939, e-mail info@apress.com, or visit http://www.apress.com.

The source code for this book is available to readers at http://www.apress.com in the Source Code/ Download section. You will need to answer questions pertaining to this book in order to successfully download the code.

To my wife, Lakshmi, for her support and patience, and our two-year-old son, Yash, who is a big source of inspiration

—Raghu R. Kodali

To my wife, Laurel, and our young bear cubs, Nicholas, Patrick, and Jacob

—Jonathan Wetherbee

Contents at a Glance

Contents

█CHAPTER 4   Advanced Persistence Features 103

Foreword

EJB 3 is a very important milestone for the specification. Not only is it significantly easier to use, but also for the first time (in my opinion), the specification is now built around the proven needs of the development community, standardizing existing best practices instead of being the result of design by committee. The reader of this book is most likely a developer, so I will present some historical context of how EJB came to be and why it matters today, from the perspective of developers.

I speak at conferences fairly often, and at a certain point during a talk I will ask the audience how many have used EJB. Usually, 90 percent put up their hand. Then, I ask them, "How many of you have used EJB as distributed objects—meaning, where you have a separate physical tier for your business logic and a separate tier for your presentation (servlets/JSP) tier?" Usually only 15 percent of the 90 percent will put up their hand. These results have been consistent at conferences I've spoken at in North America, Europe, and Japan. The result still never ceases to amaze me, since the early days of EJB forced you to apply distributed semantics on your code, which is useful on large-scale multi–physical tier projects—but in fact, most of the EJB audience was using it as a local framework for their small-to-medium-sized web apps.

Why is this so? If you look at the wider context of the times (1999 to 2003), it starts to make sense. If you look at the core values that EJB 1+ proposed, you could boil them all down to three simple categories:

- *Framework benefits*: At the time, if you were doing any kind of web or enterprise development in Java, you were living in a proprietary, confusing world; or you were using nuts-and-bolts tools like RMI and servlets, and creating your own frameworks. Couple that with the fact that during this time, most software developers were new, attracted by the dot-com boom—the industry was just waiting to be given a standard, agreed-upon way to do enterprise development. EJB provided that—a standard framework for handling transactions, security, stateful components, object persistence, and so on. Having a standard framework solved a real and present need—since at the time there was no open source movement and there were no web frameworks.

- *Distribution benefits*: EJB standardized a programming model and platform for building business logic with distributed objects. Hot on the heels of RMI and CORBA, this too was needed. If you wanted to do distributed objects, EJB was the answer.

- *Component benefits*: This is where things got nutty. In my opinion, Sun was reacting to the success of the Visual Basic (VB) component market and dreamed of having a similarly active market in the area of Java business components. I remember the early days when documentation and marketing around EJB centered on component reuse. There were even attempts at building online marketplaces for EJB components. As a result, EJB gained a lot of weight in the APIs, deployment, and package semantics in order to have EJB components' binaries run consistently well across app servers.

In particular, the Java community was really interested in standards/solutions for persistence, as there were only a few solutions at the time for object persistence—and rolling your own O/R mapper is no easy task.

So that's where we came from. Now let's step forward to the EJB 2.1 time frame, for which we'll fast forward to circa late 2003/early 2004. When giving this talk at conferences, I then proceed to where the community is going, in terms of these three value propositions (this is before EJB 3 plans were unveiled):

- *Framework*: At this point, we had open source frameworks that provided transactionality, pooling, security, and all the other good programming model benefits of EJB—and they did it much more simply and way better. Tools like XDoclet and Spring, and methodologies such as AOP, were bringing all the framework benefits of EJB to lighter-weight environments. Most notably, entity beans were almost universally criticized as being poor as an O/R mapping solution (indeed, they were designed around persisting components, not objects), and Hibernate rose to the most popular O/R mapping solution in Java, making entity beans irrelevant.

- *Distribution*: RMI was no longer the de facto standard for remoting in Java; other open source APIs/protocols now existed. Also, SOA (service-oriented architecture) principles frowned on certain distribution cases in which remote objects may have been used. EJB 2.0's introduction of the local interfaces felt like a hack, which also must have further complicated the spec in many ways.

- *Components*: Who cares? The enterprise component market is dead. When Sun was eyeing the success of the VB market, they failed to notice that that marketplace consisted mostly of UI widgets and "utility"-type components that are reusable across projects. We did not see things like payroll classes or the notion of a "user" captured as a VB component. The fact is, business logic is generally not reusable across projects, and so all the weight added to EJB was not necessary. Binary compatibility between EJB JARs was also a feature that had not really been used. It was common to simply add the EJB source to your build and package it at build time for different application servers. If building reusable components was not an objective of the EJB specification team, perhaps we would have had something closer to EJB 3 back in 2001.

Now, bringing the survey question I started off with back into perspective, notice that the majority of people were *not* using EJB for its component or distribution benefits. The majority of people were using it for its framework benefits, and those benefits were better served by lightweight open source. In 2003, I think the only real value proposition EJB brought to the table was its use as a distributed object framework for real large-scale systems—where it was originally intended to be used to begin with. Thus, as I would tell the audience at the talk, "You've all misused EJB." The implication here being that the 15 percent who actually used EJB to distribute their business logic across physical tiers did not misuse it—they were already dealing with a situation in which they had decided that distribution was necessary and EJB certainly was the right technology choice for that.

So where are we today? EJB 3 has finally been rebuilt to be optimized for the 85 percent of the audience, based on best practices that had been established in the community by frameworks like Spring and Hibernate. Instead of a specification for building distributed, transactional, persistent components, we now have a specification for a powerful, easy-to-use, POJO-based framework providing transactions, security, O/R mapping, and distribution. The additions of basic interception, dependency injection, and annotation-driven configuration also bring to EJB 3 proven best practices that have become popular in the community over the last few years.

Things have gotten so much better that there will not be a new edition of my own book, *EJB Design Patterns*, which came out in 2002. For many of the patterns, there were workarounds to make EJB more usable for the 85 percent, and luckily those have all been addressed.

EJB 3 finally serves the needs of developers, and it is thus a great time to be reading this book.

Floyd Marinescu
Author, EJB Design Patterns
Cofounder and chief editor, InfoQ.com Enterprise Software Development Community
Creator, TheServerSide.com (J2EE community)

About the Authors

RAGHU R. KODALI is a consulting product manager and SOA evangelist for Oracle Fusion Middleware. A native of India, Raghu has worked in the software industry for over ten years as a developer, consultant, and presales engineer in emerging technologies. He is responsible for J2EE features, and has expertise in SOA technologies, web services, and application development frameworks. Raghu has been the lead product manager for EJB design-time features in Oracle JDeveloper since the EJB 1.1 specification. His current area of focus is evangelizing service-oriented infrastructure and implementing service-oriented applications.

Prior to his career in product management, Raghu held presales and marketing positions in Oracle Asia Pacific. Before joining Oracle, he worked as a software developer in Singapore. Raghu has spoken at many international conferences, including Oracle Open World, JavaOne, JavaZone, JAOO, Sun Technology Days, and EclipseWorld. He has also written numerous articles for many leading IT magazines, including *Java Developers Journal*, *Java Pro*, *SOA Web Services Journal*, *JavaWorld*, and *ODTUG Technical Journal*. Raghu holds a Master of Science degree in computer applications.

JONATHAN WETHERBEE is a consulting engineer and tech lead for EJB development tools on Oracle's JDeveloper IDE. He has over ten years of experience in development at Oracle, working on a variety of O/R mapping tools and holding responsibility for Oracle's core EJB toolset since EJB 1.1.

Prior to joining Oracle's development staff, Jonathan was a product manager for Oracle's CASE (computer-aided software engineering) tools. In 1999, he received a patent for his work on integrating relational databases in an object-oriented environment. Jonathan received a Bachelor of Science degree in cognitive science from Brown University.

PETER ZADROZNY brings over 20 years of experience to StrongMail Systems, where he serves as chief technology officer. Zadrozny joined StrongMail Systems from Oracle, where he was vice president and chief evangelist for Oracle Application Server. Previously, Zadrozny served as chief technologist of BEA Systems for Europe, the Middle East, and Africa—a role he held since launching WebLogic's operations in Europe in 1998. Prior to BEA, Zadrozny held executive and technical positions in many countries around the world for companies such as Macromedia, McKesson, Electronic Data Systems, Petróleos de Venezuela, and Sun Microsystems, for whom he started operations in Mexico.

Zadrozny authored *J2EE Performance Testing with BEA WebLogic Server*, coauthored *Professional J2EE Programming with BEA WebLogic Server*, and is the founding editor of *WebLogic Developer's Journal*. He has written numerous technical papers and articles, and is a frequent speaker on technology issues around the world. Zadrozny holds a degree in computer engineering from Universidad Simón Bolivar in Caracas, Venezuela.

About the Technical Reviewer

TOM MARRS is a principal architect with CIBER, where he specializes in SOA. He designs and implements mission-critical business applications using the latest SOA, J2EE, and open source technologies; he also provides architecture evaluation and developer training and mentoring services.

Tom is a coauthor of *JBoss at Work: A Practical Guide*, he speaks regularly at software conferences, and he reviews best-selling technical books for major publishers. An active participant in the local technical community, Tom recently founded the Denver JBoss Users Group (www.denverjbug.org) and has served as president of the Denver Java Users Group (www.denverjug.org).

Acknowledgments

While only few names are mentioned here, I must say that I've been lucky enough to have a strong team with representation from friends, family, colleagues at work, and special people from the publishing house. Without this swat team, we would still only be thinking about the book.

I would like to thank my friend Peter Zadrozny, who encouraged and convinced me that I could do this book, and who introduced me to Apress. Without his experience, craft, and guidance, this book would not have been possible.

Thanks to Sofia Marchant, Damon Larson, and Kelly Winquist at Apress, for being patient and helping us through the process of putting our chapters together and making it all happen.

It is tough to work on a book when you have a day job to take care of. Thanks to my manager Roel Stalman for encouraging me to take on this book project and keeping keen interest.

I would also like to thank Floyd Marinescu for agreeing to write the foreword for this book, and for highlighting facts about EJB technology based on his experiences.

A special thanks goes to my friend Sri Rajan, who is inspiring as always. Sri helped us to work on the performance part of the book by providing the hardware and letting us use it for a few months.

To my dad, Chandra Sekhara Kodali, who has always taught me that patience and perseverance will always pay off in the long run, and who has always encouraged me to reach new heights.

To my wife, Lakshmi, and our two-year-old son, Yash, for patiently waiting for me during my long hours of writing this book.

Raghu R. Kodali

This book is borne of the efforts and insights of many people who provided both technical input and pure inspiration throughout its life. In particular, I would like to thank John Bracken and Doug Clarke for many design meetings and discussions of EJB and JPA best practices. Chris Carter and Michel Trudeau supported me on my quest, even when it took my attentions away from JDeveloper. They knew that the insights gained from researching, testing, and writing this book would surely pay dividends back to the team. Raghu Kodali has shown constant grace, patience, and wisdom during our numerous conversations and dealings with book matters. Dave Clark offered me an excellent forum to test out my knowledge and garner feedback. Steve Anglin, Sofia Marchant,

Damon Larson, Kelly Winquist, and the excellent editorial and publication teams at Apress proved they are truly experts in their domain.

With the technical help from all of the above, writing a book on this topic that I love dearly would have been a mere marathon, if it weren't for all of the diversions of everyday life! For these welcome distractions, I have the following people to thank: David Silver provided much-needed head clearings in the middle of the grind. Our conversations, punctuated by long runs in the park, were pure soul satisfaction. Adam Beyda has given me a lifetime of insight and perspective on what really matters. Moby Coquillard's practical guidance and navigation through the psychological waters of writing a book was essential.

To my parents, Andrea and Peter Wetherbee, who have provided love and encouragement, and a constant reminder that you are my biggest fans. And Bob and Holly Spain, I could not have done it if you had not graciously taken the kids for so many weekends, and freed me up to do my research and writing.

In the end, the primary motivation for punching this thing through came from my desire to spend time again with my wife, Laurel, and our boys. This has been the busiest year we've ever been through together, and there is no doubt—we have been truly blessed with interesting times!

Jonathan Wetherbee

CHAPTER 1

■ ■ ■

Introduction to the EJB 3 Architecture

When we set out to write this book, our goal was to present Enterprise JavaBeans (EJB) 3 to developers, with a keen eye to how this technology can be used in everyday, real-world applications. EJB 3 is a deep spec, spanning three documents, and it addresses the needs of beginning developers and hardcore power users alike. That's a large audience to satisfy, and as a reference guide, the EJB 3 spec documents cover it well. In writing a book about how to *use* EJB 3, we had to narrow our audience; but we believe that we've written a book that will serve the needs of a majority of Java EE developers.

This book is targeted at developers who are experienced with Java, have built single- or multi-tier applications using earlier versions of EJB or other technologies, and are ready to take on the challenges (and rewards) of building enterprise applications using cutting-edge technology. Recognizing that a combined 800 pages of reference material can be daunting, we provide an on-ramp for developers, unfolding EJB 3 one section at a time, and giving you the information and code examples you need to roll up your sleeves and get to work.

As each chapter unfolds, you will not only learn about a new area of the spec, but you will learn through specific examples how to apply it to your own applications. Many of these samples come directly from the comprehensive, end-to-end, Java EE Enterprise Wines Online application covered in Chapters 7 and 12, so you can see how they fit into a bigger picture. You are encouraged to take these examples and run with them. Try them out in your favorite IDE or development environment, and change them around and try new things. EJB 3—and particularly the new out-of-the-container persistence features that let you use entities (formerly, entity beans) outside the EJB container—gives you a lot to work with. Once you're comfortable with the basics of building, deploying, and testing, you'll find that EJB 3 components are not only powerful, but easy to build and use.

Together, we the authors have built a number of applications using EJB 3 in concert with other players in the Java EE stack, and we have attempted to capture in this book advice about the practical patterns we have learned, the strategies we have found successful, and some pitfalls to avoid. Most chapters in this book are dedicated to exploring specific areas of EJB 3, but we have also included chapters on migrating from EJB 2.x to 3, gauging the performance of your EJB 3 applications, and deploying to the Java EE app server of your choice. We've also included an introductory "Getting Started" section at the end of this chapter to get you set up to run the many useful sample applications sprinkled throughout the book.

We hope this book will serve not only as a reference guide for information on EJB 3, but also as a how-to guide and repository of practical examples that you can refer back to as you build your own applications. Enjoy!

An Introduction to EJB

Around 1996, as Java was becoming bolstered by the emergence of technologies (such as RMI and JTA) that addressed the needs of large-scale applications, the need arose for a business component framework that could unify these technologies and incorporate them under a standard development model. EJB was born to fill this need. Over the past 10 years, it has evolved to encompass numerous features (while ejecting others) and has matured into a robust and standard framework for deploying and executing business components in a distributed, multiuser environment.

What Is EJB?

EJB 3 is defined by JSR 220: Enterprise JavaBeans 3. Whereas the previous versions of EJB were captured in a single document, this JSR now spans three documents (listed following). The first document provides a synthesis of the high-level features of the new release, and focuses on the new simplified development model for building EJB components. The last two documents address the technical details of the core enterprise bean framework and the persistence model, respectively.

- *EJB 3 Simplified API* gives a high-level overview of the new EJB 3 development model.

- *EJB Core Contracts and Requirements* focuses on session and message-driven beans.

- *Java Persistence API* addresses entities and the persistence framework.

What emerges from these three documents that comprise the EJB 3 spec is both a component model and a framework.

The EJB Component Model

As a component model, EJB defines three object types that developers may build and customize, as follows:

- *Session beans* perform business service operations and orchestrate transaction and access control behavior.

- *Message-driven beans* (MDBs) are invoked asynchronously in response to external events, through association with a messaging queue or topic.

- *Entities* are objects that have unique identities and represent persistent business data.

Session and message-driven beans are EJBs, and are often referred to collectively as enterprise beans. In earlier versions of EJB, entities were referred to as entity beans, and also fell into this category. In EJB 3, however, entities are managed by a persistence provider and not the EJB container, and are no longer considered true enterprise beans.

The EJB Framework

The EJB framework provides the supporting environment in which EJB components operate. This includes container transaction and security services, pooling and caching of resources, component life cycle services, concurrency support, and more—all of which we will explore throughout this book. EJB components specify the details of how they wish to interact with their supporting container using EJB-specific metadata that is either captured by the container and applied to the EJB's behavior at run time, or interpreted at the time an EJB component is deployed to an EJB container and used to construct wrapping.

Core Features of EJB

Throughout its life, EJB has maintained its focus on delivering components imbued with a handful of core features.

Declarative Metadata

One of the hallmarks of the EJB component model is the ability for developers to specify the behavior of both enterprise beans and entities *declaratively* (as opposed to *program-matically*), using their choice of JDK 5.0 annotations and/or XML descriptors. This greatly simplifies the development process, since much customization can be added to a bean without having to write any logic in Java. To accommodate developer preference and application flexibility, EJB 3 offers developers their choice of both annotations and XML, with the ability to use both methods simultaneously within the same EJB or entity, for specifying behavior in metadata. In cases in which the same piece of metadata is defined both in an annotation and in XML, the XML declaration takes precedence in resolving the conflict. Additional benefits of this approach are explored later, in the "EJB 3 Simplified Development Model" section of this chapter.

Configuration by Exception

Coupled with the ability to specify behavior declaratively is the strong use of intelligent defaults in EJB 3. Much behavior is attached automatically to an EJB or entity without it being declared explicitly, such as the transactional behavior of session bean methods, and the names of the table and columns that persist an entity and its public properties. An annotation, or its counterpart in XML, needs to be explicitly specified only when non-default behavior is desired. In the most common cases, in which default behavior is desired, this practice leads to very sparse, clean code. This development model is known as *configuration by exception,* because only in exceptional (non-default) cases is it necessary to explicitly configure the behavior of the bean.

Scalability

Large-scale applications demand the ability to scale well as the client load increases. The EJB server employs resource pooling to maximize object reuse, utilizes a persistence cache to avoid repeatedly querying or creating the same objects, and implements an optimistic locking strategy in the middle tier to reduce load on the relational database management system (RDBMS) and avoid concurrency locking issues.

Transactionality

The Java Transaction API (JTA) defines a standard API for distributed transactions, and the EJB server acts as a JTA transaction manager to EJBs. Since its inception, the EJB spec has defined a standard model for declaratively specifying container-managed transactional behavior on enterprise beans.

Multiuser Security

Method-level access control may be specified declaratively on EJBs, enforcing user- and role-level privileges defined by application server administrators.

Portability

Spec-compliant enterprise beans are deployable to any application server that implements EJB, at least in theory. In practice (and this was particularly true of releases prior to EJB 3), vendors provided their own metadata definitions that enterprise bean developers grew to rely upon, locking them into a particular vendor's implementation. As EJB has matured, it has grown to incorporate many of these formerly platform-specific features, so that EJBs implemented today are far more portable than in the past.

Reusability

EJBs are loosely coupled components. An EJB may be reused and packaged into multiple applications, though it must be bundled with, or have access to, other dependent EJBs.

Persistence

Entity beans—in EJB 3 replaced by plain old Java object (POJO) classes known simply as entities—represent persistent domain objects with unique identities. An entity class corresponds to a database table, and each entity instance is represented by a single row in that table.

Progression of the EJB Spec

Each time a new version of the EJB spec was introduced, it included new, significant features to address popular demand and adopt emerging technologies. Here is a brief summary of how the EJB spec has progressed since its birth in 1996, or more importantly, since its first commercial implementations in 1998.

EJB 1.0

The initial release, 1.0, began with support for stateful and stateless service objects, called session beans, and optional support for persistent domain objects, called entity beans. For portability, EJBs were made accessible through a special remote interface that offered portability and remotability, but incurred the overhead of a remoting infrastructure and pass-by-value semantics.

EJB 1.1

The follow-up release, 1.1, mandated support among vendors for entity beans, and introduced the XML deployment descriptor to replace storing metadata in a special serialized class file.

EJB 2.0

EJB 2.0 addressed the overhead and pass-by-value shortcomings of remote interfaces by introducing the local interface. Only clients running inside the J2EE container could access an EJB through its local interface—but pass-by-reference method calls allowed for more efficient interchanges between components. Also introduced was a new type of EJB, the message-driven bean (MDB), which could participate in asynchronous messaging systems. Entity beans gained support for container-managed relationships (CMRs), allowing bean developers to declaratively specify persistent relationships between entity beans that were managed by the EJB container. Also, Enterprise JavaBeans Query Language (EJB QL) was introduced, which gave the ability to query entity bean instances using a language that resembled SQL.

EJB 2.1

EJB 2.1 added support for Web Services, allowing a session bean to expose an endpoint interface, and a timer service that allowed EJBs to be invoked at designated times or intervals. EJB 2.1 also provided expanded EJB QL functions, and an XML schema was introduced as a replacement for the DTD that defined the `ejb-jar.xml` deployment descriptor.

EJB 3

For EJB 3, the most significant change is that entity beans have been replaced by POJOs (plain old Java objects)—referred to now as entities—that can be run outside an EJB container, and so require no special interfaces or EJB-specific code in the entity class itself. Session beans no longer require home or EJB-specific component interfaces, although they continue to logically support both remotable and non-remotable (ordinary) interfaces. Both of these changes, along with many others, are consistent with the new design philosophy of EJB 3, centered on a simplified development model.

EJB 3 Simplified Development Model

This latest revision of the EJB specification, EJB 3, is a significant departure from earlier releases. The architects of EJB 3 set out to redesign the development experience, to introduce a far simplified development model that would reduce the complexity of the enterprise beans themselves, and at the same time incorporate many of the ideas found in peer technologies. The consensus is in: the spec has been widely hailed as having achieved these goals, and in so doing has overcome many of the problems that prevented earlier versions of EJB from becoming widely adopted.

XML and Annotations

If you are familiar with earlier versions of EJB, one of the first things you will notice in EJB 3 is that it is no longer necessary to capture EJB metadata in a deployment descriptor. EJB 3 lets you store your EJB metadata inside your bean source using JDK 5.0 annotations. This isn't to say that XML deployment descriptors have gone away; they are still alive and well, and are preferred by many developers over annotations. Using XML decouples the Java source from the EJB metadata, allowing the same entity or enterprise bean classes to be used in different contexts, where the context-specific information is captured in the XML and doesn't "pollute" the bean class.

Many users will prefer to use annotations, though—and to avoid wading into a religious war (vocal proponents on both sides abound), we suggest you choose for yourself. A simple rule we follow is this: if we need to decouple our entity and bean classes from their EJB 3 metadata, as when we want to use the same entity classes with two different entity inheritance strategies, we put our metadata in XML. Otherwise, we stick with annotations. And don't forget, you can always mix and match, relying on the firm policy that whenever metadata is specified for an element using both XML and annotations, the XML always wins. This allows any role (see the "EJB Roles" section later in the chapter) downstream of the bean developer to override metadata settings without having to update the Java source, since overrides can be applied exclusively to the XML descriptors.

Note A more advanced strategy that we also recommend is to use annotations only when defining behavior on an enterprise bean or an entity that is truly integral to its definition, such as the relationship type of an entity relationship field, or the transactional requirements of a method on a session bean. Anything that could reasonably be overridden, such as the name of the table that an entity maps to, or the details of a value generator used for populating the primary key on an entity, would go in the XML descriptor, where it can be specified at deploy time by an application assembler, perhaps in consultation with a database administrator. While there is no harm in specifying default values using annotations in the Java source file, this approach recognizes the difference between firm metadata that ought not to be modified, and loose metadata that may be freely modified without changing the behavior of the enterprise bean or entity.

Dependency Injection

After an EJB is instantiated inside the Java EE container, but before it is handed out to a client, the container may initialize property data on the instance according to rules defined for that enterprise bean. This feature is called dependency injection, and was popularized by the Spring Framework. Unlike Spring, however, EJB allows this information to be specified not only in XML, but also using JDK 5.0 annotations on the EJB itself.

░Note Injection uses a "push" model to push data out to the bean, and occurs regardless of whether the bean actually uses the data. If there is a chance that the data will not be used, the bean may elect to avoid incurring the cost of the resource derivation by performing a Java Naming and Directory Interface (JNDI) lookup in Java code to "pull" the data only if it is actually (or likely to be) used.

Common examples of dependency injection use are as follows:

- Injecting an `EntityManager` into a session bean for interacting with entities in a persistence unit

- Injecting a `UserTransaction` into a session bean that manages its transaction demarcation

Interceptors: Callback Methods

Both enterprise beans and entities may designate some of their methods, or methods on separate classes, to be called when certain life cycle events occur. For instance, a session bean may indicate that a certain method should be called after the bean has been instantiated, but before it has been handed off to a client. This method may initialize state information on the bean, or look up resources using JNDI, or any other action it wishes, provided that it does not require a transactional context. Such callback methods are called interceptors, and allow bean developers to participate programmatically in the interaction between an enterprise bean, or an entity, and its container.

POJO Implementation

EJB 3 has taken great strides to eliminate the trappings that beset enterprise bean classes and their required interfaces in earlier EJB releases. Similar to complaints over having to define XML metadata to specify even the most basic bean behavior, developers found it burdensome to have to write custom interfaces to handle an enterprise bean's factory support, and inconvenient to require a session bean's interfaces to extend EJB-specific interfaces. All these limitations have been addressed in EJB 3.

Home methods are no longer mandated, although they're still supported. For session beans and MDBs, a default constructor replaces the no-argument `ejbCreate()` method required by earlier EJB specs.

For entities, the `Home` interface is replaced by an `EntityManager` instance that serves as a single-instance factory for managing entity life cycle operations, including query execution.

Intelligent Use of Defaults

An excellent example of how EJB 3 simplifies the development process is its leveraging of default, assumed values to provide rich behavior with no coding or declarative metadata required. For instance, by simply marking a POJO with the @Entity annotation, all of its public properties automatically become persistent fields, and the table and column names take on derived values that match the entity and field names. An annotation or XML element is only required when overriding the default behavior of a particular area. Only when the table name does not match the entity name is the @Table annotation required. Great care has been taken to ensure that the default values match the most common usages, so that any given annotation is not required most of the time—leading to leaner, more clutter-free code.

> **Note** One consequence of relying on default behavior is that the class does not describe its full behavior anywhere, so you need to have a good understanding of the default behavior that is being applied. IDEs can be useful in deriving and displaying the enterprise bean or entity with its fully defaulted values explicitly shown.

Distributed Computing Model

Essential to any enterprise application is the ability to execute tasks and run components in separate Java threads or processes. Through the RMI-based remoting services, clients in an application client tier may access EJBs running in an application server anywhere on the network. The pass-by-value behavior of remote interface methods provides a coarse-grained model designed to reduce network traffic between clients and servers that are loosely connected to each other.

EJB Roles

The EJB spec defines seven roles for individuals involved in the different stages of defining an enterprise bean or entity, or in providing services and API implementation to enterprise beans. This book is targeted at the three roles involved in defining enterprise beans and their associated metadata. In practice, one or more of these roles may be performed by the same individual, and certain tasks may be performed by one role and overridden by another; but it is useful to understand the logical partitioning of tasks in the EJB development process. We will refer to these roles in various sections throughout the book.

The Enterprise Bean Provider

The Enterprise Bean Provider, also known as the Bean Provider, has the responsibility of defining and implementing the business logic and structure of an enterprise bean. This includes defining the Java class, implementing service methods, specifying transactional and security information declaratively on the bean and its methods, injection or lookup of required resources, and anything else that can be applied to the enterprise bean class.

Applied to entities, the Bean Provider defines the persistent structure of the entity and its relationships with other entities. The provider may define mapping and primary key–generation behavior, but this role is generally limited to defining the logical dependencies and structure of the entity.

The Application Assembler

The Application Assembler combines EJBs into EJB modules and entities into persistence archives, and then combines these modules together with other Java EE modules to produce an application. This task requires resolving references between enterprise beans and entities. The Application Assembler must work with the interfaces and metadata defined for the EJB and entity components, but needs not be familiar with the implementation details.

The Deployer

The Deployer takes an application that has been assembled by the Application Assembler and deploys it to a particular EJB container. The Deployer must resolve all external dependencies defined by the EJB component, mapping them to concrete resources installed in the application server environment. In the case of entities, the Deployer may provide or override the details of the live database objects that the entities will map to.

How This Book Is Organized

To orient you to the structure of the remainder of this book, here is a brief summary of each chapter. There is no requirement that you read these chapters in order. Each one is coupled to example programs that may be run independently of each other. Topics are introduced progressively, however, and so if you find a reference in one chapter to a term or concept that is not defined in that chapter, chances are it was defined in an earlier chapter of the book.

Chapter 1: Introduction to the EJB 3 Architecture

This chapter opens by introducing the book and offering an orientation to EJB. This orientation covers the EJB framework and component model, the core features of EJB, the history of EJB, the EJB 3 simplified development model, and the EJB distributed computing model. This chapter concludes with a "Getting Started" section to help you install the GlassFish Java EE reference implementation and run the sample applications provided with this book.

Chapter 2: EJB 3 Session Beans

Chapter 2 explores EJB's primary service object, the session bean. Session beans are examined in their many roles: as entity facades, as service components both with and without state, as timer-driven objects, and as the primary orchestrators of transaction and security services.

Chapter 3: Entities and the Java Persistence API

The new Java Persistence API (JPA) is introduced, along with the various persistence services that are available to support entities both within a Java EE container and outside of one. This chapter covers basic O/R mappings and introduces the Java Persistence Query Language, or JPQL.

Chapter 4: Advanced Persistence Features

Delving into more advanced persistence concepts, this chapter describes the new support offered in the JPA for mapping entity inheritance hierarchies. Examples of the three supported inheritance mapping strategies identify the strengths and weaknesses of each approach, to help you decide which one best suits the particular needs of your application. This chapter also covers the ID (primary key) generators introduced in the JPA, for autopopulating ID values using a database sequence or table.

Chapter 5: EJB 3 Message-Driven Beans

This chapter describes how you can use MDBs to add asynchronous, event-driven behavior to your application. JMS, Java's messaging API, is explained and demonstrated in this chapter's code examples.

Chapter 6: EJB 3 and Web Services

Session beans provide an excellent implementation for Web Services, and this chapter explores EJB's support for this fine marriage of technologies.

Chapter 7: Integrating Session Beans, Entities, Message-Driven Beans, and Web Services

After covering all the different component model types individually, Chapter 7 brings them together into an integrated Java EE application. We think you will find it particularly useful to see how everything fits together to produce a running application.

Chapter 8: Transaction Support in EJB 3

EJB offers rich transaction service support, and makes it easy for Bean Providers to declaratively specify custom container-provided transactional behavior on an enterprise bean. EJB also allows enterprise beans to opt out of this model, and control their own transaction demarcation behavior. This chapter applies two alternative transactional models to a single logical scenario for exploring the pros and cons of each approach.

Chapter 9: EJB 3 Performance and Testing

This chapter provides an invaluable look at how to gauge the performance of your EJB components, to help you decide which of the many options EJB offers is right for your application. In addition to explaining how to set up performance tests, we present some performance test cases that we have run, complete with our assessments of the results.

Chapter 10: Migrating EJB 2.x Applications to EJB 3

If you have an existing EJB 2.0 or 2.1 application, chances are you will want to migrate it to EJB 3, either to leverage the performance benefits of the new persistence framework or to take advantage of the simplified development experience. This chapter walks you through the many steps you must take when migrating EJBs and EJB clients to 3, and provides an example migration case.

Chapter 11: EJB 3 Deployment

Assembly and deployment are rolled into this chapter, as we cover the tasks required of the Application Assembler and Deployer roles. This chapter discusses packaging EJB and persistence modules, assembling modules in different ways into an enterprise archive (EAR) file, resolving references between modules and between EJBs packaged into different modules, and binding resource requirements to concrete resources installed in the target application server environment.

Chapter 12: EJB 3 Client Applications

In this chapter, we walk you through application architectures and different programming models that you can use to build applications, including the pros and cons of each approach. Once we have done that, we settle on one application architecture—developing web applications using JavaServer Faces (JSF) technology. We then drill down into the JSF architecture and concepts, and focus on integrating JSF user interface components and the JSF navigation model with the EJB 3 back-end application that we developed in Chapter 7.

Finally, we also explain how to use a lightweight application client container to execute your session beans in a pure Java SE environment. This lightweight container provides EJBs that execute in its environment with some of the services (such as container injection) that are offered by a true EJB container.

Getting Started

This section of the chapter will help you get ready with all the required software after installation and configuration, and work with the samples in the following chapters. At the time of writing this book, the EJB 3 specification had been going through rapid changes. No implementations were fully compliant with the final version of the specification. Oracle Application Server and JBoss had early implementations of the specifications that allowed the developer community to get hands-on experience with draft specifications.

GlassFish is an open source application server that implements the newest features in the Java EE 5 platform. GlassFish is the reference implementation for all the specifications in the Java EE 5 platform, including the EJB 3 specification.

Oracle provided the reference implementation for the JPA part of the EJB 3 specification by donating the code from the popular object/relational framework Oracle TopLink. JPA and EJB 3 implementation in GlassFish were evolving as we were writing this book. We decided to base the samples in this book on the GlassFish application server, as it is the reference implementation for Java EE 5, and we weren't sure when other vendors and open source containers would be able to roll out production class application servers that have support for the final specification of EJB 3. The book also makes heavy use of other Java EE 5 specifications, such as JAX-WS 2.0 and JSF 2.0, and many new features of the Java EE 5 platform, such as dependency injection in web and application client containers. As of this writing, there were no other open source or vendor containers that supported other Java EE 5.0 specifications required to run the samples in the book.

Due to the availability of Windows XP machines, we use Windows XP to run the GlassFish application server and the samples in this book. By no means are the samples or code in this book operating system specific, however. With some minor tweaks to the environment settings, you will be able to run the samples and the GlassFish application server in other operating systems (such as Linux) as well.

■**Note** You can find more details on the GlassFish application server at the following web site, which also contains a comprehensive FAQ: https://glassfish.dev.java.net/public/faq/GF_FAQ_2.html.

The remaining sections of this chapter will cover the following:

- Prerequisites for installing the GlassFish application server

- Installing the GlassFish application server

- Environment variables setup

- Starting and testing the GlassFish installation

Even if you are already familiar with the GlassFish application server and have the environment set up, we recommend that you read through the following sections, as running the sample code in the rest of the chapters depends on this setup being done correctly.

Prerequisites for Installing the GlassFish Application Server

Installing the GlassFish application server is pretty straightforward. You need to make sure that the machine is installed and configured with Java 2 Standard Edition (J2SE) version 5, and Apache Ant version 1.6.2. Ant is included with GlassFish; you can either use it or configure the environment properties to use another installation. The GlassFish project recommends that you use the Ant, which is bundled with its install.

To be certain which version of the JDK is installed on your machine, open a command prompt window and enter the following command:

```
C:\>java -version
```

This command will print out the JDK version that is installed on the machine and configured in the environment variables (see Figure 1-1). You should have a JDK version of 1.5.0 or higher.

Note We haven't tested the setup using the Java SE 6.0 (Mustang) beta version.

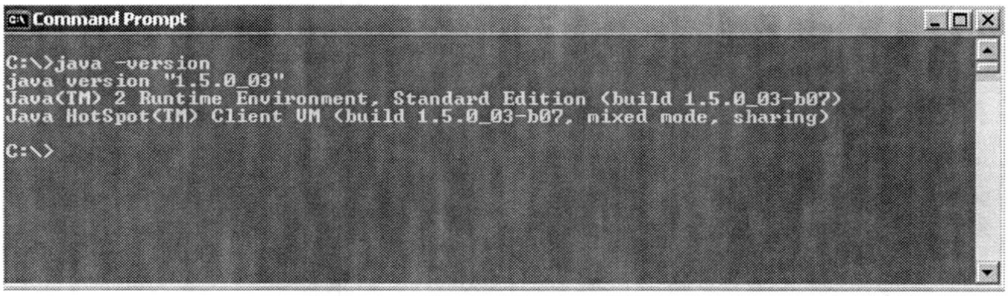

Figure 1-1. *Printing the JDK version*

If the version of J2SE installed and configured on your machine meets the requirements, you are set to start installation of the GlassFish application server.

Note If your machine isn't set up with J2SE version 5, you can download and install J2SE from the following web site: `http://java.sun.com/j2se/1.5.0/download.jsp`.

Installing the GlassFish Application Server

The GlassFish application server can be downloaded from `http://glassfish.dev.java.net/public/downloadsindex.html`.

Note URLs are subject to change. If the preceding URL doesn't work, navigate from the GlassFish home page (`http://glassfish.dev.java.net`).

At the time of writing, we had to use different builds, as GlassFish was being continuously updated to accommodate the specification changes and bugs. We tested our samples in GlassFish version 1, build 48, which is the Java EE 5 release, but the persistence unit developed in this chapter couldn't be deployed due to a bug (the details of which can be seen at `https://glassfish.dev.java.net/issues/show_bug.cgi?id=557`). As a result, we had to start using GlassFish version 2, and we settled on version 2, build 3. We don't expect significant changes to either installation or configuration, or massive feature changes from the final build of version 1 (build 48).

Download GlassFish version 2, build 3 to the directory in which you want to install it. We have downloaded the JAR file into a directory named Software in the C: drive. Open a command prompt window and change directory to the location at which you have the downloaded GlassFish JAR file.

Enter the following command (see Figure 1-2) and press Enter:

C:\Software>java -Xmx256m -jar glassfish-installer-v2-b03.jar

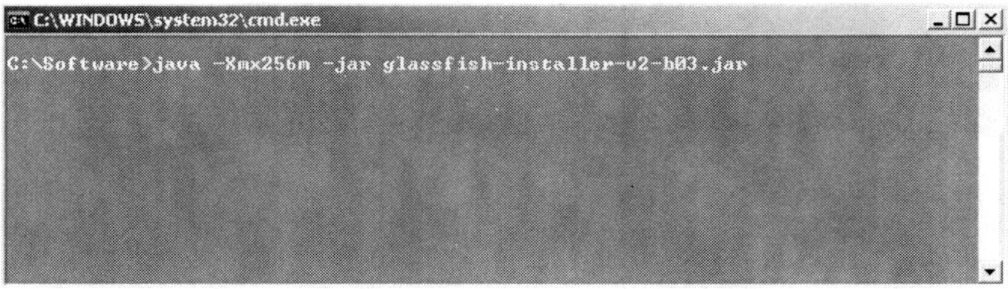

Figure 1-2. *Installing GlassFish*

This command will prompt for a license agreement dialog initially. Read the agreement, and scroll down and press the Accept button. The GlassFish installer JAR will be unzipped into the C:\Software\GlassFish directory.

Using the same command prompt window that you used to run the preceding command, change directory to C:\Software\GlassFish.

We need Ant software to set up the GlassFish application server, so as recommended, we will make use of the Ant software that is bundled with GlassFish.

In the command prompt window, enter the following command (see Figure 1-3) and press Enter:

C:\Software\Glassfish>.\lib\ant\bin\ant -f setup.xml

Figure 1-3. *Setting up the GlassFish application server*

This command will set up the GlassFish application server domain, port numbers, and administrator account, among other things. After successful execution of the preceding command, your GlassFish application server will be ready to be used. In the next sections, we will show you how to set up environment variables, and start and verify the installed GlassFish application server.

Environment Variables Setup

Since we are going to use the same environment variables to work with the samples in the rest of the chapters, it makes sense to add these variables to the system properties. These environmental properties can be used as shortcuts to selected directories where we have installed GlassFish, Ant, and the source code for the samples.

We will set up the environmental variables shown in Table 1-1.

Table 1-1. *Environment Variables*

Variable	Description
JAVA_HOME	The path to the directory in which J2SE is installed (we have installed it in C:\software\JDK15)
GLASSFISH_HOME	The path to the directory in which GlassFish is installed (we have installed it in C:\software\Glassfish)
ANT_HOME	The path to the directory in which Ant is installed (we are using Ant that comes with the GlassFish install located in C:\software\Glassfish\lib\ant\)

Once these environment variables are set up as system properties, we can refer to them as %JAVA_HOME%, %GLASSFISH_HOME%, and %ANT_HOME%.

To set these variables, open the Control Panel on your Windows XP machine, and click the System icon to bring up the System Properties dialog. Select the Advanced tab (see Figure 1-4).

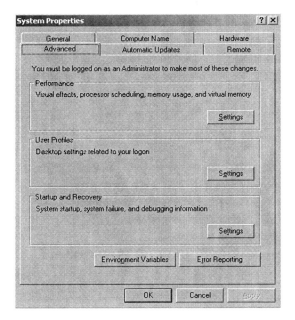

Figure 1-4. *The System Properties dialog*

Click the Environment Variables button, and you will see the Environment Variables pop-up dialog (see Figure 1-5).

Figure 1-5. *The Environment Variables dialog*

Click the New button at the bottom of the User Variables section, and the New User Variable dialog will appear. Enter JAVA_HOME in the Variable name field and C:\software\ jdk15 in the Variable value field, as shown in Figure 1-6. Click the OK button.

■**Note** Substitute the directory in which you have installed J2SE for C:\software\jdk15.

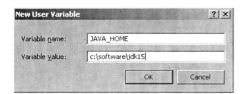

Figure 1-6. *The New User Variable dialog*

Similar to the preceding step, add two more environment variables, GLASSFISH_HOME and ANT_HOME. Substitute the directory names in which you have installed the GlassFish application server. Figure 1-7 shows the Environment Variables dialog after adding the values.

Figure 1-7. *The completed Environment Variables dialog*

Click OK on the Environment Variables and System Properties dialogs.

Starting and Testing the GlassFish Installation

Assuming all the preceding steps have been executed successfully, you are ready to start the GlassFish application server and run a few tests to ensure that you are set to run the samples in this book.

Starting GlassFish

The GlassFish application server provides the `asadmin` command-line utility for administrative tasks including starting and shutting down the GlassFish application server domains. The GlassFish application server comes with the following default values:

- `domain.name=domain1`

- `instance.name=server`

- `admin.user=admin`

- `admin.password=adminadmin`

- `admin.port=4848`

- `instance.port=8080`

- `orb.port=3700`

- `imq.port=7676`

- `https.port=8181`

If you notice any port conflicts with the existing software on your machine, edit `%GLASSFISH_HOME%/setup.xml` with new port values and rerun `ant -f setup.xml` from the `%GLASSFISH_HOME%` directory.

■**Note** By no means is this section of the chapter a user guide for the GlassFish application server. For more information on GlassFish, see `https://glassfish.dev.java.net/downloads/quickstart/index.html`.

Open a command prompt window in the %GLASSFISH_HOME% directory. Change directory to %GLASSFISH_HOME%/bin, and run the following command:

asadmin start-domain domain1.

You will see the GlassFish startup messages in the command prompt window, as shown in Figure 1-8.

Note domain1 is the default domain that gets set up during the installation of GlassFish.

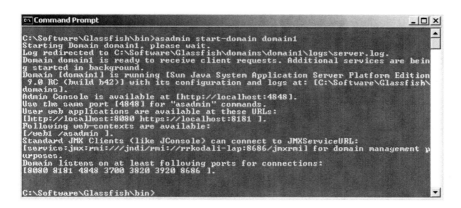

Figure 1-8. *Starting GlassFish*

Testing GlassFish

Once GlassFish has been successfully started, you can test whether the server is able to accept the basic HTTP requests. To do so, open a browser, type in the URL http://localhost:8080/, and you will be able to see the page shown in Figure 1-9 if the server is up and running.

Note Substitute localhost with the machine name or IP address if you are trying to access it from a machine other than the one on which GlassFish is installed. If you changed the port number during installation, use that port instead of 8080.

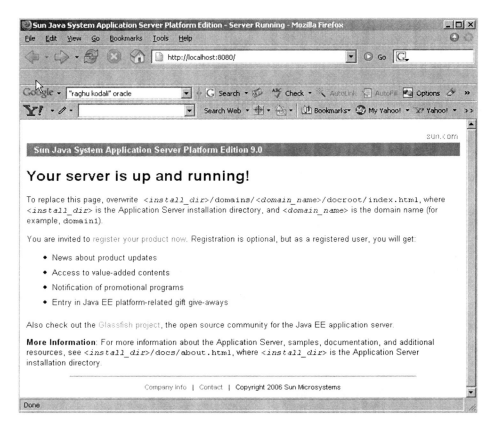

Figure 1-9. *Testing GlassFish*

The next step is to test the access to the administration console. In the browser, type in the URL http://localhost:4848/, and you will be able to see the administration console login page, as shown in Figure 1-10.

Note Substitute localhost with the machine name or IP address if you are trying to gain access from a machine other than the one on which GlassFish is installed. If you changed the port number during installation, use that port instead of 4848.

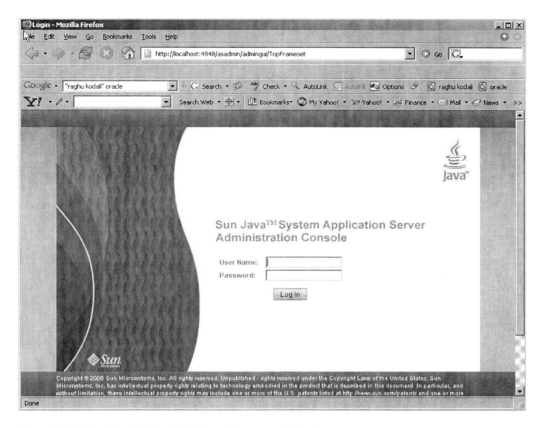

Figure 1-10. *The GlassFish administration console login page*

On the administration console login page, enter admin as the username and adminadmin as the password, and click the Log In button. You will be able to see the administration console, as shown in Figure 1-11.

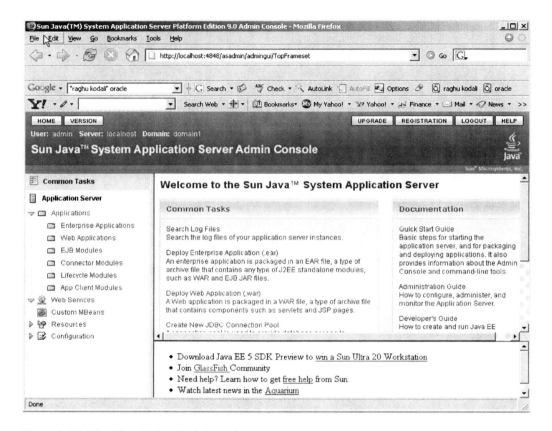

Figure 1-11. *The GlassFish administration console*

Stopping GlassFish

With all the preceding setup done, one last thing to learn is how to stop the running GlassFish application server using the asadmin command-line utility. In the command prompt window that you used to start GlassFish, run the following command:

```
asadmin stop-domain domain1
```

You should see a message telling you that domain1 has stopped, as shown in Figure 1-12.

Figure 1-12. *Stopping GlassFish*

Conclusion

This chapter opened with an introduction to the book and EJB. This orientation covered essential information about the core features of EJB, the EJB framework, and the component model. This included a brief overview of the history of EJB, the EJB 3 simplified development model, and the EJB distributed computing model.

In the "How This Book Is Organized" section, we provided a summary of each chapter to illustrate the general flow of the chapters, and to help you decide which areas to focus on first, should you wish to read the chapters out of sequence.

The chapter concluded with a "Getting Started" section to help you install and configure the GlassFish Java EE reference implementation, set up required environment properties, and verify that the installation was successful. With this, you now have the required software infrastructure to run the code samples in this book and examine the many features of EJB 3 over the following chapters.

CHAPTER 2
■■■
EJB 3 Session Beans

Introduction

This chapter will discuss EJB 3 session beans, the core business service objects used by EJB client applications. You'll gain an understanding of the new and simplified EJB 3 session bean model, with insight into the following topics:

- Types of session beans, both stateful and stateless, and when to use which

- The bean class, business interfaces, and business methods

- Callback methods

- Interceptors

- Exception handling

- Client view

- Dependency injection with annotations related to session beans

Introduction to Session Beans

Session beans are Java components that run in either stand-alone EJB containers or EJB containers that are part of standard Java Platform, Enterprise Edition (Java EE) application servers. These Java components are typically used to model a particular user task or use case, such as entering customer information or implementing a process that maintains a conversation state with a client application. Session beans can hold the business logic for many types of applications, such as human resources, order entry, and expense reporting applications.

Types of Session Beans

Session beans are of two types, as follows:

- *Stateless*: This type of bean does not maintain any conversational state on behalf of a client application.

- *Stateful*: This type of bean maintains state, and a particular instance of the bean is associated with a specific client request. Stateful beans can be seen as extensions to client programs that are running on the server.

We will drill down into more specifics of stateless and stateful beans in the following sections.

When Do You Use Session Beans?

Session beans are used to write business logic, maintain a conversation state for the client, and model back-end processes or user tasks that perform one or more business operations. Typical examples include the following:

- A session bean in a human resources application that creates a new employee and assigns the employee to a particular department

- A session bean in an expense reporting application that creates a new expense report

- A session bean in an order entry application that creates a new order for a particular customer

- A session bean that manages the contents of a shopping cart in an e-commerce application

- A session bean that leverages transaction services in an EJB 3 container (removing the need for an application developer to write the transaction support)

- A session bean used to address deployment requirements when the client applications are not colocated on the same server

- A session bean that leverages the security support provided by the container on the component or method level

Session beans can be used in traditional 2-tier or 3-tier architectures with professional/ rich client applications, or in 3-tier web-based applications. These applications can be deployed in different logical and physical tier combinations. In the next section, we will investigate some of the possible combinations.

3-Tier Architecture with Rich Client

Figure 2-1 shows a typical architecture for a session bean in 3 tiers, with a rich client front-end application that has some data entry screens used by end users like customer service representatives, bank tellers, and so on. These client applications can be developed using Java Swing technology with the Java Platform, Standard Edition (Java SE), or they can be plain old Java objects (POJOs) that are run from the command line. Generally, the end user launches the client application from his desktop, enters some data, and triggers an event by pressing some user interface component such as a Submit button. The general workflow may look something like this:

1. User action establishes a connection to the session bean running in the EJB container using remote method invocation (RMI).

2. The client application invokes one or more business methods in the session bean.

3. The session bean processes the request and validates data—by interacting with databases, enterprise applications, legacy systems, and so on—to perform a certain business operation or task.

4. The session bean finally sends a response back to the client application, either through data collections or simple objects that contain acknowledgment messages.

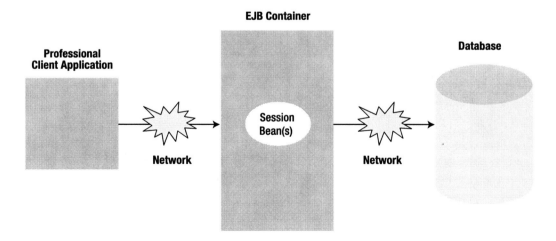

Figure 2-1. *Session beans in a 3-tier architecture*

3-Tier Architecture for a Web Application

This architecture, as shown in Figure 2-2, is typically front-ended by a web application running in the browser of a desktop or laptop machine. These days, other types of client devices, such as PDAs, cell phones, and telnet devices, are also being used to run these applications. The web application running in a browser or mobile device renders the user interface (data entry screens, Submit buttons, etc.) using web technologies such as JavaServer Pages (JSP), JavaServer Faces (JSF), or Java Servlets. Typical user actions, such as entering search criteria or adding certain items to the web application shopping cart, will invoke/call session beans running in an EJB container via one of the aforementioned web technologies. Once the session bean gets invoked, it processes the request and sends a response back to the web application, which formats the response as required, and then sends the response on to the requesting client device (browser, PDA, telnet, etc.).

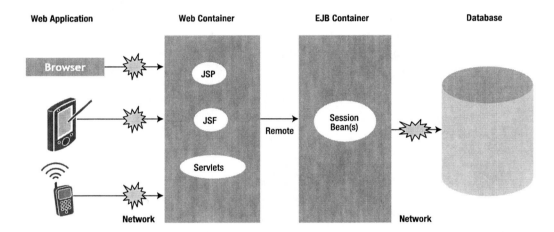

Figure 2-2. *Session beans in a 3-tier architecture with a web application*

In the 3-tier architecture just discussed, the client application (which is the web application) and the session beans can be run within the same instance of an application server (colocated) or from different instances running on the same machine. They can also be run in physically separate machines that have an instance of an application server.

Stateless Session Beans

Stateless session beans are comprised of the following elements:

- Business interfaces, which contain the declaration of business methods that are going to be visible to client applications

- A bean class, which contains the business method implementation to be executed

The Bean Class

A stateless session bean class is any standard Java class that has a class-level annotation of @Stateless. If deployment descriptors are used instead of annotations, then the bean class should be denoted as a stateless session bean. If you use both annotations and deployment descriptors (mixed mode), then the @Stateless annotation must be specified if any other class-level or member-level annotations are specified in the bean class. If both annotations and deployment descriptors are used, then the settings or values in the deployment descriptor will override the annotations in the classes during the deployment process.

To illustrate the use of stateless session beans, we will create a SearchFacade session bean that provides various search facilities to client applications regarding available wines. The workflow is as follows:

1. Users of the application will type in or choose one or more search criteria, which will be submitted to the SearchFacade session bean.

2. The SearchFacade bean will access back-end databases to retrieve the requested information. To simplify the code examples in this chapter, we will actually retrieve the list of hard-coded values within the bean class. In later chapters, we will augment the SearchFacade bean to access the back-end database.

3. The bean returns to the client applications the information that satisfied the search criteria.

Listing 2-1 shows the definition of the SearchFacade bean. In the following sections of this chapter, we will build the code that will show the preceding workflow in action. SearchFacadeBean is a standard Java class with a class-level annotation of @Stateless.

Listing 2-1. *SearchFacadeBean.java*

```java
package com.apress.ejb3.chapter02;

import javax.ejb.Stateless;

@Stateless(name="SearchFacade")
public class SearchFacadeBean implements SearchFacade, SearchFacadeLocal {
    public SearchFacadeBean() {
    }
}
```

The Business Interface

A stateless session business interface is a standard Java interface that does not extend any EJB-specific interfaces. This interface has a list of business method definitions that will be available for the client application. Every session bean must have a business interface that can be implemented by the bean class, generated at design time by tools such as Oracle JDeveloper, NetBeans, or Eclipse; or generated at deployment time by the EJB container.

Business interfaces can use annotations as well, as described in the following list:

- The @Remote annotation can be used to denote the remote business interface.

- The @Local annotation can be used to denote the local business interface.

If no annotation is specified in the interface, then it is defaulted to the local interface.

If your architecture has a requirement whereby the client application (web application or rich client) has to run on a different Java Virtual Machine (JVM) from the one that is used to run the session beans in an EJB container, then you need to use the remote interface. The separate JVMs can be on the same physical machine or on separate machines. If your application architecture is going to use the same JVM for both the client application and the session beans, then use the local interface.

It is possible that your application architecture requires both remote and local interfaces. For example, an enterprise might have an order entry application that is developed using session beans that have business methods for submitting new orders and also addressing administrative tasks, such as data entry for the products. Potentially, you could have two different client applications that access the back-end order entry application, as follows:

- A web client application (as shown in Figure 2-3) that can be run in the same JVM as the session bean and used to submit new orders

- A rich client application (as shown in Figure 2-4) that runs on an end-user desktop machine and is used by the administrator for data entry purposes

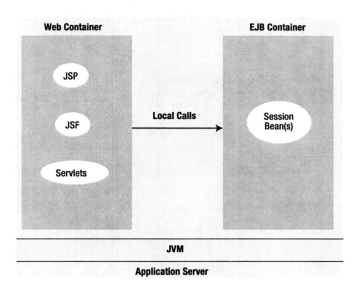

Figure 2-3. *A web client using local interfaces of session beans*

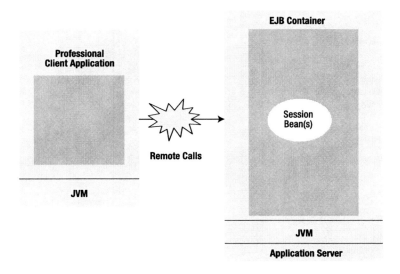

Figure 2-4. *A rich client using remote interfaces of session beans*

The SearchFacade session bean has both remote and local interfaces, as shown in Figure 2-5.

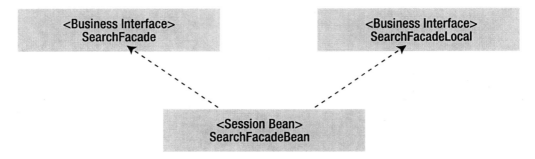

Figure 2-5. *The business interfaces of the SearchFacade session bean*

Listing 2-2 shows the code snippet for the SearchFacade remote business interface, with an @Remote annotation and a wineSearch() method declaration. The wineSearch() method takes one parameter that represents the type of the wine, and returns a list of wines that match the wine type criteria.

Listing 2-2. *SearchFacade.java*

```
package com.apress.ejb3.chapter02;

import java.util.List;

import javax.ejb.Remote;

@Remote
public interface SearchFacade {
    List wineSearch(String wineType);
}
```

Listing 2-3 shows the code snippet for the SearchFacade local business interface, with an @Local annotation and a wineSearch() method declaration.

Listing 2-3. *SearchFacadeLocal.java*

```
package com.apress.ejb3.chapter02;

import java.util.List;
```

```
import javax.ejb.Local;

@Local
public interface SearchFacadeLocal {
    List wineSearch(String wineType);
}
```

Business Methods

The methods implemented in the bean class must correspond to the business methods declared in the remote or local business interfaces. They are matched up based on the convention that they have the same name and method signature. Other methods in the bean class that do not have the corresponding declaration in the business interfaces will be private to the bean class methods.

The SearchFacade bean implements one method, wineSearch(), which has been declared in both remote and local business interfaces. The wineSearch() method returns a static wines list based on the type of wine. Listing 2-4 shows the implementation for wineSearch().

Listing 2-4. *SearchFacadeBean.java*

```
package com.apress.ejb3.chapter02;

import java.util.ArrayList;
import java.util.List;

import javax.ejb.Stateless;

@Stateless(name="SearchFacade")
public class SearchFacadeBean implements SearchFacade, SearchFacadeLocal {
    public SearchFacadeBean() {
    }

    public List wineSearch(String wineType) {
        List wineList = new ArrayList();
        if (wineType.equals("Red"))
            {
            wineList.add("Bordeaux");
            wineList.add("Merlot");
            wineList.add("Pinot Noir");
            }
```

```
        else if (wineType.equals("White"))
            {
            wineList.add("Chardonnay");

            }

        return wineList;
    }
}
```

Dependency Injection

In Chapter 1, we introduced the concept of dependency injection as a programming design pattern. In this section, we will look into using dependency injection in stateless session beans.

EJB 3 containers provide the facilities to inject various types of resources into stateless session beans. Typically, in order to perform user tasks or process requests from client applications, the business methods in the session bean require one or more types of resources. These resources can be other session beans, data sources, or message queues.

The resources that the stateless session bean is trying to use can be injected using annotations or deployment descriptors. Resources can be acquired by annotation of instance variables or annotation of the setter methods. Listing 2-5 shows an example of setter and instance variable–based injection of myDb, which represents the data source.

Listing 2-5. *Data Source Injection*

```
    @Resource
    DataSource myDb;
```

or

```
    @Resource
    public void setMyDb(DataSource myDb) {
        this.myDb = myDb;
    }
```

You typically use the setter injections to preconfigure or initialize properties of the injected resource.

Callback Methods

There will be certain instances or use cases in which the application using session beans requires fine-grained control over things like an object's creation, removal, and so on. For example, the SearchFacade session bean might need to perform some database initialization when it is created, or close some database connections when it is destroyed. The application can gain fine-grained control over the various stages of the bean life cycle via methods known as *callback methods*. A callback method can be any method in the session bean that has callback annotations. The EJB container calls these methods at the appropriate stages of the bean's life cycle (bean creation and destruction).

Following are two such callbacks for stateless session beans:

- PostConstruct: Denoted with the @PostContruct annotation. Any method in the bean class can be marked with this annotation.

- PreDestroy: Denoted with the @PreDestroy annotation. Again, any method in the bean class can be marked with this annotation.

PostContruct callbacks happen after a bean instance is instantiated in the EJB container. If the bean is using any dependency injection mechanisms for acquiring references to resources or other objects in its environment, PostConstruct will occur after injection is performed and before the first business method in the bean class is called.

In the case of the SearchFacade session bean, you could have a business method, wineSearchByCountry(), that would return the wine list for a particular country, and have a PostConstruct callback method, initializeCountryWineList(), that would initialize the country's wine list whenever the bean gets instantiated. Ideally, you would load the list from a back-end datastore; but in this chapter, we will just use some hard-coded values that get populated into a HashMap, as shown in Listing 2-6.

Listing 2-6. *The PostConstruct Method*

```
@PostConstruct
public void initializeCountryWineList()
    {
    //countryMap is HashMap
    countryMap.put("Australia", "Sauvignon Blanc");
    countryMap.put("Australia", "Grenache");
    countryMap.put("France","Gewurztraminer");
    countryMap.put("France","Bordeaux");
    }
```

The PreDestroy callback happens before the container destroys an unused or expired bean instance from its object pool. This callback can be used to close any connection pool that has been created with dependency injection, and also to release any other resources.

In the case of the SearchFacade session bean, we could add a PostConstruct callback method (destroyWineList()) into the SearchFacade bean, which would clear the country wine list whenever the bean gets destroyed. Ideally, during PostContruct, we would close any resources that have been created with dependency injection; but in this chapter, we will just clear the HashMap that has the countries and wine list. Listing 2-7 shows the destroyWineList() code.

Listing 2-7. *The PreDestroy Method*

```
@PreDestroy
public void destroyWineList()
    {
    countryMap.clear();
    }
```

Callback methods defined on a bean class should have the following signature:

```
public void <METHOD>()
```

Callback methods can also be defined on a bean's listener class; these methods should have the following signature:

```
public void <METHOD>(Object)
```

where Object may be declared as the actual bean type, which is the argument passed to the callback method at run time.

Interceptors

The EJB 3 specification provides annotations called *interceptors,* which allow you to intercept a business method invocation. An interceptor method can be defined for session and message-driven beans (MDBs). We will show you the usage of interceptors in the session bean context.

There are number of use cases for interceptors in a typical application, in which you would find a need to perform a certain task before or after the business method is invoked. For example, you may wish to do one of the following:

- Perform additional security checks before a critical business method that transfers more than $100,000 dollars

- Do some performance analysis to compute the time it takes to perform the task

- Do additional logging before or after the method invocation

You can either add an @AroundInvoke annotation on a particular method, or you can define an interceptor class whose methods are invoked before a business method is invoked in the bean class. An interceptor class is denoted by the @Interceptor annotation on the bean class with which it is associated. In the case of multiple interceptor classes, the @Interceptors annotation is used. Methods that are annotated with @AroundInvoke should have the following signature:

```
public Object <METHOD>(InvocationContext) throws Exception
```

The definition of InvocationContext is as follows:

```
package javax.ejb;

public interface InvocationContext {
    public Object getBean();
    public java.lang.reflect.Method getMethod();
    public Object[] getParameters();
    public void setParameters(Object[] params);
    public EJBContext getEJBContext();
    public java.util.Map getContextData();
    public Object proceed() throws Exception;
}
```

The following list describes the methods in the preceding code:

- getBean() returns the instance of the bean on which the method was called.

- getMethod() returns the method on the bean instance that was called.

- getParameters() returns the parameters for the method call.

- setParameters() modifies the parameters used for the method call.

- getEJBContext() gives the interceptor methods access to the bean's EJBContext.

- getContextData() allows values to be passed between interceptor methods in the same InvocationContext instance using the Map returned.

- proceed() invokes the next interceptor, if there is one, or invokes the target bean method.

In the `SearchFacade` session bean, we can add an interceptor that logs the time taken to execute each business method when invoked by the client applications. Listing 2-8 shows a time log method that will print out the time taken to execute a business method. `InvocationContext` is used to get the name of bean class and the invoked method name. Before invoking the business method, current system time is captured and deducted from the system time after the business method is executed. Finally, the details are printed out to the console log using `System.out.println`.

Listing 2-8. *The Interceptor Method*

```
@AroundInvoke
public Object TimerLog (InvocationContext ctx) throws Exception
    {
    String beanClassName = ctx.getClass().getName();
    String businessMethodName = ctx.getMethod().getName();
    String target = beanClassName + "." + businessMethodName ;
    long startTime = System.currentTimeMillis();
    System.out.println ("Invoking " + target);
        try {
            return ctx.proceed();
            }
        finally {
            System.out.println("Exiting " + target);
            long totalTime = System.currentTimeMillis() - startTime;
            System.out.println("Business method " + businessMethodName +
            "in " + beanClassName + "takes " + totalTime + "ms to execute");
            }
    }
```

Stateful Session Beans

Similar to stateless session beans, stateful beans comprise a bean class and a business interface.

The Bean Class

A stateful session bean class is any standard Java class that has a class-level annotation of `@Stateful`. If deployment descriptors are used instead of annotations, the bean class should be denoted as a stateful session bean. In the case of mixed mode, in which you are using annotations *and* deployment descriptors, the @Stateful annotation must be specified if any other class-level or member-level annotations are specified in the class.

To illustrate a stateful session bean, we will create a ShoppingCart session bean that will keep track of the items added to a user's shopping cart and their respective quantities. In this chapter, we will use hard-coded values for the shopping cart to illustrate the state and conversation maintenance between the client and stateful session bean. Listing 2-9 shows the definition of a ShoppingCart session bean.

Listing 2-9. *ShoppingCartBean.java*

```
package com.apress.ejb3.chapter02;

import javax.ejb.Stateful;

@Stateful(name="ShoppingCart")
public class ShoppingCartBean implements ShoppingCart, ShoppingCartLocal {
    public ShoppingCartBean() {
    }
}
```

There will be certain use cases in which the application wants to be notified by the EJB container before or after transactions take place, and then use these notifications to manage data and cache. A stateful session bean can receive this kind of notification by the EJB container when it implements the javax.ejb.SessionSynchronization interface. This is an optional feature. There are three different types of transaction notifications that the stateful session bean receives from the EJB container, as follows:

- afterBegin: Indicates that a new transaction has begun

- beforeCompletion: Indicates that the transaction is going to be committed

- afterCompletion: Indicates that a transaction has been completed

For example, the ShoppingCart session bean could implement the javax.ejb. SessionSynchronization interface to get an afterCompletion notification, so that it can clear out the shopping cart cache.

The Business Interface

Business interfaces for stateful session beans are similar to those for stateless session beans, and are annotated in the same way, using @Local and @Remote annotations. The ShoppingCart session bean has both remote and local interfaces, as shown in Figure 2-6.

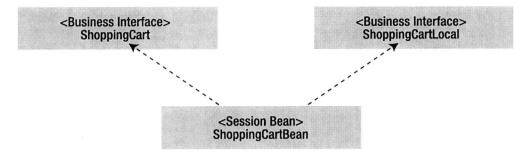

Figure 2-6. *Business interfaces for ShoppingCart*

We will primarily use the local interface from our web application. The remote interface is added to facilitate unit testing of the bean in this chapter.

Listings 2-10 and 2-11 show the remote and local ShoppingCart business interfaces, with @Remote and @Local annotations, respectively.

Listing 2-10. *ShoppingCart.java*

```
package com.apress.ejb3.chapter02;

import javax.ejb.Remote;

@Remote
public interface ShoppingCart {
}
```

Listing 2-11. *ShoppingCartLocal.java*

```
package com.apress.ejb3.chapter02;

import javax.ejb.Local;

@Local
public interface ShoppingCartLocal {
}
```

Alternatively, you can use the coding style shown in Listing 2-12, in which you can specify the @Local and @Remote annotations before specifying @Stateful or @Stateless with the name of the business interface.

Listing 2-12. *ShoppingCartBean.java*

```
package com.apress.ejb3.chapter02;



import javax.ejb.Local;
import javax.ejb.Remote;
import javax.ejb.Stateful;

@Local({ShoppingCartLocal.class})
@Remote({ShoppingCart.class})
@Stateful(name="ShoppingCart")

public class ShoppingCartBean implements ShoppingCart, ShoppingCartLocal {
    public ShoppingCartBean() {
    }
}
```

■**Note** In this book, we will follow the earlier convention, in which @Local and @Remote annotations are marked on the business interfaces.

Business Methods

Business methods in stateful session beans are similar to those in stateless session beans. We will augment the ShoppingCart bean by adding business methods that will add and remove wines from the shopping cart, and return a list of cart items.

Listing 2-13 shows the ShoppingCart bean implementing the addWineItem(), removeWineItem(), and getCartItems() methods.

Listing 2-13. *ShoppingCartBean.java*

```
package com.apress.ejb3.chapter02;
import java.util.ArrayList;

import javax.ejb.Stateful;

@Stateful(name="ShoppingCart")
```

```
public class ShoppingCartBean implements ShoppingCart, ShoppingCartLocal {
    public ShoppingCartBean() {
    }
    public ArrayList cartItems;

    public void addWineItem(String wine) {
       cartItems.add(wine);
    }

    public void removeWineItem(String wine) {
       cartItems.remove(wine);
    }

    public void setCartItems(ArrayList cartItems) {
        this.cartItems = cartItems;
    }

    public ArrayList getCartItems() {
        return cartItems;
    }
}
```

Callback Methods

Stateful session beans support callback events for construction, destruction, activation, and passivation. Following are the callbacks that map to the preceding events:

- PostConstruct: Denoted with the @PostConstruct annotation. Any method in the bean class can be marked with this annotation.

- PreDestroy: Denoted with the @PreDestroy annotation.

- PreActivate: Denoted with the @PreActivate annotation.

- PrePassivate: Denoted with the @PrePassivate annotation.

The PostContruct callback happens after a bean instance is instantiated in the EJB container. If the bean is using any dependency injection mechanism for acquiring references to resources or other objects in its environment, the PostConstruct event happens after injection is performed and before the first business method in the bean class is called.

In the case of the ShoppingCart session bean, we could have a business method called initialize() that initializes the cartItems list, as show in Listing 2-14.

Listing 2-14. *The PostConstruct Method*

```
@PostConstruct
public void initialize()
    {
    cartItems = new ArrayList();
    }
```

The PreDestroy callback happens after any method with an @Remove annotation has been completed. In the case of the ShoppingCart session bean, we could have a business method called exit() that writes the cartItems list into a database. In this chapter, we will just print out a message to the system console to illustrate the callback. Listing 2-15 shows the code for the exit() method, which has the @PreDestroy annotation.

Listing 2-15. *The PreDestroy Method*

```
@PreDestroy
public void exit()
    {
        // items list into the database.
        System.out.println("Saved items list into database");
    }
```

The @Remove annotation is a useful life cycle method for stateful session beans. When the method with the @Remove annotation is called, the container will remove the bean instance from the object pool after the method is executed. Listing 2-16 shows the code for the stopSession() method, which has the @Remove annotation.

Listing 2-16. *The Remove Method*

```
@Remove
public void stopSession()
    {
    // The method body can be empty.
    System.out.println("From stopSession method with @Remove annotation");
    }
```

The `PrePassivate` callback kicks in when a stateful session bean instance is idle for too long. During this event, the container might passivate and store its state to a cache. The method tagged with `@PrePassivate` is called before the container passivates the bean instance.

The `PostActivate` event gets raised when the client application uses a passivated stateful session bean again. A new instance with restored state is created. The method with the `@PostActivate` annotation is called when the bean instance is ready.

Interceptors

There are some minor differences between interceptors for stateless and stateful session beans. `AroundInvoke` methods can be used with stateful session beans. For stateful session beans that implement `SessionSynchronization`, `afterBegin` occurs before any methods that have `AroundInvoke` annotations, and before the `beforeCompletion()` callback method.

Exception Handling

The EJB 3 specification outlines two types of exceptions:

- Application exceptions

- System exceptions

Application exceptions are exceptions related to execution of business logic that the client should handle. For example, an application exception might be raised if the client application passes an invalid argument, such as the wrong credit card number.

System exceptions, on the other hand, are caused by system-level faults, such as Java Naming and Directory Interface (JNDI) errors, or failure to acquire a database connection. A system exception must be a subclass of a `java.rmi.RemoteException`, or a subclass of a `java.lang.RuntimeException` that is not an application exception.

From the EJB application point of view, application exceptions are done by writing application-specific exception classes that subclass the `java.lang.Exception` class.

In the case of a system exception, the application catches particular exceptions—such as a `NamingException` that results from a JNDI failure—and throws an `EJBException`. In this particular chapter, our examples aren't using any resources as such—but there are more examples of system exceptions in the later chapters.

Client View for Session Beans

A session bean can be seen as a logical extension of a client program or application, where much of the logic and data processing for that application happens. A client application typically accesses the session object through the session bean's client view interfaces, which are the business interfaces that were discussed in the earlier sections.

A client application that accesses session beans can be one of three types:

Remote: Remote clients run in a separate JVM from the session beans that they access, as shown in Figure 2-4. A remote client accesses a session bean through the bean's remote business interface. A remote client can be another EJB, a Java client program, or a Java servlet. Remote clients have location independence, meaning that they can use the same API as the clients running in the same JVM.

Local: Local clients run in the same JVM, as shown in Figure 2-3, and access the session bean through the local business interface. A local client can be another EJB, or a web application using Java Servlets, JavaServer Pages (JSP), or JavaServer Faces (JSF). Local clients are location dependent. Remote and local clients are compared in Table 2-1.

Web Services: You can publish stateless session beans as web services that can be invoked by Web Services clients. We will discuss Web Services and clients in Chapter 6.

Table 2-1. *Considerations for Choosing Between Local and Remote Clients*

Remote	Local
Loose coupling between the bean and the client	Lightweight access to a component
Location independence	Location dependence
Expensive remote calls	Must be colocated with the bean
Objects must be serialized	Not required
Objects are passed by value	Objects are passed by reference

In some cases, the session beans need to have both local and remote business interfaces to support different types of client applications. A client can obtain a session bean's business interface via dependency injection or JNDI lookup. Before invoking the methods in the session bean, the client needs to obtain a stub object of the bean via JNDI. Once the client has a handle to the stub object, it can call the business methods in the session bean. In the case of a stateless session bean, a new stub can be obtained on every invocation. In the case of a stateful session bean, the stub needs to be cached on the client side so that the container knows which instance of the bean to return on subsequent calls. Using dependency injection, we can obtain the business interface of the SearchFacade session bean with the following code:

```
@EJB SearchFacade searchFacade;
```

If the client accessing the session bean is remote, the client can use JNDI lookup once the context interface has been obtained with the right environment properties. Local clients can use JNDI lookup as well, but dependency injection results in simpler code. Listing 2-17 shows the SearchFacadeTest client program's JNDI code, which looks up the SearchFacade bean, invokes the wineSearch() business method, and prints out the returned list of wines.

Note If the remote client is a Java application or command-line program, an application client container can be used to invoke the session beans. Application client containers support dependency injection for remote clients. We will discuss application client containers in Chapter 12, along with other types of client applications.

Listing 2-17. *SearchFacadeClient.java*

```java
package com.apress.ejb3.chapter02.client;

import com.apress.ejb3.chapter02.SearchFacade;
import java.util.List;
import javax.naming.InitialContext;
import javax.naming.NamingException;

public class SearchFacadeTest {
    public SearchFacadeTest() {
    }

    public static void main(String[] args) {
        SearchFacadeTest searchFacadeTest = new SearchFacadeTest();
        searchFacadeTest.doTest();
    }

    @EJB
    static SearchFacade searchFacade;

    void doTest(){
        InitialContext ic;

        try {
            ic = new InitialContext();
            System.out.println("SearchFacade Lookup");
```

```
            System.out.println("Searching wines");
            List winesList = searchFacade.wineSearch("Red");
            System.out.println("Printing wines list");
            for (String wine:(List<String>)winesList ){
                System.out.println(wine);
            }
        } catch (NamingException e) {
            e.printStackTrace();
        }
    }
}
```

Listing 2-18 shows the ShoppingCartTest client program, which looks up the stateful
ShoppingCart session bean, calls the addWineItem() business method to add a wine to the
shopping cart, calls the getCartItems() business method to get the items in the cart, and
finally prints the list of wines in the shopping cart.

Listing 2-18. *ShoppingCartTest.java*

```
package com.apress.ejb3.chapter02.client;

import com.apress.ejb3.chapter02.ShoppingCart;

import java.util.ArrayList;

import java.util.List;

import javax.naming.InitialContext;
import javax.naming.NamingException;

public class ShoppingCartTest {
    public ShoppingCartTest() {
    }

    public static void main(String[] args) {
        ShoppingCartTest shoppingCartTest = new ShoppingCartTest();
        shoppingCartTest.doTest();
    }

@EJB
static ShoppingCart shoppingCart;
```

```
    void doTest(){
        InitialContext ic;

        try {
            ic = new InitialContext();
            System.out.println("ShoppingCart Lookup");
            System.out.println("Adding Wine Item");
            shoppingCart.addWineItem("Zinfandel");
            System.out.println("Printing Cart Items");
            ArrayList cartItems = shoppingCart.getCartItems();
            for (String wine:(List<String>)cartItems ){
                System.out.println(wine);
            }
        } catch (NamingException e) {
            e.printStackTrace();
        }
    }
}
```

Packaging, Deploying, and Testing the Session Beans

Session beans need to be packaged into EJB JAR (.jar) files before they are deployed into EJB containers. In the case of some EJB containers or application servers, packaged EJB archives need to be assembled into Enterprise Archive (EAR) files before deployment. EJB containers or application servers provide deployment utilities or Ant tasks to facilitate deployment of EJBs. Java IDEs (integrated development environments) like Oracle JDeveloper, NetBeans, and Eclipse also provide deployment features that allow developers to package, assemble, and deploy EJBs to application servers. Packaging, assembly, and deployment are covered in detail in Chapter 10.

So far in this chapter, we have developed one stateless session bean (SearchFacade) and one stateful session bean (ShoppingCart). The following sections will walk you through the steps to package, assemble, deploy, and test these session beans.

Prerequisites

Before performing any of the steps detailed in the next sections, complete the "Getting Started" section of Chapter 1, which will walk you through the installation and environment setup required for the samples in this chapter.

■**Note** We assume that the source code for this chapter's samples is located in the Z: drive. Replace Z: with the location of the directory into which you have downloaded the source.

Compiling the Session Beans

From the DOS console, execute the following javac command to compile the SearchFacade and ShoppingCart session beans, along with their business interfaces. Figure 2-7 shows the command being executed from the z:\Chapter02-SessionSamples\SessionBeanSamples directory.

Z:\Chapter02-SessionSamples\SessionBeanSamples>%JAVA_HOME%/bin/javac -classpath ➥ %GLASSFISH_HOME%\lib\javaee.jar -d ./classes src\com\apress\ejb3\chapter02*.java

Figure 2-7. *Compiling the session beans*

In the downloaded source code for this chapter's samples, you will see the Ant build script (build.xml). You can alternatively use the following Ant task to compile the session beans:

Z:\Chapter02-SessionSamples\SessionBeanSamples>%ANT_HOME%/bin/ant ➥ Compile-SessionSamples

■**Note** If you are using the Ant task for compiling, make appropriate changes to the build.properties file to reflect the settings for the GlassFish application server that you have installed.

Packaging the Session Beans

Once the source code for the session beans is compiled, you need to package the compiled classes into an EJB JAR file. Execute the following command from the DOS console:

```
Z:\Chapter02-SessionSamples\SessionBeanSamples\classes>%JAVA_HOME%/bin/jar cvf ➡
.. \archive\SessionSamples.jar .\com
```

Note The preceding command is run from the `classes` directory.

Figure 2-8 shows the command being executed from the `Z:\Chapter02-SessionSamples\ SessionBeanSamples\classes` directory, and the files being added to the generated JAR file.

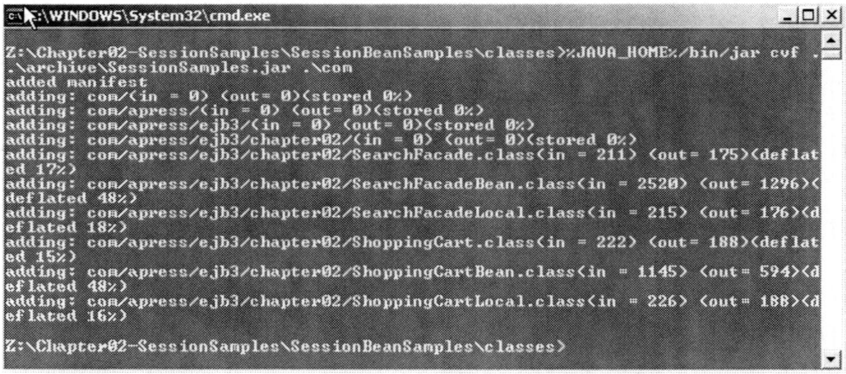

Figure 2-8. *Packaging the session beans*

Alternatively, you can use the following Ant task to package the session beans:

```
Z:\Chapter02-SessionSamples\SessionBeanSamples>%ANT_HOME%/bin/ant ➡
Package-SessionBeans
```

The generated `SessionSamples.jar` file will be stored in the `archive` directory.

Note If you are using the Ant task for packaging, make the appropriate changes to the `build.properties` file to reflect the settings for the GlassFish application server you have installed.

Deploying the Session Beans

Once you have compiled and packaged the session beans, you can deploy the generated JAR file (SessionSamples.jar) to the GlassFish application server. You can deploy the JAR file from the GlassFish administration console—however, for practical purposes, you'll want to automate these tasks as much as possible. You should use the following command-line utilities and Ant task for deployment.

From the DOS console, execute the following command:

```
Z:\Chapter02-SessionSamples\SessionBeanSamples>%GLASSFISH_HOME%/bin/asadmin.bat ➥
deploy --host localhost --port 4848 --user admin --passwordfile %GLASSFISH_HOME%\ ➥
asadminpass --upload=true --target server ➥
Z:\Chapter02-SessionSamples\SessionBeanSamples\archive\SessionSamples.jar
```

Figure 2-9 shows the command being executed from the z:\Chapter02-SessionSamples\ SessionBeanSamples directory.

Figure 2-9. *Deploying the session beans*

Alternatively, you can use the following Ant task to deploy the session beans:

```
Z:\Chapter02-SessionSamples\SessionBeanSamples>%ANT_HOME%/bin/ant ➥
Deploy-SessionBeans
```

■**Note** If you are running the GlassFish application server on a different machine, replace localhost with that machine name in the command-line arguments. Similarly, if you are running on a different port, replace 4848 with the number of the port that you are using. If you are using the Ant task for deployment, make the appropriate changes to the build.properties file to reflect the settings for the GlassFish application server you have installed.

Compiling the Client Programs

From the DOS console, execute the following `javac` command to compile the
`ShoppingCartTest` and `SearchFacadeTest` classes.

```
Z:\Chapter02-SessionSamples\SessionBeanSamples>%JAVA_HOME%/bin/javac -classpath ➡
%GLASSFISH_HOME%\lib\javaee.jar;.\classes\ -d ./classes ➡
 src\com\apress\ejb3\chapter02\client\*.java
```

Figure 2-10 shows the command being executed from the `Z:\Chapter02-SessionSamples\`
`SessionBeanSamples` directory.

Figure 2-10. *Compiling the client programs*

Alternatively, you can use the following Ant task to compile the client programs:

```
Z:\Chapter02-SessionSamples\SessionBeanSamples>%ANT_HOME%/bin/ant ➡
Compile-ClientPrograms
```

Running the Client Programs

Once the client programs are compiled, you can invoke the business methods in the
deployed `ShoppingCart` and `SearchFacade` session beans using the GlassFish application
client container that supports dependency injection. You will assemble the client and its
dependent classes into a JAR file, which will enable you to specify the JAR file as an argument to the application client container.

■**Note** The application client container will be covered in detail in Chapter 12.

Execute the following command in the DOS shell to run SearchFacadeTest:

Z:\Chapter02-SessionSamples\SessionBeanSamples\archive>%GLASSFISH_HOME%/bin/➥
appclient.bat -client searchfacadeclient.jar

Figure 2-11 shows the output printed to the console after successful execution of the client program.

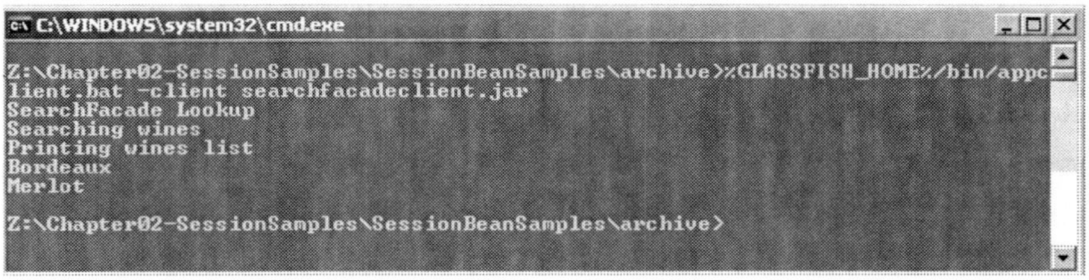

Figure 2-11. *The SearchFacadeTest client results*

Execute the following command in the DOS shell to run ShoppingCartTest:

Z:\Chapter02-SessionSamples\SessionBeanSamples\archive>%GLASSFISH_HOME%/bin/➥
appclient.bat -client shoppingcartclient.jar

Figure 2-12 shows the output printed to the console after successful execution of the client program.

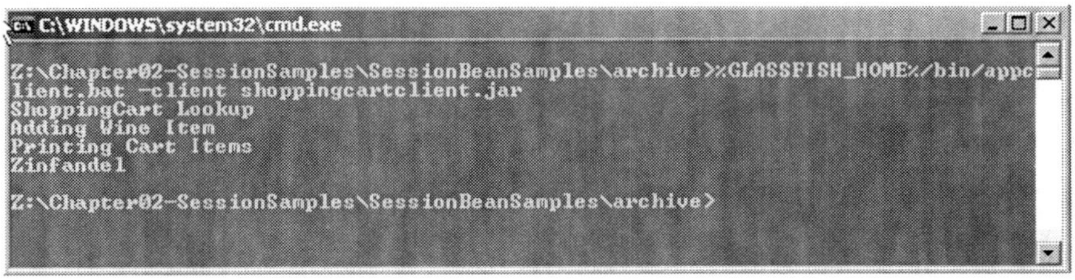

Figure 2-12. *The ShoppingCartTest client results*

Conclusion

This chapter has covered EJB 3 session bean details using a specific set of examples. We looked at the new and simplified EJB 3 model for developing session beans using standard Java language artifacts, such as Java classes and interfaces. We looked at session beans, and some typical use cases in which session beans can be used for developing applications. We discussed two different types of session beans (stateless and stateful), including the differences between them and some general use cases for each. We covered session bean usage in 2-tier and 3-tier application architectures. We discussed the usage of dependency injection in stateless and stateful beans. We considered ways to gain fine-grained control over application flow, including the use of callback methods and interceptors in stateless and stateful beans, as well as the use of annotations like `@PostContruct` and `@PreDestroy`. We looked at what is required to compile/build, package, and deploy session beans to the GlassFish application server. Finally, we looked at running the sample client programs using the GlassFish application client container.

In the next two chapters, we will drill down into the Java Persistence API (JPA) so that you can learn how to map POJOs to database tables and perform query and CRUD operations.

CHAPTER 3

■■■

Entities and the Java Persistence API

Now that you have explored how EJB provides business services through session beans, we turn your attention to entities—persistent data objects that represent tables in a database. The entity model introduced in EJB 3.0 is defined in its own document—the Java Persistence API (JPA). The new JPA is widely regarded as a tremendous improvement over the entity beans model defined in earlier versions of EJB. For the 3.0 release, EJB has borrowed unabashedly from both proprietary and open source models, such as TopLink, Hibernate, and Spring, which have gained traction as popular alternatives to the often heavyweight and cumbersome persistence directives required by earlier EJB revisions. Consequently, like session beans, entities are now simple POJOs (plain old Java objects). While the EJB persistence model has grown in reach and ability, entities themselves have conveniently become largely decoupled from their supporting persistence framework, allowing them to be used both inside and outside a Java EE container.

In the spirit of this book, the two chapters on persistence will cover the most commonly used features, describing their use through practical examples using our online wine store application. This chapter will get you started writing entity classes and using the key persistence features; the next chapter will explore more advanced persistence features. These chapters explain, through examples, the major areas of the persistence programming model—however, they are not meant to be a substitute for the expansive JPA specification. We encourage you to refer to the JPA spec when you're ready to explore details that go beyond the scope of this discussion.

Table 3-1 summarizes what we'll be covering in this chapter.

Table 3-1. *Key Topics in This Chapter*

Concept	Description
An entity example	We begin with a simple JavaBean, and progressively add annotations required to transform it into a simple entity, and then beyond.
Primary entity annotations	Further refining the requirements of an entity, the entity class must have a no-argument `public` or `protected` constructor, and must not be `final`. Entities define their persistent structure through their JavaBeans property accessors or instance variables, and may include custom methods as well.
The `EntityManager`	The `EntityManager` object provides persistence services, including transaction management and query, merge, remove, find, and refresh operations. It is central to an understanding of the EJB 3.0 persistence framework.
Entity life cycle	An entity instance may go through many formal states during its life as an in-memory Java object. Understanding these different states will help you know when the entity is in a consistent or inconsistent state with the back-end database, and how to reconcile these differences within a transactional context.
Object/relational (O/R) mapping	EJB defines declarative markup through annotations and/or XML descriptors to map entity fields to table columns in a relational database management system (RDBMS).
Entity relationships	Entity classes may hold unary and collection references to themselves or to other entities. Note that in EJB 3.0, relationship fields are no longer bidirectionally maintained by the container.
Java Persistence Query Language (JPQL)	JPQL supports queries, along with bulk update and delete operations. Queries may be defined either statically, as named queries, or dynamically. Queries may take bind parameters and return Java objects, including entity instances.
Forward generation vs. reverse engineering	As a practical consideration when designing your entity classes, consider whether the entity class is the primary design object, or whether the database schema is the source of truth. In the former case, the database serves mainly to persist the entity data, whereas in the latter case, the entity class serves to adapt the table into Java.
Example application: `InventoryManager`	Finally, we give an example application demonstrating all of the concepts in this chapter in a simple, working model.

An Entity Example

Let's take a look at how you can transform a simple JavaBean into an entity, and progressively customize it to add functionality and flexibility.

A Simple JavaBean: Customer.java

We begin with a simple JavaBean, shown in Listing 3-1. This class has properties as defined by the JavaBeans standard. Each property on the JavaBean is represented to the world outside the bean through a pair of property accessor methods. For each property, a getter method retrieves its data and a setter method assigns it. Internally, these property accessor methods read and write to a private, dedicated instance variable on the JavaBean class.

Listing 3-1. *A Simple JavaBean*

```
public class Customer {
  private long customerId;
  private String name;

  public long getCustomerId() { return customerId; }
  public void setCustomerId(long customerId) { this.customerId = customerId; }

  public String getName() { return name; }
  public void setName(String name) { this.name = name; }
}
```

A Simple Entity: Customer.java

Listing 3-2 shows the Customer.java JavaBean after it has been transformed into an entity.

Listing 3-2. *A Simple Entity*

```
@Entity
public class Customer {
  @Id
  private long customerId;
  private String name;
```

```
    public long getCustomerId() { return customerId; }
    public void setCustomerId(long customerId) { this.customerId = customerId; }

    public String getName() { return name; }
    public void setName(String name) { this.name = name; }
}
```

The only changes required were to add the @Entity and @Id annotations. These are the minimum metadata requirements to transform this class into an entity.

The @Entity Annotation

The @Entity annotation is required to identify this class as an entity at the time the entity is deployed. When entities are deployed in a persistence archive (JAR file), they may be accompanied by non-entity classes. This annotation, or its equivalent declaration in the orm.xml file, tells the container to look for further annotations on the class, and otherwise handle its O/R mappings, allow it to participate in queries and persistent relationships with other entities, and undergo byte weaving or other procedures when they are later instantiated by the persistence provider. All classes that are not marked as entities are ignored by the container during deployment.

The @Id Annotation

The @Id annotation indicates which field (there may be several) is the entity's primary key, or identifier. The value in the identifier field (or fields) must be unique across all entity instances of the entity type Customer so that it can uniquely identify this entity. In the case that the primary key spans multiple columns in the table, a composite primary key is required, and the @Id fields may be replaced by a single field that is annotated @EmbeddedId. We will discuss how to specify composite keys later in the chapter.

Comparison with EJB 2.x

The fundamental EJB 3.0 persistence coding construct is the entity class. Before EJB 3.0, the entity bean served as the primary persistence object, and was comprised of a bean class and a local and/or remote component and home interface. In the 3.0 release, most of the trappings of the entity bean have been stripped away, or simplified away through strong use of defaults and annotations. What remains is simply the entity bean class, known now as the entity class, or more simply still, the entity. While it is equally valid to specify persistence metadata in an XML descriptor, for brevity all examples in this chapter use JDK (Java SE Development Kit) 5.0 annotations. As in the rest of the EJB 3.0 realm, each declarative construct specified by an annotation has a corresponding representation in the XML descriptor for the persistence unit (collection of colocated entities), and so may be equivalently specified in XML. The decision whether to use annotations or XML is entirely a matter of personal choice.

Configuration by Default

The previous two annotations were specified explicitly. Given the EJB 3.0 simplified development model that leverages configuration by default, you will not be surprised to find out that a lot of other metadata in this example is implied by default. Before exploring these default settings, it is worth considering why the @Entity and @Id annotations were chosen to be specified explicitly, rather than implied implicitly.

The @Entity annotations could have been the default settings for each class deployed through a persistence archive, and a hypothetical @NotEntity annotation could have been used to specify a non-entity class; but following the pattern set by session and message-driven beans, the explicit opt-in pattern was chosen instead.

Similarly, all fields could have been assumed to be part of the primary key, but in practice, only a small subset (usually only one) of an entity's properties typically comprises an entity's primary key. The spec designers felt that it makes better sense in this case to use the opt-in pattern of explicitly specifying @Id on primary key fields, implying that all columns are not part of the primary key. This type of decision characterizes the configuration-by-default approach, in which annotations are not required for the more common cases and are only used when an override is needed.

The next section will examine some of the behavior that this Customer.java entity acquired by default, and show how you can override this default behavior.

An Entity with Defaults Exposed: Customer.java

Listing 3-3 shows the same entity, with some of its defaults shown.

Listing 3-3. *An Entity with Defaults Shown*

```
@Entity(name="Customer")
@Table(name="CUSTOMER")
public class Customer {
  @Id
  @Column(name="CUSTOMERID", table="CUSTOMER", unique=true,
          nullable=false, insertable=true, updatable=true)
  private long customerId;
```

```
@Basic(fetch=FetchType.EAGER)
@Column(name="NAME", table="CUSTOMER")
private String name;

    ...
}
```

Each entity has a name, and unless otherwise specified, this name defaults to the unqualified class name, which is in this case Customer. This name is used when referring to the entity in query statements (Java Persistence Query Language, JPQL, is covered in Chapter 4), and is typically specified when the unqualified class name is awkward or is a reserved name in JPQL.

The @Table Annotation

An entity instance typically represents a single row in a table, and exposes each column value in that row through a corresponding property on the entity. Consequently, an entity must map to a table in a database, and that table is specified using the @Table annotation. Its name defaults to the entity name. Since databases do not all support mixed-case table names, this translates to a table named CUSTOMER.

The @Column Annotation

Similarly, each field declared on the entity maps by default to a column with the same name, and so the customerId and name fields map to the CUSTOMERID and NAME columns in the CUSTOMER table. The @Column annotation may also be used to override default column type information, as well as column-level constraints, such as to indicate that the column is optional, insertable, and/or updatable. Ordinarily, it is only necessary to specify this level of detail when you are relying on the container to create the table when an entity is deployed.

The @Basic Annotation

Entity fields that are of simple Java types such as String or int (like the customerId and name fields) are automatically configured by the JPA to use the @Basic annotation. Arrays of simple types, and any other type that implements the Serializable interface, may also be marked @Basic.

The persistence framework provides automatic conversion of column data types to certain Java types, and EJB persistence providers will attempt to define a suitable default column type when generating tables for entity classes during deployment. Most numeric, string, and date types will be converted automatically.

Table 3-2 presents a list of Java types that can be annotated @Basic and mapped automatically.

Table 3-2. *Field/Property Types That Are Valid for Simple Mappings*

Java Type
Java primitive types (int, long, char, etc.)
Primitive wrapper types (Integer, Long, Char, etc.)
Java serializable types
User-defined serializable types
enums
java.lang.String
java.math.BigInteger
java.math.BigDecimal
java.util.Date
java.util.Calendar
java.sql.Date
java.sql.Time
java.sql.Timestamp
byte[]
Byte[]
char[]
Character[]

Additional Field Types

There are a number of other type specifiers that may be applied to different types of columns. For instance, an entity may also hold references to other entities, and these references are represented by properties on the entity as well. We will look at some examples of how to specify these relationship properties later in this chapter.

An entity may have methods beyond its property access methods, but typically these are limited to support methods for managing add and remove operations from collection relationship properties.

Coding Requirements

In addition to the @Entity annotation and a primary key specifier, the minimal coding requirements for an entity are that it have a public or protected default (no argument) constructor and that the class is not final. In this Customer example, a default constructor was implied, since in the absence of any non-default constructors on a public class, a default constructor is assumed by Java. Non-default constructors may be specified on an entity as well, and are often used for initializing the entity with its mandatory properties.

The java.io.Serializable Interface

Entities that will be passed by value, as when passed by remote session beans to Java SE clients that are external to the EJB container, must implement the java.io.Serializable marker (no method) interface. Implementing this interface indicates to the compiler that it must enforce all fields on the entity class to be serializable, so that any instance can be serialized to a byte stream and passed using remote method invocation (RMI) over HTTP.

Placing Annotations on Instance Variables vs. JavaBean Property Accessors

When defining an entity class, the Bean Provider may choose to place member-level annotations on either the entity instance variables or on the corresponding JavaBean property accessors for those instance variables. As with the decision between specifying metadata using annotations or XML, this is largely a matter of personal preference. However, whereas mixing and matching annotations and XML metadata is allowed, the Bean Provider must choose, for any given entity, whether to annotate the entity's instance variables or its property accessors. If the entity is part of an entity hierarchy (see a discussion on this in Chapter 4), this choice applies to all entities in the hierarchy. This decision is made implicitly, when the Bean Provider first annotates a class member and places the annotation on either the instance variable or its property accessor. Once made, the Bean Provider is of course free to switch to the alternative approach; but by the time the entity is deployed, only one approach may be used across the entire entity class (hierarchy), or else an exception will be raised during entity deployment.

Regardless of where the member-level annotations are specified, the entity's instance variables must not be public, and clients of that entity, including related entities, must always access an entity's properties through accessor methods. It is up to the entity provider to decide which property accessors to make public, exposing them to clients, and which to make protected—making them available only to the persistence provider. When annotating instance variables, the entity need not define any property accessor methods, if desired.

By policy, only the persistence framework and the class methods themselves are allowed to access these fields directly. For both access types, clients must access field data through public accessor or other methods on the entity class.

There are several material consequences of choosing one approach over the other—these are discussed in the following sections.

Entity Data Access

When annotations are specified on the entity's instance variables, the persistence manager accesses the instance variables directly when reading and writing persistent property to and from the entity. When annotating property accessors instead of instance variables, the persistence manager reads and writes property data through these property accessors.

Annotating the entity's instance variables directly avoids the overhead of method calls and provides a slight performance optimization, since the persistence manager talks directly to the fields. Annotating the property accessors provides a simple way for the Bean Provider to intercept and perform custom logic during all attempts to read and write property data.

This latter option affords the Bean Provider a chance to lazily derive persistent property values on demand, if desired. However, be aware that any validation or side-effect code on the property accessor methods will be called during entity state transitions. As you'll see in the next chapter, if the Bean Provider wishes to initialize transient data or refine persistent data at the time the entity's persistent state is first loaded, or prior to saving changes out to persistent storage, it is preferable to perform these steps using entity life cycle callback methods. Using the combination of field-level annotations and entity life cycle callbacks has the benefit that validation and other code in the setter methods will only be called when a client calls the setter, and not when the entity is being instantiated from persistent store by the framework.

Another consideration is how the entity behaves when it is involved in a query. This is a similar issue, since a query statement may both retrieve and update field data on an entity—so it is important to be aware of any possible side effects of using property accessors.

Property Name

The second material impact of choosing whether to annotate instance variables or property accessors occurs when the property accessor expresses a default field name that is different from the instance variable name. When annotating property accessors, the logical property name is derived from the getter using the JavaBean property-naming convention; whereas if the instance variable is annotated, the logical property name becomes the instance variable's name.

Example: Annotating Instance Variables

The code snippet in Listing 3-4 demonstrates instance variable annotation, and illustrates validation and side-effect code. In this example, the entity provider narrows the client interface to expose only the get/setZipCode() methods, but specifies both zipCodeInt and zipCodeStr properties to the persistence provider. Placing annotations on the instance variables provides a clean separation between the entity's client-side API and its persistence-side interface.

Listing 3-4. *An Entity That Uses Instance Variable Annotations*

```
@Entity
public class Address implements Serializable {
{
    @Column (name="ZIP")
    private int zipcodeInt;

    @Transient
    private String zipCodeStr;

    public String getZipcode() {
        if (zipcodeStr==null && zipCodeInt > 0) {
            zipcodeStr = convert(zipcodeInt);
        }
        return zipcodeStr;
    }
    public void setZipcode(String zipcode) throws IllegalArgumentException {
        // Validate the zipcode String, to make sure it reduces cleanly to
        // either a 5- or 9- digit integer, and assign it to the internal
        // persistent 'zipcodeInt' class field
        ...
        zipcodeStr = zipcode;
        zipcodeInt = convert(zipcode);
    }

    private int convert(String zipCode) {...}
    private String convert(int zipCode) {...}
}
```

The get/setZipCode() methods allow the entity to lazily transform the internal data into a client-friendly String representation, but only when requested. No property accessors are even specified for the zipCodeInt instance variable.

The @Transient Annotation

You may not wish to make all fields or properties of an entity class persistent. Derived or transient fields may be annotated @Transient to indicate that they should be ignored by the persistence framework. The zipCodeStr instance variable is marked @Transient, indicating that it should not be managed by the persistence provider. This instance variable serves only to cache the derived value.

Example: Annotating Property Accessors

Listing 3-5 demonstrates how a Bean Provider may use side-effect code when annotating an entity's property accessors.

Listing 3-5. *An Entity That Uses Property Accessor Annotations*

```
@Entity
public class Address implements Serializable {
{
    private long addressId;
    private int zipCode;
    private String city;

    @Id
    public long getAddressId() {return addressId;}
    public void setAddressId(long addressId) {this.addressId = addressId;}

    public int getZipCode() {return zipCode;}
    public void setZipCode(int zipCode) {this.zipCode = zipCode;}

    public String getCity() {
        //  Derive the city from the zipcode property, if available
        if (city == null && zipCode > 0) {
          city = deriveCityFromZip();
        }
        return city;
    }
    public void setCity(String city) {
        this.city = city;
    }
}
```

Placing the @Id annotation on the getAddressId() property accessor disambiguates the access policy, indicating that property accessors should be used by the persistence provider. Forcing the persistence provider to assign data through the property accessor affords the entity the opportunity to "clean up" the city data coming from the database. Also, knowing that the city field will be obtained by the persistence manager through its getter method allows the entity to lazily calculate its value only when requested through the getCity() accessor. Should the usage of this entity involve many calls to setZipCode() before the entity is persisted (or merged) out to the database, it is more efficient to defer deriving the city value until it is actually requested. Were this entity to use instance variable access, it would be necessary to eagerly update the city field each time the zipCode was assigned, since a request could come at any time to merge the entity changes into the database. As mentioned earlier, however, the use of entity life cycle callback methods could avoid the overhead of eagerly deriving this value.

Access Type Summary

The JPA offers two models for how the persistence provider accesses the field data on an entity—directly, through instance variables, and indirectly, through property accessors. In the general case, we have found that annotating an entity's instance variables is preferable to annotating its property accessors. You rarely have a need to validate data coming in from the persistent store, and any side-effect code in setter methods typically ought to be performed lazily, not eagerly at the time the entity is instantiated. Furthermore, field-level annotations allow you to decouple the public property types exposed through that field's get/set methods from the underlying column representation. For instance, you may want to expose the zipCode property as a String through the getZipcode()/setZipcode() methods, but convert it internally to an integer, using a field of type Integer, for persistence to an INTEGER column in the database. Finally, the use of entity life cycle callback methods provides the opportunity for additional initialization or preparation, both after the entity data is loaded and before it is saved.

Declaring the Primary Key

An entity must declare its primary key. The primary key serves to uniquely identify an entity instance among all of the instances of the entity type. A primary key may be simple, represented by a single field of a basic Java class like String or Long, as in the previous Customer.java example. Alternatively, a primary key may be complex—represented by a composite class comprised of multiple elementary fields or properties.

The underlying column or columns on the entity's table that are mapped to by the primary key field or fields may be formally bound by a database primary key constraint, but this is not a requirement. It is, however, required that the primary key column value or values for any entity instance resolve to a unique value across all instances of that entity. Database constraints are useful in enforcing this requirement, and in their absence, care should be taken to ensure that unique values are assigned by application.

Simple Primary Key

A simple primary key is declared by annotating a single basic-type field on the entity class with the @Id annotation (see Listing 3-6). A basic-type field is a basic Java type (a list of basic types is shown in Table 3-2).

Listing 3-6. *An Entity with a Simple Primary Key*

```
@Entity
public class Customer1 implements Serializable {
    @Id
    private Integer id;
    private String name;

    public Customer1() {}
    public Customer1(Integer id) {this.id = id;}

    public Integer getId() { return id; }
    public void setId(Integer id) { this.id = id; }

    public String getName() { return name; }
    public void setName(String name) {this.name = name;}
}
```

Note that we could eliminate the usefulness of an alternate constructor in our entity class by using a database sequence to populate the PK value automatically. Listing 3-7 shows how this might look.

Listing 3-7. *An Entity with a Simple Primary Key That Is Populated Using @GeneratedValue*

```
@Entity
@SequenceGenerator(name = "Customer1Sequence", sequenceName = "CUSTOMER1_SEQ",
                   initialValue = 100, allocationSize = 20)
public class Customer1 implements Serializable {
    @Id
    @GeneratedValue(strategy = GenerationType.SEQUENCE,
```

```
                              generator = "Customer1Sequence")
        private Integer id;
        private String name;

        public Integer getId() { return id; }
        public void setId(Integer id) { this.id = id; }

        public String getName() { return name; }
        public void setName(String name) {this.name = name;}
}
```

The @GeneratedValue Annotation

The @GeneratedValue annotation tells the persistence framework to autopopulate this column with the specified sequence generator, which must be defined on one of the entities in your persistence archive (it is defined directly on the Customer1 entity). An @SequenceGenerator annotation defines a sharable sequence generator, which can either define a new framework-generated sequence or refer to an existing sequence in your database. ID generators will be explored more fully in Chapter 4.

Composite Primary Key

If an entity's primary key maps to multiple database columns, it uses a complex, or composite, primary key. This may be represented in one of two ways on the entity class. The entity may declare each field in the composite key directly on the entity class—annotating each one with @Id—and specify a composite key class that provides these exact same fields in an @IdClass annotation. Alternatively, the entity may designate a single, complex field to represent its primary key, by annotating that field with @EmbeddedId. The class type of the @EmbeddedId field is the entity's composite key class. This composite key class is annotated @Embeddable and must specify the mapping details for each of its fields. These fields will end up mapping to the base table on the entity. With either approach, the composite primary key class must override the hashcode() and equals(Object obj) methods on java.lang.Object.

Listing 3-8 shows how these options look.

Listing 3-8. *An Entity with a Composite Primary Key Using @IdClass*

```
@Entity
@IdClass(Customer2PK.class)
public class Customer2 implements Serializable {
    @Id
    private Integer customerId;
    @Id
    private String name;

    public Integer getCustomerId() { return customerId; }
    public void setCustomerId(Integer customerId) { this.customerId = customerId; }

    public void setName(String name) { this.name = name; }
    public String getName() { return name; }
}
```

The @IdClass Annotation

@IdClass identifies an ordinary POJO (such as the example in Listing 3-9) that does not require any metadata. Any mapping details required for the primary key fields are specified on the fields on the entity.

Listing 3-9. *A Simple POJO That Serves As a Composite Primary Key*

```
public class Customer2PK implements Serializable {
    private Integer id;
    private String name;

    public void setId(Integer id) { this.id = id; }
    public Integer getId() { return id; }

    public void setName(String name) { this.name = name; }
    public String getName() { return name; }
}
```

The composite primary key class must conform to the access type (annotated instance variables vs. property accessors) of the entity, and all its fields or properties must have matching fields or properties on the entity class. The corresponding fields on the entity must be annotated @Id.

The @EmbeddedId Annotation

Alternatively, the entity may designate one of its fields or properties to be its composite primary key, by annotating it @EmbeddedId (see Listing 3-10).

Listing 3-10. *An Entity Using an @EmbeddedId Annotation*

```
@Entity
public class Customer3 {
  @EmbeddedId
  private Customer3PK customerId;

  public Integer getCustomerId() { return customerId; }
  public void setCustomerId(Integer customerId) { this.customerId = customerId; }
}
```

The @Embeddable Annotation

Every @EmbeddedId must reference a class that is marked @Embeddable. Listing 3-11 shows the corresponding embeddable composite key class.

Listing 3-11. *An @Embeddable Composite Key Class*

```
@Embeddable
public class Customer3PK {
  Long id;
  String name;

  public void setId(Long id) { this.id = id; }
  public Long getId() { return id; }

  public void setName(String name) { this.name = name; }
  public String getName() { return name; }

  public int hashcode() {. . .}
  public boolean equals(Object obj) {. . . }
}
```

The composite key class Customer3PK must be annotated @Embeddable. Unlike in the @IdClass case, its instance variables or property accessors may have @Column annotations to specify their mapping details.

Summary of Entity Examples

The basic @Entity and @Id annotations are sufficient to define an entity class, making the on-ramp to coding entities very straightforward. As you become more familiar with the annotations available to you, and as your requirements become more demanding, you can simply add annotations to your entities to achieve powerful persistence features. We just covered the very basics in this section. We'll now turn our attention away from the entity class itself and toward the EntityManager and some other important services in the persistence framework. Later, we'll return to explore more annotations that satisfy more complex needs.

The Persistence Archive

Until now, we have referred to the persistence archive as the encapsulation of a group of colocated entities that are deployed simultaneously in a JAR file. This archive defines the entities and related non-entity classes that are bundled together for deployment. We now take a closer look at the contents of this archive.

The persistence.xml File

A persistence archive requires a persistence.xml file (introduced in EJB 3.0) in its META-INF directory. This file groups subsets of entities in the archive into what are known as persistence units. A persistence.xml file must define at least one persistence unit, and the same entity may be included in multiple persistence units within the same persistence.xml file.

Listing 3-12 demonstrates an example of a persistence.xml file.

Listing 3-12. *An Example persistence.xml File*

```xml
<?xml version="1.0" encoding="windows-1252" ?>
<persistence xmlns:xsi="http://www.w3.org/2001/XMLSchema-instance"
            xsi:schemaLocation="http://java.sun.com/xml/ns/persistence
                http://java.sun.com/xml/ns/persistence/persistence_1_0.xsd"
            xmlns="http://java.sun.com/xml/ns/persistence" version="1.0">
  <persistence-unit name="Chapter03-Unit">
   <provider>
      oracle.toplink.essentials.ejb.cmp3.EntityManagerFactoryProvider
   </provider>
   <jta-data-source>jdbc/wineappDS</jta-data-source>
   <class>com.apress.ejb3.ch03.Customer</class>
  </persistence-unit>
  <persistence-unit name="Chapter03-Unit-JSE">
```

```
    <class>com.apress.ejb3.ch03.Customer</class>
    <properties>
      <property name="jdbc.driver" value="oracle.jdbc.driver.OracleDriver"/>
      <property name="jdbc.url"
                value="jdbc:oracle:thin:@localhost:1521:ORCL"/>
      <property name="jdbc.user" value="jwetherb"/>
      <property name="jdbc.password" value="jwetherb"/>
      <property name="platform.class.name"
value="oracle.toplink.essentials.platform.database.oracle.OraclePlatform"/>
    </properties>
  </persistence-unit>
</persistence>
```

This persistence.xml file defines two persistence units, Chapter03-Unit and
Chapter03-Unit-JSE; the Customer class is defined in both. The first persistence unit is used
by Java EE clients (like session beans), whereas the second unit is configured for use by
Java SE clients (like the CustomerService.java class shown in Listing 3-14). Specifying different configuration settings in the two persistence units allows you to insulate the client
from the configuration details of the persistent units, and makes an entity that is run in
both Java SE and EE environments appear virtually the same in both cases.

The EntityManager

The EntityManager, also introduced in EJB 3.0, is the client's gateway to entity management services offered by the EJB 3.0 persistence framework. Client sessions must obtain
an EntityManager instance before interacting with persistent entity instances. The
EntityManager provides support for querying, updating, refreshing, and removing
existing entity instances, and registering entity classes to create new persistent objects
with identity.

Persistence Context

The EntityManager maintains a cache of instances within a transactional context called a
persistence context. The persistence context allows the EntityManager to track modified,
created, and removed entity instances, and to reconcile entity instances with changes
that were committed by external transactions concurrent with the EntityManager's own
transaction.

Entity instances queried through the EntityManager may be freely passed to clients
both inside and outside the EJB container. Clients may access and update the entity data
as they would an ordinary Java object. To apply changes back to the persistent store, the

client calls the merge() method on the EntityManager, within a transactional scope, and the EntityManager persists the state of the entity data into the back-end store.

Acquiring an EntityManager Instance

An EntityManager instance can be acquired both from within the EJB container (Java EE) and outside it (Java SE). This offers clients the flexibility to interact with persistent entity beans in a uniform way, without regard to whether the persistence code is running inside or outside the Java EE container.

A Session Bean Using Container Injection

Listing 3-13 gives an example of a session bean acquiring an EntityManager instance through container injection.

Listing 3-13. *A Session Bean Injected with an EntityManager Instance*

```
@Stateless
public class CustomerManager {
    @PersistenceContext("Chapter03-Unit")
    private EntityManager em;

    public void createCustomer() {
        final Customer cust = new Customer();
        cust.setName("Moneybags MgGee");
        em.persist(cust);
    }
}
```

In this example, we use container injection to obtain an EntityManager instance that is bound to the Chapter03-Unit persistence unit, which includes our Customer entity. We then use this EntityManager to persist a new Customer instance. Note that this example assumes that an ID generator or other service exists to autopopulate the primary key of the new instance.

A Java SE Service Client Using an EntityManagerFactory

There are times when container injection is not an option, or when more control over the life cycle of the EntityManager is desired by the application. In such cases, the client can obtain an EntityManager by first acquiring an EntityManagerFactory. The javax.persistence. Persistence class serves as a factory for acquiring an EntityManagerFactory, and it may be used from both a Java EE environment and a Java SE environment. Listing 3-14 shows how an ordinary Java SE service client would obtain an EntityManager.

Listing 3-14. *A POJO That Serves As an Entity Façade*

```
public class CustomerService {
  public static void main(String[] args) {
    final EntityManagerFactory emf =
      Persistence.createEntityManagerFactory("Chapter03-Unit");
    final EntityManager em = emf.createEntityManager();
    final Customer cust = new Customer();
    cust.setName("Best Customer Ever");
    em.persist(cust);
  }
}
```

Here we create an EntityManagerFactory that is again bound to the Chapter03-Unit persistence unit, which includes our Customer entity. We then create an EntityManager instance from that factory and use it to persist a new Customer instance.

Looking Up the EntityManager Through JNDI

A third option, available also through both Java SE and EE environments, is to look up the EntityManagerFactory, or the EntityManager itself, through Java Naming and Directory Interface (JNDI). Listing 3-15 shows an example of how this is done from within a session bean.

Listing 3-15. *EntityManager Lookup Through JNDI*

```
@Stateless
@PersistenceContext(name="Chapter03-Unit")
public class CustomerServiceBean implements CustomerService {
    @Resource SessionContext ctx;
    public void performService() {
        EntityManager em = (EntityManager)ctx.lookup("Chapter03-Unit");
        ...
    }
}
```

The injected SessionContext resource provides a JNDI namespace for acquiring other resources at run time.

Transaction Support

The EntityManager also exposes methods to begin, commit, and roll back transactions, for use with resource-local (non-JTA) transactions. This topic is covered in depth in Chapter 8.

The Entity Life Cycle

An entity instance may go through many formal states during its life as an in-memory Java object. Understanding these different states will help you know when the entity is in a consistent or inconsistent state with the back-end database, and how to reconcile these differences within a transactional context.

An entity instance will typically go through many states of persistence during its lifetime as a Java object. In EJB 3.0, entity classes are completely transparent. They are created using ordinary constructors instead of the Home and LocalHome factory interfaces of earlier EJB versions. They may be freely passed to and from the EJB container and between clients, and they may be updated by a client without the overhead of a call back to the EJB container.

The Life Cycle of a New Entity Instance

Let's take a look at the life cycle of a newly created persistent entity instance. In its life, the entity may visit the new, managed, detached, and removed states.

New Entity Instance

A client creates a new entity instance by using one of the entity's Java constructors. This is a significant simplification over earlier EJB specifications, which required that users define create() factory methods on the entity bean's Home and/or LocalHome interfaces. The default (no argument) constructor is required of all entity classes, but additional constructors may be defined as well. The client may live outside or within an EJB container. At the point of construction, it is in the new state, and does not yet have persistent identity because it has not been associated with an EntityManager's persistence context. The client is free to call any of its methods and assign data values, and all updates to the entity are kept local to the entity class.

Managed Entity Instance

To turn this entity class into a persistent object, the client acquires an `EntityManager` instance and calls the `EntityManager.persist()` method. Listing 3-16 shows a code snippet from a session bean that acquires the `EntityManager` through injection, and then persists the entity instance passed as a parameter to the `persistEntity()` method.

Listing 3-16. *Example Showing How an Entity Instance Is Made Persistent*

```
@Stateless
public class MySessionEJB implements MySession {
  @PersistenceContext("Chapter03-Unit")
  private EntityManager em;

  public Object persistEntity(Object entity) {
    return em.persist(entity);
  }
}
```

When the entity is made persistent, it is added to a persistence context as a managed instance. Being managed affords the entity the following advantages.

By default, all fields on the entity are designated to be lazily loaded by the persistence provider. While a lazy designation is really only a hint (see the "Lazy vs. Eager Field Bindings" section later in the chapter), lazy field binding can be seamlessly performed only on managed instances.

When an entity is managed, changes made to it may be tracked by the persistence manager to optimize subsequent `EntityManager.merge()` operations. For instance, change tracking may be handled directly on the entity instance, using byte weaving provided by the persistence provider when the entity was instantiated. This is particularly important when managing a network of related entities, so that a minimum of effort is required to calculate the change set when the network of entities is merged back to the persistence context.

In general, there is no guarantee that a call to `EntityManager.persist()` will cause an SQL `INSERT` statement to be performed immediately. It is up to the persistence manager to decide whether to perform this step immediately, or at a later time but prior to committing the transaction. In this example, however, we can assume that a transaction was created and committed by the EJB container during the course of the `persistEntity()` method call—so the entity was not only inserted but committed as well.

Sequence values may have been assigned to the entity instance, and other side-effect code may have been executed during this step as well.

Detached Entity Instance

The entity remains in a managed state for the life of the persistence context that contains it, or until it is removed from the database. If one of these events occurs, or if the instance is passed by value to a client, it becomes a detached entity instance and is no longer associated with a persistence context. Detached entities do not undergo change tracking or other internal optimizations. In particular, the persistence provider is not available to lazily bind fields that were not already bound at the time the entity became detached; and attempting to access a detached entity's field that has not yet been bound will throw a runtime exception. To merge its state back into the persistence context and make it a managed instance again, you need to pass a detached entity to the EntityManager.merge() method.

While an entity instance returned from an EntityManager.merge() call is managed, changes are not propagated immediately to the persistent storage; they merely update the entity itself. Suppose the client modifies the entity:

```
entity = mySession.persistEntity(entity);
entity.setName( "foo" );
```

At this point, the change has been applied only to the entity instance, and no changes have been propagated to the persistence context or to the database. To apply these changes to the persistence context, you would call the EntityManager.merge() operation, as follows:

```
// Assumes the EntityManager em was obtained, possibly through injection
em.merge( entity );
```

This updates the persistence context cache, and possibly updates the row in the underlying database as well, depending on the transactional settings in effect.

Removed Entity Instance

An entity becomes a removed instance when its remove() method is called. The row (or rows, if this entity maps to multiple tables) that represents its persistent state will be removed when the context transaction is committed.

O/R Mapping

We have examined a number of annotations that define the general behavior of an entity. Let us now explore the annotations involved in the O/R mapping of persistent fields or properties on the entity to table columns in the database.

The heart of an entity class is the list of fields or properties that define its persistent structure. These fields or properties that define its persistent state must map to columns in a database table. It is the job of the persistence framework to load this state from the database into an entity instance before it is handed out to a client, and to copy this state back out to the rows of the table when it is persisted. Whereas in earlier versions of EJB, this O/R mapping information was specific to the various container-managed persistence (CMP) providers, in EJB 3.0, this mapping markup is now part of the specification. Like nearly every part of EJB 3.0, users have the choice of specifying this information through annotations, or using XML in the orm.xml file.

The @Table Annotation (Revisited)

The @Table annotation lets you specify details about the base table that an entity is mapped to. Listing 3-17 shows the @Table annotation definition.

Listing 3-17. *The @Table Annotation*

```
@Target({TYPE}) @Retention(RUNTIME)
public @interface Table {
    String name() default "";
    String catalog() default "";
    String schema() default "";
    UniqueConstraint[] uniqueConstraints() default {};
    boolean specified() default true; // For internal use only[27]
}
```

Each entity identifies a database table that will hold its persistent data, as follows:

```
@Entity
@Table(name="ADDRESSES")
public class Address implements Serializable {
    . . .
}
```

Here, the @Table annotation is used to override the default table name for the Address entity. In the absence of an @Table annotation, the default table name is the same name as the entity class itself (it would default to "ADDRESS" in this example). The @Table annotation also allows you to specify database schema and constraint information, for use when the table is generated during deployment. An entity may also map to more than one table by specifying the @SecondaryTable annotation.

Note The predefined annotation types @Target and @Retention may be specified on an annotation def-inition to provide information to the compiler about the annotation. The @Target annotation identifies the program element (in our example, a part of a class) that can accept the annotation. The @Retention anno-tation is used to indicate whether the annotation should be available only in the Java source file, or also in the compiled class file. When @Retention(SOURCE) is specified, the annotation is useful as documentation and may be used by a design-time tool like an integrated development environment (IDE); but the annotation usage is not compiled into the .class file. When @Retention(RUNTIME) is specified, the information is also compiled into the .class file and so may be obtained through Java reflection, for use by deployment or runtime tools like the EJB container.

The @Column Annotation (Revisited)

Entity class fields or properties are mapped to database columns using the @Column anno-tation. Again, if no @Column annotation is defined for a field through its instance variable or property accessor, the mapped column name gets its name from the field.

Listing 3-18 gives the definition of the @Column annotation.

Listing 3-18. *The @Column Annotation*

```
@Target({METHOD, FIELD}) @Retention(RUNTIME)
public @interface Column {
    String name() default "";
    boolean unique() default false;
    boolean nullable() default true;
    boolean insertable() default true;
    boolean updatable() default true;
    String columnDefinition() default "";
    String secondaryTable() default "";
    int length() default 255;
    int precision() default 0; // decimal precision
    int scale() default 0; // decimal scale
}
```

As you can see, it is possible to fully specify a column's attributes if desired. This is useful when you want to give deploy-time directives to generate custom column defini-tions. Most typically, you will use the name attribute to decouple the column name from the field or property name, as when the column name is too utilitarian or cryptic.

Here, the field `identifier` is told to map to a column called ID, releasing the naming dependency that binds them by default:

```
@Entity
@Table(name="ADDRESSES")
public class Address implements Serializable {
    . . .
    @Column(name="ID")
    String identifier;
    . . .
}
```

Complex Mappings

More complex mappings, including those involving multiple tables per entity, complex data types, embedded classes, and inheritance hierarchies, will be covered in the next chapter. For now, let us examine how relationships between entities are mapped.

Entity Relationships

Entities may hold single-value and collection references to themselves or to other entities. Additionally, relationships may be exposed as relationship fields on either one or both entities involved in the relationship. For those of you familiar with EJB 2.1, be aware that in EJB 3.0, relationship fields are no longer bidirectionally maintained by the container. Updating the field at one end of a bidirectional relationship no longer causes the field at the other end to be automatically updated as well. When mapping a relationship field, the target entity is always represented by its primary key. The source, or owning, end of the relationship may be mapped to a foreign key on the source entity's table, but there is no requirement that an actual database foreign key constraint be specified on the underlying columns.

Let's take a look at how EJB 3.0 lets you define relationships.

@OneToOne

Following is the definition of the @OneToOne relationship annotation:

```
@Target({METHOD, FIELD}) @Retention(RUNTIME)
public @interface OneToOne {
    Class targetEntity() default void.class;
    CascadeType[] cascade() default {};
```

```
    FetchType fetch() default EAGER;
    boolean optional() default true;
    String mappedBy() default "";
}
```

The @OneToOne relationship is represented by a single-value entity reference at one or both ends of the relationship. One relationship field will map to columns on its table that reference the primary key columns on the table at the other end of the relationship.

Here is an example in which Customer uses Address, but Address knows nothing about its usage by Customer, and so does not have a relationship field in its class:

```
@Entity
public class Customer implements Serializable {
    . . .
    @OneToOne
    @JoinColumn(name="MAILING_ADDRESS_REF",
                referencedColumnName="ADDRESS_PK")
    protected Address address;
    . . .
}
```

To make this a bidirectional relationship, simply add a relationship field to Address that points back to Customer:

```
@Entity
public class Address implements Serializable {
    . . .
    @OneToOne(mappedBy="address")
    protected Customer customer;
    . . .
}
```

Note that by using the (mappedBy="address") attribute, there is no need to redundantly specify the @JoinColumn information on the Address.customer field. Also, the entity type at the other end of the relationship is derived from the customer field type.

If you were then to make the relationship unidirectional, but in the opposite direction, you would just move the @JoinColumn annotation from Customer.address onto Address. customer, and then remove the Customer.address field.

@OneToMany and @ManyToOne

The @OneToMany relationship annotation is added to a Collection relationship field, where the entity at the other end either does not have a relationship field, or has a single-value relationship field pointing back to this entity. If there is a field on the entity at the other end of the relationship, it will be annotated @ManyToOne, indicating that it is an entity that is part of a Collection, and that it knows the entity type that owns the Collection. As with an @OneToOne relationship field, specifying a mappedBy attribute on an @OneToMany relationship is enough to identify the mapping used for both relationship fields.

```
@Entity
public class Orders implements Serializable {

    . . .

    @OneToMany(mappedBy="orders")
    protected Collection<OrderItems> orderItemsCollection;

    . . .

}

@Entity
public class OrderItems implements Serializable {

    . . .

    @ManyToOne
    @JoinColumn(name="SELECTION_REF", referencedColumnName="SELECTION_PK")
    protected Orders orders;

    . . .

}
```

Note that by using generic collection types (Collection<OrderItems>), the persistence framework is able to determine the entity type at the other end of the relationship. With that, all that is needed to resolve the mapping for the @OneToMany side is the field or property name on that entity, which in this case is orders.

@ManyToMany

The @ManyToMany annotation is assigned to a Collection relationship field to indicate that the target entity also has a Collection of the source entity type. This type of mapping requires an @JoinTable, commonly known as an intersection table. The join table holds references back to the primary keys of the entities at either end of the relationship. In the example that follows, the intersection table EJB_PROJ has two columns: EMP_ID is a reference column back to the ID primary key column on the EMPLOYEE table, and PROJ_ID is a reference column pointing to the ID primary key column on the PROJECT table.

```
@Entity
public class Employee {

    . . .

    @ManyToMany(mappedBy="employees", cascade=PERSIST)
    @JoinTable(table=@Table(name="EMP_PROJ"),
```

```
                    joinColumns={@JoinColumn(name="EMP_ID",
                                 referencedColumnName="ID")},
                    inverseJoinColumns={@JoinColumn(name="PROJ_ID",
                                          referencedColumnName="ID")})
    protected Collection<Project> projects;
    . . .
}


@Entity
public class Project {
    . . .
    @ManyToMany(mappedBy="projects")
    protected Set<Employee> employees;
    . . .
}
```

Use of the (mappedBy="projects") attribute on @ManyToMany allows the mapping information contained in the @JoinTable annotation to be shared by both relationship fields.

Lazy vs. Eager Field Bindings

By default, and for performance reasons, all field values are designated to be fetched
lazily, due to the fact that the implied fetch attribute found on each of the field mappings
(@Basic, @OneToMany, etc.) holds a default value of FetchType.LAZY. This default FetchType.
LAZY value is in fact only a hint, and the persistence manager is not bound to honor the
request. For many fields, including nearly all simple values, it would be a significant bur-
den to lazily fault in the fields of an entity as they are actually required, so the persistence
manager generally ignores the FetchType.LAZY directive and loads them eagerly anyhow.

When the non-default value FetchType.EAGER is specified on a field mapping, however,
this is not an optional request. When a field is so decorated, the persistence manager is
obliged to eagerly bind its value when the entity is instantiated. This is particularly relevant when dealing with relationship fields. A relationship field may be annotated with the
fetch=FetchType.EAGER attribute to ensure that should the entity become detached, it will
still be possible for clients to traverse that relationship field to access the related entity
instances.

When an entity is managed, relationship values will be bound at the time they are
first requested. However, when an entity is instantiated and then detached, as when it
is serialized and passed to a remote client, it may be desirable to prebind all of its relationship fields eagerly. In this case, you can override the default fetch values and set
(fetch=FetchType.EAGER) on the relationship fields. Be aware of the consequences of this
action, however, since this may cause a storm of cascaded loading if the eagerly loaded
collections in turn eagerly load their referenced objects, and so on.

Cascading Operations

Entities that are related to other entities may cascade certain life cycle operations across references. This allows an operation on one entity to propagate to certain other related entities. The cascade options are defined through annotations on the individual relationship fields, so you can precisely control the cascading behavior. Here are the cascade options:

```
public enum CascadeType {
    ALL,
    PERSIST,
    MERGE,
    REMOVE,
    REFRESH
}
```

For example, a Customer entity that holds a reference to an exclusively owned Address entity may wish to have all operations on the Customer propagated to the Address instance.

```
@Entity
public class Customer {

    . . .

    @OneToOne(cascade=ALL)
    protected Address address;

    . . .

}
```

When an EntityManager operation like persist() or remove() is called on the Customer entity, the operation will be called also on the Address instance held in the address field, and on any cascading fields of that Address instance, and so on.

Use of these cascade annotation attributes allows the entity developers to declaratively and succinctly specify cascading behavior, and saves the client from having to keep track of the network of instances that need to be manipulated when a persist(), merge(), remove(), or refresh() life cycle operation is performed on a top-level instance.

JPQL

EJB defines its own query language to support entity-based queries along with bulk update and delete operations. JPQL shares much in common with SQL, with the primary difference being that the primary structures are entities and fields, instead of tables and columns. Like SQL, JPQL queries may be defined either statically, through declared @NamedQuery annotations, or as dynamic statements submitted to the EntityManager and processed at run time. Queries may take bind parameters, and their returned results may be entities or ordinary Java objects.

By expressing queries in terms of entities and their fields, JPQL statements become independent of the underlying schema. Thus, a JPQL query need not change when an entity's mappings are modified.

JPQL queries are executed by the EntityManager on the persistence context, so query results will include uncommitted data that is pending in the context transaction.

@NamedQuery and @NamedQueries

```
@Target({TYPE}) @Retention(RUNTIME)
public @interface NamedQuery {
    String name();
    String queryString();
}
@Target({TYPE}) @Retention(RUNTIME)
public @interface NamedQueries {
    NamedQuery [] value ();
}
```

An entity may declare named JPQL statements inside @NamedQuery annotations to define reusable queries. An @NamedQuery consists simply of a name and a queryString containing the JPQL text. @NamedQuery names must be unique across the persistence unit.

```
@Entity
@NamedQueries({
  @NamedQuery(name="findAllInventory",
            queryString="select object(o) from Inventory o"),
  @NamedQuery(name="findInventoryByYear",
            queryString="select object(o) from Inventory o where o.year=:year"),
  @NamedQuery(name="findInventoryByRegion",
            queryString="select object(o) from Inventory o where o.region=?1 ")
})
public class Inventory implements Serializable {
    . . .
}
```

Binding Query Parameters

Queries may take bind parameters, either as named parameters or indexed parameters. To invoke the queries from the previous section, client code, such as a session bean, might issue the following calls:

```
@Stateless
public class InventoryManagerBean implements InventoryManager,
                                             InventoryManagerLocal {
    . . .
    /** <code>select object(o) from Inventory o</code> */
    public List<Inventory> findAllInventory() {
        return em.createNamedQuery("findAllInventory").getResultList();
    }

    /** <code>select object(o) from Inventory o where o.year=:year</code> */
    public List<Inventory> findInventoryByYear(Object year) {
        return em.createNamedQuery("findInventoryByYear").setParameter("year",
year).getResultList();
    }

    /** <code>select object(o) from Inventory o where o.region=?1 </code> */
    public List<Inventory> findInventoryByRegion(Object p1) {
        return em.createNamedQuery("findInventoryByRegion").setParameter(0,
p1).getResultList();
    }
    . . .
}
```

Note that the findInventoryByYear query takes a named parameter, :year, whereas findInventoryByRegion uses an indexed parameter, ?1. These approaches are equivalent, but require different setParameter() calls when binding the parameters prior to query execution time, as shown in the previous sample code.

Dynamic Queries

So far, we have shown example queries that are defined through the @NamedQuery annotation on an entity class. It is also possible to execute queries dynamically, by passing query strings that may be constructed on the fly at run time.

Listing 3-19 shows an example of how this is done.

Listing 3-19. *Example of Dynamic JPQL Usage*

```
@Stateless
public class InventoryManagerBean implements InventoryManager,
                                             InventoryManagerLocal {
    . . .
    /** <code>select object(o) from Inventory o</code> */
    public List<Inventory> findAllInventory() {
        return em.createQuery("select o from Inventory o").getResultList();
    }
    . . .
}
```

Bulk Update and Delete Operations

JPQL may also be used to perform bulk update and delete operations across multiple instances of a specific entity class, including subclass instances. These JPQL statements may also take parameters, and return the number of entity instances affected by the operation. An example of a bulk delete operation is shown in Listing 3-20.

Listing 3-20. *Example of a Bulk Delete Statement in JPQL*

```
@Stateless
public class InventoryManagerBean implements InventoryManager,
                                             InventoryManagerLocal {
    . . .
    /**
     * Perform a bulk delete of empty Inventory items
     */
    public int bulkDeleteEmptyInventory() {
        return em.createQuery("delete from Inventory o where o.quantity =
0").executeUpdate();
    }
    . . .
}
```

Bulk delete and update statements are also executed through the EntityManager's query engine, using the EntityManager.createQuery() call. They may also be specified either declaratively, through @NamedQuery elements, or dynamically, as shown in Listing 3-20.

■**Caution** Care should be taken when performing bulk update and delete operations, since they bypass the `PersistenceContext` and can lead to cache inconsistency. They are essentially translated straight into SQL and executed without observing optimistic locking checks or following cascade rules specified on relationship fields. As a rule of thumb, bulk operations should be performed in their own transaction context, or else at the beginning of a transaction. If a `PersistenceContext` whose `type` is `PersistenceContextType.EXTENDED` is used, make sure you call `EntityManager.flush()` after performing a bulk operation. That way, no entities will exist in the cache following the bulk operation that might be out of date or removed.

Complex Queries

We will cover more advanced areas of JPQL in the next chapter, including queries that return ordinary, non-entity Java objects, and native queries written in SQL that may return results that are converted into entity instances.

Forward Generation vs. Reverse Engineering

One of the decisions an application designer has to make when approaching EJB entity classes is whether to design them top-down or bottom-up—that is, whether to first create the entities and let the database schema follow, or whether to create the database schema first. It is of course possible to build both entities and tables in parallel, but in many cases, one or the other of these objects is fixed, and the other must be built to match.

Forward Generation == Persistence

In the top-down model, the entity class serves as the source of truth, and the database schema is created to provide persistence for the entity class data. The underlying table(s) can be generated as a side effect of deploying the entity class; you may wish to specify metadata in `@Table`, `@Column`, and related annotations to guide the deployment tool in generating the structure of the schema.

Reverse Engineering == Adaption

In the bottom-up approach, the database schema is the source of truth: the schema is fixed, and the Java objects—entity classes—exist to adapt the database objects into the Java world. This process, typically provided through an IDE using an EJB reverse engineering tool, generates a default entity class for each table and a default field for each column.

Which One Is Right for Your Project?

Both approaches are equally common in real-world development projects. Your needs will dictate which tools you will want to use to glue the database to the entity beans. You may think of the issue as one of persistence vs. adaption: does the database schema exist solely to provide persistence for the entity beans, or are you adapting the database schema into the Java space? Consider this question when you begin to create your entity beans.

Example Application: CustomerOrderManager

In the CustomerOrderManager example, we show how a session bean may serve as a façade for a handful of entities. Our CustomerOrderManager session bean exposes CRUD (create, retrieve, update, delete) operations as service methods, allowing clients to access and manipulate Customer, CustomerOrder, and Address entities. These service methods on the session façade provide transaction, access control, and other enterprise-level services, and allow the persistence framework to handle the interface between the Java data objects (entities) and the underlying RDBMS.

Customer.java

The Customer.java class, shown in Listing 3-21, hosts a pair of named queries and has a simple primary key. It holds two unidirectional @ManyToOne relationships with the Address entity, implemented through the billingAddress and shippingAddress fields. It also has a bidirectional @OneToMany relationship with CustomerOrder, exposed through the customerOrderList field. Note that the property accessors for the customerOrderList field are complemented by addOrderList() and removeOrderList() methods. These methods should be used by clients when adding or removing a CustomerOrder from a Customer, to ensure that the relationship fields on both entity classes involved are properly updated with the correct relationship information.

Listing 3-21. *Customer.java*

```
package com.apress.ejb3.ch03;

import java.io.*;
import java.util.*;
import javax.persistence.*;
```

```java
@Entity
@NamedQueries({
  @NamedQuery(name = "Customer.findAll", query = "select o from Customer o"),
  @NamedQuery(name = "Customer.findByEmail", query = "select o from Customer o where
email = :email")
})
public class Customer
  implements Serializable {
  protected String email;
  @Id
  @Column(nullable = false)
  protected Long id;
  @OneToMany(mappedBy = "customer")
  protected List<CustomerOrder> customerOrderList;
  @ManyToOne
  @JoinColumn(name = "BILLING_ADDRESS", referencedColumnName = "ID")
  protected Address billingAddress;
  @ManyToOne
  @JoinColumn(name = "SHIPPING_ADDRESS", referencedColumnName = "ID")
  protected Address shippingAddress;

  public String getEmail() {
    return email;
  }

  public void setEmail(String email) {
    this.email = email;
  }

  public Long getId() {
    return id;
  }

  public void setId(Long id) {
    this.id = id;
  }

  public List<CustomerOrder> getCustomerOrderList() {
    return customerOrderList;
  }
```

```
  public void setCustomerOrderList(List<CustomerOrder> customerOrderList) {
    this.customerOrderList = customerOrderList;
  }

  public CustomerOrder addCustomerOrder(CustomerOrder customerOrder) {
    getCustomerOrderList().add(customerOrder);
    customerOrder.setCustomer(this);
    return customerOrder;
  }

  public CustomerOrder removeCustomerOrder(CustomerOrder customerOrder) {
    getCustomerOrderList().remove(customerOrder);
    customerOrder.setCustomer(null);
    return customerOrder;
  }

  public Address getBillingAddress() {
    return billingAddress;
  }

  public void setBillingAddress(Address address) {
    this.billingAddress = address;
  }

  public Address getShippingAddress() {
    return shippingAddress;
  }

  public void setShippingAddress(Address address) {
    this.shippingAddress = address;
  }
}
```

CustomerOrder.java

An instance of the CustomerOrder entity, shown in Listing 3-22, represents an order placed by a customer. For this example, we have eliminated the related OrderItem entities for brevity. The full-blown Apress Wines Online application, which includes a number of other entities as well, is explored in Chapter 7.

Listing 3-22. *CustomerOrder.java*

```java
package com.apress.ejb3.ch03;

import java.io.*;
import java.sql.*;
import javax.persistence.*;

@Entity
@NamedQuery(name = "CustomerOrder.findAll",
  query = "select o from CustomerOrder o")
@Table(name = "CUSTOMER_ORDER")
public class CustomerOrder
  implements Serializable {
  protected String city;
  @Column(name="CREATION_DATE")
  protected Timestamp creationDate;
  @Id
  @Column(nullable = false)
  protected Long id;
  protected String state;
  protected String status;
  protected String street1;
  protected String street2;
  protected Long version;
  @Column(name="ZIP_CODE")
  protected String zipCode;
  @ManyToOne
  @JoinColumn(name = "CUSTOMER_ID", referencedColumnName = "ID")
  protected Customer customer;

  public CustomerOrder() {
  }

  public String getCity() {
    return city;
  }

  public void setCity(String city) {
    this.city = city;
  }
```

```java
public Timestamp getCreationDate() {
  return creationDate;
}

public void setCreationDate(Timestamp creationDate) {
  this.creationDate = creationDate;
}

public Long getId() {
  return id;
}

public void setId(Long id) {
  this.id = id;
}

public String getState() {
  return state;
}

public void setState(String state) {
  this.state = state;
}

public String getStatus() {
  return status;
}

public void setStatus(String status) {
  this.status = status;
}

public String getStreet1() {
  return street1;
}

public void setStreet1(String street1) {
  this.street1 = street1;
}
```

```java
  public String getStreet2() {
    return street2;
  }

  public void setStreet2(String street2) {
    this.street2 = street2;
  }

  public Long getVersion() {
    return version;
  }

  public void setVersion(Long version) {
    this.version = version;
  }

  public String getZipCode() {
    return zipCode;
  }

  public void setZipCode(String zipCode) {
    this.zipCode = zipCode;
  }

  public Customer getCustomer() {
    return customer;
  }

  public void setCustomer(Customer customer) {
    this.customer = customer;
  }
}
```

Address.java

The final entity in this example is Address, shown in Listing 3-23. The Address entity is referenced by the Customer entity, but holds no relationship field of its own, making the references from Customer unidirectional.

Listing 3-23. *Address.java*

```java
package com.apress.ejb3.ch03;

import java.io.*;
import javax.persistence.*;

@Entity
@NamedQuery(name = "Address.findAll", query = "select o from Address o")
public class Address
  implements Serializable {
  protected String city;
  @Id
  @Column(nullable = false)
  protected Long id;
  protected String state;
  protected String street1;
  protected String street2;
  protected Long version;
  @Column(name="ZIP_CODE")
  protected Long zipCode;

  public Address() {
  }

  public String getCity() {
    return city;
  }

  public void setCity(String city) {
    this.city = city;
  }

  public Long getId() {
    return id;
  }

  public void setId(Long id) {
    this.id = id;
  }
```

```java
  public String getState() {
    return state;
  }

  public void setState(String state) {
    this.state = state;
  }

  public String getStreet1() {
    return street1;
  }

  public void setStreet1(String street1) {
    this.street1 = street1;
  }

  public String getStreet2() {
    return street2;
  }

  public void setStreet2(String street2) {
    this.street2 = street2;
  }

  public Long getVersion() {
    return version;
  }

  public void setVersion(Long version) {
    this.version = version;
  }

  public Long getZipCode() {
    return zipCode;
  }

  public void setZipCode(Long zipCode) {
    this.zipCode = zipCode;
  }
}
```

CustomerOrderManager.java

The CustomerOrderManager session bean serves as a façade for the three entities shown previously, and offers an interface to the persist(), merge(), and remove() methods on EntityManager. It is shown in Listing 3-24.

Listing 3-24. *CustomerOrderManager.java*

```java
package com.apress.ejb3.ch03;

import java.util.List;
import javax.ejb.Stateless;
import javax.persistence.EntityManager;
import javax.persistence.PersistenceContext;

@Stateless(name = "SessionEJB")
public class CustomerOrderManager
  implements SessionEJB {
  @PersistenceContext(unitName = "Chapter03-Unit")
  private EntityManager em;

  public CustomerOrderManager() {
  }

  public Object mergeEntity(Object entity) {
    return em.merge(entity);
  }

  public Object persistEntity(Object entity) {
    em.persist(entity);
    return entity;
  }

  /** <code>select o from Customer o</code> */
  public List<Customer> queryCustomerFindAll() {
    return em.createNamedQuery("Customer.findAll").getResultList();
  }

  public void removeCustomer(Customer customer) {
    customer = em.find(Customer.class, customer.getId());
    em.remove(customer);
  }
```

```java
/** <code>select o from CustomerOrder o</code> */
public List<CustomerOrder> queryCustomerOrderFindAll() {
  return em.createNamedQuery("CustomerOrder.findAll").getResultList();
}

public void removeCustomerOrder(CustomerOrder customerOrder) {
  customerOrder = em.find(CustomerOrder.class, customerOrder.getId());
  em.remove(customerOrder);
}

/** <code>select o from Address o</code> */
public List<Address> queryAddressFindAll() {
  return em.createNamedQuery("Address.findAll").getResultList();
}

public void removeAddress(Address address) {
  address = em.find(Address.class, address.getId());
  em.remove(address);
}

/** <code>select o from Customer o where email = :email</code> */
public List<Customer> queryCustomerFindByEmail(Object email) {
  return em.createNamedQuery("Customer.findByEmail").setParameter("email",
email).getResultList();
}
}
```

CustomerOrderClient.java

Listing 3-25 shows a simple Java SE client that creates a new Address instance, associates it with a new Customer instance, and persists Customer. It concludes by querying Customer back again through a named query that takes Customer's email property as a query parameter.

Listing 3-25. *CustomerOrderClient.java*

```java
package com.apress.ejb3.ch03.client;

import com.apress.ejb3.ch03.Address;
import com.apress.ejb3.ch03.Customer;
import com.apress.ejb3.ch03.SessionEJB;
```

```
import javax.naming.Context;
import javax.naming.InitialContext;
import javax.naming.NamingException;

public class CustomerOrderClient {
  public static void main(String [] args) {
    try {
      final Context context = new InitialContext();
      SessionEJB sessionEJB = (SessionEJB)context.lookup("SessionEJB");
      final Address address = new Address();
      address.setCity("San Mateo");
      address.setState("CA");
      address.setZipCode(94402L);
      final Customer customer = new Customer();
      customer.setEmail("wayzout@gmail.com");
      customer.setBillingAddress(address);
      sessionEJB.persistEntity(customer);

      for (Customer cust : sessionEJB.queryCustomerFindByEmail("wayzout@gmail.com"))
  {
        System.out.println("Customer ID is " + cust.getId());
      }
    }
    catch (Exception ex) {
      ex.printStackTrace();
    }
  }
}
```

persistence.xml

To deploy this example, you will need a `persistence.xml` file that declares a named persistence unit that can be referenced by the session bean (see Listing 3-26).

Listing 3-26. *persistence.xml*

```
<?xml version="1.0" encoding="windows-1252" ?>
<persistence xmlns:xsi="http://www.w3.org/2001/XMLSchema-instance"
             xsi:schemaLocation="http://java.sun.com/xml/ns/persistence
http://java.sun.com/xml/ns/persistence/persistence_1_0.xsd"
             xmlns="http://java.sun.com/xml/ns/persistence">
```

```
    <persistence-unit name="Chapter03-Unit">
        <provider>oracle.toplink.essentials.ejb.cmp3.EntityManagerFactoryProvider
    </provider>
        <jta-data-source>jdbc/wineappDS</jta-data-source>
        <class>com.apress.ejb3.ch03.Address</class>
        <class>com.apress.ejb3.ch03.Customer</class>
        <class>com.apress.ejb3.ch03.CustomerOrder</class>
    </persistence-unit>
</persistence>
```

Conclusion

This chapter introduced the EJB 3.0 entity programming model and a few of the essential services offered by the JPA. We examined how a simple JavaBean can be transformed into an entity simply by adding a couple of annotations. We then extended this example to illustrate how you can further refine your entities to add greater flexibility by declaratively specifying additional annotations on the entity class.

We explored the essential services of the JPA: the persistence archive, the persistence unit, the persistence context, and the EntityManager. We walked through the entity life cycle states to examine an entity's behavior as it transitions between the following states: new, managed, detached, and removed.

The section on O/R mapping explored how entities map to their underlying tables, and how you can control the basic mapping to allow a field to map to a column with a different name. We then delved into entity relationships and discussed the relationship field types supported by the JPA: @OneToOne, @OneToMany, @ManyToOne, and @ManyToMany.

A discussion of JPQL ensued, with examples of how to declare and execute named queries, and how to use dynamic as well as bulk update and delete queries.

We concluded with a sample application that illustrated how related entities interact, and how they can be fronted through a session façade that is in turn called from a Java SE client.

CHAPTER 4

■ ■ ■

Advanced Persistence Features

We have organized the persistence sections of this book into three main chapters. The previous chapter introduced EJB 3 entities and the JPA, and gave you a starting point for creating entities, wiring up O/R mappings, and writing queries that retrieve them. With an understanding of these concepts, you can create and build applications with powerful, persistent entities that run inside an EJB container.

In this chapter, we build upon this knowledge and explore areas of the Java Persistence API (JPA) that offer greater flexibility and power to your applications, including the following:

- How to define and work with entity inheritance hierarchies, including abstract entities and mapped superclasses

- How to build precise and custom queries with Java Persistence Query Language (JPQL) and native SQL

- How to configure and use entities both inside and outside a Java EE container

- How to determine the choices you need to make when deciding how to organize the boundaries of persistence units

The third main area of the Persistence API, covered in Chapter 8, involves transaction management. The container provides you with options for managing the life cycle of the EntityManager, control over the longevity of your persistence context, and the use of either Java Transaction API (JTA) or resource-local transactions. With good knowledge of the way EJB 3 supports transactions and how you can apply this technology, you will have the tools to build full-scale, persistent enterprise applications.

As with the rest of this book, this chapter covers many of the concepts defined in the JSR 220 Java Persistence API, but it is not intended to fully supplant it. Indeed, users are strongly encouraged to consult the spec as a reference document and a resource for exploring these concepts in even greater depth. We focus here on translating the spec into its applied use, providing examples of how the new persistence features can be used to accomplish your real-world goals of building component-based enterprise Java applications.

■**Note** As discussed in the previous chapter, entities may designate their persistent state to be defined by either their instance variables or bean property accessors. To improve readability in this chapter, we use the term *field* to refer generically to the persistent members of an entity, leaving open the detail of how the entity declares its persistent properties.

Mapping Entity Inheritance Hierarchies

Java has supported single class inheritance—in which a non-interface class may extend a single other class—since its inception. While it has been common practice to exploit the code reuse and polymorphism benefits of inheritance in many areas of the business domain, data inheritance has not been well handled in the EJB persistence domain until now. This has been a major shortcoming, since in the real world, data is often hierarchical, and the lack of standard, built-in support for inheritance of data objects has required countless workarounds and headaches. Leveraging the ease of use of JDK 5.0 annotations, EJB 3 delivers declarative support for defining and mapping entity inheritance hierarchies, including abstract entities and polymorphic relationships and queries.

■**Note** An *abstract entity* is an entity class that contains the `abstract` modifier and therefore cannot be instantiated in its own right. An abstract entity must be an intermediate class in an entity inheritance hierarchy—it may not itself be a leaf entity since it may only be instantiated through one of its subentities. Correspondingly, all leaf entities in an entity inheritance hierarchy must be concrete, and therefore instantiable. An abstract entity exists to provide a common data structure for its subentities and to represent its subentities through polymorphic relationships with other entities.

Much of the new entity inheritance support is borne of the work of designers and tool developers who have over the years come up with ways to roll their own O/R mappings, and EJB 3 has conveniently adopted several alternative inheritance mapping approaches that derive from these efforts.

Within a given entity inheritance hierarchy, a single inheritance strategy applies to all entities in the hierarchy. Additionally, all entities in a hierarchy must use the same primary key type, regardless of the inheritance strategy. This makes it reasonable for the container to support polymorphic relationships, regardless of the mapping strategy employed for the class hierarchy.

Also note that any time a table's limitation of 256 columns becomes a factor, entities are free to distribute their field mappings across joined rows in multiple tables.

Getting Started

All the code snippets in this chapter exist in runnable form that you can download and execute directly in your local environment, together with SQL scripts for creating the corresponding tables and sequences in your local database. Since these examples deal only with entities, we can leverage the outside-the-container support offered in the JPA and skip the step of deploying these entities into a Java EE container. You will see that a simple Java class is sufficient to create an `EntityManager` that can interact with these entities and drive example tests. Seeing these concepts in action is likely to clear up any questions left unanswered here, and the samples should provide a useful launchpad for testing out your own ideas as well.

Entity Inheritance Mapping Strategies

EJB 3 provides declarative support for three main implementation strategies that dictate how the entities in a hierarchy map to underlying tables. We will examine each strategy by applying it to a sample entity hierarchy, and explore the strengths and weaknesses of each approach. This comparison is intended to help you decide how to map each of the entity hierarchies in your own application.

Sample Entity Hierarchy

To illustrate how these three strategies are manifested in code, Figure 4-1 shows a sample entity hierarchy that demonstrates both inheritance and polymorphic relationships.

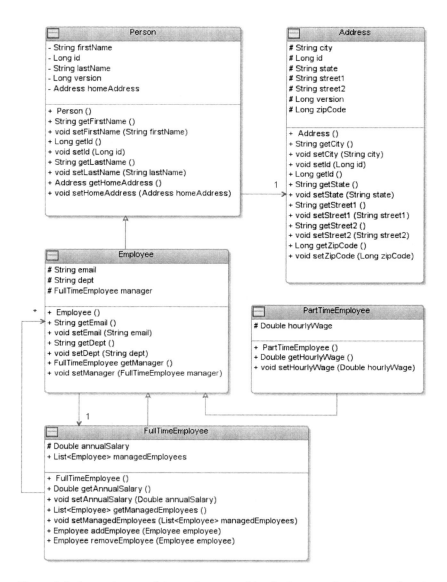

Figure 4-1. *An entity type hierarchy, rooted in the base entity Person, showing relationships to entities both inside and outside the hierarchy*

In this example, the Person entity serves as the root class in an entity hierarchy, and is extended by the Employee entity. Employee is further specialized to produce two other entities: FullTimeEmployee and PartTimeEmployee.

The root Person entity and the intermediate Employee entity are both abstract in our example. Only the leaf entities FullTimeEmployee and PartTimeEmployee, and the stand-alone entity Address, are concrete and instantiable. Note that even abstract entities may be involved in relationships with other entities, and as you will see from the code that follows, abstract entities may also be used in JPQL statements. Whenever a non-leaf entity is referenced, that reference implicitly assumes that the actual concrete implementation being referenced may be that entity or any of its subclass entities. Non-leaf entities may also be concrete, though—and had we chosen to do this in our example, we could have made these base classes concrete.

In this example, the root Person entity holds a single-value reference to an Address instance, represented by the homeAddress field on Person. This relationship is inherited by all subclasses of Person, so all instances of Employee (FullTimeEmployee and PartTimeEmployee) can refer to their homeAddress field as well. Note that there is no corresponding field on Address referencing Person, so this is a unidirectional relationship. From our coverage of entity relationships in the previous chapter, you will recall that this is a one-to-one relationship.

■**Note** A relationship between two entities that is exposed through a field on only one of the entities is known as a unidirectional relationship. A relationship exposed through fields on both entities involved is known as a bidirectional relationship.

In addition, we have defined a one-to-many, bidirectional relationship between a FullTimeEmployee (a manager) and a collection of Employees (its managedEmployees). Because this relationship is exposed through fields at both ends of the relationship (in this case, the two entities involved are actually the same entity, Employee), this is a bidirectional, one-to-many relationship.

As you look at each example, you will see how the Java source files are essentially constant across the three inheritance mapping strategies. Only the annotations for declaring the inheritance strategies, and some details like the table names, separate the entities in one example from another. This is a key benefit—the chosen inheritance strategy can be replaced without impacting the entities' Java API. In the three sections that follow, we will illustrate how each mapping strategy can be applied to this hierarchy.

Object/Relational Inheritance Mapping Strategies

Now that we have defined our entity hierarchy, let's look at how each of the three O/R strategies supported natively by EJB 3 can be used to map this Person entity hierarchy, and the associated Address entity, to a relational schema. Here is a summary of each strategy defined by the InheritanceType enum:

```
public enum InheritanceType
{ SINGLE_TABLE, JOINED, TABLE_PER_CLASS };
```

- `SINGLE_TABLE`: Single-table-per-class inheritance hierarchy. This is the default strategy. The entity hierarchy is essentially flattened into the sum of its fields, and these fields are mapped down to a single table.

- `JOINED`: Common base table, with joined subclass tables. In this approach, each entity in the hierarchy maps to its own dedicated table that maps only the fields declared on that entity. The root entity in the hierarchy is known as the base table, and the tables for all other entities in the hierarchy join with the base table. This strategy is not mandated of persistence providers for EJB 3 spec compliance, so be aware that it may not be supported on all platforms.

- `TABLE_PER_CLASS`: Single-table-per-outermost concrete entity class. The third inheritance mapping option is also not required of JPA containers for compliance with the final draft of the EJB 3 spec, so portable applications should avoid it until it is officially mandated or at least widely supported. This strategy maps each leaf (i.e., outermost, concrete) entity to its own dedicated table. Each such leaf entity branch is flattened, combining its declared fields with the declared fields on all of its superentities, and the sum of these fields is mapped onto its table.

The @GeneratedValue Annotation

In each of the inheritance strategy examples, we use the `@GeneratedValue` annotation to autopopulate the `id` field for both the `Person` entity hierarchy and the stand-alone `Address` entity. Specifying an ID generator in metadata allows the persistence provider to assign an entity its ID value before the entity is actually saved as a row in the database. Declarative specification of the `@GeneratedValue` annotation is certainly easier than assigning the ID in application code, and is also an optimization over the alternative of autopopulating the ID value using a database trigger. Since the ID value is used when persisting relationship mappings, this saves the persistence manager the trouble of querying the row back again from the database to retrieve the trigger-populated value. Details on how to customize sequence- or table-based ID generators are provided later in the chapter.

We will now explore each strategy, discussing its strengths and weaknesses, and illustrating its use through examples.

Single-Table-per-Class Inheritance Hierarchy (InheritanceType.SINGLE_TABLE)

The default inheritance mapping strategy is `SINGLE_TABLE`, in which all the entities in the class hierarchy map onto a single table. A dedicated discriminator column on this table identifies the specific entity type associated with each row, and each entity in the hierarchy is given a unique value to store in this column. By default, the discriminator value for an entity is its entity name, although an entity may override this value using the @DiscriminatorValue annotation. This approach performs well for querying, since only a single table is involved, and if your type hierarchy can abide by the practical limitations, this is probably the best approach to use.

Figure 4-2 shows a diagram of a schema that maps our example entities using the SINGLE_TABLE strategy. We have chosen to prefix these tables with CH04_ST_ to avoid conflicts with the PERSON and ADDRESS tables in our example schema that are used by the full Enterprise Wines Online application.

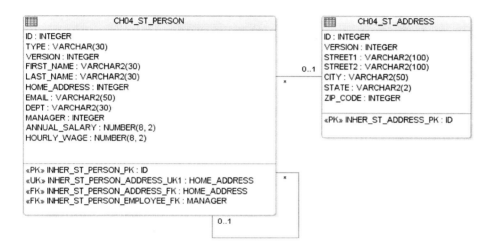

Figure 4-2. *The CH04_ST_PERSON table holds all entity instances in the entity hierarchy rooted by Person. The CH04_ST_ADDRESS table holds the associated Address instances.*

All the properties across the entity hierarchy rooted by the Person entity map to columns on a single table, CH04_ST_PERSON. This table holds a foreign key reference, bound to the HOME_ADDRESS column, to CH04_ST_ADDRESS, which is mapped to the Address entity. This column also has a unique key constraint, ensuring that each row in the CH04_ST_ADDRESS table corresponds to, at most, one row in the CH04_ST_PERSON table. It also holds a foreign key reference, using the MANAGER column, back to itself. This foreign key is not constrained to be unique, indicating that multiple rows may hold the same value in their MANAGER column.

Example Entity Classes

Listings 4-1 through 4-4 show how the entities in the Person hierarchy are mapped using the SINGLE_TABLE inheritance strategy. The strategy is declared on the root entity in the hierarchy, and applies to all subentities in the hierarchy as well. Annotations introduced in the example entities that have not yet been covered are explained in the sections that follow.

Listing 4-1. *Person.java, an Abstract Root Entity in a SINGLE_TABLE Inheritance Hierarchy*

```
/*
 * Person:  An abstract entity, and the root of a SINGLE_TABLE hierarchy
 */
@Entity
@Inheritance(strategy = InheritanceType.SINGLE_TABLE)
@DiscriminatorColumn(name = "TYPE")
@NamedQuery(name = "Person.findAll", query = "select o from Person o")
@SequenceGenerator(name = "PersonIdGenerator",
                   sequenceName = "CH04_ST_PERSON_SEQ", initialValue = 100,
                   allocationSize = 20)
@Table(name = "CH04_ST_PERSON")
public abstract class Person
  implements Serializable
{
  @Column(name = "FIRST_NAME")
  private String firstName;
  @Id
  @Column(nullable = false)
  @GeneratedValue(generator="PersonIdGenerator")
  private Long id;
  @Column(name = "LAST_NAME")
  private String lastName;
  @Version
  private Long version;
  @OneToOne(cascade = { CascadeType.ALL })
  @JoinColumn(name = "HOME_ADDRESS", referencedColumnName = "ID")
  private Address homeAddress;

  public Person() {
  }

  /* get/set methods... */
}
```

Listing 4-2. *Employee.java, an Abstract Intermediate Entity in a SINGLE_TABLE Inheritance Hierarchy*

```
/*
 * Employee:  An abstract entity
 */
@Entity
@NamedQuery(name = "Employee.findAll", query = "select o from Employee o")
public abstract class Employee
  extends Person
  implements Serializable
{
  protected String email;
  protected String dept;
  @ManyToOne(cascade = { CascadeType.ALL })
  @JoinColumn(name = "MANAGER", referencedColumnName = "ID")
  protected FullTimeEmployee manager;

  public Employee() {
  }

  /* get/set methods... */
}
```

Listing 4-3. *FullTimeEmployee.java, a Concrete Leaf Entity in a SINGLE_TABLE Inheritance Hierarchy*

```
/*
 * FullTimeEmployee:  A concrete leaf entity */
@Entity
@NamedQuery(name = "FullTimeEmployee.findAll",
            query = "select o from FullTimeEmployee o")
@DiscriminatorValue("FullTimeEmployee") // Illustrating the default value
public class FullTimeEmployee
  extends Employee
  implements Serializable
{
  @Column(name = "ANNUAL_SALARY")
  protected Double annualSalary;

  @OneToMany(mappedBy = "manager", cascade = { CascadeType.ALL })
  public List<Employee> managedEmployees;
```

```
    public FullTimeEmployee() {
    }

    /* get/set methods... */
}
```

Listing 4-4. *PartTimeEmployee.java, a Concrete Leaf Entity in a SINGLE_TABLE Inheritance Hierarchy*

```
/*
 * PartTimeEmployee:  A concrete leaf entity
 */
@Entity
@NamedQuery(name = "PartTimeEmployee.findAll",
            query = "select o from PartTimeEmployee o")
public class PartTimeEmployee
  extends Employee
  implements Serializable
{
  @Column(name = "HOURLY_WAGE")
  protected Double hourlyWage;

  public PartTimeEmployee() {
  }

  /* get/set methods... */
}
```

Outside of this entity hierarchy lives the Address entity, shown in Listing 4-5. This entity is the target of a unidirectional @OneToOne relationship with the root (and abstract) Person entity shown previously.

Listing 4-5. *Address.java, a Concrete Stand-Alone Entity*

```
/*
 * Address:  A standalone entity
 */
@Entity
@NamedQuery(name = "Address.findAll", query = "select o from Address o")
@SequenceGenerator(name = "AddressIdGenerator",
                   sequenceName = "CH04_ST_ADDRESS_SEQ", initialValue = 100,
```

```
                          allocationSize = 20)
@Table(name = "CH04_ST_ADDRESS")
public class Address
  implements Serializable
{
  protected String city;
  @Id
  @Column(nullable = false)
  @GeneratedValue(generator="AddressIdGenerator")
  protected Long id;
  protected String state;
  protected String street1;
  protected String street2;
  @Version
  protected Long version;
  @Column(name = "ZIP_CODE")
  protected Long zipCode;

  public Address() {
  }

  /* get/set methods... */
}
```

Let's take a look at some of the annotations that were introduced in this example.

The @JoinColumn Annotation

An Employee entity has a manager field of type FullTypeEmployee, and is mapped this way:

```
@ManyToOne(cascade = { CascadeType.ALL })
@JoinColumn(name = "MANAGER", referencedColumnName = "ID")
protected FullTimeEmployee manager;
```

The manager field is of type FullTimeEmployee and maps to the to the MANAGER column, identified by the name = "MANAGER" attribute on the @JoinColumn annotation. The MANAGER column is a foreign key reference to the table mapped by the FullTypeEmployee entity, which in this case is the same CH04_ST_PERSON table. The @JoinColumn's referencedColumnName = "ID" attribute designates the target column on that table. Because this field maps to the foreign key column, it is considered the *owning* end of the relationship.

The cascade = { CascadeType.ALL } attribute indicates that any operation performed on this entity, Employee, must also be applied to FullTimeEmployee instances referenced by this relationship field. For example, if a new Employee instance is created and assigned a FullTimeEmployee as its manager, the act of persisting the Employee instance through EntityManager.persist() will also cause the referenced FullTimeEmployee instance to be persisted as well, if it has not been persisted already.

The entity at the other end of this bidirectional relationship, FullTimeEmployee, holds the managedEmployee field.

```
@OneToMany(mappedBy = "manager", cascade = { CascadeType.ALL })
public List<Employee> managedEmployees;
```

Since we have already specified the mapping on the owning end, this field can simply refer to that manager field, using the mappedBy = "manager" attribute. This managedEmployees field contains a list of Employee instances, which in practice will be concrete FullTimeEmployee and/or PartTimeEmployee instances. The managedEmployees field is also marked cascade = { CascadeType.ALL }, and so operations applied to the managing FullTimeEmployee will be propagated to all Employee instances in the managedEmployees list.

The @DiscriminatorColumn Annotation

By default, the persistence manager looks for a column named DTYPE in the root entity's table (CH04_ST_PERSON, in this case). In our example, we have named the discriminator column TYPE, so we explicitly annotate this setting, using the @DiscriminatorColumn(name = "TYPE") annotation. Were we to use a column named DTYPE, we could have skipped this annotation altogether, and accepted the default value.

The @DiscriminatorValue Annotation

Each concrete entity declares, either explicitly or by tacitly accepting the default, a unique discriminator value that serves to identify the concrete entity type associated with each row in the table. The discriminator value defaults to the entity name, and in this example we have accepted this default value for each of the entities in the hierarchy. When adapting legacy tables and data into EJB 3 (it is necessary to map preexisting discriminator values to entities with dissimilar names), you can use the @DiscriminatorValue annotation to specify the discriminator value to use for each entity in the hierarchy that requires an override.

Pros and Cons of the SINGLE_TABLE Strategy

Table 4-1 offers a look at some of the strengths and weaknesses of the SINGLE_TABLE entity inheritance strategy.

Table 4-1. *Pros and Cons of the SINGLE_TABLE Inheritance Strategy*

Considerations	Pros and Cons
Design-time considerations	This mapping approach works well when the type hierarchy is fairly simple and stable. Adding a new type to the hierarchy and adding fields to existing supertypes simply involves adding new columns to the table; though in particularly large deployments, this may have an adverse impact on the index and column layout inside the database. If your hierarchy may outgrow the column limitations of a single table, which is typically 256 columns, or if for some reason you need to map more than one very large field to inline LOB (Locator OBject) columns, you may have to introduce an @SecondaryTable mapping. In this case, it might be wiser to adopt one of the approaches that follow.
Performance impact	This strategy is very efficient for querying across all types in the hierarchy, or specific types. No table joins are required by the internal persistence framework—only a WHERE clause listing the type identifiers. In particular, relationships involving types that employ this mapping strategy are very performant.

Sample Client Code

As we mentioned in the "Getting Started" section of this chapter, we have put together sample client code to test the inheritance examples, along with the other examples that appear later in this chapter. Listing 4-6 shows a client that tests the previously shown entities that use the SINGLE_TABLE inheritance mapping strategy. Interestingly, this same client code can be used for all the other examples as well, provided that you update the PERSISTENCE_UNIT field to point to the persistence unit that we have defined for each of the examples.

Listing 4-6. *EntityClient.java, a Sample Entity Client That Illustrates Creating and Retrieving the Entities Defined in Figure 4-1*

```
/*
 * Sample entity client that obtains an EntityManager running outside of a
 * Java EE container, and illustrates CRUD operations on a handful of entities
 */
public class EntityClient
{
  private static final String PERSISTENCE_UNIT = "Ch04_SingleTable-JSE";
```

```java
public static void main(String[] args) {
    // Use the EntityManagerFactory to obtain an EntityManager for
    // PERSISTENCE_UNIT. From the EntityManager, acquire an EntityTransaction
    // instance.
    final EntityManagerFactory emf =
        Persistence.createEntityManagerFactory(PERSISTENCE_UNIT);
    final EntityManager em = emf.createEntityManager();
    final EntityTransaction et = em.getTransaction();

    // Clear out any previous test data. Due to "cascade" settings on the
    // "homeAddress" relationship field, removing a Person will remove its
    // Address as well.
    final List<Person> people =
        em.createNamedQuery("Person.findAll").getResultList();

    try {
        et.begin();
        for (Person person: people) {
            System.out.println("Removing " + person.getLastName());
            em.remove(person);
        }
        et.commit();
    }
    catch (Exception e) {
        if (et.isActive()) {
            et.rollback();
        }
    }

    // Create some entities and wire them together
    final FullTimeEmployee ftEmp = new FullTimeEmployee();
    ftEmp.setFirstName("Jon");
    ftEmp.setLastName("Wetherbee");
    ftEmp.setEmail("laterdaze@wayzout.com");
    ftEmp.setAnnualSalary(123.45);
    ftEmp.setDept("Magistry");

    final Address ftAddress = new Address();
    ftAddress.setCity("San Mateo");
    ftAddress.setState("CA");
    ftAddress.setStreet1("28 Barbary Lane");
    ftAddress.setZipCode(94402L);
```

```
ftEmp.setHomeAddress(ftAddress);

final PartTimeEmployee ptEmp = new PartTimeEmployee();
ptEmp.setFirstName("John Paul");
ptEmp.setLastName("Jones");
ptEmp.setEmail("led@zep.com");

ftEmp.addEmployee(ptEmp);

//  Perform a persist operation inside a transaction. Note that no
//  transaction context was required before this, during entity creation
//  and association. Also note that we have set up "cascade" settings on
//  all relationships, so persisting our FullTimeEmployee causes a cascading
//  persist of its related PartTimeEmployee and Address entities.
try {
  et.begin();
  em.persist(ftEmp);
  et.commit();
}
catch (Exception e) {
  if (et.isActive()) {
    et.rollback();
  }
}

//  Now we query back all FullTimeEmployee entities, and print out some
//  details
final List<FullTimeEmployee> ftEmps =
  em.createNamedQuery("FullTimeEmployee.findAll").getResultList();
for (FullTimeEmployee mgr: ftEmps) {
  System.out.println(mgr.getFirstName());
  System.out.println(mgr.getLastName());
  System.out.println(mgr.getEmail());

  //  Traverse the managedEmployees relationship field
  for (Employee emp: mgr.getManagedEmployees()) {
    System.out.println(emp.getFirstName());
    System.out.println(emp.getLastName());
    System.out.println(emp.getEmail());
```

```
            //  Traverse back through the manager relationship field to its
            //  homeAddress relationship field, and print some of its fields
            final Address mgrHomeAddress = emp.getManager().getHomeAddress();
            System.out.println(mgrHomeAddress.getStreet1());
            System.out.println(mgrHomeAddress.getCity());
            System.out.println(mgrHomeAddress.getState());
            System.out.println(mgrHomeAddress.getZipCode());
        }
    }

    //  Ad-hoc JPQL to demonstrate polymorphic relationship usage
    final String stmt = "select o from Employee o " +
      "where o.homeAddress.city = 'San Mateo'";
    final List<Employee> emps = em.createQuery(stmt).getResultList();
    for (Employee emp : emps)
    {
      System.out.println(emp.getFirstName());
      System.out.println(emp.getLastName());
    }
  }
}
```

Common Base Table with Joined Subclass Tables (InheritanceType.JOINED)

In the JOINED strategy, each entity in the hierarchy introduces its own table, but only to map fields that are declared on that entity type. The root entity in the hierarchy maps to a root table that defines the primary key structure to be used by all tables in the entity hierarchy, as well as the discriminator column and optionally a version column. Each of the other tables in the hierarchy defines a primary key that matches the root table's primary key, and optionally adds a foreign key constraint from their ID column(s) to the root table's ID column(s). The non-root tables do not hold discriminator type or version columns. Since each entity instance in the hierarchy is represented by a virtual row that spans its own table as well as the tables for all of its superentities, it eventually joins with a row in the root table that captures this discriminator type and version information. Querying all the fields of any type requires a join across all the tables within the supertype hierarchy.

Figure 4-3 illustrates the schema that maps our entities using the JOINED inheritance strategy. As in the previous example, we have prefixed the tables with the strategy indicator, in this case CH04_JOIN_, so that all the tables in these examples can be loaded into a single test schema without danger of name collision.

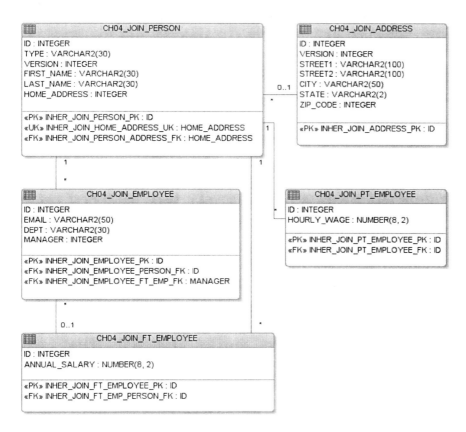

Figure 4-3. *A schema that maps our example entities using the JOINED strategy. Each entity in the hierarchy has its own table to persist its declared fields. The table CH04_JOIN_ADDRESS holds associated Address instances.*

Example Entity Classes

Let's now take a look at the entity classes that map to the previous schema. We have omitted the class bodies for each of these entities, since the only differences between these entities and the ones shown in the previous SINGLE_TABLE strategy example lie in the entity's class-level annotations. Listings 4-7 through 4-10 show the entities in the Person hierarchy, while Listing 4-11 shows the Address entity.

Listing 4-7. *Person.java, an Abstract Root Entity in a JOINED Inheritance Hierarchy*

```
/*
 * Person:  An abstract entity, and the root of a JOINED hierarchy
 */
@Entity
@Inheritance(strategy = InheritanceType.JOINED)
@DiscriminatorColumn(name = "TYPE")
@NamedQuery(name = "Person.findAll", query = "select o from Person o")
@SequenceGenerator(name = "PersonIdGenerator",
                    sequenceName = "CH04_JOIN_PERSON_SEQ", initialValue = 100,
                    allocationSize = 20)
@Table(name = "CH04_JOIN_PERSON")
public abstract class Person
  implements Serializable
{
  /* The class body is identical across all inheritance strategies */
}
```

Listing 4-8. *Employee.java, an Abstract Intermediate Entity in a JOINED Inheritance Hierarchy*

```
/*
 * Employee:  An abstract entity
 */
@Entity
@NamedQuery(name = "Employee.findAll", query = "select o from Employee o")
@Table(name = "CH04_JOIN_EMPLOYEE")
public abstract class Employee
  extends Person
  implements Serializable
{
  /* The class body is identical across all inheritance strategies */
}
```

Listing 4-9. *FullTimeEmployee.java, a Concrete Leaf Entity in a JOINED Inheritance Hierarchy*

```
/*
 * FullTimeEmployee:  A concrete leaf entity
 */
@Entity
@NamedQuery(name = "FullTimeEmployee.findAll",
```

```
              query = "select o from FullTimeEmployee o")
@Table(name = "CH04_JOIN_FT_EMPLOYEE")
public class FullTimeEmployee
  extends Employee
  implements Serializable
{
  /* The class body is identical across all inheritance strategies */
}
```

Listing 4-10. *PartTimeEmployee.java, a Concrete Leaf Entity in a JOINED Inheritance Hierarchy*

```
/*
 * PartTimeEmployee:  A concrete leaf entity
 */
@Entity
@NamedQuery(name = "PartTimeEmployee.findAll",
             query = "select o from PartTimeEmployee o")
@Table(name = "CH04_JOIN_PT_EMPLOYEE")
public class PartTimeEmployee
  extends Employee
  implements Serializable
{
  /* The class body is identical across all inheritance strategies */
}
```

Listing 4-11. *Address.java, a Concrete Stand-Alone Entity*

```
/*
 * Address:  A standalone entity
 */
@Entity
@NamedQuery(name = "Address.findAll", query = "select o from Address o")
@SequenceGenerator(name = "AddressIdGenerator",
                    sequenceName = "CH04_JOIN_ADDRESS_SEQ", initialValue = 100,
                    allocationSize = 20)
@Table(name = "CH04_JOIN_ADDRESS")
public class Address
  implements Serializable
{
  /* The class body is identical across all inheritance strategies */
}
```

You can see from the highlighted differences that they are very minimal. Ignoring table name differences, which are thrown in simply out of our desire to avoid name collisions with the tables in the other examples, only the @Inheritance annotation has changed. Besides its table and sequence names, the Address entity is identical to Listing 4-5, the previous example of the SINGLE_TABLE strategy.

Pros and Cons of the JOINED Strategy

Table 4-2 offers a look at some of the strengths and weaknesses of the JOINED entity inheritance strategy.

Table 4-2. *Pros and Cons of the JOINED Inheritance Strategy*

Considerations	Pros and Cons
Design-time considerations	Introducing a new type to the hierarchy, at any level, simply involves interjecting a new table into the schema. Subtypes of that type will automatically join with that new type at run time. Similarly, modifying any entity type in the hierarchy by adding, modifying, or removing fields affects only the immediate table mapped to that type. This option provides the greatest flexibility at design time, since changes to any type are always limited to that type's dedicated table.
Performance impact	This approach does not suffer from the use of UNION operations, but inherently requires multiple JOIN operations to perform just about any query. Querying across all instances initially involves only a single query of the topmost base entity's table to retrieve a list of all primary keys of instances in the hierarchy. Due to the presence of the discriminator column in the base entity's table, resolution of these instances into entity classes can be efficient, depending on the lazy loading strategies employed by the persistence manager implementation.

Single-Table-per-Outermost Concrete Entity Class (InheritanceType.TABLE_PER_CLASS)

Support for the final inheritance mapping strategy is optional for persistence providers. It is not required for compliance with the EJB 3 spec, so portable applications should avoid it until it is officially mandated or at least widely supported. This inheritance mapping option maps each outermost concrete entity to its own, dedicated table. Each table maps all of the fields in that entity's entire type hierarchy; since there is no shared table, no columns are shared. The only table structure requirement is that all tables must share a common primary key structure, meaning that the name(s) and type(s) of the primary key column(s) must match across all tables in the hierarchy.

For good measure, Figure 4-4 illustrates our third type hierarchy using the joined table approach, which demonstrates the use of the single-table-per-outermost entity subclass strategy. The tables are required to share nothing in common except the structure of their primary key, and since the table implicitly identifies the entity type, no discriminator column is required. With this inheritance mapping strategy, only concrete entities—FullTimeEmployee, PartTimeEmployee, and Address in our example—require tables.

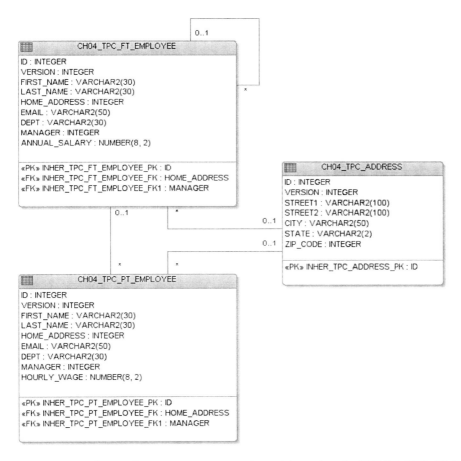

Figure 4-4. *A schema that maps our example entities using the TABLE_PER_CLASS strategy. Concrete leaf entities are mapped to dedicated tables that contain columns that map all of their declared and inherited fields.*

Example Entity Classes

Listings 4-12 through 4-15 show how the entities mapped to these tables are annotated. Since only the class-level annotations are different from the previous strategy, the method bodies are stripped out.

Listing 4-12. *Person.java, an Abstract Root Entity in a TABLE_PER_CLASS Inheritance Hierarchy*

```
/*
 * Person:  An abstract entity, and the root of a TABLE_PER_CLASS hierarchy
 */
@Entity
@Inheritance(strategy = InheritanceType.TABLE_PER_CLASS)
@DiscriminatorColumn(name = "TYPE")
@NamedQuery(name = "Person.findAll", query = "select o from Person o")
@SequenceGenerator(name = "PersonIdGenerator",
                   sequenceName = "CH04_TPC_PERSON_SEQ", initialValue = 100,
                   allocationSize = 20)
@Table(name = "CH04_TPC_PERSON")
public abstract class Person
  implements Serializable
{
  /* The class body is identical across all inheritance strategies */
}
```

Listing 4-13. *Employee.java, an Abstract Intermediate Entity in a TABLE_PER_CLASS Inheritance Hierarchy*

```
/*
 * Employee:  An abstract entity
 */
@Entity
@NamedQuery(name = "Employee.findAll", query = "select o from Employee o")
@Table(name = "CH04_TPC_EMPLOYEE")
public abstract class Employee
  extends Person
  implements Serializable
{
  /* The class body is identical across all inheritance strategies */
}
```

Listing 4-14. *FullTimeEmployee.java, a Concrete Leaf Entity in a TABLE_PER_CLASS Inheritance Hierarchy*

```
/*
 * FullTimeEmployee:  A concrete leaf entity
 */
@Entity
@NamedQuery(name = "FullTimeEmployee.findAll",
            query = "select o from FullTimeEmployee o")
@Table(name = "CH04_TPC_FT_EMPLOYEE")
public class FullTimeEmployee
  extends Employee
  implements Serializable
{
  /* The class body is identical across all inheritance strategies */
}
```

Listing 4-15. *PartTimeEmployee.java, a Concrete Leaf Entity in a TABLE_PER_CLASS Inheritance Hierarchy*

```
/*
 * PartTimeEmployee:  A concrete leaf entity
 */
@Entity
@NamedQuery(name = "PartTimeEmployee.findAll",
            query = "select o from PartTimeEmployee o")
@Table(name = "CH04_TPC_PT_EMPLOYEE")
public class PartTimeEmployee
  extends Employee
  implements Serializable
{
  /* The class body is identical across all inheritance strategies */
}
```

The Address class in the TABLE_PER_CLASS example is identical to the previous examples, aside from the table and sequence names we have chosen.

Pros and Cons of the TABLE_PER_CLASS Strategy

Table 4-3 offers a look at some of the strengths and weaknesses of the TABLE_PER_CLASS entity inheritance strategy.

Table 4-3. *Pros and Cons of the TABLE_PER_CLASS Inheritance Strategy*

Considerations	Pros and Cons
Design-time considerations	As new outermost concrete types are introduced into the hierarchy, new tables are added. This is nice because no existing tables (nor their data) need be aware. However, since each type maps all of its supertype fields as well, introducing a new field on a base class, or a new base entity itself, requires modifying the tables for all affected subtypes across the hierarchy to map any newly introduced fields.
Performance impact	Querying across multiple types requires a UNION select statement, which is not very performant, but querying a single type is very efficient, since only one table is involved in the query. Relationships involving supertypes in this hierarchy should be avoided, since they will necessarily require this UNION operation to resolve to concrete subtype instances.

Comparison of O/R Implementation Approaches

Now that we have explored the three inheritance mapping implementations, let's look at some of the characteristics of a class inheritance hierarchy to consider when choosing which implementation approach to use for your type hierarchies. The following list contains subjective questions about your own entity hierarchies. They do not have precise answers, but are meant to stimulate design consideration when building your application.

- Class hierarchies can be static, with a fixed number of subtypes, or they can be dynamic, with varying numbers of subtypes. How often will you need to incorporate new subtypes into your hierarchy?

- Hierarchies can be deep, with lots of subclasses, or they can be shallow, with only a few. How granular is your hierarchy?

- The types in a hierarchy may diverge greatly, with very different sets of properties on the subclasses than the base class, or with very little difference in properties. How much do the persistent property sets of your entities diverge from one another?

- Will other entities define relationships with classes in this type hierarchy, and if so, will the base classes frequently be the referenced type?

- Will types in this hierarchy be frequently queried, updated, or deleted? How will the presence or absence of SQL JOIN or UNION operations impact your application's performance?

- During the life of your application, how frequently will you be updating the structure of the type hierarchy itself? The impact of this type of change varies for each inheritance strategy, with considerations that include the following:

    - Adding or removing new types to the hierarchy (as when refactoring classes).

    - Adding, removing, or modifying fields on an entity in the hierarchy.

    - Adding, removing, or modifying relationships involving types in this hierarchy.

■**Note** A comparison of the performance of these three inheritance strategies, along with details on how to set up your own performance comparison tests, is explored in Chapter 9. Check out the results of our performance tests, and test your own entity hierarchies as you build them, to help you decide which strategy makes best sense in the context of your application.

Using Abstract Entities, Mapped Superclasses, and Non-Entity Classes in an Inheritance Hierarchy

Within an entity class hierarchy, EJB 3 allows both non-entity classes and abstract classes to be intermixed. Let's look at how we map these classes.

Abstract Entity Class

As shown in the previous section on inheritance hierarchies, EJB 3 entities may be either concrete or abstract. An abstract entity is simply an entity that cannot be instantiated—in can still be involved in entity relationships and queries, and its fields are persisted following the mapping strategy for its type hierarchy. Listing 4-16 is an example of one of our abstract entities.

Listing 4-16. *Person.java, an Abstract Root Entity in a JOINED Inheritance Hierarchy*

```
/*
 * Person:  An abstract entity, and the root of a JOINED hierarchy
 */
@Entity
@Inheritance(strategy = InheritanceType.JOINED)
@DiscriminatorColumn(name = "TYPE")
@NamedQuery(name = "Person.findAll", query = "select o from Person o")
@SequenceGenerator(name = "PersonIdGenerator",
                   sequenceName = "CH04_JOIN_PERSON_SEQ", initialValue = 100,
                   allocationSize = 20)
@Table(name = "CH04_JOIN_PERSON")
public abstract class Person
  implements Serializable
{
  ...
  @OneToOne(cascade = { CascadeType.ALL })
  @JoinColumn(name = "HOME_ADDRESS", referencedColumnName = "ID")
  private Address homeAddress;
  ...
}
```

Not only is the abstract Person entity queryable (here we have defined a
"Person.findAll" named query), it also holds an association with the Address entity that is
shared by all of its subclasses. Although Person is abstract, it can specify its own mappings
and its own table. It just won't have its own discriminator value, since there will never be
a concrete entity instance of the base class Person.

Mapped Superclass (@MappedSuperclass)

A mapped superclass is a non-entity class that is nonetheless recognized by the persistence manager, and that declares persistent fields and their mappings. Since it is not an
entity, it may not be the target of persistent entity relationships, nor may it be used in
queries. It may, however, provide persistent properties common to any entities that
extend it, whether directly or indirectly. Starting with the previous inheritance example,
let us transform the root entity, Person, into a mapped superclass. Listings 4-17 and 4-18
show the transformed classes.

Listing 4-17. *Person.java, an Abstract Mapped Superclass (Non-Entity)*

```
/*
 * Person:  An abstract non-entity mapped superclass
 */
@MappedSuperclass
@SequenceGenerator(name = "PersonIdGenerator",
                   sequenceName = "CH04_MS_PERSON_SEQ", initialValue = 100,
                   allocationSize = 20)
public abstract class Person
  implements Serializable
{
  @Column(name = "FIRST_NAME")
  private String firstName;
  @OneToOne(cascade = { CascadeType.ALL })
  @JoinColumn(name = "HOME_ADDRESS", referencedColumnName = "ID")
  private Address homeAddress;
  @Id
  @Column(nullable = false)
  @GeneratedValue(generator="PersonIdGenerator")
  private Long id;
  @Column(name = "LAST_NAME")
  private String lastName;
  @Version
  private Long version;

  public Person() {
  }

  /* get/set methods */
}
```

Listing 4-18. *Employee.java, an Abstract Root Entity in a SINGLE_TABLE Entity Inheritance Hierarchy, and a Subclass of a Mapped Superclass*

```
/*
 * Employee:  A root entity in a JOINED inheritance hierarchy, and a subclass
 * of the mapped superclass Person
 */
@Entity
@Inheritance(strategy = InheritanceType.JOINED)
@DiscriminatorColumn(name = "TYPE")
```

```
@NamedQuery(name = "Employee.findAll", query = "select o from Employee o")
@Table(name = "CH04_MS_EMPLOYEE")
public class Employee
  extends Person
  implements Serializable
{
  protected String email;
  protected String dept;

  public Employee() {
  }

  /* get/set methods */
}
```

The Person class becomes a mapped superclass (@MappedSuperclass) and all of its class-level annotations are moved onto Employee, which becomes the new root entity in the hierarchy. While a mapped superclass may not be referenced through a persistence relationship field, it may have persistence relationship fields of its own, so the homeAddress field that references the Address entity is perfectly legal. Also note that we can continue to define the @Id and @Version fields on the mapped superclass, and we can even continue to specify an ID generator for the id field. Entities that extend this mapped superclass map these fields, along with all other fields defined on the mapped superclass, onto their own tables.

Non-Entity Class

Entities may also make use of non-entity classes within their type hierarchies. An entity may subclass a non-entity class, or may be extended by a non-entity class. Such classes may be concrete or abstract, and so may be instantiable, but their fields will not be persistable or maintained by the EJB persistence framework. They also may not participate at all in persistent entity relationships or JPQL queries. If a class in a type hierarchy serves only as an organizing construct for its subclasses, and is not involved in entity relationships (and there is no other reason to mark it as an entity), then it is best left as an ordinary class. It can always be turned into an entity later by annotating it or designating it an entity in the XML descriptor.

Embedded Non-Entity Class Usage (@Embeddable and @Embedded)

Finally, an entity may embed a non-entity class for its own private use. Such classes are marked @Embeddable and may hold mapping metadata for their persistent fields. A class marked @Embeddable may be used as a field type in an entity. When used in this way, the field is marked @Embedded and the fields on the embeddable class map to the owning entity's table. Embeddable classes have no persistent identity of their own, and instances of embeddable classes may not be passed around among entities. They are generally used for their convenience as a field organization tool, allowing a set of persistent fields to be encapsulated as a single field on the owning entity. As an example, let us transform our Address entity (Listing 4-19) into an embeddable class, and embed it as a field on the Person entity (Listing 4-20).

Figure 4-5 shows the CH04_EMB_PERSON table we will use that contains columns for the fields found on the Address entity.

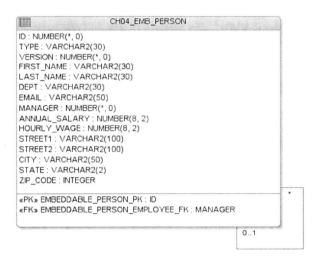

Figure 4-5. *Table CH04_EMB_PERSON holds columns for all fields in the Person entity hierarchy, as well as fields from an embedded Address field.*

Listing 4-19. *Address.java, an Embeddable Non-Entity Class*

```
/*
 * Address:  An embeddable non-entity class
 */
@Embeddable
public class Address
  implements Serializable
{
  protected String city;
  protected String state;
  protected String street1;
  protected String street2;
  @Column(name = "ZIP_CODE")
  protected Long zipCode;

  public Address() {
  }

  /* get/set methods */
}
```

Listing 4-20. *Person.java, an Entity That Holds an @Embedded homeAddress Field*

```
/*
 * Person:  An abstract entity, and the root of a SINGLE_TABLE hierarchy
 */
@Entity
@Inheritance(strategy = InheritanceType.SINGLE_TABLE)
@DiscriminatorColumn(name = "TYPE")
@NamedQuery(name = "Person.findAll", query = "select o from Person o")
@SequenceGenerator(name = "PersonIdGenerator",
                   sequenceName = "CH04_EMB_PERSON_SEQ", initialValue = 100,
                   allocationSize = 20)
@Table(name = "CH04_EMB_PERSON")
public abstract class Person
  implements Serializable
{
  @Column(name = "FIRST_NAME")
  private String firstName;
```

```
@Id
@Column(nullable = false)
@GeneratedValue(generator="PersonIdGenerator")
private Long id;
@Column(name = "LAST_NAME")
private String lastName;
@Version
private Long version;
@Embedded
private Address homeAddress;

public Person() {
}

/* get/set methods */
}
```

When a Person instance is persisted, if its homeAddress field is not null, all of the values of fields on its homeAddress instance are saved into columns we have added to the CH04_EMB_PERSON table.

Polymorphic Relationships

As shown in the previous examples, entity relationships can be specified between both concrete and abstract entities in a hierarchy. You can define a relationship with any entity in an inheritance hierarchy, and it will implicitly involve subtypes of that entity as well. Even persistent entity relationship fields declared on mapped superclasses are polymorphic. A relationship that implicitly includes subtypes in this way is known as a polymorphic relationship.

In EJB 3, relationships may be defined against any other entity class, including abstract supertype entities in a hierarchy. This support for polymorphic relationships complements EJB 3's support for mapping class hierarchies, and provides a powerful construct for querying entities at any level across an entity type hierarchy. In the previous example entity hierarchy, the FullTimeEmployee.manager-to-Employee.managedEmployees relationship illustrates a one-to-many, bidirectional relationship between the concrete FullTimeEmployee (manager) and its collection of abstract Employee (managedEmployee) instances. This example shows a relationship between entities within the same hierarchy, but could just as easily be defined between entities in separate entity hierarchies.

Relationship Mapping

Mapping polymorphic relationships requires no special knowledge about the inheritance table mapping strategy for either entity in the relationship. This is evident from the fact that the relationship field mappings remained identical across our sample entity classes as we applied each of the three inheritance mapping strategies. All relationships map to the primary key of the target class, a mapping assumption made possible because of the spec requirement that all classes in a class hierarchy share a common primary key structure, even if each subclass maps to its own table. The mapping information defined for each entity is sufficient for the EJB persistence framework to resolve base type references onto the actual subclass instances. Relationship fields are derived automatically using JOIN and UNION statements, and these queries are further constrained by the use of WHERE clauses that refer to discriminator column values.

Polymorphic JPQL Queries

Similarly, JPQL queries can select or join entities of a supertype class, and any instances of subtypes matching the query criteria will be returned in the query result list. What's more, queries may use internal JOIN clauses to bind references to types anywhere along a supertype hierarchy, with the only restriction being that the left and right side of the JOIN clause resolve to a common base type.

In the previous inheritance hierarchy, the "Person.findAll" and "Employee.findAll" named queries defined on the abstract Person and Employee entities are examples of polymorphic queries. Instances returned from these queries are all concrete entities—either FullTimeEmployee or PartTimeEmployee.

By way of example, let us look at some code from our sample client. Listing 4-21 queries all Employee instances whose home address is somewhere in San Mateo. The query is issued on the abstract Employee entity, and it traverses through the homeAddress relationship field defined on the root Person entity. Any entities that are returned from this will be concrete, either FullTimeEmployee or PartTimeEmployee.

Listing 4-21. *Code Snippet That Demonstrates Polymorphic Relationship Usage in JPQL*

```
// Ad-hoc JPQL to demonstrate polymorphic relationship usage
final String stmt = "select o from Employee o " +
  "where o.homeAddress.city = 'San Mateo'";
final List<Employee> emps = em.createQuery(stmt).getResultList();
for (Employee emp : emps)
{
  System.out.println(emp.getFirstName());
  System.out.println(emp.getLastName());
}
```

Using Native SQL Queries

JPQL offers the ability to reference entity fields by name, and join with other entities through relationships, without regard to the underlying mapping details. This offers a fair degree of independence between the database schema definer and the query definer roles—but there are times when you'll want to take control of the query to leverage specific indexes, return sparse data sets, or otherwise just issue a query that is more easily expressed in SQL. EJB 3 lets you do this easily, and even offers support for mapping the query results back to entities if you desire.

As an example, you may wish to use a native SQL query to return just the name and primary key column data from a table that happens to map to one of your entities. The queried name values could then be presented to the user through a combo box, and only when the user chooses a name would you go out to the EntityManager and bind that name's corresponding primary key value to an entity instance, using the EntityManager. find(Object primaryKey) call. Had you used JPQL to return a collection of fully loaded entities, instead of just the sparse key and name data set, you would have queried more data fields than necessary, causing more resources to be consumed than were actually needed.

The example in Listing 4-22, which you can find online at the Apress web site (www.apress.com), shows how to issue a native SQL query and then map the results back to entity instances, using an @SqlResultSetMapping declaration.

Listing 4-22. *Code Snippet That Demonstrates Native SQL Support in JPQL*

```
//  Example of native SQL usage. Assumes the following annotation has been
//  defined on one of the classes in the persistence unit:
//
//  @SqlResultSetMapping(name = "EmployeeResults",
//                       entities = { @EntityResult(entityClass = Employee.class,
//                                                  discriminatorColumn = "TYPE"
//                                                  )})
System.out.println("Using a native SQL query to find employees in the " +
                   "department 'Magistry'...");
final List<Employee> employeesWithEmail =
  em.createNativeQuery("select o.id, o.type " +
                       "from ch04_emb_person o where o.dept = ?1",
                       "EmployeeResults").
                       setParameter(1, "Magistry").getResultList();
```

```
System.out.println("The following employees were found:");
for (Employee employee: employeesWithEmail) {
  System.out.println(employee.getFirstName());
  System.out.println(employee.getLastName());
  System.out.println(employee.getDept());
}
```

When using an @SqlResultSetMapping to map the results back to entity classes, an implicit EntityManager.find(Object primaryKey) is performed to populate each entity instance. This is what allows us to see the firstName, lastName, and dept fields of the Employee instances (actually, its concrete subentity instances), even though they were not part of the native SQL query.

Composite Primary Keys and Nested Foreign Keys

When mapping entities to a new schema, it is good practice to designate a single, dedicated column to be the primary key column, as we have done in the previous examples. An entity's primary key value may not be updated once it has been assigned. Also, dedicating a column to hold the primary key instead of using a name or other column that holds meaningful property data eliminates potential conflicts that might arise should a user wish to modify a significant field that happens to be part of the primary key. It is also desirable to follow a single approach that is common to all your entities, and use of a single dedicated column for the primary key is a simple pattern that we have found to work well.

However, there are cases in which the schema has already been defined and is being adapted into Java as EJB entities, and cases in which, for other reasons, a composite primary key is required. A legacy case we run into a lot occurs when a composite primary key includes columns, such as foreign key columns, that are also involved in relationships to other entities. On top of this, these relationships are necessarily mandatory (since all primary key columns must be NOT NULL), so you will need to be careful how you persist your entity graphs when you need to persist such related entities, to avoid NOT NULL constraints when the row data is inserted during the EntityManager.persist() call.

There are two ways you can use a composite primary key to implement your entity's identity, which are described in the following sections.

Using an Embedded Composite Key (@EmbeddedId)

If the fields of the composite key do not represent useful property data that you consider part of the entity definition, you can designate a single entity field to be the primary key field, and set its type to be the composite key class type. This composite key class is marked @Embedded. Its fields will be mapped as if they were part of the entity itself, but will only be accessible to clients through the composite field.

The embedded composite key field on the entity is annotated @EmbeddedId. In Listing 4-23, extended from the Ch04_Embedded example source code (and albeit somewhat contrived), we have removed the @Id Long id primary key field from Person, and changed the homeAddress field to be Person's new primary key field. This allows us to reuse the @Embedded Address class from a previous example. The persistent fields on Address become Person's composite primary key fields.

Listing 4-23. *Person.java, Illustrating Usage of a Composite Primary Key Using an @EmbeddedId Annotation*

```java
/*
 * Person:  An abstract entity, and the root of a SINGLE_TABLE hierarchy,
 * demonstrating use of an @Embedded Address field as its @EmbeddedId
 */
@Entity
@Inheritance(strategy = InheritanceType.SINGLE_TABLE)
@DiscriminatorColumn(name = "TYPE")
@NamedQuery(name = "Person.findAll", query = "select o from Person o")
@SequenceGenerator(name = "PersonIdGenerator",
                   sequenceName = "CH04_EMB_PERSON_SEQ", initialValue = 100,
                   allocationSize = 20)
@Table(name = "CH04_EMB_PERSON")
@IdClass (Address.class)
public abstract class Person
  implements Serializable
{
  @Column(name = "FIRST_NAME")
  private String firstName;
  private Long id;
  @Column(name = "LAST_NAME")
  private String lastName;
  @Version
  private Long version;
  @EmbeddedId
  private Address homeAddress;

  public Person() {
  }

  /* get/set methods */
}
```

To transform the Person class to use an embedded ID, we removed the @Id annotation from the id field, added the @IdClass class-level annotation, and annotated the homeAddress field with @EmbeddedId. To fit this entity back into our sample entity hierarchy, the manager relationship field on Person's Employee subentity would need to be modified to map to all the columns in the new primary key.

Exposing Composite Key Class Fields Directly on the Entity Class (@IdClass)

An alternative approach to mapping a composite primary key, shown in Listing 4-24, is to declare fields explicitly on the entity class for each field in the primary key class, but annotate each of them @Id. If any of the fields on the primary key double as useful properties on your entity, you will probably want to take this approach. You then define a new composite key class that declares each of these @Id fields, taking care that they exactly match the key class fields in name and type.

Listing 4-24. *Person.java, Illustrating Usage of a Composite Primary Key Representing Multiple @Id Fields*

```
/*
 * Person:  An abstract entity, and the root of a SINGLE_TABLE hierarchy,
 * demonstrating use of an @Embedded Address field as its @EmbeddedId
 */
@Entity
@Inheritance(strategy = InheritanceType.SINGLE_TABLE)
@DiscriminatorColumn(name = "TYPE")
@NamedQuery(name = "Person.findAll", query = "select o from Person o")
@SequenceGenerator(name = "PersonIdGenerator",
                   sequenceName = "CH04_ST_PERSON_SEQ", initialValue = 100,
                   allocationSize = 20)
@Table(name = "CH04_EMB_PERSON")
@IdClass (PersonPK.class)
public abstract class Person
  implements Serializable
{
  @Column(name = "FIRST_NAME")
  private String firstName;
  @Id
  @Column(nullable = false)
  @GeneratedValue(generator="PersonIdGenerator")
  private Long id;
```

```
@Id
@Column(name = "LAST_NAME")
private String lastName;
@Version
private Long version;
@EmbeddedId
private Address homeAddress;

public Person() {
}


/* get/set methods */
}
```

In this example, both the `id` and `lastName` fields are now marked `@Id`. We have added an `@IdClass` annotation that identifies `PersonPK` as the composite primary key class, shown in Listing 4-25.

Listing 4-25. *PersonPK.java, a Composite Primary Key Class*

```
public class PersonPK
  implements Serializable
{
  private Long id;
  private String lastName;

  public PersonPK();

  /* get/set methods */
}
```

This composite key class requires no special annotations. It is primarily used when looking up a `Person` instance through its primary key, using the `EntityManager.find()` method.

Mapping Relationships That Use Composite Keys

When defining a relationship in which the inverse entity uses a composite primary key, the owning entity must map its relationship field to columns of the corresponding type. This requires use of the `@JoinColumns` annotation (or equivalent XML metadata). If these columns happen to be nested in the owning entity's primary key, or if they are otherwise NOT NULL constrained, then the relationship must be bound at the time the

EntityManager.persist() operation is called to persist this entity into the persistence context, or at least by the time EntityManager.flush() is called to issue the database INSERT call.

In the following example, the PersonPK composite primary key class contains two fields—id and addressId—that are mandatory (NOT NULL) since they are part of the primary key. Since the addressId and the relationship field homeAddress both map to the same ADDRESS_ID column, and only one of these fields may be insertable and updatable, we must mark one of the fields to be read-only. In Listing 4-26, the relationship field homeAddress is marked as read-only by assigning the insertable=false, updatable=false attributes on the @JoinColumn annotation.

Listing 4-26. *Person.java, with a Composite Primary Key That Maps to a Column That Is Shared by Both an Ordinary @Id Field and a Relationship Field*

```
/*
 * Person:  An abstract entity, and the root of a SINGLE_TABLE hierarchy,
 * demonstrating use of a composite key that contains a field whose mapped
 * column is also mapped to a relationship field.
 */
@Entity
@Inheritance(strategy = InheritanceType.SINGLE_TABLE)
@DiscriminatorColumn(name = "TYPE")
@NamedQuery(name = "Person.findAll", query = "select o from Person o")
@SequenceGenerator(name = "PersonIdGenerator",
                   sequenceName = "CH04_ST_PERSON_SEQ", initialValue = 100,
                   allocationSize = 20)
@Table(name = "CH04_EMB_PERSON")
@IdClass (PersonPK.class)
public abstract class Person
  implements Serializable
{
  @Id
  @Column(name = "ADDRESS_ID")
  private Long addressId;
  @Id
  @Column(nullable = false)
  @GeneratedValue(generator="PersonIdGenerator")
  private Long id;
  @Column(name = "FIRST_NAME")
  private String firstName;
  @Column(name = "LAST_NAME")
  private String lastName;
```

```
@Version
private Long version;
@OneToOne(cascade = { CascadeType.ALL })
@JoinColumn(name = "HOME_ADDRESS",
            referencedColumnName = "ID"
            insertable = false, updatable = false)
private Address homeAddress;

public Person() {
}

/* get/set methods */
}
```

When using this Person class, you may retrieve data through the homeAddress relationship field, but you may not update this field. Its value must be populated at the time the entity is persisted, and since it is part of the entity's primary key, it may not subsequently be modified.

Support for Optimistic Locking (@Version)

As shown in the previous examples, you can use the @Version annotation to designate a field to be used by the EntityManager to perform optimistic locking for merge operations and concurrency management. Optimistic locking is a useful performance optimization that offloads work that would otherwise be required of the database. Databases typically offer a pessimistic locking service that allows the database client (in our case, the JPA EntityManager) to lock a row in a table to prevent another client from updating it while the EntityManager is applying some changes. This is an effective mechanism to ensure that two clients do not modify the same row at the same time, but requires expensive, low-level access checks inside the database. An alternative to pessimistic locking is to move concurrency control into a database client like the EntityManager, and employ an optimistic locking strategy. Using a dedicated @Version column, the EntityManager follows a couple of simple rules. Whenever it sends a modified entity out to the database, as during a commit or flush operation, it looks at the current value of the entity instance's @Version field, queries the current state of that entity's row from the database, and compares the version values. If they are the same, it increments the entity instance's @Version field (or whatever field is annotated @Version) and sends the change out to the database, causing an UPDATE statement to be executed. If the version values are different, that means that some other client modified the row between the time the row was last queried by the EntityManager and loaded into an entity instance, and the time that instance was flushed back out to the database. When such a difference is detected, we call it a concurrency exception, and the `EntityManager` throws an exception and rolls back its transaction. The client of the `EntityManager` needs to anticipate that a concurrency exception might occur, and be prepared to resolve the conflict, typically by notifying the user of the conflict so that the entity can be refreshed.

The use of a dedicated `@Version` column on an entity allows the `EntityManager` to perform optimistic locking simply by comparing the value of the `@Version` field stored in the entity instance with the value of the `VERSION` column in the database. If you don't specify an `@Version` field, the `EntityManager` has to walk through each field in the entity instance and compare its value to its corresponding, mapped column in the database, which is far more laborious. A declared `@Version` field will be autopopulated by the persistence framework and should not be updated by application code.

The bottom line is that it's not a requirement to use an `@Version` field, but it's good practice to define an `@Version` field on your entities to allow the `EntityManager` to take advantage of this optimization.

Support for Autogenerated Primary Key Values (@GeneratedValue)

In addition to built-in optimistic locking support through the `@Version` column, EJB 3 provides several convenient ways to autopopulate primary key columns when an entity is persisted. You can declare that a field's value should be populated using the following:

- An automatic mechanism maintained by the persistence framework (`strategy=GenerationType.AUTO`)

- A custom database sequence (`strategy=GenerationType.SEQUENCE` or `GenerationType.IDENTITY`)

- A custom database table, emulating a pseudo-sequence (`strategy=GenerationType.TABLE`)

We found the autopopulated PK feature to be very high on the convenience scale, saving us from coding this up for each entity in our application. We recommend explicitly defining the sequence details, since even with the default setting `strategy=AUTO`, the persistence provider you are using will probably require you to install a sequence or table in the database schema that hosts the entity tables. Once installed, the `AUTO` case generates unique identifiers for any `@Id` field that is annotated `@GeneratedValue` or `@GeneratedValue`➥ (`strategy=GenerationType.AUTO`), and at least leaves the entity class a little less cluttered. Listing 4-27 demonstrates usage of the default ID generation feature.

Listing 4-27. *Person.java, Employing a Default ID Generator*

```
@Entity
@Inheritance(strategy = InheritanceType.JOINED)
@DiscriminatorColumn(name = "TYPE")
@Table(name = "CH04_JOIN_PERSON")
@NamedQuery(name = "findAllPerson", query = "select object(o) from Person o")
public abstract class Person implements Serializable {
    @Id
    @GeneratedValue
    private Long id;
    /* ... */
}
```

The SQL scripts to generate all the tables and sequences for the examples in this chapter are available for download from the Apress web site (www.apress.com); but to give you an idea, Listing 4-28 gives the DDL to create any of the ID generator sequences used in these examples.

Listing 4-28. *SQL DDL Statement for Creating an ID Generator Sequence in an Oracle Database*

```
CREATE SEQUENCE CH04_EMB_PERSON_SEQ
  INCREMENT BY 50
  START WITH 100
  MINVALUE 1
  CACHE 20;
```

Listing 4-29 gives an example of a table-based ID generator declaration.

Listing 4-29. *TABLE_ID_GENERATOR @TableGenerator Annotation Declaration*

```
@TableGenerator(name = "TABLE_ID_GENERATOR", table = "EJB_TAB_ID_GEN",
                pkColumnName = "ID_NAME", valueColumnName = "SEQ_VALUE",
                pkColumnValue = "SEQ_GEN")
```

Finally, Listing 4-30 gives the SQL DDL that would be used to generate this table in an Oracle database.

Listing 4-30. *SQL DDL Statement for Creating an ID Generator Table in an Oracle Database*

```
CREATE TABLE EJB_TAB_ID_GEN (
  ID_NAME VARCHAR2(4000),
  SEQ_VALUE NUMBER(*, 0)
);
```

Interceptors: Entity Callback Methods

EJB 3 provides support for a number of callback methods, or interceptors, that allow you to add your own custom code when certain life cycle events occur on an entity or a mapped superclass. You can register interceptors to be invoked when certain life cycle events occur on specific entity types, or broadly whenever a life cycle event occurs on any entity. The latter case is one of the few times when you must use XML to specify metadata, since the effect is applied globally, across all entities in the persistence unit.

The following annotations may be applied to methods to indicate that they are entity callback methods:

- PrePersist

- PostPersist

- PreRemove

- PostRemove

- PreUpdate

- PostUpdate

- PostLoad

Callback methods may be declared by annotating a specific method with that callback name (for instance, @PrePersist). Alternatively, callback classes may be registered for an entity (or a mapped superclass) to intercept one or more life cycle events on one or more entity types. Multiple interceptor methods may be registered for any given entity life cycle event, and they are executed in the order in which they are specified.

Entity callback methods can be used to validate an entity's contents prior to the entity being persisted, and to populate transient, derived fields following instantiation. Listing 4-31 shows how you might plug an @PreUpdate interceptor into the FullTimeEmployee entity in your company's payroll system to give all employees from a certain ZIP code an automatic raise. (Wishful thinking!)

Listing 4-31. *FullTimeEmployee.java, Employing an Illicit Entity Callback to Finally Stick It to the Man!*

```
@Entity
@Inheritance
public class FullTimeEmployee extends Employee {
  ...
  @PreUpdate
  public void wishfulThinking() {
    if (getHomeAddress().getZipCode() == 94402) {
      setSalary(getSalary() + 10000);
    }
  }
  ...
}
```

Conclusion

We have covered a fair bit of ground in this chapter, and with this information you should be ready to go out and build some powerful entities that are configured to best suit your application domain. Table 4-4 provides a summary of the key concepts we covered in this chapter.

Table 4-4. *Summary of the Key Concepts in This Chapter*

Concept	Description
Mapping entity inheritance hierarchies	EJB 3 provides built-in support for three common O/R mapping strategies for entity class inheritance hierarchies. We examined the strengths and weaknesses of each approach, and offered examples of common use cases that map best to each strategy.
Using abstract entities, mapped superclasses, and non-entity classes in an inheritance hierarchy	EJB 3 offers flexible solutions when it comes to mixing entities with abstract and non-entity classes in a type hierarchy. Entities may be either concrete or abstract. Only entity classes may be queried or serve as the targets of mapped entity relationships, but entities may still make use of non-entity classes, both by embedding them and by extending them or being extended by them. We showed some examples that mix these options together to illustrate their use.

Continued

Table 4-4. *Continued*

Concept	Description
Polymorphic relationships	Relationships can be specified between entities, including abstract supertype entities in a hierarchy. This lets you define a relationship with entities anywhere along an inheritance hierarchy that will implicitly involve subtypes of that entity as well.
Polymorphic JPQL queries	Similarly, JPQL queries can select or join entities of a supertype class, and any instances of subtypes matching the query criteria will be returned in the query result list.
Using native SQL queries	The `EntityManager` lets you issue native SQL queries, as an overture to experienced SQL developers and as an optimization to avoid the overhead of querying across all of an entity's fields when only a few are actually needed. We provided an example of how to use an `@SqlResultSetMapping` annotation to map the results of a native SQL query to entity type, so that the results could be seamlessly integrated into an EJB application.
Composite primary keys and nested foreign keys	We explored the different types of composite primary key usage, showing how to use an `@EmbeddedId` field and multiple `@Id` fields. When an entity's primary key maps to columns that are also involved in relationships to other entities (as when the primary key contains one or more columns that are also part of a foreign key), things can get a little bit dicey. We provided some examples of how to deal with this situation.
Support for optimistic locking	Using the `@Version` annotation, you can designate a field (one that is common to all entities in your inheritance hierarchy) to be used by the `EntityManager` to perform optimistic locking when managing concurrency, such as during merge operations. This field will be autopopulated by the persistence framework and should not be updated by application code.

Concept	Description
Support for autogenerated primary key values	EJB 3 offers declarative support for the automatic population of @Id fields with unique values. We provided examples of how to declare both database sequence- and table-based ID generators.
Interceptors: entity callback methods	You can designate methods on your entity class, or on a helper class of your choosing, to handle entity life cycle callbacks. We listed the callback methods available to you, and explained how to use them to register your own custom methods that will be called during life cycle events.

## CHAPTER 5

EJB 3 Message-Driven Beans

Introduction

This chapter discusses the need for message-oriented architecture. It introduces Java Message Service (JMS), the typical architecture for messaging applications, and details the concepts behind EJB 3 message-driven beans (MDBs). The chapter also covers annotations, dependency injection, and interceptors in relation to MDBs.

Message-Oriented Architecture

Today's IT organizations have tens of applications and services that perform such well-defined tasks as inventory, billing, expense reporting, and order entry. With the evolution of the Internet and e-business, enterprises have started to think about how different applications can work independently, but at the same time be a part of an information workflow process.

This new demand brings us to the concept of integrating existing applications, as well as building new applications that work coherently with existing applications. Integrating existing applications with new applications becomes a very complex task, first because of the large number of applications that most enterprises have, and second because of their complex business workflow.

Messaging is one of the most viable solutions for integrating existing and new applications in an asynchronous communication and loosely coupled transaction model. Asynchronous messaging allows applications to communicate by exchanging messages independently, without them having to be hard-wired to each other. An application or business process sending a message does not have to wait for the receiver, as long as both sender and receiver understand and agree on message format and intermediate destination.

What Is JMS?

JMS is a standard Java EE API that allows applications to send and receive messages asynchronously. JMS is analogous to JDBC (Java Database Connectivity), which provides a standard API to connect to several types of databases (Oracle, DB2, MySQL, etc.). Likewise, JMS provides a standard API to connect to several types of messaging systems (IBM MQ, SonicMQ, etc.).

JMS architecture consists of the following:

JMS provider: A messaging system (as shown in Figure 5-1) that handles the routing and delivery of messages. A JMS provider can be a messaging component of an application server (such as OracleAS, BEA WebLogic, IBM WebSphere, etc.). JMS providers are also known as JMS servers.

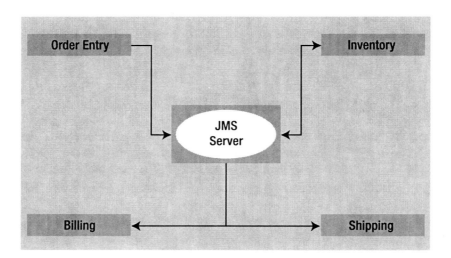

Figure 5-1. *A JMS messaging system*

JMS client: Any Java application or Java EE component that uses the JMS API to either consume or produce a JMS message.

JMS consumer: A JMS client application that consumes JMS messages. The inventory, billing, and shipping applications shown in Figure 5-1 are JMS message consumers.

JMS producer: A JMS client that generates the message. The order entry application shown in Figure 5-1 is a JMS message producer.

JMS message: A message consisting of a header, properties, and a body. The header identifies the message, the properties provide additional attributes that are specific to the application and provider, and the body contains the content of the message. The JMS specification provides support to send and receive different types of messages. Table 5-1 shows the message types and descriptions.

Table 5-1. *JMS Message Types*

Message Type	Description
ByteMessage	Consists of a series of bytes
MapMessage	Consists of a set of name/value pairs
ObjectMessage	Consists of a serialized Java object
StreamMessage	Consists of a sequence of primitive data types
TextMessage	Consists of strings

Messaging Application Architecture

Generally, two different classes of messaging applications exist:

- The point-to-point (P2P) model

- The publish-subscribe (pub-sub) model

The P2P model is based on message queues, where a queue holds the JMS messages sent by the JMS client application. Message producers and consumers decide upon a common queue to exchange messages.

The P2P model is used if there is one and only one message consumer for each message. For example, the order entry system shown in Figure 5-2 sends a new order into the message queue, which is picked up by the inventory system. Similarly, the message sent by the inventory system is consumed by the shipping system, and the message from the shipping system is consumed by the billing system.

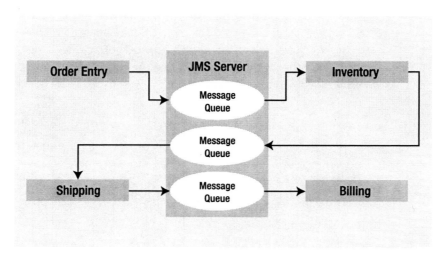

Figure 5-2. *A JMS messaging system using queues*

The pub-sub model is based on topics, where the topic is the destination address of the message. Multiple recipients or JMS consumers can retrieve each message. In this model, publishers are not always aware of possible subscribers. The pub-sub model is used for broadcast-type applications, as shown in Figure 5-3, in which a message is delivered for more than one JMS client. Topics are defined in the messaging server, each having a unique name. Each message, with its associated subject, gets published and delivered to all subscribers.

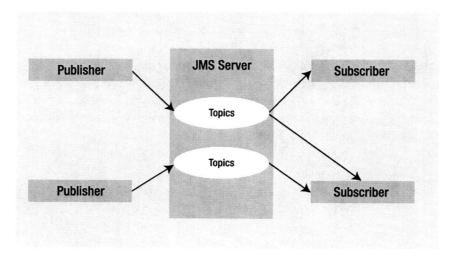

Figure 5-3. *A JMS messaging system using topics*

Using MDBs

An MDB is an asynchronous message consumer that processes messages delivered via JMS. While MDBs do the job of processing the messages, the EJB container in which the MDBs run take care of the services (transactions, security, resources, concurrency, message acknowledgement, etc.), letting the bean developer focus on the business logic of processing messages. Traditional JMS applications would have to custom write some of these services. MDBs are stateless in nature, which means that EJB containers can have numerous instances of MDBs execute concurrently to process hundreds of JMS messages coming in from various applications or JMS producers, and also provide quality of service (QoS)—such as high availability and reliability for enterprise applications.

EJB client applications cannot access MDBs directly as they can with session beans and entities. The only way to communicate with an MDB would be by sending a JMS message to the destination that the MDB is listening to. Any Java application or Java EE component using the JMS API can be the message provider for the MDB by sending messages to queues or topics.

When Do You Use MDBs?

Earlier in the chapter, we discussed the need for asynchrony in enterprises. Asynchronous messaging provides loose coupling between applications, systems, and services, thus providing greater flexibility and change management for applications and systems. MDBs provide a standard messaging component model that achieves the goal of asynchronous and message-oriented architecture in enterprises.

Figure 5-4 shows a message-oriented application that has order entry, inventory, billing, and shipping systems that communicate asynchronously to handle a workflow that starts with a new purchase order and ends when the order gets shipped to the customer. An order entry system captures a new order from a customer, processes the order, and sends it into a designated message queue (in Figure 5-4, the New Order queue). The inventory system picks up the message from the queue and checks whether the inventory is available. If not, it sends a message to the Suppliers queue; if the order can be shipped, then it puts a message into the Order Ready queue. This new message is picked up by the billing system, which processes the billing for the customer and puts a message back into the Shipping queue. Finally, the shipping application picks up the message, gets the order shipped to the customer, and sends an e-mail that has tracking information to the customer.

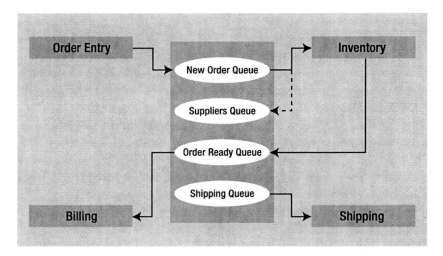

Figure 5-4. *An order-to-shipping JMS messaging system*

MDB Classes

Unlike a session bean, an MDB doesn't have any business interfaces. It has only the following:

- A message-driven class

- An optional callback listener class

- An optional interceptor class

An MDB class is any standard Java class that has a class-level annotation @MessageDriven. If deployment descriptors are used instead of annotations, the bean class should be denoted as an MDB class. In the case of mixed mode, in which you are using annotations and deployment descriptors, the @MessageDriven annotation must be specified if any other class-level or member-level annotations are specified in the bean class. The @MessageDriven annotation parameters can be used to specify the JMS queues or topics that the bean is listening to. Table 5-2 details the parameters.

Table 5-2. *The @MessageDriven Annotation*

Parameter	Description
ActivationConfigProperty	The set of properties used to specify the destination name and type
description	A description of the bean class
mappedName	The physical Java Naming and Directory Interface (JNDI) name of the topic or queue that the MDB is listening to
messageListener	The interface name of the interface class that the MDB is extending
name	The name of the MDB, if it has to be a different name than the bean class

To illustrate the use of an MDB, we will create the use case shown in Figure 5-5. We will have an application client, which will be a Java command-line program that invokes a business method in the OrderProcessing session bean. The OrderProcessing session bean will create and send a JMS message to a topic registered/configured in the GlassFish application server. An MDB, StatusMailer, will listen to the topic and process the incoming message. The message received will contain details for the customer, and it will be used to send an e-mail notification to the customer regarding their order status. This simple use case will allows us to demonstrate how MDBs work, and how to inject different types of resources in session beans and MDBs.

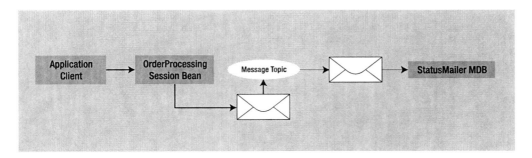

Figure 5-5. *A sample MDB use case*

Listing 5-1 shows the definition of a StatusMailer MDB. We have marked the StatusMailerBean class with the @MessageDriven annotation.

Listing 5-1. *StatusMailerBean.java*

```
package com.apress.ejb3.chapter05;

import javax.ejb.MessageDriven;

@MessageDriven
public class StatusMailerBean {
}
```

An MDB class has one method, onMessage(), that gets invoked by the EJB container on the arrival of a message in the queue/topic that the MDB is listening to. The onMessage() method contains the business logic on how to process the incoming message. The onMessage() method contains one parameter, which is the JMS message. In the case of the StatusMailer bean, the onMessage() method checks whether the message is of MapMessage type, and it then gets the customer information from the message, creates an e-mail message about the order status, and sends an e-mail to the customer. Listing 5-2 shows the onMessage() method code. In a try block, we start by checking whether the message received is of type MapMessage, as we are expecting. If it is, then we use getStringProperty() to retrieve the values of the from, to, subject, and content attributes in the message.

Listing 5-2. *The onMessage Method Code*

```
public class StatusMailerBean {


    public void onMessage(Message message){
        try {
            if (message instanceof MapMessage) {
                MapMessage orderMessage = (MapMessage)message;
                String from = orderMessage.getStringProperty("from");
                String to = orderMessage.getStringProperty("to");
                String subject = orderMessage.getStringProperty("subject");
                String content = orderMessage.getStringProperty("content");
            }
```

```
        else {
            System.out.println("Invalid message ");
            }


    } catch (Exception ex)  {
        ex.printStackTrace();
    }



    }
}
```

In addition to marking the standard Java class with the `@MessageDriven` annotation, the following additional requirements apply to an MDB class:

- The MDB class must implement the message listener interface. In the case of JMS, this will be `javax.jms.MessageListener`.

- The class cannot be final or abstract.

- The class should have a no-argument public constructor that is used by the EJB container to create instances of the bean class.

If both annotations and deployment descriptors are used, the settings or values in the deployment descriptor will override the annotations in the classes during the deployment process.

Configuration Properties

Bean developers can provide configuration properties along with MDB classes, which get used at deployment time. The EJB container uses these properties to configure the bean and link it to the appropriate JMS provider. These configuration properties can be set using the `@ActivationConfigProperty` annotation. This annotation can be provided as one of the parameters for the `@MessageDriven` annotation. Listing 5-3 shows the `@MessageDriven` annotation with properties for the `StatusMailer` MDB. We have defined two `ActivationConfigProperty` annotations that specify the logical destination name and the destination type.

Listing 5-3. *The @MessageDriven Annotation with Properties for the StatusMailer MDB*

```
@MessageDriven(activationConfig= {
@ActivationConfigProperty(propertyName="destinationName",➡
propertyValue="StatusMessageTopic"),➡
@ActivationConfigProperty(propertyName="destinationType",➡
propertyValue="javax.jms.Topic")
}, mappedName="StatusMessageTopic")

public class StatusMailerBean implements javax.jms.MessageListener
{


}
```

In the following sections, we will show what additional properties can be set for MDBs.

Message Acknowledgment

The EJB container provides a message acknowledgment service. There are two message acknowledgment modes, as follows:

- `Auto-acknowledge`

- `Dups-ok-acknowledge`

In the case of `Auto-acknowledge`, the message delivery acknowledgment happens after the `onMessage()` method. This property is useful for applications that require no duplicate messages. For example, a new order should be received by the inventory system once and only once. In the case of `Dups-ok-acknowledge`, the acknowledgment is done lazily, which means that there might be duplicate delivery of messages, but it reduces the overhead for the session in terms of immediate acknowledgement. For example, an e-mail message that gets sent out during the order process can possibly allow duplicate messages. We can use the `@ActivationConfigProperty` annotation to specify the message acknowledgment property. Listing 5-4 shows the property set to allow duplicates.

Listing 5-4. *The @ActivationConfigProperty Annotation*

```
@MessageDriven(
activationConfig= {
@ActivationConfigProperty(propertyName="acknowledgeMode", ➡
propertyValue="Dups-ok-acknowledge")}
)
```

The Message Selector

The message selector allows filtering of incoming messages based on the selection criteria provided by the bean developer using the @ActivationConfigProperty annotation. This property is useful for restricting the messages that the bean receives. For example, the MDB that processes the incoming orders might only process orders pertaining to red and white wines. The property name used to specify is messageSelector.

Message Destination

The message destination describes whether the MDB listens on a queue or topic. Bean developers can provide the description in the bean using the @ActivationConfigProperty annotation. The value of the property must be either javax.jms.Queue or javax.jms.Topic. For example, a new order may need to be processed by an inventory system as a next step in the workflow; in this case, the order entry system doesn't have to broadcast the new order message. Both the order entry and inventory system can agree on a particular destination. Listing 5-3 shows the code to specify destination name and type.

Subscription Durability

If the bean is designed to listen to a topic, then the bean developer can further specify the durability of the message. The topic can be either Durable or Non-Durable. Usage of Durable topics ensures reliability for the applications. They ensure that messages are not missed, even if the EJB container is temporarily offline. For example, we may need to make sure that the new purchase orders received from client applications are not lost if the EJB container goes down. All purchase orders have to be reliably processed by the MDBs. We can use the @ActivationConfigProperty annotation to specify the durability using the subscriptionDurability property. Listing 5-5 shows the code to set the property to Durable. If this property is not set, the default of Non-Durable will be assumed by the container.

Listing 5-5. *The Code to Set the Property to Durable*

```
@MessageDriven(
activationConfig= {
@ActivationConfigProperty(propertyName=" subscriptionDurability ", ➥
propertyValue="Durable")}
)
```

In the StatusMailer MDB, we will create properties using the @ActivationConfig➥ Property annotation. The message's destinationName is set to StatusMessageTopic, and destinationType is set to javax.jms.Topic. We will use the mappedName parameter to specify the physical destination name of the topic. In our case, it is the same as destinationName. Listing 5-6 shows the StatusMailer MDB in its current state of completion.

Listing 5-6. *StatusMailerBean.java*

```
package com.apress.ejb3.chapter05;

import javax.ejb.ActivationConfigProperty;
import javax.jms.Message;
import javax.ejb.MessageDriven;
import javax.jms.MapMessage;

@MessageDriven(activationConfig= {
@ActivationConfigProperty(propertyName="destinationName", ➥
propertyValue="StatusMessageTopic"), ➥
@ActivationConfigProperty(propertyName="destinationType", ➥
propertyValue="javax.jms.Topic")
}, mappedName="StatusMessageTopic")

public class StatusMailerBean implements javax.jms.MessageListener{


    public void onMessage(Message message){
        try {
            if (message instanceof MapMessage) {
                MapMessage orderMessage = (MapMessage)message;
                String from = orderMessage.getStringProperty("from");
                String to = orderMessage.getStringProperty("to");
                String subject = orderMessage.getStringProperty("subject");
                String content = orderMessage.getStringProperty("content");
             }
            else {
                System.out.println("Invalid message ");
                }
```

```
        } catch (Exception ex)  {
            ex.printStackTrace();
        }


    }

}
```

Dependency Injection in MDBs

MDBs can use dependency injection to acquire references to resources such as JavaMail, EJBs, or other objects. The resources that an MDB tries to acquire and use must be available in the container context or environment context.

In the sample use case from Figure 5-5, we talked about creating an e-mail after the message is processed, and sending the order status to the customer via e-mail. In order to do this in the StatusMailer message bean, we need to acquire a JavaMail session so that we can create an e-mail and send it. JavaMail is an API that provides a platform-independent framework for building mail applications. The JavaMail API is available with the Java EE platform.

We can acquire a JavaMail session in an MDB using dependency injection. Listing 5-7 shows the completed StatusMailer MDB using dependency injection and the JavaMail API. The @Resource annotation is used to inject a JavaMail session with the name mail/wineappMail, which has been registered as a mail resource in the GlassFish application server. The injected mail session is used to create javax.mail.Message, and the setter methods are used to create the headers and content of the mail message. Finally, the send() method in the javax.mail.Transport class is used to send the created message.

Listing 5-7. *The Completed StatusMailer MDB Using Dependency Injection and the JavaMail API*

```
package com.apress.ejb3.chapter05;
import javax.annotation.Resource;
import javax.ejb.ActivationConfigProperty;
import javax.jms.Message;
import javax.ejb.MessageDriven;
import javax.jms.MapMessage;
import javax.mail.Transport;
import javax.mail.internet.InternetAddress;
import javax.mail.internet.MimeMessage;
```

```
@MessageDriven(activationConfig= {
@ActivationConfigProperty(propertyName="destinationName", ➥
propertyValue="StatusMessageTopic"), ➥
@ActivationConfigProperty(propertyName="destinationType", ➥
propertyValue="javax.jms.Topic")
}, mappedName="StatusMessageTopic")

public class StatusMailerBean implements javax.jms.MessageListener{

@Resource(name="mail/wineappMail" )
private javax.mail.Session ms;

    public void onMessage(Message message){
        try  {
            if (message instanceof MapMessage) {
                MapMessage orderMessage = (MapMessage)message;
                String from = orderMessage.getStringProperty("from");
                String to = orderMessage.getStringProperty("to");
                String subject = orderMessage.getStringProperty("subject");
                String content = orderMessage.getStringProperty("content");
                javax.mail.Message msg = new MimeMessage(ms);
                msg.setFrom(new InternetAddress(from));
                InternetAddress[] address = {new InternetAddress(to)};
                msg.setRecipients(javax.mail.Message.RecipientType.TO, address);
                msg.setSubject(subject);
                msg.setSentDate(new java.util.Date());
                msg.setContent(content, "text/html");
                System.out.println("MDB: Sending Message...");
                Transport.send(msg);
                System.out.println("MDB: Message Sent");
             }
            else {
                System.out.println("Invalid message ");
                }


        } catch (Exception ex)  {
            ex.printStackTrace();
        }


    }

  }
```

Callback Methods

There will be certain instances in which an application that uses MDBs requires fine-grained control. Two life cycle event callbacks are supported for MDBs:

- `PostConstruct`

- `PreDestroy`

The `PostConstruct` callback occurs before the first message listener method invocation on the bean, and after the container has performed the dependency injection. The `PreDestroy` callback occurs when the MDB is removed from the pool or destroyed.

For example, a `PostConstruct` callback can be used to initialize some attributes or resources, and a `PreDestroy` callback can be used to clean up or release the acquired resources.

Callback methods defined on an MDB class should have the following signature:

```
public void <METHOD> ()
```

Callback methods can also be defined on a bean's listener class, in which case the methods should have the following signature:

```
public void <METHOD>(Object)
```

where `Object` may be declared as the actual bean type, which is the argument passed to the callback method at run time.

Callback methods can be any methods in the MDB that have callback annotations. The following rules apply for these methods:

- The method should be public.

- The method cannot be final or static.

- The return type should be `void`.

The methods can take either zero or one argument, as shown previously. A callback listener class is denoted by the `@CallbackListener` annotation on the MDB class with which it is associated.

Interceptors

The EJB 3 specification provides annotations called *interceptors,* which allow you to intercept a business method invocation. Interceptor methods can be defined for MDBs.

You can add either an @AroundInvoke annotation or an <around-invoke-method> element in the deployment descriptor for a particular method, or you can define an interceptor class whose methods are invoked before the onMessage() method is invoked in the MDB class. An interceptor class is denoted using the @Interceptor annotation on the MDB class with which it is associated. In the case of multiple interceptor classes, the @Interceptors annotation is used. Only one AroundInvoke method may be present on the bean class or on any given interceptor class. An AroundInvoke method cannot be an onMessage() method of the MDB class.

AroundInvoke methods should have the following signature:

```
public Object <METHOD>(InvocationContext) throws Exception
```

The definition of InvocationContext is as follows:

```
package javax.ejb;

public interface InvocationContext {
    public Object getBean();
    public java.lang.reflect.Method getMethod();
    public Object[] getParameters();
    public void setParameters(Object[] params);
    public EJBContext getEJBContext();
    public java.util.Map getContextData();
    public Object proceed() throws Exception;
}
```

The following list describes each of the methods:

- getBean(): Returns the instance of the bean on which the method was called

- getMethod(): Returns the method on the bean instance that was called

- getParameters(): Returns the parameters for the method call

- setParameters(): Allows modification of the parameters for the method call

- getEJBContext(): Gives the interceptor methods access to the bean's EJBContext

- getContextData(): Allows values to be passed between interceptor methods in the same InvocationContext instance using the Map returned

- proceed(): Invokes the next interceptor if there is one, or invokes the target bean method

Exception Handling

The EJB 3 spec outlines two types of exceptions: application exceptions and system exceptions. For more general information on these exceptions, see the "Exception Handling" section of Chapter 2. In the case of an MDB, the listener method must not throw a `java.rmi.RemoteException`, or in general, a runtime exception. The client assumes that the message consumer continues to exist even though a runtime exception has occurred. If the client sends a message after a runtime exception is thrown, then the EJB container delegates the messages to a different MDB instance. Also, if you allow an exception to "escape" an MDB, the message isn't considered to be consumed, and it goes back on the queue/topic. Then, the offending message gets redelivered. This is known as the "poison message" problem.

Callback methods can throw runtime exceptions. A runtime exception thrown by a callback method that executes within a transaction causes that transaction to be rolled back. Callback methods must not throw application exceptions.

Client View

To a client application, an MDB is simply a message consumer. A client application can be any Java client of a Java EE component that is using the JMS API to send a message. From the perspective of the client application, the existence of an MDB is completely hidden behind the destination or endpoint for which the MDB is the message listener.

A client's JNDI namespace may be configured to include the destinations or endpoints of MDBs installed in multiple EJB containers located on multiple machines on a network. The actual locations of an enterprise bean and EJB container are, in general, transparent to the client using the enterprise bean.

References to message destinations can be injected via the `@Resource` annotation (which is in the `javax.annotation` package) or via JNDI lookup in cases in which the resource has been defined in the deployment descriptor.

In the use case discussed earlier and shown in Figure 5-5, we have a session bean that is acting as an intermediary between the client application and the message topic. The client application invokes a business method in the session bean and the session becomes the client or JMS message producer that is creating and sending the message. To illustrate this, we will create a stateless session bean, `OrderProcessing`, with one business method, `SendOrderStatus()`. Listing 5-8 shows the code for the `OrderProcessing` session bean. We are using the `@Resource` annotation to inject the `TopicConnectionFactory` and `Topic` that the `StatusMailer` MDB is listening to. We will use some hard-coded values in the session bean to simulate the customer e-mail address and the content for the e-mail. In the `try` block, we create a connection to the `statusMessageTopicConnectionFactory` and start the connection. Using the created session, we create a topic session and topic producer with the createSession() and createProducer() methods. Finally, we create a MapMessage object, populate the message with the e-mail address, subject, and content, and send the message to the Topic using the send() method.

Listing 5-8. *OrderProcessingBean.java*

```java
package com.apress.ejb3.chapter05;
import javax.annotation.Resource;
import javax.ejb.Stateless;
import javax.jms.Connection;
import javax.jms.JMSException;
import javax.jms.MapMessage;
import javax.jms.MessageProducer;
import javax.jms.Session;
import javax.jms.Topic;
import javax.jms.TopicConnectionFactory;

@Stateless(name="OrderProcessing")
public class OrderProcessingBean implements OrderProcessing {
    public OrderProcessingBean() {
    }

    @Resource(mappedName="StatusMessageTopicConnectionFactory")
    private  TopicConnectionFactory statusMessageTopicCF;

    @Resource(mappedName="StatusMessageTopic")
    private  Topic statusTopic;


    public String SendOrderStatus() {
        String from = "wineapp@localhost";
        String to = "wineapp@localhost";
        String content = "Your order has been processed " + ➥
"If you have questions" + ➥
        " call EJB3 Application with order id # " + "1234567890";


        try {
            System.out.println("Before status TopicCF connection");
             Connection connection = statusMessageTopicCF.createConnection();
            System.out.println("Created connection");
```

```
            connection.start();
            System.out.println("started connection");
            System.out.println("Starting Topic Session");
            Session topicSession = connection.createSession(false,
                    Session.AUTO_ACKNOWLEDGE);

            MessageProducer publisher = topicSession.createProducer(statusTopic);
            System.out.println("created producer");
            MapMessage message =topicSession.createMapMessage();
                    message.setStringProperty("from", from);
                    message.setStringProperty("to", to);
                    message.setStringProperty("subject", "Status of your ➥
wine order");
                    message.setStringProperty("content", content);
            System.out.println("before send");
            publisher.send(message);
            System.out.println("after send");
        }
        catch (JMSException e) {
            e.printStackTrace();
        }

        return "Created a MapMessage and sent it to StatusTopic";
    }
}
```

One last thing we need to do to complete the use case discussed in Figure 5-5 is to come up with the client application that will look up the OrderProcessing session bean and invoke the SendOrderStatus() message. Listing 5-9 shows the code for the client application. In the try block of the doIt() method, we are doing a JNDI lookup of the OrderProcessing session bean and calling the SendOrderStatus() business method.

Listing 5-9. *StatusMessageClient.java*

```
package com.apress.ejb3.chapter05.client;
import java.util.List;
import javax.ejb.EJB;
import com.apress.ejb3.chapter05.OrderProcessing;
import java.rmi.RemoteException;
import javax.naming.InitialContext;
import javax.naming.NamingException;
```

```
public class StatusMessageClient {
    public StatusMessageClient() {
    }

    public static void main(String[] args) {
        StatusMessageClient messageClient = new StatusMessageClient();
        messageClient.doIt();
    }

    private void doIt() {
    System.out.println("Performing logic in doIt() ");

        InitialContext ic;

        try {
            ic = new InitialContext();
            System.out.println("OrderProcessing session bean lookup to be done");
            OrderProcessing orderProcessing = ➥
(OrderProcessing)ic.lookup("com.apress.ejb3.chapter05.OrderProcessing");
            System.out.println("Invoking SendOrderStatus() business method now");
            System.out.println(orderProcessing.SendOrderStatus());
            System.out.println("Done !!!");

        } catch (NamingException e) {
            e.printStackTrace();
        }
        catch (RemoteException re){
            re.printStackTrace();
        }

    }
}
```

In the next section, we will look at packaging, deploying, and running the use case we have worked on.

Packaging, Deploying, and Testing MDBs

MDBs need to be packaged into EJB JAR (Java Archive) files before they can be deployed into EJB containers. These EJB archives can then be deployed. (For some EJB containers or application servers, they need to be assembled into EAR [Enterprise Archive] files). Most EJB containers or application servers provide deployment utilities or Ant tasks to facilitate deployment of EJBs to their containers. Java integrated development environments (IDEs) like Oracle JDeveloper, NetBeans, and Eclipse also provide deployment features that allow developers to package, assemble, and deploy EJBs to application servers. Packaging, assembly, and deployment aspects are covered in detail in Chapter 10.

In this chapter, we have developed one stateless session bean (OrderProcessing) and one MDB (StatusMailer). JMS providers have to be configured with queues and topics that will be used by the client application and MDB accordingly before the MDBs are deployed.

The following sections describe the steps to package, assemble, deploy, and test these MDBs and session beans.

Prerequisites

Before performing any of the steps detailed in the next sections, complete the "Getting Started" section of Chapter 1, which will walk you through the installation and environment setup required for the samples in this chapter.

▮Note We will assume that the source code for this chapter's samples is located in the Z: drive. Substitute this with the location of the directory in which you have downloaded the source.

Compiling the Session Beans and MDBs

From the DOS console, execute the following javac command to compile the StatusMailer MDB and the OrderProcessing session bean, along with its business interface. Figure 5-6 shows the command being executed from the Z:\Chapter05-MDBSamples\MDBSamples directory.

```
Z:\Chapter05-MDBSamples\MDBSamples>%JAVA_HOME%/bin/javac -classpath ➥
%GLASSFISH_HOME%\lib\javaee.jar -d ./classes src\com\apress\ejb3\chapter05\*.java
```

Figure 5-6. *Compiling the session beans and MDBs*

In the downloaded source code for this chapter's samples, you will see the Ant build script (build.xml). You can alternatively use the following Ant task to compile the session beans and MDBs:

```
Z:\Chapter05-MDBSamples\MDBSamples>%ANT_HOME%/bin/ant Compile-MDBSamples
```

■**Note** If you are using the Ant task to compile the beans, make appropriate changes to the build. properties file to reflect the settings for the GlassFish application server that you have installed.

Packaging the Session Beans and MDBs

Once the source code for session beans and MDBs is compiled, you will package the compiled classes into an EJB JAR file. Execute the following command in the DOS console:

```
Z:\Chapter05-MDBSamples\MDBSamples\classes>%JAVA_HOME%/bin/jar cvf ➥
..\archive\MDBSamples.jar .\com
```

■**Note** The command is run from classes directory.

Figure 5-7 shows the command being executed from the Z:\Chapter05-MDBSamples\ MDBSamples\classes directory, and the files being added to the generated JAR file.

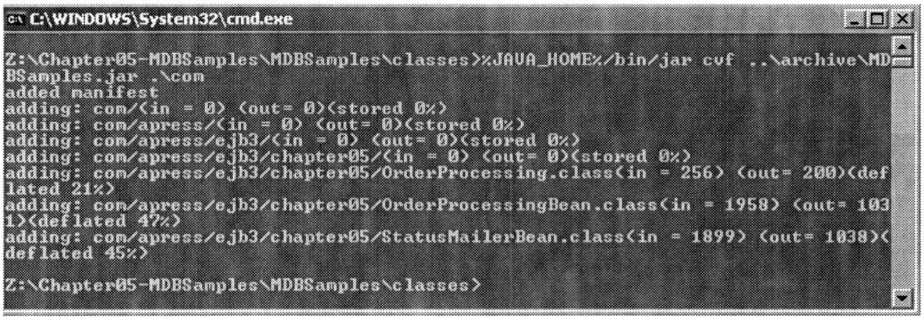

Figure 5-7. *Packaging the session beans and MDBs*

Alternatively, you can use the following Ant task to package the session beans and MDBs:

Z:\Chapter05-MDBSamples\MDBSamples>%ANT_HOME%/bin/ant Package-MDB

The generated MDBSamples.jar file will be stored in the archive directory.

■**Note** If you are using the Ant task for packaging the beans, make appropriate changes to the build.properties file to reflect the settings for the GlassFish application server that you have installed.

Creating the JMS and JavaMail Resources

The StatusMailer MDB makes use of JMS and JavaMail resources. Before the MDBSamples.jar file can be deployed to GlassFish, these resources have to be preconfigured.

Execute the following command in the DOS window. This will create a JMS Topic➥ ConnectionFactory that will be used by the OrderProcessing session bean to send a message to the topic that will be consumed by StausMailer.

Z:\Chapter05-MDBSamples\MDBSamples>%GLASSFISH_HOME%/bin/asadmin.bat ➥
create-jms-resource --host localhost --port 4848 --user admin -passwordfile ➥
%GLASSFISH_HOME%\asadminpass -restype ➥
javax.jms.TopicConnectionFactory StatusMessageTopicConnectionFactory

Figure 5-8 shows the creation of the JMS resource StatusMessageTopicConnectionFactory.

Figure 5-8. *Creating the JMS TopicConnectionFactory*

Execute the following command in the DOS window. This will create a JMS Topic.

```
Z:\Chapter05-MDBSamples\MDBSamples>%GLASSFISH_HOME%/bin/asadmin.bat ➥
create-jms-resource --host localhost --port 4848 --user admin -passwordfile ➥
%GLASSFISH_HOME%\asadminpass --restype javax.jms.Topic ➥
--property imqDestinationName=StatusMessageTopic StatusMessageTopic
```

Figure 5-9 shows the creation of the JMS resource StatusMessageTopic.

Figure 5-9. *Creating the JMS Topic*

> **Note** If you are running GlassFish on a different machine, substitute that machine name for localhost in the command-line arguments. Similarly, if you are running on a different port, substitute the port number you are running for 4848. If you are using the Ant task for creating the beans, make appropriate changes to the build.properties file to reflect the settings for the GlassFish application server that you have installed.

Alternatively, you can use the following Ant task to create the JMS resources:

```
Z:\Chapter05-MDBSamples\MDBSamples>%ANT_HOME%/bin/ant CreateJMSResources
```

Execute the following command in the DOS console to create a JavaMail resource that will be used by the `StatusMailer` MDB to send out e-mail messages:

```
Z:\Chapter05-MDBSamples\MDBSamples>%GLASSFISH_HOME%/bin/asadmin.bat ➥
create-javamail-resource --host localhost --port 4848 --user admin ➥
-passwordfile ~ %GLASSFISH_HOME%\asadminpass --mailhost localhost ➥
-mailuser wineapp@localhost --fromaddress wineapp@localhost mail/wineappMail
```

Figure 5-10 shows the creation of the JavaMail resource.

Figure 5-10. *Creating the JavaMail resource*

Alternatively, you can use the following Ant task to create a JavaMail resource:

```
Z:\Chapter05-MDBSamples\MDBSamples>%ANT_HOME%/bin/ant CreateJavaMailResources
```

Note We have used the Apache Java Enterprise Mail Server (aka James) to demonstrate the ability to send e-mail messages using the JavaMail API. Apache James can be downloaded from `http://james.apache.org`. If you are using a different e-mail server, substitute the appropriate values for the `mailhost`, `mailuser`, and `fromaddress` parameters in the command-line arguments and Ant build script shown previously.

Deploying the Session Beans and MDBs

Now you can deploy the generated JAR file (`MDBSamples.jar`) to the GlassFish application server. You could deploy the JAR file from the GlassFish administration console—but for all practical purposes, you'll want to automate these tasks as much as possible. Therefore, we'll demonstrate the use of the command-line tools and Ant task for deployment.

From the DOS console, execute the following command:

```
Z:\Chapter05-MDBSamples\MDBSamples>%GLASSFISH_HOME%/bin/asadmin.bat deploy ➥
--host localhost --port 4848 --user admin –passwordfile ➥
%GLASSFISH_HOME%\asadminpass --upload=true --target server ➥
z:\Chapter05-MDBSamples\MDBSamples\archive\MDBSamples.jar
```

Figure 5-11 shows the sample application being deployed successfully.

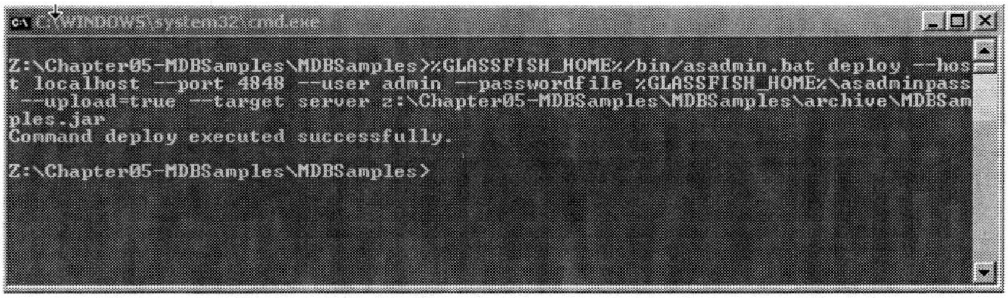

Figure 5-11. *Deploying the MDBs and session beans*

Alternatively, you can use the following Ant task for deployment:

```
Z:\Chapter05-MDBSamples\MDBSamples>%ANT_HOME%/bin/ant Deploy-MDB
```

▦**Note** If you are running the GlassFish application server on a different machine, substitute that machine name for `localhost` in the command-line arguments. Similarly, if you are running on a different port, substitute the port number you are running for `4848`. If you are using the Ant task for deployment, make appropriate changes to the `build.properties` file to reflect the settings for the GlassFish application server that you have installed.

Compiling the Client Programs

From the DOS console, execute the following `javac` command to compile the `StatusMessageClient` class:

```
Z:\Chapter05-MDBSamples\MDBSamples>%JAVA_HOME%/bin/javac –classpath ➥
%GLASSFISH_HOME%\lib\javaee.jar;.\classes -d ./classes ➥
src\com\apress\ejb3\chapter05\client\*.java
```

Figure 5-12 shows the client class being compiled using `javac`.

Figure 5-12. *Compiling the client programs*

Alternatively, you can use the following Ant task to compile the client programs:

`Z:\Chapter05-MDBSamples\MDBSamples>%ANT_HOME%/bin/ant Compile-ClientPrograms`

Running the Client Programs

Once the client programs are compiled, you can invoke the business methods in the deployed `OrderProcessing` session bean, which will create a message and send it to the `Topic` that the `StatusMailer` MDB is listening to. We are going to use the application client container that comes with the GlassFish application server to run the client programs.

■**Note** The application client container will be covered in detail in Chapter 12.

Execute the following command in the DOS shell to run the `StatusMessageClient`:

`Z:\Chapter05-MDBSamples\MDBSamples\classes>%GLASSFISH_HOME%\bin\appclient.bat ➥`
`com.apress.ejb3.chapter05.client.StatusMessageClient`

Figure 5-13 shows the messages printed out to the DOS shell.

```
C:\WINDOWS\system32\cmd.exe

Z:\Chapter05-MDBSamples\MDBSamples\classes>%GLASSFISH_HOME%\bin\appclient.bat co
m.apress.ejb3.chapter05.client.StatusMessageClient
Performing logic in doIt()
OrderProcessing session bean lookup to be done
Invoking SendOrderStatus() business method now
Created a MapMessage and sent it to StatusTopic
Done !!!

Z:\Chapter05-MDBSamples\MDBSamples\classes>
```

Figure 5-13. *The StatusMessageClient result*

Once the StatusMessageClient successfully runs, you should be able to see an e-mail message, as shown in Figure 5-14.

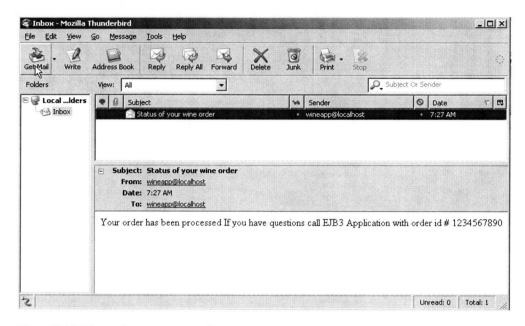

Figure 5-14. *The order status e-mail message*

Conclusion

In this chapter, we have introduced you to the concept of message-oriented middleware, and why enterprises are looking at loosely coupled applications that can converse in an asynchronous fashion.

We covered message application architecture with the P2P and pub-sub models, and discussed why messaging is one of the best ways to implement asynchronous applications. We looked at JMS in detail, including different JMS components such as providers, consumers, clients, and different types of messages. We looked at MDBs and the different artifacts that can make them. We covered the different configuration properties of MDBs and how they can be set using annotations. We explained dependency injection in MDBs, using the specific example of injecting a JavaMail resource. We discussed what it takes to compile, package, deploy, and test MDBs, along with information on how you can create different types of resources in the GlassFish application server. Finally, we covered running sample client programs using the application client container in GlassFish, and viewing the output and receiving e-mail messages sent by MDBs.

In the next chapter, we will drill down into web services, including how you can publish session beans as web services and invoke web services from EJB applications.

## CHAPTER 6

EJB 3 and Web Services

Introduction

This chapter will explain Web Services, introduce the core Web Services standards (SOAP, WSDL, UDDI), and discuss the evolution of Web Services support in the Java EE platform. We will also drill down on how you can publish EJB 3 stateless session beans as web services. Finally, we will discuss how to invoke the published web service from a command-line Java client program and a stateless session bean.

What Are Web Services?

Web services fundamentally constitute some kind of business logic or functionality available in an application or module and exposed via a service interface to a client application (commonly known as service consumer). The consumer of the web service doesn't have to know any implementation details of the web service—the client is able to access or invoke the web service with the information provided in the service interface. This architecture fundamentally provides a loosely coupled model in which the consumer doesn't have to be aware of technology or infrastructure details particular to the implementation of the business logic exposed as a web service.

The Web Services Architecture Working Group of the W3C (World Wide Web Consortium) provides the following definition for a web service:

> *A Web service is a software system designed to support interoperable machine-to-machine interaction over a network. It has an interface described in a machine-processable format (specifically WSDL). Other systems interact with the Web service in a manner prescribed by its description using SOAP messages, typically conveyed using HTTP with an XML serialization in conjunction with other Web-related standards.*

While the concept of abstracting out the details to an interface has been used in several languages and distributed architectures (e.g., EJB and CORBA), the key difference in Web Services is the usage of standards to describe the abstraction, invocation, and registration of services.

Web Services architecture goes by the find-bind-execute model, in which you find the required service in a registry, get the description of the service, bind it to the service (create the message that will be sent to the service based on the description), and finally execute or invoke the service. Figure 6-1 shows the find-bind-execute model. UDDI, WSDL, and SOAP are the standards that make this find-bind-execute model ubiquitous and different from earlier computing models.

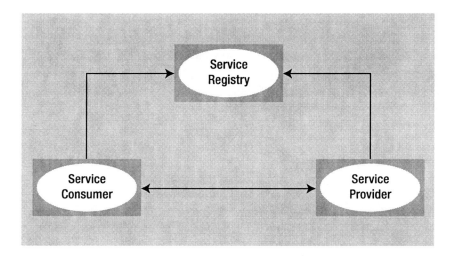

Figure 6-1. *Web Services architecture*

UDDI

Universal Description, Discovery, and Integration (UDDI) provides a standards-based approach to locating a web service, and information on invoking that service. It also provides additional metadata about the service. UDDI helps you to dynamically bind web services instead of having to hard-wire them to an external interface, and also helps to provide taxonomy. Businesses or service providers can provide basic contact information (including identification), categorization for the service, information that describes its behavior, and the actual location of the web service.

UDDI, which is currently in version 3, has evolved over the last few years. Version 1 focused on providing a registry for services, while version 2 focused on aligning the specification with other Web Services specifications and flexible taxonomies. The current version focuses on delivering support for secure interaction of private or public implementations of the services. Several companies, including Oracle, SAP, IBM, Cisco, Infravio, and Systinet, are members of the UDDI technical committee for the Organization for the Advancement of Structured Information Standards (OASIS). Most of the application server vendors (such as Oracle, IBM, and BEA) either provide a UDDI registry as a standard component that comes with their application server, or an OEM UDDI registry (from Systinet or other registry providers) as part of their middleware platform.

WSDL

Web Services Description Language (WSDL) is a technology that is used to describe the interface of a service using XML. WSDL is a standard developed by the W3C, to which several vendors and individuals have contributed over the last few years. WSDL describes what a service does, how to invoke its operations, and where to find it.

WSDL details can be split into two categories: service interface definition details and service implementation definition details. The service interface definition is an abstract or reusable service definition that can be instantiated and referenced by multiple service implementation definitions. It contains the following WSDL elements, which comprise the reusable portion of the service description. We will use a credit check web service as an example to introduce the service interface definition elements listed here:

```
<definitions>
<types>
<message>
<portType>
<binding>
```

The <definitions> Element

The <definitions> element allows you to specify global declarations of namespaces that are visible through the WSDL document. It acts as a container for service description. Listing 6-1 shows an example <definitions> element that defines a target namespace and other namespaces that are referred to by a credit service.

Listing 6-1. *The <definitions> Element in CreditService.wsdl*

```
<?xml version="1.0" encoding="UTF-8" standalone="yes"?>
<definitions targetNamespace="http://www.apress.com/ejb3/credit" ➥
name="CreditService" xmlns:tns="http://www.apress.com/ejb3/credit" ➥
xmlns:xsd="http://www.w3.org/2001/XMLSchema" ➥
xmlns:soap="http://schemas.xmlsoap.org/wsdl/soap/" ➥
xmlns="http://schemas.xmlsoap.org/wsdl/">
```

The <types> Element

The <types> element is used to define the data types for the <message> element. XML schema definitions (XSDs) are most commonly used to specify the data types. Listing 6-2 shows an example <types> element that provides the schema location for the credit service.

Listing 6-2. *The <types> Element in CreditService.wsdl*

```
<types>
  <xsd:schema>
<xsd:import namespace="http://www.apress.com/ejb3/credit"➥
    schemaLocation="CreditServiceBeanService_schema1.xsd"/>
  </xsd:schema>
</types>
```

The <message> Element

The <message> element is used to define the format of data exchanged between a web service consumer and a web service provider. Listing 6-3 shows an example of two <message> elements: CreditCheck and CreditCheckResponse.

Listing 6-3. *The <message> Element in CreditService.wsdl*

```
<message name="CreditCheck">
  <part name="parameters" element="tns:CreditCheck"/>
</message>
<message name="CreditCheckResponse">
  <part name="parameters" element="tns:CreditCheckResponse"/>
</message>
```

The <portType> Element

The <portType> element is used to specify the operations of the web service. Listing 6-4 shows the <portType> element for the credit service with the CreditCheck operation.

Listing 6-4. *The <portType> Element in CreditService.wsdl*

```
<portType name="CreditCheckEndpointBean">
  <operation name="CreditCheck">
    <input message="tns:CreditCheck"/>
    <output message="tns:CreditCheckResponse"/>
  </operation>
</portType>
```

The <binding> Element

The <binding> element describes the protocol, data format, and security for a <portType> element. The standard bindings are HTTP or SOAP; or you can create one of your own.

The "bindings" part of the WSDL specification is flexible—it allows you to provide your own bindings environment instead of the default SOAP-over-HTTP model. This flexibility of the specification has been widely exploited by WSIF (Web Services Invocation Framework), which is an Apache open source project. WSIF provides a nice way to expose existing Java, EJB, JMS (Java Message Service), and JCA-based components as web services with native bindings that provide better performance and support native transactions. Listing 6-5 shows the <binding> element for the credit service, using SOAP-over-HTTP.

Listing 6-5. *The <binding> Element in CreditService.wsdl*

```
<binding name="CreditCheckEndpointBeanPortBinding"➥
type="tns:CreditCheckEndpointBean"> ➥
    <soap:binding transport="http://schemas.xmlsoap.org/soap/http" ➥
style="document"/>
    <operation name="CreditCheck">
      <soap:operation soapAction=""/>
      <input>
        <soap:body use="literal"/>
      </input>
      <output>
        <soap:body use="literal"/>
      </output>
    </operation>
  </binding>
```

The service implementation definition part of the WSDL document identifies a web service. It contains the following elements:

```
<service>
<port>
```

The <service> Element

The <service> element contains a collection of <port> elements, where each port is associated with an endpoint (a network address location or URL). Listing 6-6 shows an example of a <service> element for the credit service.

Listing 6-6. *The <service> Element in CreditService.wsdl*

```
<service name="CreditService">
  <port name="CreditCheckEndpointBeanPort" ➥
binding="tns:CreditCheckEndpointBeanPortBinding">
    <soap:address location="http://localhost:8080/serviceurl/"/>
  </port>
</service>
```

Listing 6-7 shows the complete WSDL document for the credit service that we are going to develop later in the chapter.

Listing 6-7. *The Complete WSDL Document for CreditService.wsdl*

```
<?xml version="1.0" encoding="UTF-8" standalone="yes"?>
<definitions targetNamespace="http://www.apress.com/ejb3/➥
credit" name="CreditService"
xmlns:tns="http://demo.org/"  xmlns:xsd="http://www.w3.org/2001/XMLSchema" ➥
xmlns:soap="http://schemas.xmlsoap.org/wsdl/soap/" ➥
xmlns="http://schemas.xmlsoap.org/wsdl/">
  <types>
    <xsd:schema>
      <xsd:import namespace="http://www.apress.com/ejb3/credit" ➥
schemaLocation="CreditService_schema1.xsd"/>
    </xsd:schema>
  </types>
  <message name="CreditCheck">
```

```
      <part name="parameters" element="tns:CreditCheck"/>
    </message>
    <message name="CreditCheckResponse">
      <part name="parameters" element="tns:CreditCheckResponse"/>
    </message>
    <portType name="CreditCheckEndpointBean">
      <operation name="CreditCheck">
        <input message="tns:CreditCheck"/>
        <output message="tns:CreditCheckResponse"/>
      </operation>
    </portType>
    <binding name="CreditCheckEndpointBeanPortBinding" ➥
  type="tns:CreditCheckEndpointBean"> ➥
      <soap:binding transport="http://schemas.xmlsoap.org/soap/http" ➥
  style="document"/>
      <operation name="CreditCheck">
        <soap:operation soapAction=""/>
        <input>
          <soap:body use="literal"/>
        </input>
        <output>
          <soap:body use="literal"/>
        </output>
      </operation>
    </binding>
    <service name="CreditService">
      <port name="CreditCheckEndpointBeanPort" ➥
  binding="tns:CreditCheckEndpointBeanPortBinding">
        <soap:address location="http://localhost:8080/serviceurl"/>
      </port>
    </service>
  </definitions>
```

SOAP

Simple Object Access Protocol (SOAP) is an XML-based protocol used for exchanging
information in a decentralized and distributed environment using XML. SOAP is a standard developed by the W3C. Fundamentally, SOAP is the default transport layer for the
web services.

A SOAP message is an ordinary XML document containing the following elements:

The required Envelope element identifies the XML document as a SOAP message. Envelope is the top-level element in the document. The envelope is required, and basically marks the start and end of the SOAP message (although messages can contain links to objects outside the envelope). The envelope contains the Header and the Body elements.

The optional Header element contains header information. When the SOAP protocol is used over HTTP, the HTTP headers provide information about the content type, content length, and recipient of the message. A header is included to add features to a SOAP message without prior agreement between the communicating parties.

The required Body element contains call-and-response information. Body is a mandatory element that contains the information for the recipient of the message.

The optional Fault element provides information about errors that occur while the message is processed. The Body element can contain an optional Fault element to report errors.

Figure 6-2 illustrates the elements of a SOAP message.

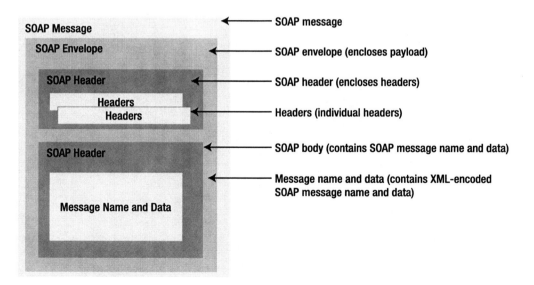

Figure 6-2. *A SOAP envelope*

When Do You Use Web Services?

Web Services provides a standard way to expose existing or new applications and data to external parties—like customers, suppliers, and partners—or across departments in an enterprise, using industry standards. Web Services can also be used to integrate heterogeneous applications and data as well. While many enterprises use web services internally, there are numerous examples of external web services that are available. Some of the popular ones are package-tracking services (provided by shippers like FedEx, UPS, and USPS). E-commerce web sites like www.amazon.com, www.yahoo.com, www.ebay.com, and www.google.com expose their core functionality using web services. Developers can subscribe and use the web services provided by these e-commerce providers to develop applications that add value to or provide seamless integration with back-end systems of these e-commerce providers.

Java EE and Web Services

The Java EE (5.0) platform has evolved over the last few years to become a mature, stable, reliable, and available platform for enterprise applications. While technologies like JDBC (Java Database Connectivity), JMS, and EJB have been in the Java EE platform right from the initial versions, only in J2EE 1.4 have the development and deployment of web services taken better shape—they've been standardized to make the web services in the Java EE platform more portable across application servers and interoperable with .NET Web Services. The common goal for the Java EE 5.0 specifications was to provide ease of development and deployment for applications and services. Some of the key specifications in Java EE that are related to web services are JAX-WS, JAXB, JAXR, SAAJ, and the JSR 181 annotations. In the following sections, we will show what these specifications are and how they can be used with EJB 3.

JAX-WS

JAX-WS (Java API for XML Web Services) defines Java APIs and annotations for accessing web services from Java applications and Java EE components like EJBs. JAX-WS provides mapping facilities between WSDL and Java interfaces, or from Java interfaces to WSDL. WSDL mapped interfaces are called service endpoint interfaces. JAX-WS also provides the client- and server-side APIs and annotations to send and receive web service requests via SOAP. The JAX-WS specification in Java EE 5.0 depends on other relevant specifications of the Java EE platform, including JSR 175, JSR 181, and JAXB. It also provides support for the latest Web Services standards like SOAP 2.0 and WSDL 2.0.

JAXB

Web Services consumers and providers use XML messages to send requests and responses. These messages could be something like a purchase order that has an XSD, which allows the parties (provider and consumer) involved to understand the purchase order. Working with XML documents using low-level language APIs can be time-consuming and can involve complex code. The JAXB (Java Architecture for XML Binding) specification in Java EE 5.0 provides standard APIs for representing XML documents as Java artifacts, so that developers can work off Java objects that represent the XML documents based on schemas (XSD). The JAXB specification facilitates unmarshalling XML documents into sets of Java objects, and marshalling sets of Java objects back into XML documents. The JAXB specification provides full support for XML schemas and binding support for JAX-WS, and leverages other Java EE specifications, such as JSR 175.

JAXR

UDDI is the standard for Web Services registry. The JAXR (Java API for XML Registries) specification defines a standard set of APIs that allow Java clients to access the registry. These APIs can also be used against XML registries other than UDDI ones.

SAAJ

Similar to the attachments you can use in e-mail messages, you can send attachments to the SOAP messages that invoke web services. SAAJ (SOAP with Attachments API for Java) defines a standard set of APIs that allow Java SE or EE components to construct SOAP messages with attachments.

JSR 181

Annotations have been introduced into Java SE with the 5.0 version. JSR 181 (Web Services Metadata for the Java Platform) defines a standard set of annotations that can be used to simplify web service development. These annotations can be used with Java classes or EJB session beans that can be JAX-WS components.

EJB 3 Stateless Session Beans As Web Services

Web Services endpoints described using WSDL are stateless in nature. Stateless session beans also share the same statelessness and are well suited for developing web services.

The EJB 3 specification relies on other Web Services specifications in the Java EE platform—including JAX-WS, JAXB, and JSR 181—to either consume web services or publish stateless session beans as web services.

A service endpoint interface (SEI) is an interface that is mapped to a web service. JAX-WS provides this mapping layer. In order to develop a new web service, you can take either the bottom-up or top-down approach, both of which are described following.

In case of the bottom-up approach, you start with an SEI and an implementation that can be published as a web service. In this process, web service artifacts like WSDL documents are generated at deployment time or by the administrative tools or utilities provided by Java EE (5.0) application servers. For example, Oracle Application Server provides a command-line utility, called Web Service Assembler (WSA), that provides the capability for generating a WSDL document and other required artifacts to publish a component as a web service and package it for deployment.

In the top-down case, you start with a WSDL document and generate an SEI using tools that implement JAX-WS. Once you have an SEI, you can add the implementation behind it. The WSA command-line tool mentioned previously can be used for the top-down approach as well.

In the case of EJB 3 stateless session beans, you need to use the annotations provided in the JAX-WS and JSR 181 specifications to mark the business interfaces and/or bean classes so that the right set of web service artifacts will be generated during deployment time. Java EE specifications require that the annotations added to components be processed at deployment time to generate the right set of artifacts. EJB stateless session beans with web service annotations are no different; they are also processed at deployment time by the deployment utilities provided by the application servers. There will be one stateless session bean for each SEI.

Developing a New Web Service

Stateless session beans are implemented using the programming model described in Chapter 2. In the case that you want to make a stateless session bean as a web service, you will need the following classes:

- A bean class (implementation)

- A web service endpoint interface (optional)

- Additional business interfaces if the bean class has local or remote clients

Creating a Bean Class

A stateless session bean class is any standard Java class that has a class-level annotation of @Stateless. Unlike earlier versions of the EJB specification, the 3 version doesn't mandate the requirement of SEIs. Providing an SEI along with a bean class is optional. In the use case, in which the bean class will be published as a web service without any service endpoint interface, the bean class will have the additional class-level annotation @WebService. The @WebService annotation is in the javax.jws package, and marks the bean class as an implementation for a web service.

The @WebService annotation takes the parameters described in Table 6-1.

Table 6-1. *The @WebService Annotation*

Parameter	Description	Additional Info
name	The name of the web service that gets mapped to wsdl:portType.	If not specified, the name of the Java class is taken.
targetNamespace	The XML namespace used for the web service.	If not specified, it is derived from the Java package.
serviceName	The name of the web service that gets mapped to wsdl:service.	If not specified, the name of the Java class is taken.
wsdlLocation	The location of the WSDL document, which comes in handy when the bean class is implementing existing web service.	

To illustrate a stateless session bean that gets published as a web service, we will create a CreditServiceEndpointBean that will be published as CreditService.

In Listing 6-8, we have a Java class, CreditCheckEndpointBean, that has two class-level annotations: @Stateless and @WebService. The @Stateless annotation provides an additional parameter to mark the bean as CreditCheckEndpointBean. If the same class is exposed to remote or local clients, those clients will access the stateless session bean with that name. The @WebService annotation provides two additional parameters: one to mark the service name as CreditService and the other to specify the target namespace (instead of using the default Java package structure).

Listing 6-8. *CreditCheckEndpointBean.java*

```java
package com.apress.ejb3.chapter06.services;
import javax.ejb.Stateless;
import javax.jws.WebMethod;
import javax.jws.WebService;
```

```
@Stateless(name="CreditCheckEndpointBean")
@WebService(serviceName="CreditService",targetNamespace=➥
"http://www.apress.com/ejb3/credit")


public class CreditCheckEndpointBean  {


    public CreditCheckEndpointBean() {
    }

}
```

The @WebMethod annotation defined in JSR 181 allows you to customize the method that is exposed as a web service operation. If no @WebMethod annotations are specified in the bean class that has the @WebService annotation, then all valid methods are exposed as web service operations.

The @WebMethod annotation takes the parameters described in Table 6-2.

Table 6-2. *The @WebMethod Annotation*

Parameter	Description	Additional Info
operationName	The name of the wsdl:operation that matches to this method.	By default, this is the name of the Java method.
action	The action for this operation. In the case of SOAP bindings, it will be the value of the SOAPAction header.	By default, this is the name of the Java method.

In Listing 6-9, we have added the following method into the CreditCheckEndpointBean class, which will be exposed as a web service operation. The operation name is customized as CreditCheck using @WebMethod parameters. The method takes a java.lang.String parameter (which is the credit card number) and returns a java.lang.boolean value of true or false, depending on whether the credit card is valid. For simplicity's sake, we are going to return true always.

Listing 6-9. *The validateCC Method in CreditCheckEndpointBean.java*

```
@WebMethod(operationName="CreditCheck" )

public boolean validateCC(String cc){
    return true;
}
```

Web Service Endpoint Interface

JAX-WS doesn't mandate the requirement of an SEI to implement a web service endpoint. You can use the annotations provided in JSR 181 to mark the bean class as a web service and one or more business methods as web service operations. In the use case in which an SEI is defined for a stateless session bean, the following should be observed:

- The SEI must have a `javax.jws.WebService` annotation.

- One or more methods can have a `javax.jws.WebMethod` annotation.

- All method parameters and return types should be compatible with the JAXB XML schema mapping definition.

- Arguments and return types of methods must be valid JAX-RPC value types, which include Java primitives (`int`, `long`, etc.), Java classes (`String`, `Date`, etc.), Java Beans, and arrays.

- `throws` clauses must include a `java.rmi.RemoteException` in addition to any other application exceptions.

In our examples, we have decided to go with adding annotations to the bean class itself, as shown in Listings 6-8 and 6-9.

Listing 6-10 illustrates a service endpoint interface for the use case in which an SEI is provided, and Listing 6-11 shows the `CreditCheckEndpointBean` class implementing the SEI.

Listing 6-10. *A Service Endpoint Interface for the Use Case*

```
@WebService(serviceName="CreditService",targetNamespace=➥
"http://www.apress.com/ejb3/credit")
public interface CreditCheckEndpoint {

    @WebMethod(operationName="CreditCheck)
      public boolean validateCC(String cc);
}
```

Listing 6-11. *The CreditCheckEndpointBean Class Implementing the SEI*

```
public class CreditCheckEndpointBean implements CreditCheckEndpoint {


    public CreditCheckEndpointBean() {
    }

//implementation goes here

}
```

Packaging, Deploying, and Testing Web Services

Stateless session beans that have web service annotations need to be packaged into EJB Java Archive (JAR) files before they are deployed into EJB containers. These EJB archives can then be deployed. (For some EJB containers or application servers, they first need to be assembled into EAR [Enterprise Archive] files). Most EJB containers or application servers provide deployment utilities or Ant tasks to facilitate deployment of EJBs to their containers. Java integrated development environments (IDEs) like Oracle JDeveloper, NetBeans, and Eclipse also provide deployment features that allow developers to package, assemble, and deploy EJBs to application servers. Packaging, assembly, and deployment aspects are covered in detail in Chapter 11.

In this chapter, we have developed one stateless session bean (CreditCheckEndpointBean) with web service annotations. We will perform the following steps to package, assemble, deploy, and test the stateless session bean to be published as a web service.

Prerequisites

Before performing any of the steps detailed in the next sections, complete the "Getting Started" section of Chapter 1, which walks you through the installation and environment setup required for the samples in this chapter.

■**Note** We will assume that the source code for this chapter's samples is located in the Z: drive. Substitute this with the location of the directory into which you have downloaded the source.

Compiling the Session Bean

From the DOS console, execute the following `javac` command to compile
`CreditCheckEndpointBean`:

```
Z:\chapter06-WebServiceSamples\WebServiceSamples>%JAVA_HOME%/bin/javac ➥
-classpath %GLASSFISH_HOME%\lib\javaee.jar -d ./classes ➥
 src\com\apress\ejb3\chapter06\services\*.java
```

Figure 6-3 shows the command being executed from the `Z:\Chapter06-`➥
`WebServiceSamples\WebServiceSamples` directory.

Figure 6-3. *Compiling the session bean*

In the downloaded source code for this chapter's samples, you will see an Ant build
script (`build.xml`). You can alternatively use the following Ant task to compile session
beans:

```
Z:\chapter06-WebServiceSamples\WebServiceSamples>%ANT_HOME%/bin/ant ➥
Compile-WSSamples
```

■**Note** If you are using the Ant task for compiling, make appropriate changes to the `build.properties`
file to reflect the settings for the GlassFish application server you have installed.

Packaging the Session Bean

Once the source code for the session bean is compiled, you will package the compiled classes into an EJB JAR file. Execute the following command in the DOS console:

```
Z:\chapter06-WebServiceSamples\WebServiceSamples\classes>%JAVA_HOME%/bin/jar ➥
cvf  ..\archive\creditservice.jar .\com
```

Note The command is run from the `classes` directory.

Figure 6-4 shows the command being executed from the `Z:\Chapter06-WebServiceSamples\WebServiceSamples\classes` directory, and the files being added to the generated JAR file.

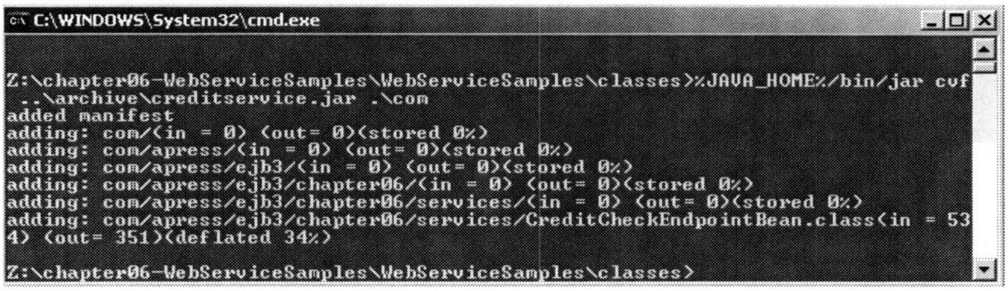

Figure 6-4. *Packaging the session bean*

Alternatively, you can use the following Ant task to package session beans:

```
Z:\chapter06-WebServiceSamples\WebServiceSamples>%ANT_HOME%/bin/ant ➥
Assemble-CreditService
```

The generated `creditservice.jar` file will be stored in the `archive` directory.

Note If you are using the Ant task for packaging, make appropriate changes to the `build.properties` file to reflect the settings for the GlassFish application server you have installed.

Figure 6-5 shows the generated JAR file using the WinZip tool. You can see that the ZIP file has only one class: CreditCheckEndpointBean.

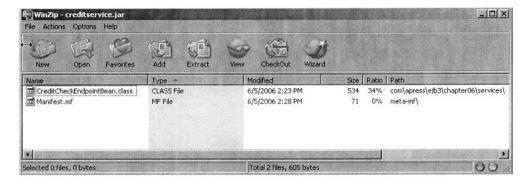

Figure 6-5. *The packaged JAR file for CreditService*

Deploying the Session Bean

Now you can deploy the generated JAR file (creditservice.jar) to the GlassFish application server. You can deploy the JAR file from the GlassFish administration console, but for all practical purposes, you'll want to automate these tasks as much as possible. You should use the following command-line tools and Ant task to deploy.

From the DOS console, execute the following command:

```
Z:\chapter06-WebServiceSamples\WebServiceSamples>%GLASSFISH_HOME%/bin/➥
asadmin.bat deploy --host localhost --port 4848 --user admin ➥
--passwordfile %GLASSFISH_HOME%\asadminpass --upload=true --target server ➥
z:\chapter06-WebServiceSamples\WebServiceSamples\archive\creditservice.jar
```

Figure 6-6 shows the sample application being deployed successfully.

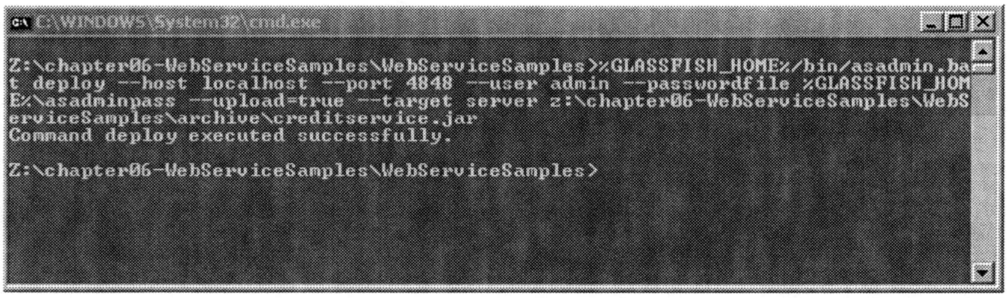

Figure 6-6. *Deploying CreditService*

Alternatively, you can use the following Ant task to deploy:

```
Z:\chapter06-WebServiceSamples\WebServiceSamples>%ANT_HOME%/bin/ant ➥
Deploy-CreditService
```

> **Note** If you are running the GlassFish application server on a different machine, substitute that machine name for `localhost` in the command-line arguments. Similarly, if you are running on a different port, replace `4848` with the number of the port on which you are running. If you are using the Ant task to deploy, make appropriate changes to the `build.properties` file to reflect the settings for the GlassFish application server you have installed.

Testing the Credit Service Using the GlassFish Console

After successful deployment, you can use the GlassFish administration console, which provides a test harness, to see if `CreditService` can be invoked properly or not.

Make sure that the GlassFish server is up and running. Launch the admin console in the browser using `http://<hostname>:<port#>/asadmin/index.html`.

> **Note** Replace `<hostname>` with the machine name on which you are running GlassFish, and `<port#>` with the number of the port on which the server is running.

Figure 6-7 shows the deployed credit service. Select `CreditCheckEndpointBean` under the Web Services node, and in the right-hand frame, click the Test button. You can view the generated WSDL document by clicking the `CreditService.wsdl` link in the right-hand frame. Clicking the Test button will launch the test harness page.

Figure 6-7. *The GlassFish administration console*

In the generated test harness page (shown in Figure 6-8), enter **12345678** as the credit card number, and click the creditCheck button.

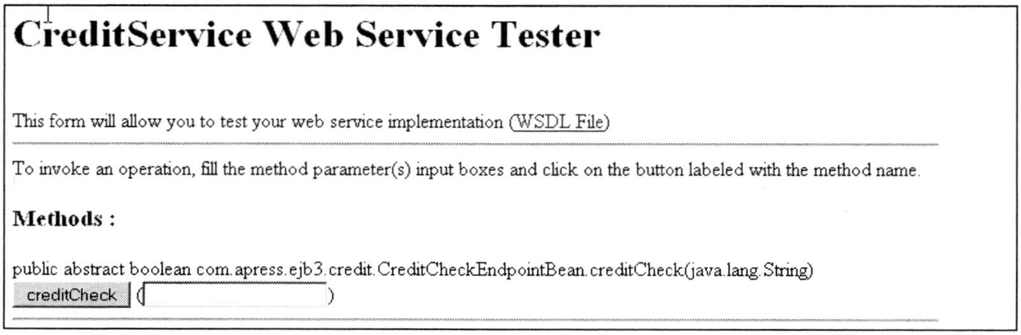

CreditService Web Service Tester

This form will allow you to test your web service implementation (WSDL File)

To invoke an operation, fill the method parameter(s) input boxes and click on the button labeled with the method name.

Methods :

public abstract boolean com.apress.ejb3.credit.CreditCheckEndpointBean.creditCheck(java.lang.String)

creditCheck (   )

Figure 6-8. *The web service test harness*

In the generated page, you can test the results with a SOAP request and response, as shown in Figure 6-9.

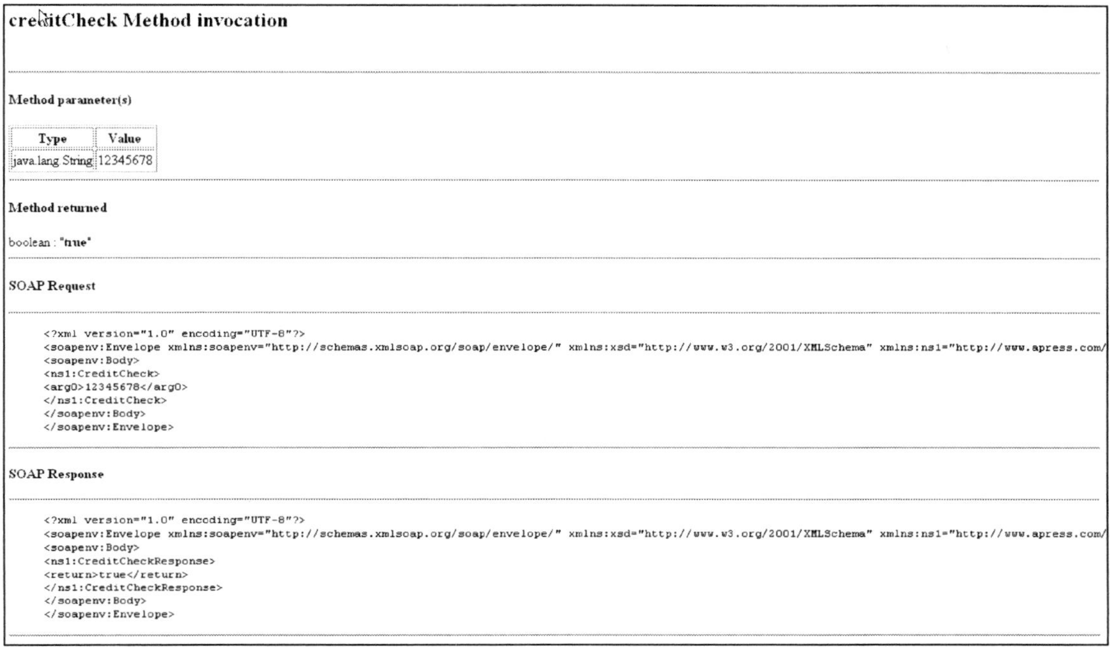

```
creditCheck Method invocation

Method parameter(s)

  Type         Value
java.lang.String 12345678

Method returned

boolean : "true"

SOAP Request

    <?xml version="1.0" encoding="UTF-8"?>
    <soapenv:Envelope xmlns:soapenv="http://schemas.xmlsoap.org/soap/envelope/" xmlns:xsd="http://www.w3.org/2001/XMLSchema" xmlns:ns1="http://www.apress.com/
    <soapenv:Body>
    <ns1:CreditCheck>
    <arg0>12345678</arg0>
    </ns1:CreditCheck>
    </soapenv:Body>
    </soapenv:Envelope>

SOAP Response

    <?xml version="1.0" encoding="UTF-8"?>
    <soapenv:Envelope xmlns:soapenv="http://schemas.xmlsoap.org/soap/envelope/" xmlns:xsd="http://www.w3.org/2001/XMLSchema" xmlns:ns1="http://www.apress.com/
    <soapenv:Body>
    <ns1:CreditCheckResponse>
    <return>true</return>
    </ns1:CreditCheckResponse>
    </soapenv:Body>
    </soapenv:Envelope>
```

Figure 6-9. *SOAP request and response messages*

So far, we have shown how to test the deployed web services using the test harness in the GlassFish administration console. In the next section, we will discuss Web Services clients, and how you can develop and run Java command client programs that can invoke web services. In our case, we will be testing against the deployed credit service.

Web Service Client View

A stateless session bean that is published as a web service can be accessed using the client view described by the WSDL document that gets generated during deployment (as shown in Listing 6-7). Since the stateless session bean is published as a web service using standards such as WSDL, any type of client application that can send and receive SOAP messages (irrespective of technology or language) can invoke it. The client application can be written using .NET or Java EE, or scripting languages such as PHP, Python, or Ruby. From the client point of view, what it sees as a contract is a WSDL document. In order to access the web service, programmatic interfaces should be generated from the WSDL document.

Web services are location independent and can be accessed remotely. If the client application invoking a web service is a Java client or other Java EE component, such as an EJB, it uses JAX-WS client APIs or annotations to invoke the web service via SOAP and HTTP.

Developing a Java Client That Accesses the Web Service

In order to access a web service via a WSDL service contract, the Java client program needs programmatic interfaces (commonly known as stubs or proxies) generated from the WSDL document. Once the stubs have been generated from the WSDL document, we can use the JAX-WS annotations to get a reference to the web service and invoke it.

We will start by generating stubs for the CreditService WSDL document. GlassFish provides the command-line utility wsimport.bat, which can generate web service stubs given a valid WSDL document. We will use this command-line utility to generate the stubs for CreditService. In the case that you are deploying the web service to other Java EE 5.0–compatible servers, these servers might also provide some tools or utilities to generate the stubs for the web service. At the time of writing this chapter, there were no other implementations available publicly.

Generating Web Service Proxy Classes

From the DOS console where the environment properties have been set, execute the following:

```
Z:\chapter06-WebServiceSamples\WebServiceSamples-keep -d ./classes/client ➥
http://<hostname>:<port#>/CreditService/CreditCheckEndpointBean?WSDL
```

■**Note** Replace <hostname> with the machine name or IP address from which the GlassFish server is running, and <port#> with the HTTP port number.

Figure 6-10 shows the generation of proxy classes using wsimport.bat.

Figure 6-10. *Web service proxy generation*

Alternatively, you can use the following Ant task to generate the web service proxy classes:

```
Z:\chapter06-WebServiceSamples\WebServiceSamples>%ANT_HOME%/bin/ant GenWSProxy
```

Once the stubs are generated and compiled, the next step is to create a client that will consume `CreditService`.

The JAX-WS specification provides `@WebServiceRef` annotations, which can be used to declare a reference to a web service, which in our case is `CreditService`.

The `@WebServiceRef` annotation can take the parameters described in Table 6-3.

Table 6-3. *The @WebServiceRef Annotation*

Parameter	Description	Additional Info
name	The name that identifies the web service reference	The name that is local to the application component using the resource
wsdlLocation	The URL pointing to the location of the WSDL document	
type	The resource type	
value	The service type	
mappedName	The physical name of the resource used to map the resource to a vendor-specific container	

Developing a Web Service Client Program

The `@WebServiceRef` annotation either provides a reference to the SEI generated by the container, or a reference to the SEI provided by the application developer. Listing 6-12 shows a Java class that is going to be a web service client. In this Java class, Credit➥ ServiceClient, we are using dependency injection to inject the credit service that we have deployed earlier as a web service. The `@WebServiceRef` annotation is used to inject the `CreditService` that has been generated as the proxy class. Once we have the injected available resource, we use that proxy class to get the web service port using the `getCreditCheckEndpointBeanPort()` method. After successfully getting the port, we can invoke the operations that are available on the port. In our case, we have defined only one operation, `creditCheck`. You can see that this is being invoked with a credit card number of 12345678.

Listing 6-12. *CreditServiceClient.java*

```java
package com.apress.ejb3.chapter06.client;
import javax.xml.ws.WebServiceRef;
import com.apress.ejb3.credit.CreditCheckEndpointBean;
import com.apress.ejb3.credit.CreditService;

public class CreditServiceClient {
    public CreditServiceClient() {
    }

@WebServiceRef(wsdlLocation="http://localhost:8080/CreditService/➥
CreditCheckEndpointBean?WSDL")
static CreditService service;

    public static void main(String[] args) {
        CreditServiceClient creditServiceClient = new CreditServiceClient();
        creditServiceClient.testCreditService();
    }

    public void testCreditService(){
        try {

        CreditCheckEndpointBean creditService = ➥
 service.getCreditCheckEndpointBeanPort();
            System.out.println(creditService.creditCheck("12345678"));

        } catch (Exception ex)  {
            ex.printStackTrace();
        }

    }
}
```

Compiling the Client Class

From the DOS console, execute the following `javac` command to compile the `CreditServiceClient` class:

```
Z:\chapter06-WebServiceSamples\WebServiceSamples>%JAVA_HOME%/bin/javac ➥
-classpath %GLASSFISH_HOME%\lib\javaee.jar;.\classes\client -d ./classes ➥
 src\com\apress\ejb3\chapter06\client\*.java
```

Figure 6-11 shows the command being executed from the `Z:\chapter06-WebServiceSamples\WebServiceSamples` directory.

Figure 6-11. *Compiling the web service client*

Alternatively, you can use the following Ant task to compile the client program:

`Z:\chapter06-WebServiceSamples\WebServiceSamples>%ANT_HOME%/bin/ant CompileWSClient`

Running the Web Service Client

Once you have compiled the client, you can invoke the `CreditService` by running the client using the GlassFish application client container, which supports dependency injection.

We will assemble the client and its dependent classes into a JAR file so that we only have to specify the JAR file as an argument to the application client container.

In the DOS command console, execute the following Ant task:

`Z:\chapter06-WebServiceSamples\WebServiceSamples>%ANT_HOME%/bin/ant Assemble-Client`

Figure 6-12 shows the execution of the Ant task to assemble the client.

```
C:\WINDOWS\System32\cmd.exe
Z:\chapter06-WebServiceSamples\WebServiceSamples>%ANT_HOME%/bin/ant Assemble-Cli
ent
Buildfile: build.xml

init:

Assemble-Client:
     [jar] Building jar: Z:\chapter06-WebServiceSamples\WebServiceSamples\archi
ve\creditserviceclient.jar

BUILD SUCCESSFUL
Total time: 0 seconds
Z:\chapter06-WebServiceSamples\WebServiceSamples>
```

Figure 6-12. *Assembling the web service client*

■Note The application client container is covered in detail in Chapter 12.

In the DOS command console, execute the following:

```
Z:\chapter06-WebServiceSamples\WebServiceSamples\archive>%GLASSFISH_HOME%/bin/ap
pclient.bat -client creditserviceclient.jar
```

Figure 6-13 shows the output after executing the client, which invokes the web service.

Figure 6-13. *The client output*

Successful invocation of the `CreditService` will print `true` in the DOS command console.

Alternatively, you can execute the following:

```
Z:\chapter06-WebServiceSamples\WebServiceSamples>%ANT_HOME%/bin/ant runclient
```

Session Beans as Web Service Clients

A session bean can be a client to a web service as well. In the sample application that we are going to build in Chapter 7, the `OrderProcessing` session bean, which coordinates the workflow, can invoke the credit service to check the validity of the credit card before starting to process the order. To act as a client to a web service, the `OrderProcessing` session bean would make use of the `@WebServiceRef` annotation—similar to what we have shown in the previous Java client sample.

Listing 6-13 shows the stateless session bean `OrderProcessFacadeBean`, which implements both local and remote business interfaces. The `@WebServiceRef` annotation is used to inject a reference to the `CreditService` WSDL document. The `PerformCheckCredit()` method in the `OrderProcessFacadeBean` session bean uses the injected reference to get the port in the `CreditService`, and invokes the `creditCheck` operation. As you can see, the process of injecting the web service, getting the port, and calling the operations from a session bean is similar to what we have done with the Java client that acted as a web service client.

Listing 6-13. *OrderProcessFacadeBean.java*

```java
@Stateless(name="OrderProcessFacade")
public class OrderProcessFacadeBean implements OrderProcessFacade,
                                               OrderProcessFacadeLocal {


    @WebServiceRef(type=CreditService.class)
    CreditService service;


    public OrderProcessFacadeBean() {
    }



    private boolean PerformCreditCheck(Individual customer){

            String ccnum  = customer.getCcNum().toString();
            CreditCheckEndpointBean creditService = ➡
 service.getCreditCheckEndpointBeanPort();
            return creditService.creditCheck(ccnum);


        }

}
```

Conclusion

In this chapter, we have introduced you to Web Services—the architecture that goes by the find-bind-execute model—and how standards like UDDI, WSDL, and SOAP have made Web Services ubiquitous as compared to earlier distributed computing models, in terms of standardization and interoperability.

We looked into the details of the UDDI, SOAP, and WSDL standards, and we demonstrated how WSDL documents and SOAP messages are constructed with a simple credit service example.

We discussed some use cases for which web services can be used, and we discussed how they fit into intranet and Internet models, including some examples of existing e-commerce sites that provide web services.

We then dived into the Java EE platform and looked at different standards (JAX-WS, JAXB, JAXR, SAAJ, and JSR 181) that are enabling developers to create web services that are portable and interoperable with the .NET platform.

We then looked at how to publish EJB 3 stateless session beans as web services using simple Web Services Metadata annotations. We developed a credit service that can be invoked from web service clients.

Finally, we looked at packaging, deploying, and testing web services using the Glass-Fish application server and Java clients, and we also looked at how this programming model is similar to invoking web services with EJBs.

So far, we have discussed the individual components of the EJB 3 specification: session beans, JPA entities, MDBs, and web services. In the next chapter, we will discuss how you can integrate all these components to build an enterprise application.

## CHAPTER 7

Integrating Session Beans, Entities, Message-Driven Beans, and Web Services

Introduction

Earlier chapters in this book have covered the individual components of EJB 3. These include session beans, entities, message-driven beans (MDBs), and stateless session beans as web services. In this chapter, we will show how you can put together these individual components into a complete Java EE 5 application, using a fictitious wine store application as an example.

Application Overview

The sample application that we are going to develop in this chapter is the Wines Online application, which provides customers (either individuals or distributors) with a variety of search criteria with which they can browse, select wines, and add them to a shopping cart. Customers need to register with the Wines Online application before they can submit orders. Once an order is submitted, the customer's credit card is validated, which triggers an order processing message and an e-mail notification to the customer on the status of the order.

Screens used by the customer to search, navigate, and submit orders are part of a simple JavaServer Faces (JSF) web application that interacts with back-end services and components developed using EJBs. In this chapter, our focus will be on developing the back-end part of the application, which can be tested with a simple Java command-line program. In Chapter 12, we will develop a JSF client for this back-end application.

As shown in Figure 7-1, the Wines Online application consists of several back-end components that are used by the client application, and these back-end components in turn make use of different types of services to perform CRUD (create, retrieve, update, delete) operations, send e-mail notifications to the customer on the order status, process the incoming orders, and verify the credit card status of the customer. We will discuss the behavior and functionality of these components in the next section.

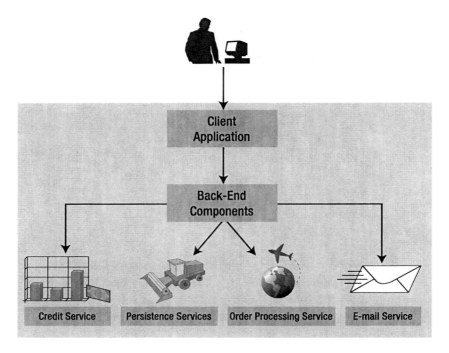

Figure 7-1. *The Wines Online application architecture*

Application Components and Services

The back-end wine store application consists of different types of EJBs that are created as components and services. The key components and services are described in the following sections.

The Shopping Cart Component

The shopping cart component manages the cart items for a registered customer who has logged into the application. This component is stateful in nature and keeps track of cart items (wines and quantity) that are added to and removed from the shopping cart. Finally, the shopping cart component transfers the order information to the order processing component.

The Search Façade Component

The search façade component allows the customer to retrieve all wines or search for wines using criteria such as year, country, and varietal. This component is a stateless session bean and it returns a list of wines based on executed search criteria.

The Customer Façade Component

The customer façade component allows customers to register themselves as members of the wine application and also retrieve customer information based on their e-mail addresses. This component is a stateless session bean.

The Order Processing Façade Component

The order processing façade component acts as a coordinator between the credit service and the order processing service. This component processes the cart items and creates a purchase order (PO) that can be consumed by the order processing service. This component is a stateless session bean.

Persistence Services

Persistence services comprise a packaged persistence unit that consists of a set of entities that are mapped to the wine store database schema. All other components and services in the back-end part of the application use this common persistence unit to perform CRUD operations.

The E-mail Service

The e-mail service is an MDB that sends out an e-mail to the customer about the status of the order submitted.

The Credit Service

The credit service is a web service that is consumed by the application. This service takes credit card information as an input message and returns the status of the credit for a particular customer. We will use the credit service developed in Chapter 6.

The Order Processing Service

The order processing service is an MDB that does the bulk of the order processing after a PO has been received.

The Wines Online Application Business Process

Figure 7-2 illustrates the process flow for the wine application. Once the shopping cart submits the customer and cart item information to the order processing façade, it verifies that the customer credit card information is accurate and the card is valid before proceeding to process the order. Once approval is received from the credit service, it creates a PO that contains the customer and order information, and submits it to the order processing service. If a negative response is received from the credit service, the order is cancelled and the e-mail service sends a notification to the customer. Once a PO is received by the order processing service, it proceeds to fulfill the order, which entails updating the inventory and sending an e-mail notification on the status of the order to the customer using the e-mail service.

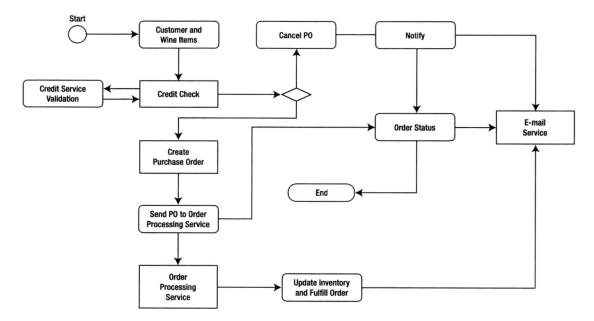

Figure 7-2. *The Wines Online application business process*

Figure 7-3 illustrates the interactions that occur among the components and services of the wine application. A step-by-step explanation of these interactions follows the diagram.

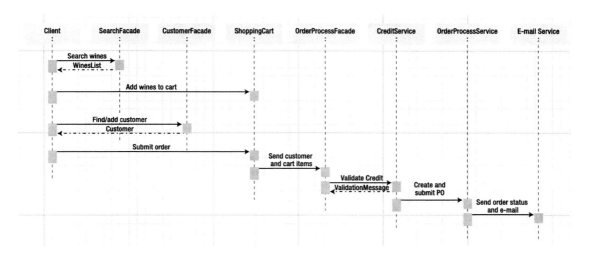

Figure 7-3. *The Wines Online application component and service interactions*

In-Depth Component/Service Walkthrough

In the following sections, we will walk through the individual component code to explain the interaction between the components and services.

Persistence Services

Persistence services make up a group of Java Persistence API (JPA) entities that are mapped to the wine store database schema using annotations. This group of entities is used as a persistence unit that is injected into other components and services to perform queries and CRUD operations on individual entities or groups of entities.

Figure 7-4 illustrates the entities, the inheritance model, and the relationships between them. The Customer entity is inherited by the Individual and Distributor entities. InventoryItem, CartItem, and OrderItem entities inherit the WineItem entity. The BusinessContact entity is inherited by the Supplier entity. The wine store persistence unit also contains different types of relationships between these entities (including one-to-one, one-to-many, and many-to-many), which will be accessed from the application code. The mappings used in these entities were covered in Chapters 3 and 4. We will focus on the code that is used in other components of this application to integrate this persistence unit.

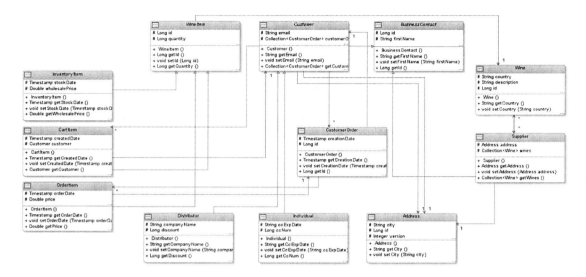

Figure 7-4. *The Wines Online persistence unit*

The Customer Façade Component

CustomerFacadeBean is as stateless session bean. This bean provides business methods to allow the client application to either query the customer based on their e-mail address or perform CRUD operations on the Customer entity in the persistence unit using an injected EntityManager via the @PersistenceContext annotation. Listing 7-1 shows the findCustomerByEmail method in CustomerFacadeBean. This method calls the named query findCustomerByEmail defined in the Individual entity of the wine store persistence unit using the createNamedQuery() method in the EntityManager.

■**Note** createNamedQuery() is a method in the javax.persistence.EntityManager interface. This method creates an instance of javax.persistence.Query for executing a named query specified in JPQL (Java Persistence Query Language) or native SQL.

Listing 7-1. *The findCustomerByEmail Method*

```
        public Individual findCustomerByEmail(Object email) {
            return ➥
(Individual)em.createNamedQuery("findCustomerByEmail").setParameter("email", ➥
email).getSingleResult();
        }
```

Listing 7-2 shows the complete code for CustomerFacadeBean, which has the business methods to perform CRUD operations using the EntityManager. This bean class has two business interfaces, CustomerFacade and CustomerFacadeLocal, which support remote and local client access. Listings 7-3 and 7-4 show the local and remote interfaces for CustomerFacadeBean.

■**Note** In Chapter 2, we provided the details on the differences between remote and client view architectures for session beans with a summary of advantages and disadvantages. Chapter 3 provided the details on the methods that are available on the EntityManager to perform the CRUD operations.

Listing 7-2. *CustomerFacadeBean.java*

```java
import com.apress.ejb3.wineapp.Customer;
import com.apress.ejb3.wineapp.Individual;
import javax.ejb.Stateless;
import javax.persistence.EntityManager;
import javax.persistence.PersistenceContext;

@Stateless(name="CustomerFacade")
public class CustomerFacadeBean implements CustomerFacade,
                                           CustomerFacadeLocal {
    @PersistenceContext(unitName="wineStoreUnit")
    private EntityManager em;

    public CustomerFacadeBean() {
    }

    public Object mergeEntity(Object entity) {
        return em.merge(entity);
    }

    public Object persistEntity(Object entity) {
        em.persist(entity);
        return entity;
    }

    public Object refreshEntity(Object entity) {
        em.refresh(entity);
        return entity;
    }
```

```
        public void removeEntity(Object entity) {
            em.remove(em.merge(entity));
        }

        public void addCustomer(Customer customer) {
            persistEntity(customer);
        }


        public Individual findCustomerByEmail(Object email) {
            return ➥
(Individual)em.createNamedQuery("findCustomerByEmail").setParameter("email", ➥
email).getSingleResult();
        }
    }
```

Listing 7-3. *CustomerFacade.java*

```
import com.apress.ejb3.wineapp.Customer;
import com.apress.ejb3.wineapp.Individual;
import javax.ejb.Remote;

@Remote
public interface CustomerFacade {
    Object mergeEntity(Object entity);

    Object persistEntity(Object entity);

    Object refreshEntity(Object entity);

    void removeEntity(Object entity);

    void addCustomer(Customer customer);

    Individual findCustomerByEmail(Object email);
}
```

Listing 7-4. *CustomerFacadeLocal.java*

```java
import com.apress.ejb3.wineapp.Customer;
import com.apress.ejb3.wineapp.Individual;
import javax.ejb.Local;

@Local
public interface CustomerFacadeLocal {
    Object mergeEntity(Object entity);

    Object persistEntity(Object entity);

    Object refreshEntity(Object entity);

    void removeEntity(Object entity);

    void addCustomer(Customer customer);

    Individual findCustomerByEmail(Object email);
}
```

■ **Note** For all the session beans in this chapter, we will be using the model in which the business interfaces are annotated with @Remote or @Local. The bean class will implement these business interfaces.

The Search Façade Component

SearchFacadeBean is a stateless session bean. This bean provides business methods that
allow the client application to query the Wine entity in the persistence unit based on
the year, country, and varietal of the wine. The persistence unit in SearchFacadeBean is
injected via the @PersistenceContext annotation. Listing 7-5 shows the complete code
for SearchFacadeBean, which has the business methods to perform search operations
using the EntityManager. This bean class has two business interfaces, SearchFacade
and SearchFacadeLocal, which support remote and local client access. The methods
findAllWine(), findWineByYear(), findWineByCountry(), and findWineByVarietal() call the
respective named queries defined in the Wine entity of the wine store persistence unit
using the createNamedQuery() method in the EntityManager, and return one or more Wine
objects in java.util.List.

Listing 7-5. *SearchFacadeBean.java*

```java
import com.apress.ejb3.wineapp.Wine;

import java.util.List;
import javax.ejb.Stateless;
import javax.persistence.EntityManager;
import javax.persistence.PersistenceContext;

@Stateless(name="SearchFacade")
public class SearchFacadeBean implements SearchFacade, SearchFacadeLocal {
    @PersistenceContext(unitName="wineStoreUnit")
    private EntityManager em;

    public SearchFacadeBean() {
    }


    /** <code>select object(o) from Wine o</code> */
    public List<Wine> findAllWine() {
        return em.createNamedQuery("findAllWine").getResultList();
    }

    /** <code>select object(o) from Wine wine where wine.year = :year</code> */
    public List<Wine> findWineByYear(Object year) {
        return em.createNamedQuery("findWineByYear").setParameter("year", ➥
year).getResultList();
    }

    /** <code>select object(o) from Wine wine where wine.country➥
 = :country</code> */
    public List<Wine> findWineByCountry(Object country) {
        return em.createNamedQuery("findWineByCountry").setParameter("country",➥
country).getResultList();
    }

    /** <code>select object(o) from Wine wine where wine.varietal ➥
 = :varietal</code> */
    public List<Wine> findWineByVarietal(Object varietal) {
        return em.createNamedQuery("findWineByVarietal").setParameter("varietal",➥
varietal).getResultList();
    }
}
```

The Shopping Cart Component

ShoppingCartBean is a stateful session bean. This bean preserves the state of a customer who is logged into the system and is currently either adding or removing wine items from the shopping cart. Once the customer submits an order, ShoppingCartBean sends the customer information to the order processing façade, which takes care of processing the order. We have decided on using a stateful session bean for this use case for the following reasons:

- There is more than one type of client application that accesses the back-end application (web, Swing, and command-line client).

- We want to show the usage of EJB 3 stateful session beans in a typical application.

■**Note** In general, there is a common belief that stateful session beans are heavyweight to store the state (as compared to storing the state on the client using an HTTP session for web clients). There is evidence that there isn't a drastic cost in terms of either performance or transactions associated with stateful session beans (see *J2EE Performance Testing with BEA WebLogic Server,* by Peter Zadrozny [Apress, 2003], for thorough coverage of this topic).

ShoppingCartBean has the business methods described in the following subsections.

Finding Customers

Listing 7-6 shows the findCustomer() method in ShoppingCartBean. This method uses the injected CustomerFacadeBean and calls the findCustomerByEmail() method to get an instance of the Individual entity. Once a Customer of type Individual is retrieved, a setCustomer() method is called, and the return value is assigned to an attribute of type Individual.

Listing 7-6. *The findCustomer Business Method*

```
public String findCustomer(Object email) {
    final Individual cust = customerFacade.findCustomerByEmail(email);
    setCustomer(cust);
    return "Customer account available";
}
```

Adding Wine Items

Listing 7-7 shows the addWineItem() method in ShoppingCartBean. This business method is called by the client application to add a particular wine item to the shopping cart, along with the quantity. The code creates a new instance of the CartItem entity and sets the quantity, wine, and time of creation using the setter methods in CartItem.

Note There is a notion of managed and unmanaged entities in the EJB 3 specification. A managed instance of an entity is one in which the persistence context is aware of and has the ability to perform transactional operations. An unmanaged object is one that is completely detached from the persistence context, and possibly created or edited by client applications.

In order to set the wine in the CartItem entity, we need to make sure that the Wine object is a managed object in the persistence context. The Wine object, which is sent by the client application, is a detached object; we need to have a managed object from the persistence context. In the following code, you will see that a call to the find() method of the EntityManager is made to retrieve a managed object before setting the Wine in the CartItem entity.

The code follows the same rule before adding CartItem to Customer. It checks whether Customer is already a managed object. If not, a call to the find() method of the EntityManager is made to retrieve a managed Customer object, and then CartItem is added to Customer. Finally, the managed Customer object is merged back into the persistence context using the merge() method.

Listing 7-7. *The addWineItem Business Method*

```
public void addWineItem(Wine wine, Long quantity) {

    CartItem cartItem = new CartItem();
    cartItem.setQuantity(quantity);
    wine = em.find(Wine.class,wine.getId());
    cartItem.setWine(wine);
    cartItem.setCreatedDate(new Timestamp(System.currentTimeMillis()));

            if(em.contains(customer)){
                customer.addCartItem(cartItem) ;
            }
            else {
```

```
                    customer = em.find(Individual.class, customer.getId());
                    customer.addCartItem(cartItem) ;
                }

        customer = em.merge(customer);
    }
```

Removing Wine Items

Listing 7-8 shows the removeWineItem() method in ShoppingCartBean. This method lets the client applications remove the items from the shopping cart when requested by the end user (via the user interface). The code checks whether Customer is a managed instance before calling the removeCartItem() method in the Customer entity, which removes the CartItem object from the CartItem list. Finally, the merge() method is called to update the Customer object and assigned back to the Customer attribute.

Listing 7-8. *The removeWineItem Business Method*

```
public void removeWineItem(CartItem cartItem) {

    if (em.contains(customer)) {
        customer.removeCartItem(cartItem);
    }
    else{
        customer = em.find(Individual.class,customer.getId());
        customer.removeCartItem(cartItem);
    }
     customer = em.merge(customer);

}
```

Submitting Orders to the Order Processing Façade

Listing 7-9 shows the SendOrderToOPC() method in ShoppingCartBean. This method is called by the client applications to submit the order when the end user finally decides to buy one or more wines. This method uses the injected OrderProcessFacadeBean and calls the ProcessOrder() method to submit the order by passing the Customer object.

■**Note** The rationale behind the naming of the SendOrderToOPC() method was that OrderProcess➡
FacadeBean, which receives the purchase orders, in effect acts as an "order processing center." With this in
mind, we decided to abbreviate "order processing center" to OPC so as to avoid an extremely long method
name.

Listing 7-9. *The SendOrderToOPC Business Method*

```
public String SendOrderToOPC() {
    try  {
        Individual customer = getCustomer();
        opcFacade.ProcessOrder(customer);


    } catch (Exception ex)  {
        ex.printStackTrace();
    }

    return "Your Order has been submitted - you will be notified about  ➡
the status via email";
    }
```

Retrieving All Cart Items

Listing 7-10 shows the getAllCartItems() method in ShoppingCartBean. This method takes
the Customer object (which is of Individual entity type) as a parameter and returns the
current list of cart items. This method will be useful when we build a JSF application, in
which we can show all the cart items in the user interface before the customer submits
the order. This method also checks whether the received Customer is a managed object.
If it is, we call the getCartItemCollection() method, which is a getter method in the
Individual entity that accesses all the cart items via the relationship specified through
the annotations. If the received customer is not a managed entity, we find the customer
first, and then call the getCartItemCollection() method.

Listing 7-10. *The getAllCartItems Business Method*

```java
public List<CartItem> getAllCartItems(Individual customer) {

    if(em.contains(customer)){
        return (List)customer.getCartItemCollection() ;
    }
    else {
        customer = em.find(Individual.class, customer.getId());
        return (List)customer.getCartItemCollection() ;
    }
}
```

The complete code for ShoppingCartBean is shown in Listing 7-11.

Listing 7-11. *ShoppingCartBean.java*

```java
import com.apress.ejb3.ch07.business.PurchaseOrder;
import com.apress.ejb3.wineapp.CartItem;
import com.apress.ejb3.wineapp.CustomerOrder;
import com.apress.ejb3.wineapp.Individual;
import com.apress.ejb3.wineapp.OrderItem;
import com.apress.ejb3.wineapp.Wine;

import java.io.Serializable;
import java.sql.Timestamp;
import java.util.ArrayList;
import java.util.Collection;
import java.util.Iterator;
import java.util.List;
import javax.annotation.Resource;
import javax.ejb.EJB;
import javax.ejb.Stateful;
import javax.persistence.EntityManager;
import javax.persistence.PersistenceContext;
```

```java
@Stateful(name = "ShoppingCart")
public class ShoppingCartBean implements ShoppingCart, ShoppingCartLocal,
                                         Serializable {
    public ShoppingCartBean() {
    }


    @PersistenceContext(unitName = "wineStoreUnit")
    private EntityManager em;

    public Individual customer;

    @EJB
    CustomerFacadeLocal customerFacade;

    @EJB
    OrderProcessFacadeLocal opcFacade;


    public Individual getCustomer() {
        return customer;
    }

    public void addWineItem(Wine wine, Long quantity) {

        CartItem cartItem = new CartItem();
        cartItem.setQuantity(quantity);
        wine = em.find(Wine.class,wine.getId());
        cartItem.setWine(wine);
        cartItem.setCreatedDate(new Timestamp(System.currentTimeMillis()));

                    if(em.contains(customer)){
                        customer.addCartItem(cartItem) ;
                    }
                    else {
                        customer = em.find(Individual.class, customer.getId());
                        customer.addCartItem(cartItem) ;
                    }

        customer = em.merge(customer);
    }
```

```java
    public void removeWineItem(CartItem cartItem) {

        if (em.contains(customer)) {
            customer.removeCartItem(cartItem);
        }
        else{
            customer = em.find(Individual.class,customer.getId());
            customer.removeCartItem(cartItem);
        }
         customer = em.merge(customer);

    }



    public void setCustomer(Individual customer) {
        this.customer = customer;

    }


        public String findCustomer(Object email) {
            final Individual cust = customerFacade.findCustomerByEmail(email);
            setCustomer(cust);
            return "Customer account available";
        }


    public String SendOrderToOPC() {
        try {
            Individual customer = getCustomer();
            opcFacade.ProcessOrder(customer);



        } catch (Exception ex)  {
            ex.printStackTrace();
        }

        return "Your Order has been submitted - you will be notified ➥
about the status via email";
    }
    public List<CartItem> getAllCartItems(Individual customer) {
```

```
        if(em.contains(customer)){
            return (List)customer.getCartItemCollection() ;
        }
        else {
            customer = em.find(Individual.class, customer.getId());
            return (List)customer.getCartItemCollection() ;
        }
    }
}
```

The Order Processing Façade Component

OrderProcessFacadeBean is a stateless session bean. This bean provides business methods that are invoked by ShoppingCartBean to submit an order, and other methods that interact with the credit and order processing services. OrderProcessFacadeBean has the business methods described in the following subsections.

Credit Check

Listing 7-12 shows the performCreditCheck() method in OrderProcessFacadeBean. This method uses the injected CreditService with the @WebServiceRef annotation to get the port of the web service. Once the port is available, the code can call the creditCheck web service operation, which takes a credit card number and returns a message on the validity of the card in true or false terms. We are using the credit service that we developed in Chapter 6.

Listing 7-12. *The performCreditCheck Business Method*

```
    private boolean performCreditCheck(Individual customer){

            String ccnum  = customer.getCcNum().toString();
            CreditCheckEndpointBean creditService = ➥
service.getCreditCheckEndpointBeanPort();
            return creditService.creditCheck(ccnum);

        }
```

Creating a Purchase Order

Listing 7-13 shows the processOrder() method in OrderProcessFacadeBean. ShoppingCartBean calls this business method when an order is submitted by the client application. This method has one parameter, which is of Individual entity type. The parameter object contains the customer information, along with the wine items (and quantity) that have been added by the customer.

To start with, the method checks whether the received entity is managed. If not, a call to the find() method of the EntityManager is made to retrieve a managed Individual object. Once the managed customer entity is grabbed, a call to the performCreditCheck() method is made to verify the credit card. If the credit card is found to be invalid, the message "Invalid Credit Card" is sent back to the client application via ShoppingCartBean.

If the credit card is valid, then a new order of CustomerOrder entity type is created. This new order is populated with the collection of CartItem entities that are related to the Customer. The price for each order item is calculated using the available retail price information for each Wine entity. A temporary list of CartItem objects is created and populated with each CartItem entity that has been added to the order.

Once all the cart items have been processed, the removeCartItem() method is called in a for loop to remove each CartItem entity from the Customer. A call to the remove() method of the EntityManager is also done to merge the updated customer back into the persistence context.

The utility class PurchaseOrder, which stores customer IDs and orders, is created, and a call to the sendPOtoMDB() method is made to send the PO to the processing service. Once the call is made, the process becomes asynchronous, and a message is sent back to the client application that the order has been sent for processing.

Listing 7-13. *The processOrder Business Method*

```
public String processOrder(Individual customer) {

  String processStatus = null;
        if (!em.contains(customer)) {
            customer = em.find(Individual.class,customer.getId());
        }

        if (performCreditCheck(customer)){
            CustomerOrder order = new CustomerOrder();
            order.setCreationDate(new Timestamp(System.currentTimeMillis()));

            try {
```

```
                        Collection<CartItem> cartCol = ➡
                    customer.getCartItemCollection();
                        Iterator cartIter = cartCol.iterator();
                    final List<CartItem> cartItems = new ArrayList();
                        while (cartIter.hasNext()) {
                                CartItem cItem = (CartItem)cartIter.next();
                                OrderItem oItem = new OrderItem();
                                Long qty = cItem.getQuantity();
                                oItem.setQuantity(qty);
                        oItem.setOrderDate(new Timestamp➡
                            (System.currentTimeMillis()));
                                oItem.setWine(cItem.getWine());
                                Wine tempWine = cItem.getWine();
                                Double d = tempWine.getRetailPrice();
                                Double price = d * cItem.getQuantity();
                                oItem.setPrice(price);
                                order.addOrderItem(oItem);
                                cartItems.add(cItem);
                        }

                        for (CartItem cartItem : cartItems) {
                                customer.removeCartItem(cartItem);
                                em.remove(em.merge(cartItem));
                        }


                        PurchaseOrder po = new PurchaseOrder();
                        po.setCustomerId(customer.getId());
                        po.setCustomerOrder(order);

                        sendPOtoMDB(po);


            } catch (Exception e) {
                e.printStackTrace();
            }

            processStatus = "Purchase Order sent for processing➡
    to the process queue";
```

```
            }
            else {
                processStatus = " Invalid Credit Card number ➥
or credit check failed";
            }
        return processStatus;
    }
```

Sending a Purchase Order to the Order Processing Service

Listing 7-14 shows the sendPOtoMDB() method in OrderProcessFacadeBean. This business method makes use of injected Java Mail Service (JMS) resources for a topic connection factory and a topic. A connection to a topic connection factory is created and the connection is started. Once a connection is available, a session is created and a MessageProducer is created with a topic. An ObjectMessage is created to take the PurchaseOrder object, and the MessageProducer is used to send the PurchaseOrder to the topic.

Listing 7-14. *The sendPOtoMDB Business Method*

```
    private void sendPOtoMDB(PurchaseOrder po) {
        //send PO to MDB now
        Connection connection = null;
        Session session = null;
        try {
            connection = poTopicCF.createConnection();
            System.out.println("Created connection");
            connection.start();
            session =
                    connection.createSession(false, Session.AUTO_ACKNOWLEDGE);
            MessageProducer producer = session.createProducer(poTopic);
            ObjectMessage objMessage = session.createObjectMessage();
            objMessage.setObject(po);
            producer.send(objMessage);
            session.close();
            connection.close();
        } catch (JMSException e) {
            e.printStackTrace();
        }
    }
```

The complete code for OrderProcessFacadeBean is shown in Listing 7-15.

Listing 7-15. *OrderProcessFacadeBean.java*

```java
import com.apress.ejb3.ch06.creditservice.CreditCheckEndpointBean;
import com.apress.ejb3.ch06.creditservice.CreditService;
import com.apress.ejb3.ch07.business.PurchaseOrder;
import com.apress.ejb3.wineapp.CartItem;
import com.apress.ejb3.wineapp.CustomerOrder;
import com.apress.ejb3.wineapp.Individual;
import com.apress.ejb3.wineapp.OrderItem;
import com.apress.ejb3.wineapp.Wine;
import java.sql.Timestamp;
import java.util.ArrayList;
import java.util.Collection;
import java.util.Iterator;
import java.util.List;
import javax.annotation.Resource;
import javax.ejb.Stateless;
import javax.jms.Connection;
import javax.jms.JMSException;
import javax.jms.MessageProducer;
import javax.jms.ObjectMessage;
import javax.jms.Session;
import javax.jms.Topic;
import javax.jms.TopicConnectionFactory;
import javax.persistence.EntityManager;
import javax.persistence.PersistenceContext;
import javax.xml.ws.WebServiceRef;

@Stateless(name="OrderProcessFacade")
public class OrderProcessFacadeBean implements OrderProcessFacade,
                                               OrderProcessFacadeLocal {
    @PersistenceContext(unitName = "wineStoreUnit")
    private EntityManager em;

    @Resource(mappedName="poTopicConnectionFactory")
    private  TopicConnectionFactory poTopicCF;

    @Resource(mappedName="PurchaseorderTopic")
    private  Topic poTopic;
```

```java
    @WebServiceRef(type=CreditService.class)
    CreditService service;


    public OrderProcessFacadeBean() {
    }

    public Object mergeEntity(Object entity) {
        return em.merge(entity);
    }

    public void removeEntity(Object entity) {
        em.remove(em.merge(entity));
    }

    public void createNewOrder(CustomerOrder newOrder) {
        persistEntity(newOrder);
    }


private boolean performCreditCheck(Individual customer){

                String ccnum  = customer.getCcNum().toString();
                CreditCheckEndpointBean creditService = ➡
                service.getCreditCheckEndpointBeanPort();
                return creditService.creditCheck(ccnum);


        }


    public String processOrder(Individual customer) {
    String processStatus = null;
            if (!em.contains(customer)) {
                customer = em.find(Individual.class,customer.getId());
            }

            if (performCreditCheck(customer)){
                CustomerOrder order = new CustomerOrder();
                order.setCreationDate(new Timestamp(System.currentTimeMillis()));

                try {
```

```
                Collection<CartItem> cartCol = ➥
                 customer.getCartItemCollection();
                Iterator cartIter = cartCol.iterator();
                final List<CartItem> cartItems = new ArrayList();
                        while (cartIter.hasNext()) {
                                CartItem cItem = (CartItem)cartIter.next();
                                OrderItem oItem = new OrderItem();
                                Long qty = cItem.getQuantity();
                                oItem.setQuantity(qty);
                                oItem.setOrderDate(new ➥
                                 Timestamp(System.currentTimeMillis()));
                                oItem.setWine(cItem.getWine());
                                Wine tempWine = cItem.getWine();
                                Double d = tempWine.getRetailPrice();
                                Double price = d * cItem.getQuantity();
                                oItem.setPrice(price);
                                order.addOrderItem(oItem);

                                cartItems.add(cItem);
                        }

                        for (CartItem cartItem : cartItems) {
                                customer.removeCartItem(cartItem);
                                em.remove(em.merge(cartItem));
                         }

                         PurchaseOrder po = new PurchaseOrder();
                         po.setCustomerId(customer.getId());
                         po.setCustomerOrder(order);

                         sendPOtoMDB(po);

        } catch (Exception e) {
            e.printStackTrace();
        }

    processStatus = "Purchase Order sent for processing to ➥
     the process queue";
```

```
            }
            else {
                processStatus = " Invalid Credit Card number or credit ➥
                check failed";
            }



        return processStatus;
    }



    private void sendPOtoMDB(PurchaseOrder po) {
        //send PO to MDB now
        Connection connection = null;
        Session session = null;
        try {
            connection = poTopicCF.createConnection();
            System.out.println("Created connection");
            connection.start();
            session =
                    connection.createSession(false, Session.AUTO_ACKNOWLEDGE);
            MessageProducer producer = session.createProducer(poTopic);
            ObjectMessage objMessage = session.createObjectMessage();
            objMessage.setObject(po);
            producer.send(objMessage);
            session.close();
            connection.close();
        } catch (JMSException e) {
            e.printStackTrace();
        }
    }


}
```

The Order Processing Service

The order processing service is an MDB. The idea behind having MDBs in the wine store
application is to show how some of the processing in an enterprise application can be
done in an asynchronous fashion, and how you can work with the EntityManager, session
beans, and other MDBs from an MDB.

■**Note** Chapter 5, which covers MDBs, describes the asynchronous architecture in detail and gives examples of some possible implementations.

OrderProcessingMDBBean is a plain old Java object (POJO) that is annotated with a class-level @MessageDriven annotation to indicate that it is an MDB. This POJO implements the mandatory onMessage() method to process the incoming messages with the help of a utility method, processOrder(). We will walk through the methods in the MDB from here.

Listing 7-16 shows the code for the onMessage() method. This method checks whether the received message is of ObjectMessage instance type, and the retrieved object is then typecast to the PurchaseOrder utility class. After that, a call to the processOrder() utility method is made to process the received PO.

Listing 7-16. *The onMessage Method in OrderProcessingMDBBean*

```
public void onMessage(Message message) {
    try {
        if (message instanceof ObjectMessage) {
            ObjectMessage objMessage = (ObjectMessage)message;
            Object obj = objMessage.getObject();
            if (obj instanceof PurchaseOrder) {
                po = (PurchaseOrder)obj;
                processOrder(po);
            }
        }
    } catch (JMSException e) {
        e.printStackTrace();
    }
}
```

Listing 7-17 shows the code for the processOrder() method. This method makes use of an injected EntityManager via the @PersistenceContext annotation to call the named query findCustomerById defined in the Individual entity using the createNamedQuery() method in the EntityManager. Once the customer is retrieved using the named query, the customer order received from the message topic is accessed and persisted using the persist() method of the EntityManager. A call to the addCustomerOrder() method in the Individual entity is made to add the new customer order to the Individual entity, and the updated Individual entity is merged back into the transaction context using the merge() method of the EntityManager.

Once the order has been added to the `Customer`, it is time to deduct the wines from the inventory tables. A `for` loop goes through all the items in the customer order, and the `Wine` entity and quantity are sent to the `deductInventory()` utility method.

After the inventory is deducted, it is time to send a status update to the customer. This is done using the e-mail service. The customer's e-mail information and order ID are retrieved from the PO object, and e-mail content is created before a call to the `sendStatus()` utility method is made.

Listing 7-17. *The processOrder Business Method*

```
private void processOrder(PurchaseOrder po) {
    Individual customer =
        (Individual)em.createNamedQuery("findCustomerById").setParameter➥
("id",customerId()).getSingleResult();
    CustomerOrder order = po.getCustomerOrder();
    em.persist(order);
    customer.addCustomerOrder(order);
    customer = em.merge(customer);
    for (OrderItem oItem: order.getOrderItemCollection()) {
        Wine wine = oItem.getWine();
        Long qty = oItem.getQuantity();
        deductInventory(wine, qty);
    }

    String from = "EJB3-WineApplication";
    String to = customer.getEmail();
    String content =
        "Your order has been processed " + "If you have questions" +
        " call Beginning EJB 3 Wine Store Application with order id # " +
        po.getCustomerOrder().getId().toString();
    sendStatus(from, to, content);


}
```

Listing 7-18 shows the code for the `deductInventory()` method. This method makes use of the injected `EntityManager` to call the named query `findInventoryItemByWine` defined in the `InventoryItem` entity. Once the inventory for the specific wine is retrieved, the quantity is updated using the `setQuantity()` setter method, and the retrieved `InventoryItem` entity is merged back into transaction context.

Listing 7-18. *The deductInventory Business Method*

```
private void deductInventory(Wine tempWine, Long deductQty) {
    InventoryItem iItem =
        (InventoryItem)em.createNamedQuery("findInventoryItemByWine").➥
setParameter("wine",tempWine).getSingleResult();
    Long newQty = iItem.getQuantity() - deductQty;
    iItem.setQuantity(newQty);
    em.merge(iItem);
}
```

Listing 7-19 shows the code for the sendStatus() method. This utility method makes use of an injected JMS resource for a topic connection factory and a topic. A connection to a topic connection factory is created and the connection is started. Once a connection is available, a session is created and a MessageProducer containing the topic is created. A Message object is created and the JMSType is set to MailMessage. After that, a series of calls to the setStringProperty() method on the Message object is made to create the to, from, subject, and content sections of the e-mail. Once all the properties are set, the message is sent out to the message topic that will be processed by the e-mail service.

Listing 7-19. *The sendStatus Business Method*

```
private void sendStatus(String from, String to, String content) {
    //send status message to MDB now
    try {
        Connection connection = statusMessageTopicCF.createConnection();

        connection.start();
        Session session =
            connection.createSession(false, Session.AUTO_ACKNOWLEDGE);

        MessageProducer producer = session.createProducer(statusTopic);
        MapMessage message = session.createMapMessage();
        message.setStringProperty("from", from);
        message.setStringProperty("to", to);
        message.setStringProperty("subject", "Status of your wine order");
        message.setStringProperty("content", content);
        producer.send(message);
        producer.close();
        session.close();
        connection.close();
```

```
        } catch (JMSException e) {
            e.printStackTrace();
        }


    }
```

The complete code for OrderProcessingMDBBean is shown in Listing 7-20.

Listing 7-20. *OrderProcessingMDBBean.java*

```java
import com.apress.ejb3.ch07.business.PurchaseOrder;

import com.apress.ejb3.wineapp.CustomerOrder;
import com.apress.ejb3.wineapp.Individual;
import com.apress.ejb3.wineapp.InventoryItem;
import com.apress.ejb3.wineapp.OrderItem;
import com.apress.ejb3.wineapp.Wine;
import javax.annotation.Resource;
import javax.ejb.MessageDriven;
import javax.jms.Connection;
import javax.jms.JMSException;
import javax.jms.MapMessage;
import javax.jms.Message;
import javax.jms.MessageListener;
import javax.jms.MessageProducer;
import javax.jms.ObjectMessage;
import javax.jms.Session;
import javax.jms.Topic;
import javax.jms.TopicConnectionFactory;
import javax.persistence.EntityManager;
import javax.persistence.PersistenceContext;

@MessageDriven(mappedName = "PurchaseorderTopic")
public class

OrderProcessingMDBBean implements MessageListener {

    private PurchaseOrder po;

    @PersistenceContext(unitName = "wineStoreUnit")
    private EntityManager em;
```

```java
    @Resource(mappedName = "StatusMessageTopicConnectionFactory")
    private TopicConnectionFactory statusMessageTopicCF;

    @Resource(mappedName = "StatusMessageTopic")
    private Topic statusTopic;

    public void onMessage(Message message) {
        System.out.println("Entered in onMessage");
        try {
            if (message instanceof ObjectMessage) {
                ObjectMessage objMessage = (ObjectMessage)message;
                Object obj = objMessage.getObject();
                if (obj instanceof PurchaseOrder) {
                    po = (PurchaseOrder)obj;
                    processOrder(po);
                }
            }
        } catch (JMSException e) {
            e.printStackTrace();
        }
    }


    private void processOrder(PurchaseOrder po) {
        Individual customer =
            (Individual)em.createNamedQuery("findCustomerById").setParameter("id",➥
po.getCustomerId()).getSingleResult();
        CustomerOrder order = po.getCustomerOrder();
        em.persist(order);
        customer.addCustomerOrder(order);
        customer = em.merge(customer);
        for (OrderItem oItem: order.getOrderItemCollection()) {
            Wine wine = oItem.getWine();
            Long qty = oItem.getQuantity();
            deductInventory(wine, qty);
        }

        String from = "EJB3-WineApplication";
        String to = customer.getEmail();
        String content =
```

```
                "Your order has been processed " + "If you have questions" +
                " call Beginning EJB 3 Wine Store Application with order id # " +
                po.getCustomerOrder().getId().toString();
            sendStatus(from, to, content);

    }


    private void deductInventory(Wine tempWine, Long deductQty) {
        InventoryItem iItem =
            (InventoryItem)em.createNamedQuery("findInventoryItemByWine").➥
setParameter("wine",tempWine).getSingleResult();
        Long newQty = iItem.getQuantity() - deductQty;
        iItem.setQuantity(newQty);
        em.merge(iItem);
    }


    private void sendStatus(String from, String to, String content) {
        //send status message to MDB now
        try {
            Connection connection = statusMessageTopicCF.createConnection();
            connection.start();
            Session session =
                connection.createSession(false, Session.AUTO_ACKNOWLEDGE);
            MessageProducer producer = session.createProducer(statusTopic);
            MapMessage message = session.createMapMessage();
            message.setStringProperty("from", from);
            message.setStringProperty("to", to);
            message.setStringProperty("subject", "Status of your wine order");
            message.setStringProperty("content", content);
            producer.send(message);
            producer.close();
            session.close();
            connection.close();
        } catch (JMSException e) {
            e.printStackTrace();
        }

    }
}
```

The E-mail Service

The e-mail service is an MDB. This MDB processes the incoming messages by sending out e-mails using an e-mail resource that is injected as a resource reference.

Listing 7-21 shows the code for the onMessage() method in the StatusMailerBean MDB. We will start by retrieving all the properties from the message, and then we will create an object of javax.mail.Message using the injected mail resource reference ms. Then the message is decorated with relevant e-mail information and the send() method is called to send the e-mail message.

Listing 7-21. *The onMessage Method in the StatusMailer MDB*

```
public void onMessage(Message message) {
    try {
        if (message instanceof MapMessage) {
            MapMessage orderMessage = (MapMessage)message;
            String from = orderMessage.getStringProperty("from");
            String to = orderMessage.getStringProperty("to");
            String subject = orderMessage.getStringProperty("subject");
            String content = orderMessage.getStringProperty("content");
            javax.mail.Message msg = new MimeMessage(ms);
            msg.setFrom(new InternetAddress(from));
            InternetAddress[] address = { new InternetAddress(to) };
            msg.setRecipients(javax.mail.Message.RecipientType.TO,
                              address);
            msg.setSubject(subject);
            msg.setSentDate(new java.util.Date());
            msg.setContent(content, "text/html");
            Transport.send(msg);

        } else {
            System.out.println("Invalid message ");
        }


    } catch (Exception ex) {
        ex.printStackTrace();
    }
}
```

The complete code for StatusMailerBean is shown in Listing 7-22.

Listing 7-22. *StatusMailerBean.java*

```
import javax.annotation.Resource;
import javax.ejb.ActivationConfigProperty;
import javax.ejb.MessageDriven;
import javax.jms.MapMessage;
import javax.jms.Message;
import javax.mail.Transport;
import javax.mail.internet.InternetAddress;
import javax.mail.internet.MimeMessage;

@MessageDriven(activationConfig =
            { @ActivationConfigProperty(propertyName = "destinationName",
                                        propertyValue =
                                        "StatusMessageTopic")
        ,
            @ActivationConfigProperty(propertyName = "destinationType",➡
 propertyValue ="javax.jms.Topic") ➡
} , mappedName = "StatusMessageTopic")

public class StatusMailerBean implements javax.jms.MessageListener {

    @Resource(name = "mail/wineappMail")
    private javax.mail.Session ms;

    public void onMessage(Message message) {
        try {
            if (message instanceof MapMessage) {
                MapMessage orderMessage = (MapMessage)message;
                String from = orderMessage.getStringProperty("from");
                String to = orderMessage.getStringProperty("to");
                String subject = orderMessage.getStringProperty("subject");
                String content = orderMessage.getStringProperty("content");
                javax.mail.Message msg = new MimeMessage(ms);
                msg.setFrom(new InternetAddress(from));
                InternetAddress[] address = { new InternetAddress(to) };
                msg.setRecipients(javax.mail.Message.RecipientType.TO,
                                address);
```

```
            msg.setSubject(subject);
            msg.setSentDate(new java.util.Date());
            msg.setContent(content, "text/html");
            Transport.send(msg);
        } else {
            System.out.println("Invalid message ");
        }


    } catch (Exception ex) {
        ex.printStackTrace();
    }
  }
}
```

The Credit Service

The credit service is a stateless session bean that is published as a web service using JSR 181 (Web Services Metadata for the Java Platform) annotations. The idea behind creating this web service is twofold:

- It shows how you can expose a stateless session bean as a web service.

- It shows how you can consume a web service from an EJB 3 application.

This web service is consumed by OrderProcessFacadeBean to check the customer's credit card. We are going to use the credit service that we developed in Chapter 6.

The Database Schema

The Wines Online application uses a single database schema to store all the information related to customers, orders, inventory, and so on. This section describes the database schema and the relationships between the tables. Figure 7-5 shows a database diagram with all the tables and relationships. The schema is designed to accommodate or showcase most of the O/R (object/relational) mappings in the JPA specification, including the different types of inheritance strategies between entities. An extra table, EJB_TAB_ID_GEN, was created to show the usage of database sequences using @SequenceGenerator and other related annotations in the specification.

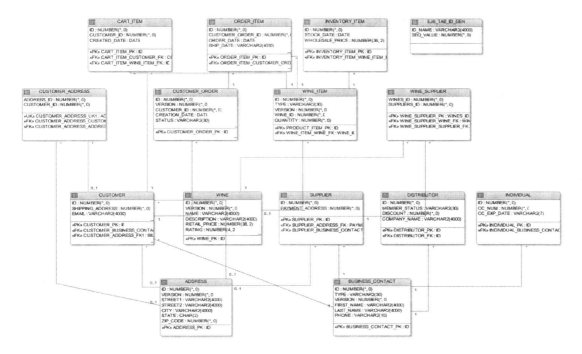

Figure 7-5. *Database diagram for the Wines Online application*

Packaging, Deploying, and Testing the Application

EJBs need to be packaged into EJB JAR (Java Archive) files before they are assembled into EAR (Enterprise Archive) files that hold all the required modules and libraries for the application. Most application servers provide deployment utilities or Ant tasks to facilitate deployment of EJBs to their containers. Java integrated development environments (IDEs) like Oracle JDeveloper, NetBeans, and Eclipse also provide deployment features that allow developers to package, assemble, and deploy applications to application servers. There is no requirement that EJBs have to be packaged into EJB JAR files and assembled into EAR files. You can also deploy the EJB JAR files themselves. In this chapter, we will assemble them into EAR files so that we can make the persistence unit a shared module, and also to set the stage for Chapter 12, in which we will be building client applications for the wine store back-end that we have just developed.

Packaging, assembly, and deployment aspects are covered in detail in Chapter 11. In this chapter, we have developed the wine store application back-end using session beans, MDBs, JPA entities, and web services. We will perform the following steps to package, assemble, deploy, and test the JSF application.

Prerequisites

Before performing any of the steps detailed in the next sections, complete the "Getting Started" section of Chapter 1, which will walk you through the installation and environment setup required for the samples in this chapter.

Note We will assume that the source code for this chapter's samples is located in the Z: drive. Substitute this with the location of the directory into which you have downloaded the source.

Deploying the Credit Service

We have built our wine store back-end application on top of the work we have done in Chapter 6, in which we implemented the credit service. If you have gone through Chapter 6 and deployed the credit service, you can skip this step—it is only necessary if you haven't deployed the credit service yet. We have bundled creditservice.jar into the archive directory so that we can deploy the JAR file if need be.

To deploy the packaged credit service JAR using the command-line utilities from GlassFish, execute the following from the DOS command window:

```
Z:\chapter07-IntegratedSamples\IntegratedSamples>%GLASSFISH_HOME%/bin/asadmin.ba
t deploy --host localhost --port 4848 --user admin --passwordfile %GLASSFISH_HOM
E%\asadminpass --upload=true --target server z:\chapter07-IntegratedSamples\Inte
gratedSamples\archive\creditservice.jar
```

Figure 7-6 shows the successful execution of the preceding command.

Figure 7-6. *Deploying the credit service*

Alternatively, you can use the following Ant task to deploy:

```
Z:\chapter07-IntegratedSamples\IntegratedSamples>%ANT_HOME%/bin/ant ➥
Deploy-CreditService
```

■**Note** If you are running the GlassFish application server on a different machine, substitute that machine name with `localhost` in the command-line arguments. Similarly, if you are running on a different port, replace `4848` with the number of the port on which you are running. If you are using the Ant task to deploy, make the appropriate changes to the `build.properties` file to reflect the settings for the GlassFish application server you have installed.

Compiling the Persistence Unit

At its core, the wine store application has all the JPA entities that are mapped to the wine store database schema. We will compile all these entities and package them as a persistence unit so that it is available to the wine store EJB module, and so that it can be used from the JSF application in Chapter 12.

From the DOS console, execute the following `javac` command to compile the JPA entities:

```
Z:\chapter07-IntegratedSamples\IntegratedSamples\PersistenceUnit>%JAVA_HOME%/bin/➥
javac -classpath %GLASSFISH_HOME%\lib\javaee.jar;%GLASSFISH_HOME%\➥
lib\toplink-essentials.jar -d ../classes src\com\apress\ejb3\wineapp\*.java
```

Figure 7-7 shows the compilation of the persistence unit.

Figure 7-7. *Compiling the persistence unit*

■**Note** The command is run from the `PersistenceUnit` directory.

If you are using `build.xml` from the downloaded source, execute the following command:

```
Z:\chapter07-IntegratedSamples\IntegratedSamples>%ANT_HOME%/bin/ant ➥
Compile-PersistenceUnit
```

Packaging the Persistence Unit

Once you have compiled all the JPA entities in the persistence unit, you will have to package the compiled classes into a JAR file. Execute the following command in the DOS console:

```
Z:\chapter07-IntegratedSamples\IntegratedSamples\classes>%JAVA_HOME%/bin/jar ➥
 -cvf ..\archive\lib\punit.jar .\com .\META-INF
```

Figure 7-8 shows the packaging of the persistence unit.

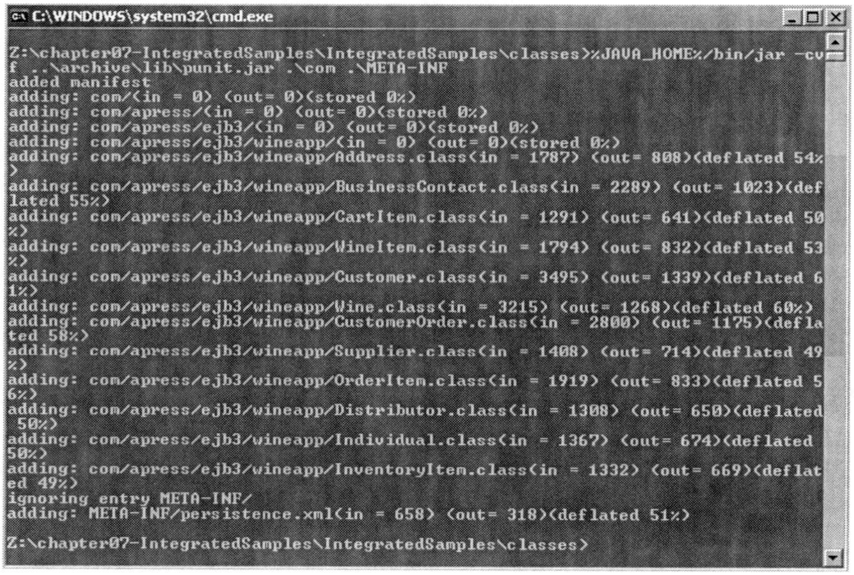

Figure 7-8. *Packaging the persistence unit*

The generated `punit.jar` file will be stored in the `archive/lib` directory to simplify the assembly of the EAR file in the later steps. If you are using `build.xml` from the downloaded source, execute the following command:

```
Z:\chapter07-IntegratedSamples\IntegratedSamples>%ANT_HOME%/bin/ant ➥
 Package-PersistenceUnit
```

Compiling the Business Services (Session Beans and MDBs)

Now that you have the persistence unit packaged properly, the next step is to compile your business services, which consist of all the session beans and MDBs that you have developed. From the DOS console, execute `javac`.

■**Note** In the classpath for `javac`, you need to include the credit service client-side proxy classes and the persistence unit classes. The credit service proxy classes were generated in Chapter 6, and we have included them in the `archive` directory to cut down on redundancy across chapters.

```
Z:\chapter07-IntegratedSamples\IntegratedSamples\WineStoreModel>%JAVA_HOME%/bin/➥
javac -classpath %GLASSFISH_HOME%\lib\javaee.jar;%GLASSFISH_HOME%\lib➥
\toplink-essentials.jar;..\archive\creditserviceclient.jar;➥
..\archive\lib\punit.jar -d ../classes src\com\apress\ejb3\chapter07➥
\business\*.java src\com\apress\ejb3\chapter07\business\mdb\*.java
```

Figure 7-9 shows successful compilation of the business services.

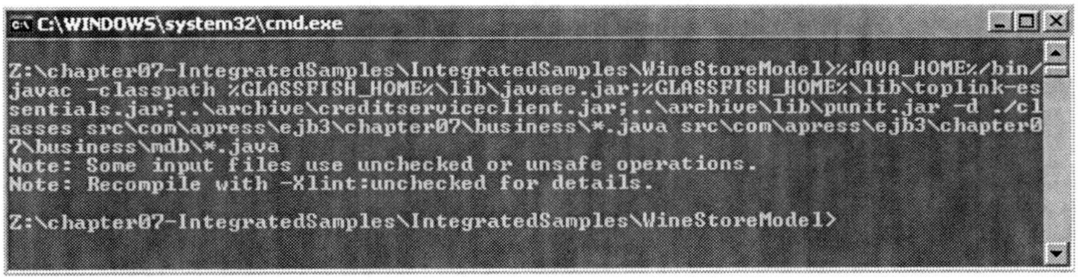

Figure 7-9. *Compiling the business services*

If you are using `build.xml` from the downloaded source, execute the following command:

```
Z:\chapter07-IntegratedSamples\IntegratedSamples>%ANT_HOME%/bin/ant ➥
Compile-BusinessServices
```

Packaging the Business Services

Once you have compiled all the session bean and MDB classes, you will have to package the compiled business service classes into a JAR file. Execute the following command in the DOS console:

```
Z:\chapter07-IntegratedSamples\IntegratedSamples\classes>%JAVA_HOME%/bin/jar ➥
 -cvf ..\archive\winestoreEJB.jar .\com\apress\ejb3\chapter07
```

Figure 7-10 shows the packaging of the business services.

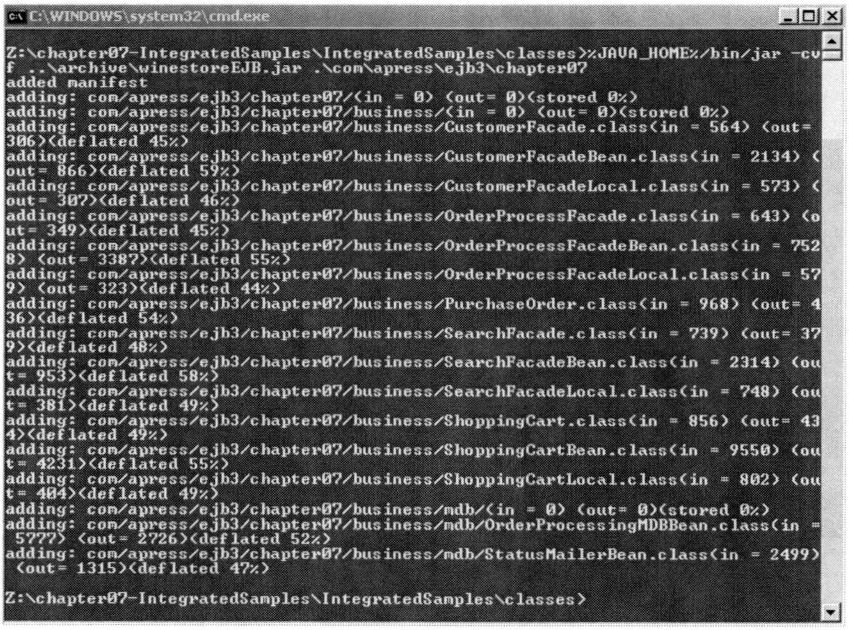

Figure 7-10. *Packaging the business services*

The generated `winestoreEJB.jar` file will be stored in the `archive` directory. If you are using `build.xml` from the downloaded source, execute the following command:

```
Z:\chapter07-IntegratedSamples\IntegratedSamples>%ANT_HOME%/bin/ant Package-Bus
InessServices
```

Assembling the Application

Now that you have packaged the persistence unit and business services, you can assemble the wine store application into an EAR file. Execute the following command from the DOS console:

```
Z:\chapter07-IntegratedSamples\IntegratedSamples\archive>%JAVA_HOME%/bin/jar ➡
 -cvf winestore.ear ./lib winestoreEJB.jar ./META-INF/application.xml
```

Figure 7-11 shows the assembly of the wine store application.

Figure 7-11. *Assembling the wine store application*

If you are using `build.xml` from the downloaded source, execute the following command:

```
Z:\chapter07-IntegratedSamples\IntegratedSamples>%ANT_HOME%/bin/ant ➡
 Assemble-WineStoreApp
```

Creating the Database Schema

We have used an Oracle database as the data server for the wine store application. Once you have downloaded the SQL scripts for this chapter, execute the following command from the DOS window after connecting to the Oracle database using SQL*Plus:

```
SQL> @runsql.sql
```

Creating Data Sources, JMS Resources, and Mail Resources

The wine store application makes use of Java Database Connectivity (JDBC) data sources from the persistence unit, JMS resources from the MDBs, and mail resources to send e-mail. Before the wine store application can be deployed to GlassFish, these resources have to be set up or preconfigured.

The persistence unit in the wine store application has defined a logical data source name, jdbc/wineappDS, in the persistence.xml deployment descriptor. We will create a JDBC connection pool that we can associate with a physical data source with the name winepool, and then we will create the data source with the name jdbc/wineappDS.

■**Note** The wine store application has been developed with the Oracle database as the data tier. Before creating the JDBC connection pool, make sure that you have copied the right version of the JDBC drivers for the Oracle database into the %GLASSFISH_HOME%/lib directory. In our case, we have copied the ojdbc14.jar file that works with Oracle 10*g*.

From the DOS command window, execute the following:

```
Z:\chapter07-IntegratedSamples\IntegratedSamples>%GLASSFISH_HOME%/bin/asadmin.bat ➥
create-jdbc-connection-pool --host localhost --port 4848 --user admin ➥
--passwordfile %GLASSFISH_HOME%\asadminpass --datasourceclassname ➥
oracle.jdbc.pool.OracleDataSource --restype javax.sql.DataSource --property ➥
DataSourceName=OracleDataSource:NetworkProtocol=tcp:DatabaseName=ORCL➥
:Password=wineapp:URL=jdbc\:oracle\:thin\:@localhost\:1521\:➥
ORCL:User=wineapp:ServiceName=ORCL:PortNumber=1521:➥
ServerName=localhost winepool
```

Figure 7-12 shows the successful creation of the JDBC connection pool.

Figure 7-12. *The JDBC connection pool*

Once the JDBC connection pool has been successfully created, we can create a JDBC data source that will make use of the connection pool. From the DOS console, execute the following:

```
Z:\chapter07-IntegratedSamples\IntegratedSamples>%GLASSFISH_HOME%/bin/asadmin.bat➥
create-jdbc-resource --host localhost --port 4848 --user admin ➥
--passwordfile %GLASSFISH_HOME%\asadminpass -- ➥
connectionpoolid winepool jdbc/wineappDS
```

Figure 7-13 shows the successful creation of the JDBC data source.

Figure 7-13. *The JDBC data source*

In the next steps, you will create the JMS resources that will be used by the MDBs.
Execute the following command in the DOS window. This will create a JMS topic connection factory that will be used by OrderProcessFacadeBean to send a message to the queue that will be consumed by OrderProcessingMDBBean.

```
Z:\chapter07-IntegratedSamples\IntegratedSamples>%GLASSFISH_HOME%/bin/asadmin.bat➥
create-jms-resource --host localhost --port 4848 --user admin --passwordfile ➥
%GLASSFISH_HOME%\asadminpass --restype javax.jms.TopicConnectionFactory ➥
poTopicConnectionFactory
```

Figure 7-14 shows the successful creation of the JMS topic connection factory.

Figure 7-14. *The JMS topic connection factory*

Execute the following command to create a JMS queue connection factory that will be used by OrderProcessingMDBBean to send a message to the queue that will be used by StatusMailerBean to send out e-mail messages to the customer:

```
Z:\chapter07-IntegratedSamples\IntegratedSamples>%GLASSFISH_HOME%/bin/asadmin.bat ➥
create-jms-resource --host localhost  --port 4848 --user admin ➥
 --passwordfile ➥ %GLASSFISH_HOME%\asadminpass ➥
 --restype javax.jms.TopicConnectionFactory ➥
StatusMessageTopicConnectionFactory
```

Figure 7-15 shows the successful creation of the connection factory.

Figure 7-15. *The JMS topic connection for the StatusMessage MDB*

Execute the following command to create a JMS topic for the PO:

```
Z:\chapter07-IntegratedSamples\IntegratedSamples>%GLASSFISH_HOME%/bin/➥
asadmin.bat create-jms-resource --host localhost --port 4848 --user admin ➥
 --passwordfile %GLASSFISH_HOME%\asadminpass --restype javax.jms.Topic ➥
 --property imqDestinationName=PurchaseOrderTopic PurchaseOrderTopic
```

Figure 7-16 shows the successful creation of the JMS topic.

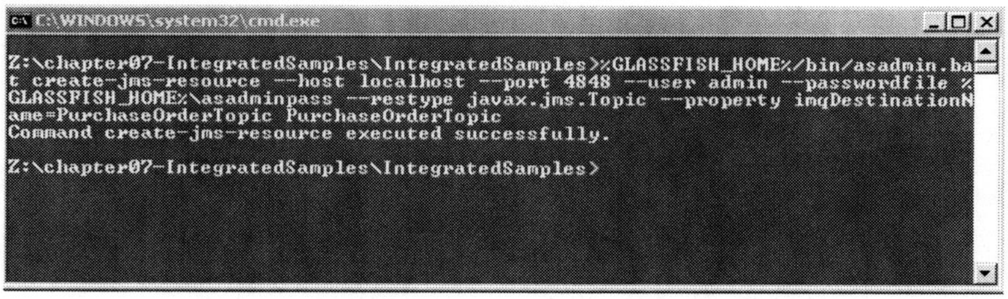

Figure 7-16. *JMS topic creation*

Execute the following command to create a JMS topic for the status e-mail message:

```
Z:\chapter07-IntegratedSamples\IntegratedSamples>%GLASSFISH_HOME%/bin/➥
asadmin.bat create-jms-resource --host localhost --port 4848 --user admin ➥
--passwordfile %GLASSFISH_HOME%\asadminpass --restype javax.jms.Topic ➥
--property imqDestinationName=StatusMessageTopic StatusMessageTopic
```

Figure 7-17 shows the successful creation of the JMS topic.

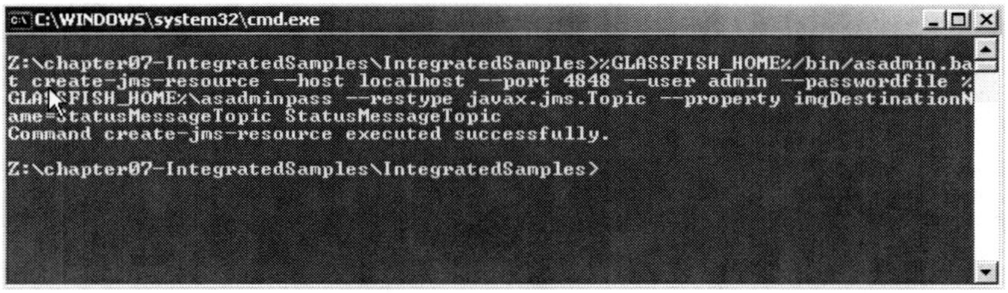

Figure 7-17. *JMS topic creation for the status e-mail message*

In this step, you will create the required JavaMail resource that will be used by
StatusMailerBean. Execute the following command:

```
Z:\chapter07-IntegratedSamples\IntegratedSamples>%GLASSFISH_HOME%/bin/➥
asadmin.bat create-javamail-resource --host localhost --port 4848 --user admin ➥
--passwordfile %GLASSFISH_HOME%\asadminpass --mailhost localhost ➥
--mailuser wineapp@localhost --fromaddress wineapp@localhost mail/wineappMail
```

Figure 7-18 shows the successful creation of the JavaMail resource.

Figure 7-18. *JavaMail resource creation*

___

■**Note** We have used the Apache Java Enterprise Mail Server (aka James) to demonstrate the ability to
send e-mail messages using the JavaMail API. Apache James can be downloaded from http://james.
apache.org. If you are using a different e-mail server, substitute the appropriate values for the mailhost,
mailuser, and fromaddress parameters in the preceding command-line and Ant build scripts.

If you are using `build.xml` from the downloaded source, execute the following command to create the resources:

```
Z:\chapter07-IntegratedSamples\IntegratedSamples>%ANT_HOME%/bin/ant ➥
CreateJavaMailResources
```

Deploying the Application

Now that you have the assembled the wine store application and all the required resources are preconfigured, your next step is to deploy the assembled wine store EAR file.

From the DOS command window, execute the following:

```
Z:\chapter07-IntegratedSamples\IntegratedSamples>%GLASSFISH_HOME%/bin/➥
asadmin.bat deploy --host localhost --port 4848 --user admin –passwordfile ➥
%GLASSFISH_HOME%\asadminpass --upload=true --target server ➥
z:\chapter07-IntegratedSamples\IntegratedSamples\archive\winestore.ear
```

Figure 7-19 shows the successful deployment of the wine store application.

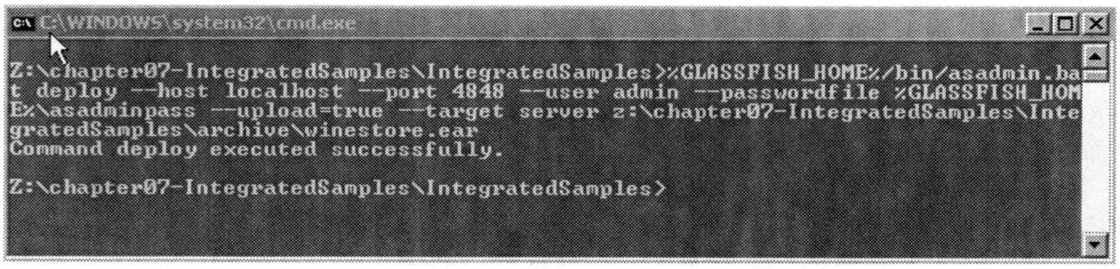

Figure 7-19. *Deploying the wine store application*

If you are using `build.xml` from the downloaded source, execute the following command:

```
Z:\chapter07-IntegratedSamples\IntegratedSamples>%ANT_HOME%/bin/ant ➥
Deploy-WineStoreApplication
```

A Simple Test Client for the Application

Client applications and different application architectures will be discussed in detail in Chapter 12. In order to test the deployed wine store application, we will develop a simple Java command-line client program. This client program will make use of the GlassFish application client container to inject the ShoppingCart and SearchFacade session beans into the wine store application to search the wines, add items to the shopping cart, and finally submit the order.

Listing 7-23 shows the code for the command-line client that works with the deployed wine store application. To start with, the client looks up the SearchFacadeBean session bean and calls the findWineByYear() method, which returns a list of wines. In order to add wines to the shopping cart, the client program looks up the ShoppingCart session bean and calls the findCustomer() method. Once the customer has been found, the client goes into a while loop and adds the list of wines retrieved from SearchFacadeBean using the addWineItem() method in the ShoppingCart bean. To keep the client simple, the quantity of each wine is set to 20. Once the client finishes adding all the wines to the shopping cart, the SendOrderToOPC() method in the ShoppingCart bean is called to submit the order.

Listing 7-23. *ShoppingCartTest.java*

```java
import com.apress.ejb3.chapter07.business.SearchFacade;
import com.apress.ejb3.chapter07.business.ShoppingCart;
import com.apress.ejb3.wineapp.Wine;
import java.util.Iterator;
import java.util.List;
import javax.ejb.EJB;

public class ShoppingCartTest {
    public ShoppingCartTest() {
    }

    @EJB
    static SearchFacade searchFacade;

    @EJB
    static ShoppingCart shoppingCart;


    public static void main(String[] args) {
        ShoppingCartTest shoppingCartTest = new ShoppingCartTest();
        shoppingCartTest.doTest();
    }


    void doTest() {
```

```java
try {


    System.out.println("invoking Search Facade");
    List yearWineList = searchFacade.findWineByYear(new Long(1991));
    Iterator yearit = yearWineList.iterator();

    while (yearit.hasNext()) {
        Wine wine = (Wine)yearit.next();
        System.out.println(wine.getName());
        System.out.println(wine.getYear());
    }

    List wineList = searchFacade.findAllWine();
    Iterator it = wineList.iterator();

    System.out.println("invoking shopping cart facade");
    System.out.println("success with shopping cart");

    System.out.println(shoppingCart.findCustomer("wineapp@localhost"));

    System.out.println("found and set customer");

    while (it.hasNext()) {
        Wine wine = (Wine)it.next();
        System.out.println(wine.getName());
        shoppingCart.addWineItem(wine, new Long(20));
        System.out.println("added cart item");
    }

    System.out.println("done with the wine loop");

    System.out.println("calling process order");
    System.out.println("Calling opc in cart");
    shoppingCart.SendOrderToOPC();
    System.out.println("done");


}
```

```
        catch (Exception ex) {
            ex.printStackTrace();
        }
    }
}
```

Running the Client Program

Once you have the client, you need to compile the client class. Execute the following from the DOS command console:

```
Z:\chapter07-IntegratedSamples\IntegratedSamples\GLassFishUnitTests>%JAVA_HOME%/
bin/javac -classpath %GLASSFISH_HOME%\lib\javaee.jar;..\archive\winestoreEJB.jar
;..\archive\lib\punit.jar -d ../classes src\com\apress\ejb3\chapter07\client\*.
java
```

Alternatively, you can execute the following task using build.xml in the downloaded source:

```
Z:\chapter07-IntegratedSamples\IntegratedSamples>%ANT_HOME%/bin/ant Compile-Client
```

Figure 7-20 shows the successful compilation of the client programs.

Figure 7-20. *Compiling the client*

Once you have compiled the client, you can invoke the wine store application by running the client using the GlassFish application client container that supports dependency injection. You will assemble the client and its dependent classes into a JAR file so that you only have to specify the JAR file as an argument to the application client container.

In the DOS command console, execute the following command:

```
Z:\chapter07-IntegratedSamples\IntegratedSamples\classes>%JAVA_HOME%/bin/jar -cvf ➥
 ..\archive\winestoreclient.jar .\com
```

Alternatively, you can execute the following Ant task:

```
Z:\chapter07-IntegratedSamples\IntegratedSamples>%ANT_HOME%/bin/ant Assemble-Client
```

Once you have assembled the client, you can invoke the wine store application by running the client.

In the DOS command console, execute the following:

```
Z:\chapter07-IntegratedSamples\IntegratedSamples\archive>%GLASSFISH_HOME%/bin/ap
pclient.bat -client winestoreclient.jar
```

Alternatively, you can execute the following Ant task:

```
Z:\chapter07-IntegratedSamples\IntegratedSamples>%ANT_HOME%/bin/ant Run-Client
```

Figure 7-21 shows the output printed from the client in the console.

Figure 7-21. *The output after executing the client*

Conclusion

In this chapter, we have given an in-depth discussion on how to integrate different types of EJBs and web services with resources like data sources, JMS topics, and JavaMail.

We looked at the conceptual design of our fictitious wine store application, and we laid out the design for the components and services that need to be built. We looked at individual components and services, and we demonstrated how to use different types of EJBs to solve specific application problems.

The extensive wine store application illustrated the various parts of typical back-end applications, which included a comprehensive persistence unit that utilized a wide range of JPA mappings, session beans that interacted with the persistence unit, MDBs, and web services using dependency injection.

We also looked at how to inject various types of resources in session beans and MDBs, and how to build asynchrony into the application using the MDBs.

Additionally, we looked into dealing with managed and detached entities from the persistence context and integrating an asynchronous model into a typical back-end application. Finally, we detailed steps on how you can package individual components and services, assemble them into a Java EE 5 application, and deploy them to the GlassFish container.

In the next chapter, we discuss the transactional services provided by the EJB container and different types of transactional models that you can use in different application architectures.

CHAPTER 8

■ ■ ■

Transaction Support in EJB 3

Much of the work surrounding the design and development of enterprise applications involves decisions about how to coordinate the flow of persistent data. This includes when and where to cache data, when to apply it to a persistent store (typically the database), how to resolve simultaneous attempts to access the same data, and how to resolve errors that might occur while data in the database is in an inconsistent state. A reliable database is capable of handling these issues at a low level—in the database tier—but these same issues can exist in the middle (application server) and client tiers as well, and typically require special application logic. For example, a database provides built-in concurrency control through pessimistic locking support, whereas an application may choose to use an optimistic locking strategy to achieve a more graceful, performant result.

One of the principal benefits of using EJB is its support for enterprise-wide services like transaction management and security control. In this chapter, we will explore how EJB offers transaction services and how you can leverage them to meet your specific requirements.

To illustrate what EJB has to offer and how to use it, we will examine a scenario from our sample Apress Wines Online application that exemplifies the aforementioned data flow issues. We will illustrate EJB's transaction support by showing ways to perform tasks that range from simple and concise to slightly more complex but more flexible. Before we dive into the examples, though, we offer an overview of some of the important transaction concepts in the EJB transaction realm, including the Java Transaction API (JTA), the many flexible transaction options available to you through declarative EJB metadata, and how transactions are handled in the persistence tier. EJB has offered these essential transaction services since its inception, so those of you who are comfortable with these concepts can skip ahead to the example section to see how they manifest themselves in an EJB 3 world involving the Java Persistence API (JPA).

What Is a Transaction?

In this section, we will explore the following questions:

- What is a transaction and why is it important to enterprise applications?

- What are the core ACID (atomicity, consistency, isolation, durability) properties that define a robust and reliable transaction?

- What is JTA, what is a distributed transaction, and what is two-phase commit?

A transaction is a group of operations that must be performed as a unit. These operations can be synchronous or asynchronous, and can involve persisting data objects, sending mail, validating credit cards, and many other events. A classic example is a banking transfer, in which one operation debits funds from one account (i.e., updates a record in a database table), and another operation credits those same funds to another account (updates another row in that same, or a different, database table). From the perspective of an external application querying both accounts, there must never be a time when these funds can be seen in both accounts. Nor can a moment exist when the funds can be seen in neither account. Only when both operations in this transaction have been successfully performed can the changes be visible from another application context. A group of operations that must be performed together in this way, as a unit, is known as a transaction.

The operations in a transaction are performed sequentially or in parallel, typically over a (relatively short) period of time. After they are all performed, the transaction is applied, or committed. If an error or other invalid condition arises during the course of a transaction, the transaction may be cancelled, or rolled back, and the operations that had thus far been performed under that transaction context are undone.

Distributed Transactions

When the operations in a transaction are performed across database or other resources that reside on separate computers or processes, this is known as a distributed transaction. Such enterprise-wide transactions require special coordination between the resources involved, and can be extremely difficult to program reliably. This is where JTA comes in, providing the interface that resources can implement and bind to, to participate in a distributed transaction.

The EJB container is a transaction manager that supports JTA, and so can participate in distributed transactions involving other EJB containers as well as third-party JTA resources, like many database management systems (DBMSs). This takes the complexity of coordinating distributed transactions off the shoulders of business application developers, so that they are free to distribute their data across the enterprise however they choose. In addition, as you will see in the following sections, EJB allows developers to choose whether to demarcate transactions explicitly—with calls to begin, commit, or roll back (cancel) a transaction—or to allow the EJB container to automatically perform transaction demarcation along method boundaries.

The ACID Properties of a Transaction

No, not the electric Kool-Aid kind. Transactions come in all shapes and sizes, and can involve synchronous and asynchronous operations, but they all have some core features in common, known as their ACID components. ACID refers to the four characteristics that define a robust and reliable transaction: atomicity, consistency, isolation, and durability. Table 8-1 describes these four components.

Table 8-1. *The ACID Properties of a Transaction*

Feature	Description
Atomicity	A transaction is composed of one or more operations that are performed as a group, known as a unit of work. Atomicity ensures that at the conclusion of the transaction, these operations are either all performed successfully (a successful commit), or none of them are performed at all (a successful rollback). At the end of a transaction, atomicity would be violated if some, but not all, of the operations completed.
Consistency	A consistent transaction has data integrity. Consistency ensures that at the conclusion of the transaction, the data is left in a consistent state, so that database constraints or logical validation rules are not left in violation.
Isolation	Transaction isolation specifies that the outside world is not able to see the intermediate state of a transaction. Outside programs viewing the data objects involved in a transaction must not see the modified data objects until after the transaction has been committed. Transaction isolation is a complex science in itself, and is largely beyond the scope of this discussion, but suffice it to say that EJB server providers typically offer configurable isolation settings that let you choose the degree to which resources within a transaction's scope can see each other's pending changes, and changes that were committed externally but during the course of the context transaction (dirty reads). There is no standard isolation setting, so portable applications should not rely on a particular configuration in their runtime environment.
Durability	The changes that result when a transaction is committed must become visible to the other applications. Committing the data into a relational database, in which the results may subsequently be queried, typically affects this requirement.

Naturally, EJB addresses all these requirements, and we will point out how each one is handled in the examples that follow.

The JTA

The JTA defines an interface for clients and transaction-aware resource managers to participate in fault-tolerant distributed transactions. EJB automatically binds to these services, so both clients and enterprise beans can conveniently participate in distributed programming without having to explicitly code logic such as the two-phase commit protocol. The primary interface for an EJB into its JTA transaction is through the `javax.transaction.UserTransaction` object interface instantiated by the EJB container and made available either through injection into the enterprise bean class or through a Java Naming and Directory Interface (JNDI) lookup.

The Two-Phase Commit Protocol

If you have programmed logic using relational databases, you may be familiar with the two-phase commit protocol. This strategy gives veto authority to resource managers participating in a distributed transaction, notifying them through a "prepare" command that a commit is about to be issued, and allowing them to declare whether they can apply their changes. Only if all resource managers indicate through unanimous consent that they are prepared to apply their changes does the final word come down from the transaction manager to actually apply the changes. Typically, resource managers perform the bulk of the changes during the "prepare" step, so the final "commit" step is trivial to execute. This reduces the likelihood that errors will occur during the "commit" step. Robust transaction managers and resource managers are capable of handling even this eventuality.

Transaction Support in EJB

This section will explore the following questions:

- What transaction services are available to enterprise bean developers?

- How do session beans, message-driven beans (MDBs), and entities interact in a transactional context?

Much of the infrastructure in the EJB server is dedicated to supporting these services, and for good reason. Not only does EJB provide a robust JTA transaction manager, it makes it accessible through declarative metadata that can be specified on interoperable, portable business components. Virtually all Java EE applications require transaction services, and EJB brings them to the application developer in a very slick package.

From its inception, the EJB framework has provided a convenient way to manage transactions and access control by letting you define the behavior declaratively on a method-by-method basis. Beyond these container-provided services, EJB lets you turn control over to your application to define transaction event boundaries and other custom behavior.

In this chapter, we look at the role transactions play in accomplishing a range of common tasks in your application. In a typical Java EE application, session beans typically serve to establish the boundaries of a transaction, and then call upon entities to interact with the database in the transactional context. Our examples mix session bean and entity operations to illustrate both the built-in (declarative) and manual behavior provided by EJB. In the spirit of the simplified development model, EJB provides a lot of its most useful features by default, so it should come as no surprise that the default transaction options are both useful and powerful.

EJB Transaction Services

The EJB transaction model is built on this JTA model, in which session beans or other application clients provide the transactional context in which enterprise services are performed as a logical unit of work. Enterprise services in the Java EE environment include the creation, retrieval, updating, and deletion of entities; the sending of JMS messages to the queue; the execution of MDBs; the firing of mail requests; the invocation of web services; JDBC operations, and much more.

EJB provides a built-in JTA transaction manager, but the real power lies in the declarative services EJB offers to bean providers. Using metadata tags instead of programmatic logic, bean providers can seamlessly participate in JTA transactions and declaratively control the transactional behavior of each business method on an enterprise bean.

EJB 3 extends this programming model by providing explicit support for both JTA transactions and non-JTA (resource-local) transactions. Resource-local transactions are restricted to a single resource manager, such as a database connection, but may result in a performance optimization by avoiding the overhead of a distributed transaction monitor.

In addition, application builders may leverage the container-provided (JTA-based) services for automatically managing transactions, or they may choose to take control of the transaction boundaries and handle the transaction begin, commit, and rollback events explicitly. Within a single application, both approaches may be used, in combination if desired. Whereas the choice of whether to have the container or the application itself demarcate transactions is defined on the enterprise bean, the decision of which type of transaction model to use—JTA or resource-local—is determined when a given EntityManager is obtained from within an application.

The persistent objects in the game—the entities—are entirely, and happily, unaware of their governing transaction framework. The transactional context in which an entity operates is not part of its definition, and so the same entity class may be used in whatever transactional context the application chooses, provided an appropriate EntityManager is created to service the entity's life cycle events.

If all of this seems a little daunting at this point, fear not. It will all make sense once we walk through some examples in code that demonstrate how all the pieces work together. It is also worth noting that EJB's built-in JTA-based transaction support is more than adequate for applications running inside the EJB container. This chapter will let you explore your options—but unless you are writing applications involving entities that live wholly outside of the EJB container, the default support is likely to serve your needs quite nicely.

Session Bean Transactional Behavior in the Service Model

This next section will explore the following questions:

- What declarative transaction support does the EJB container offer to session beans?

- What is the difference between container-managed transaction (CMT) demarcation and bean-managed transaction (BMT) demarcation? When would you choose one approach over the other?

- What are CMT attributes?

- How does EJB support the explicit demarcation of transaction boundaries?

The enterprise bean is the heart of the EJB service layer. Through session beans, the EJB container offers declarative demarcation of transaction events, along with the option to demarcate transaction events explicitly in the bean or in the application client code. Let's consider these two approaches separately, beginning with the default option: leveraging container-managed transaction demarcation using declarative markup.

Container-Managed Transaction Demarcation

The EJB container provides built-in transaction management services that are available by default to session beans and MDBs. The container demarcates transaction boundaries, and automatically begins and commits transactions based on declarative metadata provided by the bean developer.

Note Only the bean developer may assign the transaction management type of an enterprise bean. Application assemblers are permitted to override the bean's method-level container-managed transaction attributes through the `ejb-jar.xml` file, but they must use caution to avoid the possibility of deadlock. Application assemblers and deployers are not permitted to override the bean's transaction management type.

When an EJB declares its transactional behavior in metadata, the container interposes on calls to the enterprise bean's methods and applies transactional behavior at the session bean's method boundaries, providing a fixed set of options that you can specify for each method. The default behavior provided by the container is to check, immediately before invoking the method, whether a transaction context is associated with the current thread. If no transaction context is available, the container begins a new transaction before calling the method. If a transaction is available, the container allows that transaction to be propagated to the method call and made available to the method code. Then, upon returning from the method invocation, the container checks again. If the container was responsible for creating a new transaction context, it automatically commits that transaction after the method is exited. If it didn't create the transaction, then it allows the transaction to continue unaffected. By interposing on the bean's method calls, the EJB container is able to apply transactional behavior at run time that was specified declaratively at development time.

The default behavior, described previously, is but one of six CMT demarcation options provided by the container. You can attribute any one of these six demarcation options to any method on a session bean. Some of the attribute values require specific conditions to be met; when they are not met, an exception is thrown. These attributes are listed in Table 8-2.

Table 8-2. *Container Transaction Attribute Definitions*

Transaction Attribute	Behavior
MANDATORY	A transaction must be in effect at the time the method is called. If no transaction is available, a `javax.ejb.EJBTransactionRequired` exception is thrown.
REQUIRED	This is the default transaction attribute value. Upon entering the method, the container interposes to create a new transaction context if one is not already available. If the container created a transaction upon entering the method, it commits that transaction when the method call completes.

Continued

Table 8-2. *Continued*

Transaction Attribute	Behavior
REQUIRES_NEW	The container always creates a new transaction before executing a method thusly marked. If a transaction context is already available when the method is invoked, then the container suspends that transaction by dissociating it from the current thread before creating the new transaction. The container then reassociates the original transaction with the current thread after committing the intervening one.
SUPPORTS	This option is basically a no-op, resulting in no additional work by the container. If a transaction context is available, it is used by the method. If no transaction context is available, then the container invokes the method with no transaction context. Upon exiting the method, any preexisting transaction context remains in effect.
NOT_SUPPORTED	The container invokes the method with an unspecified transaction context. If a transaction context is available when the method is called, then the container dissociates the transaction from the current thread before invoking the method, and then reassociates the transaction with the thread upon returning from the method.
NEVER	The method must not be invoked with a transaction context. The container will not create one before calling the method, and if one is already in effect, the container throws javax.ejb.EJBException.

Note In general, transaction attributes may be specified on a session bean's business interface methods or web service endpoint interface, or on an MDB's listener method, but some additional restrictions apply. For more information on this, refer to section 13.3.7 of the EJB 3 Core Contracts and Requirements specification (http://java.sun.com/products/ejb).

All six attributes are typically available for session bean methods, though certain attributes are not available on a session timeout callback method, or when the session bean implements javax.ejb.SessionSynchronization. MDBs support only the REQUIRED and NOT_SUPPORTED attributes. Here is an example of how you would specify the transaction behavior on a session bean method to override the transaction behavior specified (or defaulted) at the bean level:

```
@TransactionAttribute(TransactionAttributeType.SUPPORTS)
public CustomerOrder createCustomerOrderUsingSupports(Customer customer)
  throws Exception { ... }
```

Table 8-3 illustrates an EJB's transactional behavior, dependent on its transaction attribute and the presence or absence of a transactional context at the time the session method is called. For each transaction attribute, we list on separate rows the method body and resource transactional context when a client transaction is absent (None), and when a client transaction is present (T1). Both the transaction associated with the method body code and the transaction associated with resources that are used by the method are shown.

Table 8-3. *Client and Bean Transaction States for Each of the Six Transaction Attributes*

Transaction Attribute	Client's Transaction	Transaction Associated with Business Method	Transaction Associated with Resource Managers
MANDATORY	None	Error	N/A
	T1	T1	T1
NEVER	None	None	None
	T1	Error	N/A
NOT_SUPPORTED	None	None	None
	T1	None	None
REQUIRED	None	T2	T2
	T1	T1	T1
REQUIRES_NEW	None	T2	T2
	T1	T3	T3
SUPPORTS	None	None	None
	T1	T1	T1

Table 8-3 illustrates how the container interposes on CMT-demarcated methods to propagate a transactional context differently for each transaction attribute. This table also illustrates that the transactional context used within the bean method is always the one that is in turn propagated to other methods called by that CMT bean method. Note that a client to an enterprise bean may itself be another enterprise bean.

The EJBContext.setRollbackOnly and getRollbackOnly Methods

In the case in which an exception or other error condition is encountered in a method on a CMT-demarcated enterprise bean, the bean may wish to prevent the context transaction from being committed. The bean is not allowed to roll back the transaction explicitly, but it may obtain the `javax.ejb.EJBContext` resource (through container injection or JNDI lookup) and call its `setRollbackOnly()` method to ensure that the container will not commit the transaction. Similarly, a bean method may at any time call the `EJBContext.getRollbackOnly()` method to determine whether the current transaction has been marked for rollback, whether by the current bean or by another bean or resource associated with the current transaction.

Bean-Managed Transaction Demarcation

For some enterprise beans, the declarative CMT services may not provide the demarcation granularity that they require. For instance, a client may wish to call multiple methods on a session bean without having each method commit its work upon completion. In this case, the client has two options: it can either instantiate its own JTA (or resource-local) transaction, or it can ask the session bean to expose transaction demarcation methods that the client can call to control the transaction boundaries itself.

To address this, EJB offers enterprise beans a convenient way to handle their demarcation of transaction events. To turn off the automatic CMT demarcation services, enterprise beans simply specify the `@TransactionManagement(TransactionManagementType.BEAN)` annotation or assign the equivalent metadata to the session bean in the `ejb-jar.xml` file. With BMT demarcation, the EJB container still provides the transaction support to the bean. The primary difference is that the bean makes explicit calls to begin, commit, and roll back transactions instead of using CMT attributes to declaratively assign transactional behavior to its methods. Also, the container does not propagate transactions begun by a client to beans that elect to demarcate their own transactions. While any given enterprise bean must choose one plan or the other (CMT vs. BMT demarcation) for its methods, both types of beans may interact with each other within a single transaction context.

To demarcate transactions, an enterprise bean acquires a JTA `javax.transaction.UserTransaction` instance via injection or JNDI lookup from the container. This interface provides `begin()`, `commit()`, and `rollback()` transaction demarcation methods to the bean. Similarly, non–enterprise bean clients may use a `UserTransaction` resource to demarcate transactions from an application client environment.

In the example that follows, a session bean using BMT demarcation initiates a transaction in one method that is then propagated to subsequent method calls until the transaction is finally committed in a separate method. This behavior could not be specified with the same method structure using CMT demarcation, although it would be possible to achieve the same results using a wrapper method called from a bean that employs CMT demarcation.

■Note How does the EJB server wire up a transaction context? You may be curious as to how the EJB server is able to automatically enlist database connections, and other resources obtained programmatically inside an enterprise bean, with the transaction context. Since the EJB server is providing the context for executing bean methods, it is able to interpose on these requests and perform this side-effect logic without interrupting the flow of execution within the method. That is, it intercepts the method invocation before it is performed, does some extra work (like checking the state of the transaction context, possibly creating a new one, and associating the enterprise bean with that context), and then invokes the bean method. Upon returning from the bean method invocation, it again has an opportunity to perform extra logic before returning control to the client that invoked the bean method in the first place.

Entity Transactional Behavior in the Persistence Model

This section will discuss the following questions:

- How are transactions managed in the persistence layer?

- What options does the persistence framework offer for controlling transactions involving entities?

- What is the role of the persistence context in a transaction?

- How do entities become associated with, and dissociated from, a transactional context?

If you recall from Chapter 3, a persistence unit defines a set of entity classes, and a persistence context holds the state of unique instances from a single persistence unit. At any point in time, across multiple applications executing in an application server, many persistence context instances may be actively associated with any given persistence unit, but each persistence context is associated with, at most, one transaction context.

How Entities Become Associated with a Transaction Context

From the preceding discussion about how the EJB server acts as a transaction coordinator in associating resources with a transaction context, you may have realized that the persistence context is the resource that gets associated with a transaction. In this way, a persistence context is propagated through method calls so that entities in a persistence unit can see each other's intermediate state, through their common persistence context, if they are associated with the same transaction context. Also, the restriction that only one persistence context for any given persistence unit must be associated with a given transaction context ensures that for any entity of type T with identity I, its state will be represented by only one persistence context within any transaction context.

Within an application thread, only one transaction context is available at any moment, but the EJB server is free to dissociate one persistence context from that thread and associate a new persistence context for the same persistence unit to satisfy transaction isolation boundaries. When the EJB server does this, the newly instantiated persistence context is not able to see the intermediate changes made to any entities associated with the suspended persistence context.

Container-Managed vs. Application-Managed Persistence Context

The persistence services in EJB 3 let you opt out of container-managed entity persistence altogether and manage the transaction life cycles of your entities explicitly within your application code. When an EntityManager is injected (or looked up through JNDI), it comes in as a container-managed persistence context. The container automatically associates container-managed persistence contexts with any transaction that happens to be in context at the time that the EntityManager is injected. Should an application wish to control how or whether its persistence contexts are associated with transactions, it may obtain an EntityManagerFactory (again, through container injection or JNDI lookup) and explicitly create the EntityManager instances that represent their persistence contexts. An application-managed persistence context is used when the EntityManager is obtained through an EntityManagerFactory—a requirement when running outside the Java EE container. For more information on using an application-managed EntityManager outside of a Java EE container, as in a pure Java SE environment, please see Chapters 4 and 11.

Transaction-Scoped Persistence Context vs. Extended Persistence Context

When an EntityManager is created, you may specify whether the persistence context that it manages should be bound to the life of a transaction, or whether it should span the life of the EntityManager itself. A persistence context that is created when a transaction is created, and destroyed when the transaction ends, is known as a transaction-scoped persistence context. A persistence context that is created at the time it is injected into the bean (or bound through a JNDI lookup), and is not destroyed until the EntityManager instance is itself destroyed, is called an extended persistence context. Only stateful session beans may use extended persistence contexts. At the time an EntityManager instance is created, its persistence context type is defined, and it may not be changed during the EntityManager's lifetime. The default type is transaction-scoped; to inject an EntityManager by specifying an extended persistence context, you may specify the injection directive with the following:

```
@PersistenceContext(type = PersistenceContextType.EXTENDED)
private EnterpriseManager em;
```

or you may define a persistence-context-ref element in the XML descriptor.

In the transaction examples at the end of this chapter, we will compare the behavior of a stateless session bean using a transaction-scoped persistence context with a stateful session bean that uses an extended persistence context.

JTA vs. Resource-Local EntityManager

An EntityManager may be defined to participate in either a JTA transaction or a non-JTA (resource-local) transaction. The features of JTA—most notably, support for distributed transactions—have been described previously. Resource-local EntityManagers control transactions using the EntityTransaction interface available to clients through the EntityManager.getEntityTransaction() method. This interface exposes the expected transaction demarcation methods begin(), commit(), and rollback(), along with getRollbackOnly() and setRollbackOnly() methods that are equivalent to the EJBContext methods available to enterprise beans described previously, and an isActive() method to indicate whether a transaction is currently in progress.

Container-managed EntityManagers must be JTA EntityManagers. Application-managed EntityManagers may be either JTA or resource-local, but they may only be JTA EntityManagers if the EntityManager resides in the Java EE environment.

The principal reason you might want to use a resource-local EntityManager is that while JTA provides the infrastructure for distributed transactions, resource-local transactions can provide a performance optimization by eliminating the overhead of this infrastructure.

A Transactional Scenario from the Wines Online Application

Now that we've covered the details of the transaction support offered by EJB, let's explore some cases in which these services are used, using an example scenario lifted from our sample Wines Online application.

In this scenario, we create a mock Java SE client that creates a new customer, builds up a shopping cart consisting of cart item entries, and then creates a customer order consisting of order items based on the cart items in the cart. This example was chosen for this chapter because it involves multiple operations that can be partitioned into transactional work units of greater or less granularity depending on the requirements of the client.

To illustrate the default support provided by EJB, we begin with a standard stateless session bean implementation that uses CMT demarcation. Afterward, we will demonstrate an alternative, and more flexible, implementation with a stateful session bean using BMT demarcation and an extended persistence context.

Setting Up the Examples

The following examples use the entities in the persistence unit defined for the Wines Online application, whose source lives in the Ch07_PersistenceUnit directory. The source for the session beans, OrderProcessorCMTBean.java and OrderProcessorCMTBean.java, can be found in the Ch8_XactionExamples directory. The source for the Java SE clients is in Ch08_Client.

To create the tables and ID generators that support the entities in the persistence unit, run the following SQL scripts in order from the Ch07_PersistenceUnit\database directory:

```
winestore.sql
WineStoreSchema.sql
PopulateIdGenTable.sql
```

To deploy the sample Java EE application for this chapter, deploy the Ch08_Xaction➡ Assembly.ear file found in the Ch08_Assembly\deploy directory, using Ant or the GlassFish web-based administration tool.

The Java Archive (JAR) files for the BMT and CMT sample clients are found in the Ch08_Client\deploy directory. Assuming GlassFish is installed in C:\glassfish, and the samples are installed in C:\ejb3book, the CMT client may be executed by calling the following:

```
C:\glassfish\bin\appclient.bat -client
C:\ejb3book\Ch08_Client\deploy\Ch08_CMTClient.jar
```

and the BMT client may be executed by calling the following:

```
%glassfish%\bin\appclient.bat -client
%ejb3Book%\Ch08_Client\deploy\Ch08_BMTClient.jar
```

Both examples follow the same scenario, but accomplish it using different EJB options.

Stateless Session Beans with CMT Demarcation

We begin with a default, straightforward, implementation of a stateless session bean, OrderProcessorCMTBean.java (shown in Listing 8-1). This session bean uses CMT demarcation to leverage EJB's declarative transaction support. It is followed by a simple Java SE client, OrderProcessorCMTClient.java (shown in Listing 8-2).

Listing 8-1. *OrderProcessorCMTBean.java, a Stateless Session Bean Using CMT Demarcation*

```java
@Stateless(name = "OrderProcessorCMT")
public class OrderProcessorCMTBean
  implements OrderProcessorCMT
{
  @PersistenceContext(unitName = "wineStoreUnit")
  private EntityManager em;

  public OrderProcessorCMTBean() {
  }

  /**
   *  Remove any existing Customers with email 'xaction.head@yahoo.com' and any
   *  existing Wine with country 'United States'
   */
  public String initialize() {
    StringBuffer strBuf = new StringBuffer();
    strBuf.append("Removed ");
    int i = 0;
    //  Remove any existing Customers with email 'xaction.head@yahoo.com'
    for (Individual customer: findAllCustomersByEmail("xaction.head@yahoo.com")) {
      em.remove(customer);
      i++;
    }
    strBuf.append(i);
    strBuf.append(" Customer(s) and ");

    //  Remove any existing Wine with country 'United States'
    i = 0;
    for (Wine wine: findWineByCountry("United States")) {
      em.remove(wine);
      i++;
    }
```

```java
  strBuf.append(i);
  strBuf.append(" Wine(s)");
  return strBuf.toString();
}


/**
 * Create a new CustomerOrder from the items in a Customer's cart.
 * Creates a new CustomerOrder entity, and then creates a new OrderItem
 * entity for each CartItem found in the Customer's cart.
 *
 * Using CMT w/ the default Required xaction attribute, if this method is
 * invoked without a transaction context, a new transaction will be created
 * by the EJB container upon invoking the method, and committed upon
 * successfully completing the method.
 *
 * @return a status message (plain text)
 */
public CustomerOrder createCustomerOrder(Customer customer)
  throws Exception {
  return createCustomerOrderUsingSupports(customer);
}


@TransactionAttribute(TransactionAttributeType.SUPPORTS)
public CustomerOrder createCustomerOrderUsingSupports(Customer customer)
  throws Exception {
  if (customer == null) {
    throw new IllegalArgumentException(
        "OrderProcessingBean.createCustomerOrder():  Customer not specified");
  }

  final Long custId = customer.getId();
  customer = em.merge(customer);

  if (customer == null) {
    throw new Exception("Customer with id " + custId + " not found!");
  }

  final CustomerOrder customerOrder = new CustomerOrder();
  customerOrder.setCustomer(customer);
  final Timestamp orderDate = new Timestamp(System.currentTimeMillis());
```

```
    final List<CartItem> cartItemList =
      new ArrayList(customer.getCartItemCollection());
    for (CartItem cartItem: cartItemList) {
      // Create a new OrderItem for this CartItem
      final OrderItem orderItem = new OrderItem();
      orderItem.setOrderDate(orderDate);
      orderItem.setPrice(cartItem.getWine().getRetailPrice());
      orderItem.setQuantity(cartItem.getQuantity());
      orderItem.setStatus("Order Created");
      orderItem.setWine(cartItem.getWine());
      customerOrder.addOrderItem(orderItem);

      // Remove the CartItem
      customer.removeCartItem(cartItem);
      em.remove(cartItem);
    }

    return persistEntity(customerOrder);
  }

  public <T> T persistEntity(T entity) {
    em.persist(entity);
    return entity;
  }

  /** <code>select object(cust) from Individual cust
          where cust.email = :email</code> */
  public List<Individual> findAllCustomersByEmail(Object email) {
    return em.createNamedQuery("findCustomerByEmail").
        setParameter("email", email).getResultList();
  }

  /** <code>select wine from Wine wine where wine.country = :country</code> */
  public List<Wine> findWineByCountry(Object country) {
    return em.createNamedQuery("findWineByCountry").
        setParameter("country",country).getResultList();
  }
}
```

Listing 8-2. *OrderProcessorCMTClient.java, a Java SE Client That Drives the OrderProcessorCMT Session Bean*

```java
public class OrderProcessorCMTClient
{
  public static void main(String[] args) {
    try {
      final Context context = new InitialContext();
      OrderProcessorCMT orderProcessorCMT =
        (OrderProcessorCMT)context.lookup("com.apress.ejb3.ch08.OrderProcessorCMT");

      //  Remove any existing Customers with email 'xaction.head@yahoo.com' and any
      //  existing Wine with country 'United States'.
      System.out.println(orderProcessorCMT.initialize());

      //  Create a Customer and add some CartItems and their associated Wines
      Individual customer = new Individual();
      customer.setFirstName("Transaction");
      customer.setLastName("Head");
      customer.setEmail("xaction.head@yahoo.com");
      for (int i = 0; i < 5; i++) {
        final Wine wine = new Wine();
        wine.setCountry("United States");
        wine.setDescription("Delicious wine");
        wine.setName("Xacti");
        wine.setRegion("Dry Creek Valley");
        wine.setRetailPrice(20.00D + i);
        wine.setVarietal("Zinfandel");
        wine.setYear(2000L + i);

        final CartItem cartItem = new CartItem();
        cartItem.setCreatedDate(new Timestamp(System.currentTimeMillis()));
        cartItem.setCustomer(customer);
        cartItem.setQuantity(12L);
        cartItem.setWine(wine);

        customer.addCartItem(cartItem);
      }
```

```
    //  Persist the Customer, relying on the cascade settings to persist all
    //  related Wine and CartItem entities as well. Reassign the customer,
    //  to pick up the ID value that was assigned by the EJB container when
    //  it was persisted.
    customer = orderProcessorCMT.persistEntity(customer);

    //  Create a customer order and create OrderItems from the CartItems
    final CustomerOrder customerOrder =
      orderProcessorCMT.createCustomerOrder(customer);
    for (OrderItem orderItem: customerOrder.getOrderItemCollection()) {
      final Wine wine = orderItem.getWine();
      System.out.println(wine.getName() + " with ID " + wine.getId());
    }
  }
  catch (Exception ex) {
    ex.printStackTrace();
  }
 }
}
```

Transaction Analysis

The following sections will analyze this test run from a transaction perspective.

Removing Previous Test Data

The client begins by wiping the slate clean—removing any traces of Customer and Wine entities that might have been created from previous invocations:

```
final Context context = new InitialContext();
OrderProcessorCMT orderProcessorCMT =
  (OrderProcessorCMT)context.lookup("com.apress.ejb3.ch08.OrderProcessorCMT");

//  Remove any existing Customers with email 'xaction.head@yahoo.com' and any
//  existing Wine with country 'United States'.
System.out.println(orderProcessorCMT.initialize());
```

The OrderProcessorCMT bean assumes the default TransactionManagement value—the equivalent of annotating the bean:

```
@TransactionManagement(TransactionManagementType.CONTAINER)
```

Because the initialize() method is not annotated with a TransactionAttribute override, it assumes the default transaction attribute value, the equivalent of the following:

```
@TransactionAttribute(TransactionAttributeType.REQUIRED)
```

Since the client has not begun, or inherited, a transaction, one is created and begun by the EJB container for the duration of the initialize() method, and committed upon successful completion of this method. This causes any changes made during the course of that method to be made persistent, and applied to the database so that the changes are visible to all clients henceforth.

Creating New Customer and CartItem Entity Instances in the Client

The next step for the client is to create a new Customer entity instance (actually, the concrete Individual entity subclass of the abstract Customer entity) and add some CartItem instances that reference newly created Wine instances:

```
// Create a Customer and add some CartItems and their associated Wines
Individual customer = new Individual();
customer.setFirstName("Transaction");
customer.setLastName("Head");
customer.setEmail("xaction.head@yahoo.com");
for (int i = 0; i < 5; i++)
{
  final Wine wine = new Wine();
  wine.setCountry("United States");
  wine.setDescription("Delicious wine");
  wine.setName("Xacti");
  wine.setRegion("Dry Creek Valley");
  wine.setRetailPrice(20.00D + i);
  wine.setVarietal("Zinfandel");
  wine.setYear(2000L + i);

  final CartItem cartItem = new CartItem();
  cartItem.setCreatedDate(new Timestamp(System.currentTimeMillis()));
  cartItem.setCustomer(customer);
  cartItem.setQuantity(12L);
  cartItem.setWine(wine);

  customer.addCartItem(cartItem);
}
```

Note that during this stage, entities are created that exist only in the Java client's virtual machine (VM) tier—there is no interaction during this stage with the EJB container layer. No transaction is involved in this process of creating the entity POJOs (plain old Java objects), assigning their ordinary properties, and associating them with each other.

Persisting the Customer

Having created the `Customer` and associated `CartItem` objects, the client passes the `Customer` to the `OrderProcessorCMT` bean's `persistEntity()` method. Because the relationships on the `Customer` and `CartItem` entities are annotated `cascade = {CascadeType.ALL}`, the act of persisting the `Customer` entity is cascaded to all associated entities, and so they are all persisted as well.

```
// Persist the Customer, relying on the cascade settings to persist all
// related Wine and CartItem entities as well. Reassign the customer,
// to pick up the ID value that was assigned by the EJB container when
// it was persisted.
customer = orderProcessorCMT.persistEntity(customer);
```

Also note that because we set up an ID generator on the base class (`BusinessContext`) for the `Individual` entity, its `id` field is autopopulated at the time the entity is persisted:

```
@Id
@GeneratedValue(strategy=GenerationType.TABLE, generator="TABLE_ID_GENERATOR")
@Column(nullable=false)
protected Long id;
```

Assigning the result of the `persistEntity()` callback onto the `customer` field gives us the updated instance. Because the `persistEntity()` call passes from a Java SE client to the Java EE tier, it uses pass-by-value semantics, so the customer instance does not change during the call. As such, we need to explicitly retrieve the mutated instance through the method's return value.

At the conclusion of the `persistEntity()` call, the `Customer` (`Individual`) and all associated entities are now applied to the database and available to all clients, including our own.

Creating the CustomerOrder

An instance of a `Customer` entity now exists as a persistent row in the database, so we can call `createCustomerOrder()` with `customer`, our detached copy, to create a new `CustomerOrder`, and create an `OrderItem` for each `CartItem` on the `Customer`:

```
// Create a customer order and create OrderItems from the CartItems
final CustomerOrder customerOrder =
  orderProcessorCMT.createCustomerOrder(customer);
```

Here again, the createCustomerOrder() method is not annotated with a transaction attribute, so it defaults to REQUIRED, and the EJB container creates and begins a new transaction for the duration of that method, and then commits it upon returning control to the client. Note that the implementation of the createCustomerOrder() method delegates to another method, createCustomerOrderUsingSupports(), which is annotated as follows:

```
@TransactionAttribute(TransactionAttributeType.SUPPORTS)
public CustomerOrder createCustomerOrderUsingSupports(Customer customer) {...}
```

This delegation exists purely to allow us to illustrate the transaction behavior involved when calling a method marked SUPPORTS from a method marked REQUIRED. The method called from the client, createCustomerOrder(), causes a transaction to be created that is propagated to its delegate, createCustomerOrderUsingSupports(). This latter method inherits the transaction context created by the EJB container for its caller. Had the client called createCustomerOrderUsingSupports() directly, an exception would have been thrown during its execution, when the remove() and persist() operations were called outside a transaction context.

A lot is going on inside the createCustomerOrderUsingSupports() method. Because the customer argument might be detached (in our case it is, since it is a serialized instance that was passed from a Java SE client), it needs to be turned into a managed instance:

```
customer = em.merge(customer);
```

Next, the CustomerOrder instance is created:

```
final CustomerOrder customerOrder = new CustomerOrder();
```

and populated with new OrderItems to match each CartItem in the Customer's shopping cart:

```
customerOrder.setCustomer(customer);
final Timestamp orderDate = new Timestamp(System.currentTimeMillis());
final List<CartItem> cartItemList =
  new ArrayList(customer.getCartItemCollection());
for (CartItem cartItem: cartItemList)
{
  // Create a new OrderItem for this CartItem
  final OrderItem orderItem = new OrderItem();
```

```
    orderItem.setOrderDate(orderDate);
    orderItem.setPrice(cartItem.getWine().getRetailPrice());
    orderItem.setQuantity(cartItem.getQuantity());
    orderItem.setStatus("Order Created");
    orderItem.setWine(cartItem.getWine());
    customerOrder.addOrderItem(orderItem);

    // Remove the CartItem
    customer.removeCartItem(cartItem);
    em.remove(cartItem);
}
```

As each `OrderItem` is created, its `CartItem` is removed from the `Customer` instance and is then removed from persistent storage as well.

At last, the newly populated `CustomerOrder` is persisted and returned to the caller:

```
return persistEntity(customerOrder);
```

The transaction is not committed until after the `createCustomerOrderUsingSupports()` method has completed and control is returned from the wrapper `createCustomerOrder()` method. Should anything go wrong in the course of either of these methods, the entire transaction will be rolled back, and neither this client nor any outside application will ever be aware that a `CustomerOrder` may have been created.

Does This Pass the ACID Test?

Have the core ACID requirements that characterize a valid transaction been met? Let's look at how EJB addresses each one.

Atomicity

The EJB container ensures that whenever a stateless CMT method marked REQUIRED or REQUIRES_NEW is called, if the container interposes to create a new transaction (this will always happen with REQUIRES_NEW), it will resolve that transaction upon exiting the method. If the method completes successfully, and if the bean code did not call `EJBContext.setRollbackOnly()`, the transaction will be committed. If the method throws an exception, or if `EJBContext.setRollbackOnly()` is called, the transaction will be rolled back. These two transaction attributes are the only ones for which the container may interpose to create a new transaction. For all other transaction attributes, either an externally managed transaction is involved (in which case the container will not interpose to commit it when the method is exited), or the method is called with no transaction context.

Consistency

Any database constraints or concurrency conditions (whether enforced in the database or in the EJB container) are guaranteed to be satisfied when a transaction is committed through the EJB services. Violations will result in exceptions being thrown from the EJB container, and the transaction will automatically be rolled back. A successful commit indicates that all defined constraint conditions have been met.

Isolation

This requirement is largely the responsibility of the underlying JTA resources. Each resource may expose its own configurable isolation level settings to provide varying degrees of consistency to the resources involved in a transaction. Isolation levels determine the extent to which resources within the transaction are able to see the partial (in-transaction) state of other resources involved in the transaction, and largely translate into cache consistency settings within the resource. To remain database-neutral, our example did not attempt to configure these settings.

Durability

This is also largely the responsibility of the underlying JTA resources involved in the transaction (e.g., the database or mail server). At the conclusion of a JTA transaction, any such resources are expected to be able to show the new state of the data when queried. We demonstrated this by querying the details of the new `CustomerOrder` from the client after the `createCustomerOrder()` method, and its transaction encapsulated within, had completed.

Benefits of This Approach

A principal benefit of using a default stateless session bean with CMT demarcation is that the client does not need to be concerned about beginning, ending, or otherwise coordinating the transaction logic. Also, any transaction context currently in effect on the thread in which the bean method is called is automatically propagated to that method call (if the transaction attribute is `REQUIRED` or `SUPPORTS`). Each call it makes to the Order➥ ProcessorCMT bean either completes successfully (in which case it can be assumed that the work has been applied persistently) or results in an exception (whereupon the work performed in that method is completely rolled back). It's a very simple model.

Limitations of This Approach

Sometimes simple is good, and sometimes it is too limiting. While this approach allows the client to create and manipulate new entity instances in the client tier, as when it created the Customer and CartItem instances, the client has very limited ability to manipulate existing entities in the client tier. This is because entities cannot operate in a transactional context from the Java SE client, since transactions are always begun and terminated by the EJB container before control is handed back to the client.

In the next example, we will show how using stateful session beans, coupled with BMTs and an extended persistence context, allow entities access to their transactional context while in the client tier, and so give the client greater flexibility and control over manipulating preexisting beans.

Note There has been a popular conception among EJB users that stateful session beans should be avoided for performance reasons. The performance tests that we have done strongly suggest that stateful session beans have been falsely maligned, and that when correctly used, they can actually boost performance. Furthermore, in EJB 3, their value is increased, since they provide you this PersistenceContext. EXTENDED option, allowing entity instances to be cached for use across transactions.

Stateful Session Beans with BMT Demarcation and Extended Persistence Context

To illustrate extending the reach of EJB's transaction support, here is OrderProcessor➥ BMTBean.java. This example also leverages EJB's built-in transaction support, but shows how to demarcate transactions explicitly, inside the enterprise bean code. Similar to the preceding (but different in important ways) is the stateful session bean followed by a mock Java SE client. There is no requirement that you use BMT demarcation when using stateful session beans, and in fact this option is not typically used. We show it here only to illustrate how you would use it, should you be so inclined (see Listing 8-3).

Listing 8-3. *OrderProcessorBMTBean.java, a Stateful Session Bean Using BMT Demarcation and an Extended Persistence Context*

```
public class OrderProcessorCMTClient
{
  public static void main(String[] args) {
    try {
      final Context context = new InitialContext();
      OrderProcessorCMT orderProcessorCMT =
        (OrderProcessorCMT)context.lookup("com.apress.ejb3.ch08.OrderProcessorCMT");
```

```
// Remove any existing Customers with email 'xaction.head@yahoo.com' and any
// existing Wine with country 'United States'.
System.out.println(orderProcessorCMT.initialize());

// Create a Customer and add some CartItems and their associated Wines
Individual customer = new Individual();
customer.setFirstName("Transaction");
customer.setLastName("Head");
customer.setEmail("xaction.head@yahoo.com");
for (int i = 0; i < 5; i++) {
  final Wine wine = new Wine();
  wine.setCountry("United States");
  wine.setDescription("Delicious wine");
  wine.setName("Xacti");
  wine.setRegion("Dry Creek Valley");
  wine.setRetailPrice(20.00D + i);
  wine.setVarietal("Zinfandel");
  wine.setYear(2000L + i);

  final CartItem cartItem = new CartItem();
  cartItem.setCreatedDate(new Timestamp(System.currentTimeMillis()));
  cartItem.setCustomer(customer);
  cartItem.setQuantity(12L);
  cartItem.setWine(wine);

  customer.addCartItem(cartItem);
}

// Persist the Customer, relying on the cascade settings to persist all
// related Wine and CartItem entities as well. Reassign the customer,
// to pick up the ID value that was assigned by the EJB container when
// it was persisted.
customer = orderProcessorCMT.persistEntity(customer);

// Create a customer order and create OrderItems from the CartItems
final CustomerOrder customerOrder =
  orderProcessorCMT.createCustomerOrder(customer);
for (OrderItem orderItem: customerOrder.getOrderItemCollection()) {
  final Wine wine = orderItem.getWine();
  System.out.println(wine.getName() + " with ID " + wine.getId());
}
}
```

```
    catch (Exception ex) {
      ex.printStackTrace();
    }
  }
}
```

Listing 8-4 shows `OrderProcessorBMTClient.java`, a Java SE client that drives the `OrderProcessorBMT` session bean to demonstrate EJB's BMT demarcation, using an extended persistence context.

Listing 8-4. *OrderProcessorBMTClient.java, Our Mock Java SE Client*

```
public class OrderProcessorBMTClient
{
  /**
   * OrderProcessorBMTClient creates a CustomerOrder from a Customer's
   * CartItem list. It makes explicit calls to the OrderProcessorBMT class to
   * demarcate the transaction, and demonstrates cancelling the order
   * after it has been created.
   *
   * @param args
   */
  public static void main(String[] args) {
    OrderProcessorBMT orderProcessorBMT = null;
    try {
      final Context context = new InitialContext();

      //  Look up our OrderProcessorBMT service (Stateful Session) bean
      orderProcessorBMT = (OrderProcessorBMT)context.lookup(
          "com.apress.ejb3.ch08.OrderProcessorBMT");

      //  Begin a new transaction for removing any preexisting test data
      orderProcessorBMT.beginTrans();

      //  Remove any existing Customers with email 'xaction.head@yahoo.com'
      for (Individual customer:
          orderProcessorBMT.findAllCustomersByEmail("xaction.head@yahoo.com")) {
        orderProcessorBMT.removeEntity(customer);
      }
```

```
// Remove any existing Wine with country 'United States'
for (Wine wine: orderProcessorBMT.findWineByCountry("United States")) {
  orderProcessorBMT.removeEntity(wine);
}

// Apply these changes, committing the entity removal operations
orderProcessorBMT.commitTrans();

// Create a Customer and add some CartItems and their associated Wines
Individual customer = new Individual();
customer.setFirstName("Transaction");
customer.setLastName("Head");
customer.setEmail("xaction.head@yahoo.com");
for (int i = 0; i < 5; i++) {
  final Wine wine = new Wine();
  wine.setCountry("United States");
  wine.setDescription("Delicious wine");
  wine.setName("Xacti");
  wine.setRegion("Dry Creek Valley");
  wine.setRetailPrice(20.00D + i);
  wine.setVarietal("Zinfandel");
  wine.setYear(2000L + i);

  final CartItem cartItem = new CartItem();
  cartItem.setCreatedDate(new Timestamp(System.currentTimeMillis()));
  cartItem.setCustomer(customer);
  cartItem.setQuantity(12L);
  cartItem.setWine(wine);

  customer.addCartItem(cartItem);
}

// Begin a new transaction to perform the order processing steps
orderProcessorBMT.beginTrans();

// Persist the Customer, relying on the cascade settings to persist all
// related Wine and CartItem entities as well. Reassign the customer
// to pick up the ID value that was assigned by the EJB container when
// it was persisted.
customer = orderProcessorBMT.persistEntity(customer);
```

```
    // Create a customer order and create OrderItems from the CartItems
    CustomerOrder customerOrder =
      orderProcessorBMT.createCustomerOrder(customer);

    // Query the Wines in the CustomerOrder
    for (OrderItem orderItem: customerOrder.getOrderItemCollection()) {
      final Wine wine = orderItem.getWine();
      System.out.println(wine.getName() + " with ID " + wine.getId());
    }

    // Commit the order, applying all of the changes made thus far
    orderProcessorBMT.commitTrans();
  }
  catch (Exception ex) {
    ex.printStackTrace();
    if (orderProcessorBMT != null) {
      try {
        orderProcessorBMT.rollbackTrans();
      }
      catch (Exception e) {
        e.printStackTrace();
      }
    }
  }
}
}
```

Transaction Analysis

The following sections will analyze this second test run from a transactional perspective.
We have empowered the session bean with state (i.e., Stateful), given it control over the
demarcation of its transactions, and allowed its associated persistence context to survive
from one transaction to the next.

Session Bean Declaration

This new support has arisen through the use of new annotations. You'll notice that
this session bean is annotated @Stateful, uses BMT demarcation, and injects both an
extended persistence context and a UserTransaction instance. Stateful, you will recall,
allows the enterprise bean to retain state from one client invocation to the next. In this
case, that state consists of its associated PersistenceContext and UserTransaction

instances. BMT demarcation declares that the container should not automatically interpose on method boundaries to demarcate transactions. Attempts to add TransactionAttribute qualifiers to methods on a BMT session bean will be caught and raise an exception at deployment time.

```
@Stateful(name = "OrderProcessorBMT")
@TransactionManagement(TransactionManagementType.BEAN)
public class OrderProcessorBMTBean
  implements OrderProcessorBMT
{
  @PersistenceContext(type = PersistenceContextType.EXTENDED)
  private EntityManager em;

  @Resource
  private UserTransaction ut;
  ...
}
```

The @PersistenceContext annotation holds a type property with value Persistence➡ContextType.EXTENDED, meaning that it persists from one transaction to the next, and allows associated entities to remain managed even after the transaction in which they were created has ended. The injected UserTransaction instance is this BMT bean's JTA interface onto the transaction manager, and exposes the begin(), commit(), and rollback() transaction demarcation methods.

Removing Previous Test Data

We could have initialized the test environment through a session bean method call, as we did for the preceding CMT example. However, using BMT offers us the option of performing this work interactively, in the client. This is because the OrderProcessorBMT bean's persistence context is EXTENDED, allowing the entities to remain associated with a persistence context even after control has been returned from the enterprise bean to the client.

```
    // Begin a new transaction for removing any preexisting test data
    orderProcessorBMT.beginTrans();

    // Remove any existing Customers with email 'xaction.head@yahoo.com'
    for (Individual customer :
        orderProcessorBMT.findAllCustomersByEmail("xaction.head@yahoo.com"))
    {
      orderProcessorBMT.removeEntity(customer);
    }
```

```
// Remove any existing Wine with country 'United States'
for (Wine wine : orderProcessorBMT.findWineByCountry("United States"))
{
  orderProcessorBMT.removeEntity(wine);
}

// Apply these changes, committing the entity removal operations
orderProcessorBMT.commitTrans();
```

Each call to removeEntity() is performed in the transaction that was begun on the OrderProcessorBMT bean, and puts the entity in the "removed" state in its persistence context. At the conclusion of these steps, the client calls commit() to actually perform the DBMS DELETE operations in the database and commit the transaction.

Creating New Customer and CartItem Entity Instances in the Client

As with the preceding stateless session example, the step of creating the Customer and its CartItem entity instances involves no transactions, and can be carried out entirely within the client:

```
// Create a Customer and add some CartItems and their associated Wines
Individual customer = new Individual();
customer.setFirstName("Transaction");
customer.setLastName("Head");
customer.setEmail("xaction.head@yahoo.com");
for (int i = 0; i < 5; i++)      {
  final Wine wine = new Wine();
  wine.setCountry("United States");
  wine.setDescription("Delicious wine");
  wine.setName("Xacti");
  wine.setRegion("Dry Creek Valley");
  wine.setRetailPrice(20.00D + i);
  wine.setVarietal("Zinfandel");
  wine.setYear(2000L + i);

  final CartItem cartItem = new CartItem();
  cartItem.setCreatedDate(new Timestamp(System.currentTimeMillis()));
  cartItem.setCustomer(customer);
  cartItem.setQuantity(12L);
  cartItem.setWine(wine);

  customer.addCartItem(cartItem);
}
```

It is worth noting that in earlier versions of EJB, this work would have required much more effort. In the absence of POJO entities, the client developer had two main options. Under one approach, the developer could create data transfer objects (DTOs) or follow some other similar pattern to simulate the task of creating and associating the entity objects through proxies. This network of DTO classes would then be passed into the session bean layer, as we did previously; but inside the session bean, actual entity beans would have to be explicitly created and initialized from the DTO objects.

A second approach, updating the entity beans directly from the client, is simpler to code, but potentially at the expense of higher performance costs. If the client exists outside the Java EE tier, each method call would incur the overhead of RMI/IIOP (remote method invocation over the internet inter-ORB protocol; see http://java.sun.com/➥products/rmi-iiop/) marshalling to communicate with the actual EJB object residing in the EJB container. Much of this overhead is removed when the client lives in the Java EE tier, since it could use local entity bean interfaces to communicate directly with the live entity bean; but Java SE clients like ours are forced to use remote interfaces onto the entity beans. On top of that, container-managed relationships (CMRs) are only supported on local component interfaces, so direct entity bean relationship lookups and updates were not even available to Java SE clients in the EJB 2.x world.

Persisting the Customer

We precede the step of persisting the new Customer and its CartItems by explicitly beginning a new transaction. This call could have been made inside the session bean, but there are cases in which a client will want to control transaction demarcation explicitly, and using BMT avails the client of this option.

```
// Begin a new transaction to perform the order processing steps
orderProcessorBMT.beginTrans();

// Persist the Customer, relying on the cascade settings to persist all
// related Wine and CartItem entities as well. Reassign the customer
// to pick up the ID value that was assigned by the EJB container when
// it was persisted.
customer = orderProcessorBMT.persistEntity(customer);
```

The transaction context does not extend to the client thread itself; it exists only in the session bean's thread. The call to beginTrans() establishes a transaction context on that thread that is then available to the session bean when its persistEntity() method is called.

Creating the CustomerOrder

This stage is similar to the stateless CMT example, except that the transaction has already been created, and must be explicitly committed at the conclusion.

```
// Create a customer order and create OrderItems from the CartItems
CustomerOrder customerOrder =
  orderProcessorBMT.createCustomerOrder(customer);

// Query the Wines in the CustomerOrder
for (OrderItem orderItem: customerOrder.getOrderItemCollection())
{
  final Wine wine = orderItem.getWine();
  System.out.println(wine.getName() + " with ID " + wine.getId());
}

// Commit the order, applying all of the changes made thus far
orderProcessorBMT.commitTrans();
```

Should the client wish to cancel the order at this stage, perhaps through interactive confirm/cancel buttons exposed in a client panel, the BMT option provides this possibility even after the CustomerOrder has been created.

Benefits of This Approach

The benefit of using explicit transaction demarcation is the additional degree of flexibility that it offers. The EJB server is still acting in its capacity as transaction manager, only it exposes the transaction demarcation control to the enterprise bean instead of automating this demarcation based on the transaction attribute settings on each method. While the stateless example could have prompted the user *before* creating the CustomerOrder, this approach allows the CustomerOrder to be created and validated—for example, before being submitted to the user for confirmation. BMT is not typically used, however, for the reasons mentioned in the following section.

Limitations of This Approach

It can be argued that the additional degree of flexibility is typically outweighed by the additional burdens of tracking the transaction state and avoiding misuse by session bean clients. Leaving the process of beginning and ending transactions to the mercy of the order in which clients call the session bean methods offers the possibility of dangling transactions. The client, in coordination with the bean itself, has the responsibility of cleanly ending—whether committing or rolling back—each transaction that has begun. This may be a reasonable risk if you can control how clients will use the bean—but session beans are openly published, and it may be difficult to anticipate who might use them, and how.

BMT session beans can be written to safeguard against misuse, but this safeguard code is probably going to leave the bean with behavior similar to CMT beans anyway, in which case little is gained for your efforts.

Conclusion

This chapter has defined the concepts essential to all transaction behavior and explored the transactional features offered by the EJB server and interfaces accessible to the enterprise bean developer.

We began by exploring the core ACID characteristics that define a transaction— atomicity, consistency, isolation, and durability. We introduced JTA and described the features and benefits of its distributed transaction model, including the behavior of the essential two-phase commit protocol.

We looked at how the EJB server acts as a JTA transaction manager, allowing EJBs to participate seamlessly in distributed transactions, and alleviating bean developers of the need to explicitly bind persistence or other transactional operations with transactional resources. We also detailed EJB's declarative support for these transaction services to enterprise bean developers, exploring both CMT and BMT demarcation–supported enterprise beans. For CMT beans, we described the behavior and implications of each of the six transaction attributes that may be used to define the transactional behavior of a CMT bean method. In the JPA realm, we explored the relationship between transactions and persistence contexts, and explained how extended persistence contexts may be used with stateful session beans to support entities in resolving relationships with other entities, even outside of a transactional context.

The chapter concluded with some live examples based on a scenario taken from the Wines Online application. These examples illustrated the use of CMT and BMT demarcation, extended persistence context on stateful session beans, rollback scenarios, client-controlled transactions, interactions with entities outside a transactional context using a BMT bean, and transaction context propagation between methods on a CMT bean.

In the next chapter, we will explore some techniques you can use to analyze the EJB-specific performance of your applications. Using a couple of common examples, we will demonstrate how you can set up your own tests to analyze your specific application components.

EJB 3 Performance and Testing

As developers, we are always trying to find the most efficient way to write code that delivers the highest performance. Over the years, we have learned that some of the assumptions we make are not always right and that certain programming models and techniques we use do not achieve the expected performance. The surprise here is that most of the time our expectations are defeated with models and techniques that our logic and gut feelings tell us are best.

Performance of computer systems is a very complex issue. Just think about the following: We are programming a piece of Java code that takes advantage of an infrastructure called Java Enterprise Edition (Java EE), which happens to run on top of a Java Virtual Machine (JVM). The virtual machine is hosted on an operating system, which runs on a computer that interacts with other computers using networks composed of hardware and software components. Each of these layers—the network, the computer, the operating system, the JVM, and the Java EE server—has a number of knobs that can be used to configure and optimize behavior. Each of them will present a different behavior under various usage conditions, which will inevitably impact the behavior of the other layers. Within this rather complex context it becomes a little easier to understand why our logic will not always work.

The bottom line is that we just cannot generalize when making performance statements. The only way that we can find out what performance to expect from our system is to test it in conditions as close as possible to the ones in which the code will run when in the production environment.

Every software application is unique. In order to understand the performance of your own application, you must test it yourself, according to your own definition of performance. In some situations, good performance will mean the ability to support a large number of users; in others (e.g., when the user load is small), it will simply mean being able to run as fast as possible.

In this chapter, we describe a methodology that you can use to test the performance of your systems in a consistent way. We also present tools that you can use to conduct these tests. Finally, we carry out a performance test to illustrate the methodology and the usage of the tools. The methodology and toolkit are useful in two basic situations:

- Performance testing a complete application

- Designing for performance (examining the performance costs of various aspects of the Java EE API and how certain design decisions will impact overall performance)

In the first scenario, we treat the application like a black box. We test the application under various user loads and investigate the performance of every request made by the users. The data is analyzed—requests that don't meet the required criteria are looked for, and opportunities for improving performance are identified.

While the aforementioned is useful, our advice is to performance test as early in the development cycle as possible. This way, you can use the methodology and the data you obtain from it to help you design for performance, rather than performance testing after the fact.

The example presented in this chapter focuses on designing for performance, rather than testing a complete application. If you are interested in learning more about the methodology of testing an application and performance testing in general, you can refer to *J2EE Performance Testing with BEA WebLogic Server,* by Peter Zadrozny (Apress, 2003). In this chapter, we present an adaptation of the methodology presented in the aforementioned book, which is narrowly focused on the example at hand.

The Testing Methodology

The focus of the testing methodology is consistency of data measurement. The following list gives a high-level overview of the steps that are involved in the methodology. We present them and describe them in the logical order in which they will be carried out when performing each test:

1. Define the performance criteria. We must define the relevant performance metrics for the specific application in question, and set a realistic target for that metric (e.g., a maximum acceptable response time).

2. Accurately simulate the application usage. The key aspect of this is the definition of the test scripts. These are configuration files that contain a set of requests that represent typical usage profiles of the application.

3. Define the test metrics. These include the duration of the tests, the size of the sample, the amount of initial data to exclude, and others.

4. Perform the tests.

Performance Criteria

Depending on the type of application, your focus will vary between two basic performance indicators: response time and throughput.

When working with synchronous interactive applications, we define a maximum acceptable response time. This is the maximum amount of time we are willing to wait before we get a response from the application.

For a batch or back-end application, we define the minimum acceptable throughput, typically as transactions per second (TPS)—but this has to be based on a solid understanding of exactly how a transaction will be defined in your system.

Each of these metrics is inextricably linked to one another; however, we have not been able to find any mathematical or geometrical relation between them.

Our advice is to define your performance metrics clearly and unambiguously, and to test to well-defined requirements. Not doing so is an open invitation to test and tune endlessly.

As we will be collecting data during the performance test runs, we need to have a clear understanding of the basic statistics, so let's examine them in more detail.

For the purposes of this book, we define *response time* as the length of time a client has to wait from the moment it sends a request to the moment it receives the last byte of the response from the application.

The sets of data that we collect from a performance test run consist of the individual response times of every request that makes up the test script. Each request in a test script is executed one after another, by each simulated user for a certain period of time. Our base measurement of analysis is the arithmetic mean of the response times for all users of a particular request: the average response time (ART).

Aggregate average response time (AART) is a measurement that we use extensively when analyzing performance data, and we define it as the sum of the ARTs of every individual request in a test script, divided by the number of requests in that test script.

Admittedly, AART has no real meaning in terms of how an application is performing, but it does provide an excellent indicator of how loaded the whole system is. As such, we sometimes refer to this measurement as the *load factor*. A typical AART curve when plotted against the number of simultaneous users looks as presented in Figure 9-1.

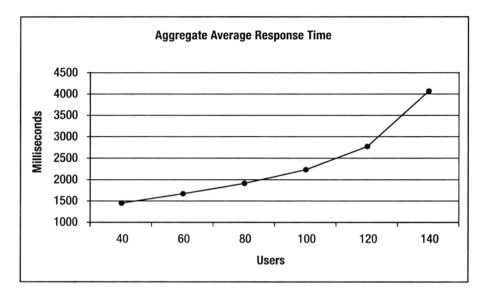

Figure 9-1. *A typical AART curve*

Throughput is not a clear-cut metric in the same way as response time. The standard way of expressing throughput is in TPS, and it is vital to understand what a transaction represents in the application being tested. It might be a single query or a specific group of queries. In a messaging system, it might be a single message; and in a servlet-based application, it might be a request. Even when there is consensus as to exactly what is being measured, the values obtained for throughput can often be misinterpreted. The reason for this is that many people regard this metric in much the same way as they regard "miles per hour": as a measurement of speed. In fact, throughput is a measure of capacity.

We can attempt to explain how throughput works in terms of a supermarket analogy. Imagine that a supermarket runs a promotion whereby ten shoppers will get for free everything they can put in their shopping carts in 15 minutes. The supermarket is the application, the shoppers are analogous to the requests (or messages), and the super-market staff that are restocking the shelves are analogous to the components of your system that are working to cope with the demand.

Even if all ten shoppers reach capacity (by completely filling their carts in 15 minutes), it doesn't necessarily mean that they've taken everything available in the supermarket. However, as we increase the number of shoppers, we will reach a point at which there are enough shoppers to empty the supermarket in that time. This point is the throughput capacity of the supermarket—the point of saturation. As we increase the number of shoppers beyond this point, we reach a point at which crowding in the aisles causes reduced shopper mobility (longer response times) and, ultimately, an actual drop in throughput.

Similar to ART, our base measurement of analysis is the arithmetic mean of the requests per second for all users of a particular request. We call this TPS.

For the purposes of analyzing performance data, and independently of the definition of throughput used for a specific performance test, we use the concept of total transactional rate (TTR). TTR is the addition of the TPS measurements of each request in a test script. TTR provides us with an excellent indicator of system capacity. Figure 9-2 shows a typical TTR curve, which reaches the point of saturation at about 100 users. At that point, it starts dropping (due to, e.g., too many shoppers).

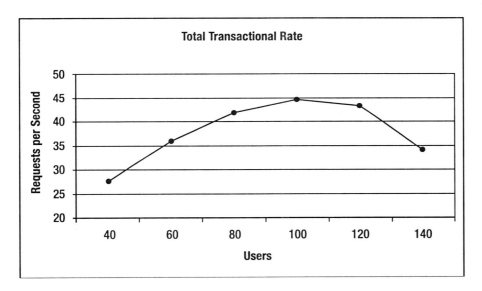

Figure 9-2. *A typical TTR curve*

The AART curve presented in Figure 9-1 is the result of data collected from the same test run as the TTR curve presented in Figure 9-2. If you review the AART curve, you can see that the response time increases in a linear fashion until it reaches 100 users. After that, the increase is more dramatic. This coincides with the TTR curve, in which the saturation point is reached at 100 users. After that, the performance of the application in general degrades. Analyzing these two curves, you can state that the application has an upper limit of 100 users under the conditions of the performance test.

Simulating Application Usage

The objective of this section of the methodology is to ensure that we are collecting our performance data in test conditions that mimic reality as closely as possible. This applies more so when performance testing whole applications, and less so when designing for performance.

For every application, there will be a number of different profiles of use that will be run concurrently. Sometimes, we will be able to simulate usage with a single test script and a single request. In other cases, it can take a dozen or so profiles, each with a different amount of requests.

A special note has to be made regarding *think time*. Also known as sleep time, this is the amount of time that elapses between the executions of each individual request in a test script. In real life, think time can be highly variable. It can be as little as a few seconds (e.g., when clicking a button that will take us to the next page), or as much as 5 to 10 minutes (e.g., when examining the transactions we made in our bank account over the last month). For the performance tests, we have adopted two basic strategies:

- *Using the real think time*: This case is used when doing a performance test of a complete, working application.

- *Using zero think time*: This case is used when performing more general investigative measurements, such as comparing programming techniques. The consequence of this is that we are not testing under realistic conditions. However, we can perform accurate comparative measurements, and once we have chosen the best scenario from these results, we can then perform tests with realistic think times.

Defining Test Metrics

The methodology is based on using a fixed number of users per test run. A performance test is made up by a number of test runs, usually increasing the user load with each subsequent test run. Some people are interested in ramping up the number of users during a single test run. We believe that this introduces a new variable that can have negative effects on the results, and is statistically incorrect from the standpoint of finding a maximum user load.

The first step is finding a representative number of simultaneous users (the lower limit) that can be increased in a regular fashion until reaching the saturation point of the application (the upper limit). We typically have a couple of additional test runs over the upper limit, just to better understand the behavior (or misbehavior) of the application.

Unfortunately, there is no exact science to choosing the upper limit up front. We usually select a random number of users and perform a couple of test runs in which the number of users is higher and lower than that initial random choice, and analyze the results to determine the direction we should go—either increasing or decreasing the number of users.

The second step is defining the sample size—that is, the length of time for which the test run will execute. To choose the actual sample size, we have to reach a compromise between two divergent interests. The first is that we want to have enough data so that the sample is statistically significant. The second is the desire to make the tests as short as possible, since we will have many test runs to do, and we don't want to spend too much time on them.

To figure out the sample size, we perform a test run using the upper limit of users, for a longer-than-usual period of time. We then plot the AART against time and analyze the curve. We are looking for a segment of the curve that is pretty much stable.

Another point that has to be made is that of data exclusion. When you first start a test, the response times are usually higher than normal. This is because all the subsystems that make up the application take a little while to get up to speed. For example, the optimizer in the JVM needs a couple of minutes to optimize the running code. The same goes for the cache of the database, which will take a little time before it is useful (and so on with other components of the application).

These unusually high response times that are seen initially only affect the first few users on a production application that will typically run for weeks. However, in our case, in which we will be testing for just a few minutes, these results will negatively skew our sample results. Because of this, we exclude the first few sets of data we collect, and start the sample when the curve has stabilized.

Thus, the sample size will start at a certain time after the actual test run has started, and will last for a certain period that provides us with enough data to deem it statistically significant.

Next is the issue of assessing the accuracy of the test results. Depending on the kind of performance test that is being conducted, you can use two different ways to measure accuracy with a high level of certainty.

For performance tests that deal with a complete application, we usually calculate the following metric, which we call the *quality of a sample*:

- quality = standard deviation / arithmetic mean

We usually apply this formula to the AART data collected.

▓**Tip** Based on our experience, acceptable quality numbers lie in the range of 0.06 to 0.2. When the quality number exceeds 0.25, we carefully analyze all the available data to find out the reason for such a low-quality sample. Sometimes, this can lead us to discard the data generated by the test run in question.

When doing tests focused on designing for performance—and more specifically, when the think time is zero—we use another method, called *calibration*. Here, we perform three test runs with the upper limit of users. We then compare the AART and TTR results of each test run against each other. The comparison is done as a percentage, and the greatest difference of all values is taken as the margin of error for the performance test.

Now that we have described all the preparation work, we can move on to describe the actual test runs that will provide us with the data that we need to perform the analysis and make the conclusions of the performance test. The actual test runs are rather mechanical and boring procedures, in which you start with a test run using the lower limit of users, increase the number of users, perform another test run, and so on, until you reach the upper limit. As mentioned earlier, you will probably want to have a couple of additional test runs in which the upper limit is exceeded.

Because the base of the methodology is consistency, you will have to reset or restart every component or subsystem that makes up the application. In our case, that will be the database and the Java EE server.

We will go over a practical example of implementing the methodology later in this chapter to illustrate how to use it.

The Grinder

The Grinder (http://grinder.sourceforge.net) is a Java-based load-testing framework that is freely available under a BSD-style open source license. The Grinder is extremely powerful, yet it's easy to use and is a lightweight toolkit. It allows you to simulate users and behaviors via test scripts across a number of machines. It consists of the following:

- A worker process, which interprets the test scripts written in Jython and performs the tests using a number of worker threads, each of which simulates a user.

- An agent process, which manages the worker processes. If you are running the simulated users on more than one computer, you will need one agent process for every computer.

- The console, which collates and displays statistics while coordinating the other processes.

A *performance test* using The Grinder is a collection of *test runs,* which can include one or more *test scripts*. A test run is the continuous sequential execution of test scripts. The test runs can last either a specific number of cycles or a specific period of time. A *cycle* is a single execution of a test script.

▨**Note** What we call a *cycle* is defined in the documentation of The Grinder as a *run,* which we find confusing.

Test scripts are used to simulate the application usage. Test scripts represent the usage profiles you want to simulate. A test script contains one or more *requests,* which resemble the typical interaction that a user of a specific profile would have with the application.

■**Note** Again, to avoid confusion, we use the word *request* instead of *test,* as defined in the documentation of The Grinder.

A Grinder test script is a Jython program, which can contain certain logic to modify the default behavior, which is the sequential execution of the requests (e.g., to execute certain requests based on the response of an already executed request).

A test script can be written by hand, or, if the simulated user interacts with the application via an HTML interface, it can be recorded. This can be done by using the TCP Proxy module, which is part of the Grinder distribution. The HTML plug-in filter of the proxy allows your interaction with an application through a web browser to be recorded. For details on how to use this functionality, please refer to the documentation.

In addition to executing URLs, The Grinder can also execute Java code as part of a request in a test script. This gives you the flexibility of simulating heavy clients, such as Swing-based clients.

Each agent process sets up a connection with the console to receive commands (such as start, stop, and reset), which it passes on to its worker processes. Each worker process sets up a connection to the console to report statistics.

In addition to the statistics presented on the console, for each test run, every worker process writes logging information and a final statistics summary to a file with a name that starts with the word out. Errors are written to a file with a name that starts with the word error. If no errors occur during a test run, no error file will be created. Detailed statistical information for every request executed is written to a file with a name that starts with the word data. These files follow a naming convention that, in addition to the words we described, also contain the name of the computer hosting the worker process and the number of the working process, as you can have more than one.

The behavior of The Grinder can be easily altered by modifying values in the configuration file, called grinder.properties. Very likely, the most common properties you will be modifying are the following:

- grinder.threads: This property specifies the number of simulated users that will execute the specified test script.

- grinder.runs: This property specifies the number of times a simulated user will sequentially execute the test script (cycles). If the value is zero, it will execute forever.

- grinder.consoleHost: This is the name or IP address of the computer running the Grinder console.

- `grinder.logProcessStreams`: Set to `true`, this property will provide extremely detailed information about the execution of every simulated user. This information appears in the `out` file. It is useful during the preliminary runs, but we strongly suggest that you set it to `false` for all the other runs, as it will degrade the performance of the test runs.

- `grinder.logDirectory`: This property specifies the directory in which you want to place the three log files described earlier.

- `grinder.script`: This is the file name of the test script to be executed.

There are many more properties available. Please consult the documentation for a full list of them.

The Grinder, along with its source code, documentation, ancillary modules, test scripts, and much more, can be found at `http://grinder.sourceforge.net`. There are also some mailing lists that you can join in order to participate in the Grinder community.

The Test Application

The test application that we have used for performance testing is a subset of the integrated Wines Online back-end application developed in Chapter 7. The user interface is developed using JavaServer Faces (JSF). Figure 9-3 shows the JSF page, which shows the list of all available wines in a list box. Users can a select wine items of their choice, enter the quantity in the input text box, and click the Add to Cart button. Users can repeat the same process to add more wines, and finally click the Submit Order button.

Figure 9-4 shows the interaction between the JSF application and the back-end wine store application. When the JSF application is launched from the browser, a call to the `getWineDisplayList()` method (which uses an injected `EntityManager` in the managed bean) is made. This gets a list of all available wines using the named query `findAllWine()`. The initial JSF page displays the retrieved list of wines. When the user adds a wine item and clicks the Add to Cart button, the `addWine()` method in the `ShoppingCart` session bean is invoked, which creates a new customer and adds the wine to the cart item of the customer. Adding a customer only happens when the `addWine()` item is called for the first time. When the user finally submits the order from the client application, the `process➥Order()` method in the `ShoppingCart` session bean is invoked, which creates a new customer order, adds all the cart items, deletes the items in the cart, and finally deducts the inventory.

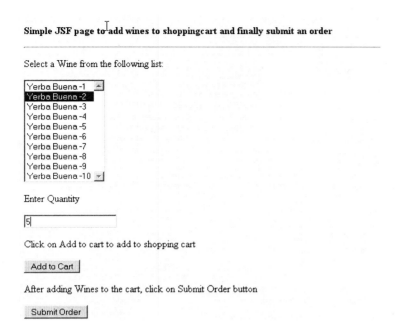

Simple JSF page to add wines to shoppingcart and finally submit an order

Select a Wine from the following list:

Enter Quantity

Click on Add to cart to add to shopping cart

Add to Cart

After adding Wines to the cart, click on Submit Order button

Submit Order

Figure 9-3. *The wine store JSF application*

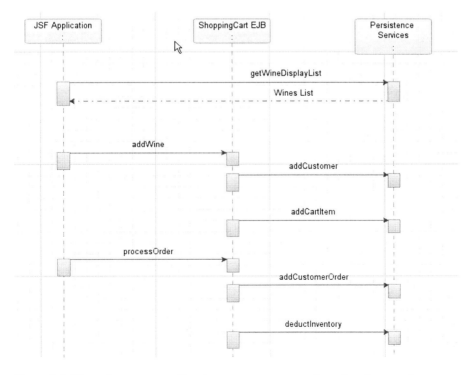

Figure 9-4. *The wine store application components and services interaction*

Figure 9-5 illustrates the Java Persistence API (JPA) entities, the inheritance model between the Java classes, and the relationships between them. The Customer entity is inherited by the Individual and Distributor entities. The InventoryItem, CartItem, and OrderItem entities inherit the WineItem entity. The BusinessContact entity is inherited by the Supplier entity. The wine store persistence unit also contains different types of relationships between these entities (including one-to-one, one-to-many, and many-to-many) that are exercised in the test application. The mappings used in these entities were covered in Chapters 3 and 4.

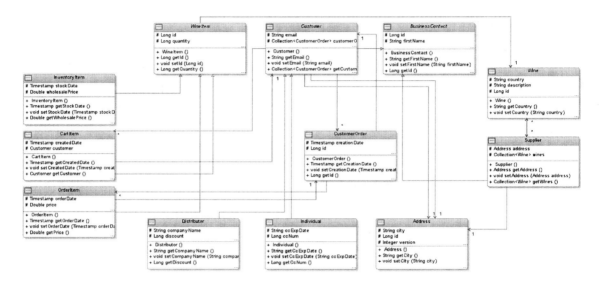

Figure 9-5. *The wine store persistence unit*

For the performance tests that we are going to run, all the previously discussed components (the JSF application, the ShoppingCart session bean, and the Java classes in the persistence unit) remain exactly the same. The only differences between the two tests are the object/relational (O/R) mapping annotations specified in the Java classes or JPA entities of the persistence unit, and the database schema that these Java classes are mapped to. The first test uses a JOINED entity inheritance strategy, in which the root entity maps to the root table in the hierarchy and the tables for all the subentities joined to that table. Figure 9-6 shows the database schema used for mapping the persistent Java classes using a JOINED inheritance strategy. In the second test, we use a SINGLE_TABLE entity inheritance strategy, in which all the entities in the class hierarchy map onto a single table, to map the persistent Java classes. Figure 9-7 shows the database schema that is used to map the second test case.

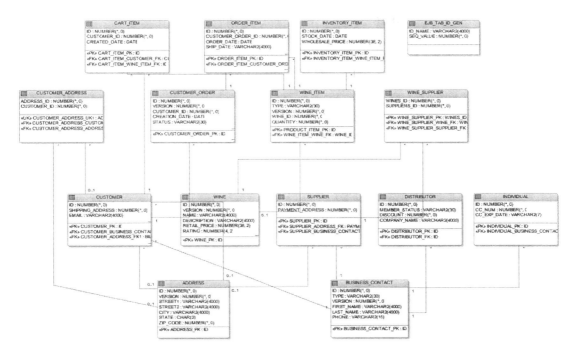

Figure 9-6. *The database schema for the JOINED entity inheritance strategy*

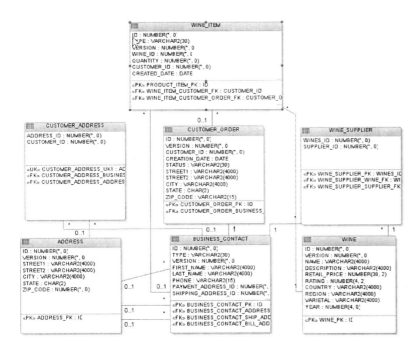

Figure 9-7. *The database schema for the SINGLE_TABLE entity inheritance strategy*

Note Inheritance strategies are explained in detail in Chapter 4.

The Performance Test

Following the methodology described earlier, and using the test program just described, we will get on with the task of comparing the inheritance models to find out which one is best under the following conditions.

The Test Environment

We have tried to mock up a typical distributed application production environment by separating the application components in different computers. Although the actual computers we use don't get close to what you will find in a real production environment, it will give you an idea of how you can set it up when it's your turn to do so. Having said that, we have been know to set up entire test environments on our laptops, just to gain a better understanding of the behavior of particular programming techniques rather simply and quickly.

Our test environment is based on four computers. The first one is designated to host the Java EE 5 server—we have named it GlassFish. The second computer is dedicated to run the database—we call it Oracle. The third computer, named Grinder, is the one on which The Grinder runs and creates the simulated load. The last computer in our environment, named Console, is the control center. This computer runs the Grinder console and collects all the data on this system.

The technical specifications of these computers and the network are presented in Table 9-1.

Table 9-1. *Test Environment Technical Specifications*

Computer	Specifications
GlassFish	Dell PowerEdge 750; Intel Pentium 4 at 2.8 GHz; 1 GB of memory; Linux ES 3.0; Java 1.5.0_05-b05
Oracle	Dell Latitude D810; Intel Pentium M at 2.13 GHz; 2 GB of memory; Windows XP Service Pack 2
Grinder	Dell PowerEdge 750; Intel Pentium 4 at 2.8 GHz; 1 GB of memory; Linux ES 3.0; Java 1.5.0_05-b05
Console	Dell Latitude X1; Intel Pentium M at 1.10 GHz; 1.24 GB of memory; Windows XP Service Pack 2
Network	Foundry Networks FastIron Edge 4802; 100 Mbps

These computers only run the corresponding software required for the tests, besides the default processes of the operating systems. The network is isolated, so the only traffic is that generated by the tests themselves.

For these tests, we used the GlassFish project, version 1, b40 promoted build, from March 8, 2006. Needless to say, this is a beta-quality server, and as such the primary focus is product stability, not performance. For the rest of the software components, we used The Grinder, version 3.0, beta 28; and the Oracle9*i* database, release 2 (9.2). We used the default settings on all the software. We realize that better performance can be obtained by fine-tuning these components, but that would be out of the scope of this book.

The Test Script

As mentioned earlier in this chapter, the idea is to create a test script that resembles as closely as possible the usage of the application in real life. Since this is a design-for-performance test, we use a test script that loosely resembles the typical usage profile of the application:

1. The user goes to the wine application web site (home).

2. The user selects a couple of bottles of one type of wine.

3. The user selects a few bottles of another type of wine.

4. The user checks out.

Since, in this example, we are comparing a couple of different inheritance models to understand which one applies best to our circumstances (design for performance), we use a zero think time.

Admittedly, tuning the database can have a major impact on the results, but that is out of the scope of this book and the reason that we use installation default values for all the software components in these tests. Also, the reality is that in a corporate environment, it is rather difficult to convince a database administrator to tune a database for one particular application when many others are using it.

The TCP Proxy module generates two files that contain Jython code. The first one has a `.py` extension, contains a high-level flow of the recorded tests, and is easily readable by humans. It is with this particular file that we interact the most. This is the file that allows us to remove the `grinder.sleeptime` directives to eliminate the think time, or change the name or IP address of the target machine running the application. The second file contains all the gory details that would make the first file unreadable. For this file's naming convention, `_tests` is appended to the file name and the `.py` extension is maintained. We review in detail the actual `wine.py` test script in the next section.

Setup

The installation of GlassFish was explained in the "Getting Started" section of Chapter 1, so we won't go over that here. You just need to make sure that the GlassFish server is up and running, and that the application is deployed with the necessary resources (JDBC connection pool and resource). One way to start the GlassFish server is to change directories to %GLASSFISH_HOME%/bin in a command shell and issue the following command:

asadmin start-domain

To stop the GlassFish server, you issue the following command:

asadmin stop-domain

The Database

Regarding Oracle, we will assume that you have it available somewhere in your network, as explaining how to install it would yield another book in itself. We do provide a set of scripts for creating and resetting the tables and associated data required for the performance test. These scripts can be found in the download package as a zipped file in the sqlscripts directory. We installed these scripts on the Oracle machine, in the D: drive, under the ejb3book\sqlscripts directory. From there, we start SQL*Plus and then execute the reset script, as shown in Figure 9-8.

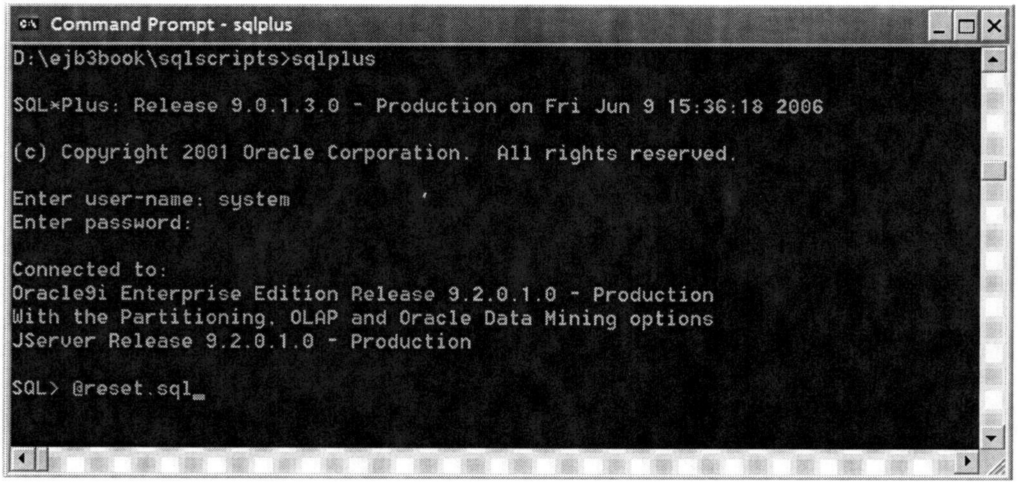

Figure 9-8. *Resetting the database*

When you execute this script, you will see a lot of lines scrolling in the window, some of them displaying messages such as "table altered" and "1 row created." At the end, you will see "Commit complete" and the SQL*Plus prompt SQL>. This means that the database reset is complete. This script basically drops or deletes the tables, creates them again, and populates them with the required data.

The Grinder

The next step is to install The Grinder on the computer dedicated to creating the simulated user load. Once you have downloaded The Grinder from http://grinder. sourceforge.net, all you have to do is unzip it in the desired directory. We installed it in the data1/grinder directory. Once you've that done, you can extract the Grinder-related files from the download package. These are in the grinder directory. We installed these files in the data1/ejb3book directory. There are four files: go, grinder.properties, wine.py, and wine_tests.py. The last two files are the actual test scripts.

Let's start by reviewing the first script, grinder.properties, shown in Listing 9-1.

Listing 9-1. *grinder.properties*

```
# Beginning EJB 3
# Chapter 9: EJB 3 Performance and Testing

# The number of worker processes
grinder.processes=1

# Number of simulated users
grinder.threads=140

# Run forever
grinder.runs=0

# Name of the machine where the console runs
grinder.consoleHost=Console

# We don't want a full detailed log file
grinder.logProcessStreams=false

# Place the log files in this directory
grinder.logDirectory=log
```

```
# Start all the simulated users at the same time
grinder.initialSleepTime=0

# Execute the test script called wine.py
grinder.script=wine.py
```

The comments in this properties file are pretty clear. You will just be changing the number of simulated users (`grinder.threads`) and the number of cycles that the test script has to run (`grinder.runs`). Just make sure that you have the correct name or IP address of the machine on which the Grinder console will be running. Other than that, you really don't need to change anything else in this properties file.

The Test Script

We had a problem with the recorded test script contained in the `wine.py` file related to the use of JSF. The issue was that JSF uses a session token that identifies the view. This value must be resubmitted to the server with the POST operation. We needed to replace the value that was recorded with the actual value returned when the view was last rendered. Interestingly enough, we found that the value was returned in the previous GET as a hidden parameter. To solve this issue, we wrote the Jython function shown in Listing 9-2, which is used throughout the test script.

Listing 9-2. *JSF View Identifier Routine*

```
def getViewState(response):
  key = 'id="javax.faces.ViewState" value="'
  start = response.index(key) + len(key)
  end = response.index('"', start)
  return response[start:end]
```

We edited the recorded test script, in which we added the function and the calls to it, and removed the think times between every request. After this, the test script (`wine.py`) looks like Listing 9-3.

Listing 9-3. *Test Script*

```
test0Response = tests[0].GET('http://glassfish:8080/wineapp/faces/winestore.jsp')

viewState = getViewState(test0Response.text)
test1Response = tests[1].POST('http://glassfish:8080/wineapp/faces/winestore.jsp',
    ( NVPair('_id_id17:selectOneListbox1', '2'),
```

```
        NVPair('_id_id17:_id_id40', '5'),
        NVPair('_id_id17:_id_id46', 'Add to Cart'),
        NVPair('javax.faces.ViewState', viewState),
        NVPair('_id_id17', '_id_id17'), ))

viewState = getViewState(test1Response.text)
test2Response = tests[2].POST('http://glassfish:8080/wineapp/faces/winestore.jsp',
    ( NVPair('_id_id17:selectOneListbox1', '5'),
      NVPair('_id_id17:_id_id40', '2'),
      NVPair('_id_id17:_id_id46', 'Add to Cart'),
      NVPair('javax.faces.ViewState', viewState),
      NVPair('_id_id17', '_id_id17'), ))

viewState = getViewState(test2Response.text)
tests[3].POST('http://glassfish:8080/wineapp/faces/winestore.jsp',
    ( NVPair('_id_id17:selectOneListbox1', '5'),
      NVPair('_id_id17:_id_id40', '2'),
      NVPair('_id_id17:_id_id51', 'Submit Order'),
      NVPair('javax.faces.ViewState', viewState),
      NVPair('_id_id17', '_id_id17'), ))
```

You can see that Test 0 calls the application (home). In Test 1, we select five bottles of wine 2; while in Test 2, we select two bottles of wine 5. Finally, Test 3 submits the order.

Running the Simulated Users

You will have to modify the next script according to where you installed the Grinder software. This is the one that we use to start the test run go. It is a very simple shell script that contains the following command:

```
java -classpath /data1/grinder/lib/grinder.jar net.grinder.Grinder
```

The Grinder Console

The final step in this setup process is installing The Grinder in the computer that will act as the control center. In our case, it's the Console computer into which we unzip the Grinder package. We do this in the C:\grinder directory. To start the console, all we do is change the directory to C:\grinder\lib, and issue the following command to bring up the console:

```
java -classpath grinder.jar net.grinder.Console
```

When you execute the go script, it will start the Grinder agent process and wait for a start signal from the console. Then click the Grinder console's start button. Figure 9-9 shows what a typical session on the Grinder computer looks like, and Figure 9-10 shows what the data collected on the Grinder console looks like.

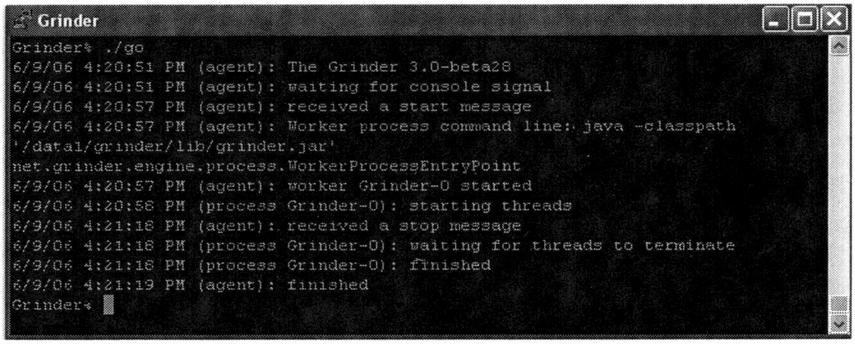

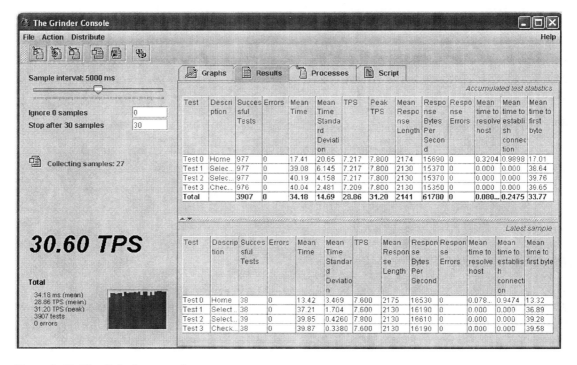

Figure 9-9. *A Grinder computer session*

Figure 9-10. *The Grinder console*

Just to make sure that things are working fine, go ahead and do a quick test with only one simulated user for one cycle. The steps are as follows:

1. Reset the database.

2. Verify that the GlassFish server is up and running with the application deployed with the necessary resources (JDBC connection pool and resource).

3. Start the Grinder console.

4. Edit the `grinder.properties` file and verify that you have only one user and one cycle.

5. Execute the `go` script to start the test run.

6. Click the start button on the Grinder console. No results will be displayed on the console because it will run for only one cycle.

7. Review the window on the Grinder computer. When it states that it has finished and is waiting for the console signal, click the stop button on the Grinder console.

8. On the Grinder computer, review the file that starts with the word `out`. This file contains a summary of the whole test run, including statistics. If there is a problem, this file and the error file will provide you with the necessary information to solve it.

Now that everything is set and ready, you can go on to the next step.

Preliminary Tests

The objective of this first set of tests is to get familiar with the application and its behavior, as well as discover any potential problems we might have with the test script or the application. As we're testing two different implementations of inheritance, it really doesn't matter which implementation we use for these preliminary tests, so we choose to conduct our initial tests with the implementation that uses multiple tables. We already performed one test run with one user for one cycle. Now we can move on to a test run for unlimited cycles and let it run for a couple of minutes. Then we'll move on to test with multiple simultaneous users for one cycle. This is done to make sure that the application and the test script can handle concurrency correctly. We will typically choose ten users. After that, we'll test ten users for unlimited cycles for a couple of minutes. Once these tests have completed successfully, we'll know that the test script and application are working fine, and we'll be ready for the next step.

We're looking to select a representative number of users for about half a dozen quick test runs that can clearly show us how the application behaves as we increase the user load.

When dealing with performance tests of full applications, we typically look for the upper limit of users when the maximum acceptable response time is reached or exceeded. Since this is a design-for-performance test, and we are not using any think time in the test script, we are going to focus on finding the number of users for which the saturation point of the application is reached. The strategy, as much as it can be called that, is to pick a number of users at random.

The test runs are short, since we don't need an exact upper limit number—just an approximation. In this case, we choose to start with 100 simultaneous users, and will collect data from the test runs for 2.5 minutes. Since we are using a sample interval of 5 seconds, we just type **30** in the Grinder console's "Stop after samples" box. To keep things simple, we will not exclude the initial data. We do this by typing **0** in the Grinder console's "Ignore samples" box. The collected statistics will present values that are a little higher than normal. This is not an issue, as these tests are just preliminary. Additionally, we don't even bother in resetting the database and restarting the GlassFish server.

We start our first test run and obtain an AART of 2,469 milliseconds.

Note You can find this information on the bottom part of the left column of the console (to the left of the square that graphically presents the TPS).

The TTR is 39.70 (you can find this information in the same place you found the AART). Next, we will try with 120 users. For this, we modify the grinder.properties file by changing the grinder.threads property to 120. We perform the next run and obtain an AART of 3,085 milliseconds and a TTR of 37.56. As the TTR for 120 users is lower than that for 100 users, we know that the saturation point is at 100 or fewer users, so our next test run will be with 80 users.

After changing the number of users in the grinder.properties file, we start the test run. We obtain an AART of 2,083 milliseconds and a TTR of 38.16. These results indicate that the saturation point is around 100 users. (Talk about a lucky guess in choosing 100 users as the initial test point.)

Based on this information, we choose to select 40 users as the lower limit and 100 users as the upper limit. The test runs will be done with 40, 60, 80, 100, 120, and 140 users. This will provide us with six reference points, which should clearly show us the behavior of the application.

Sample Size

Now that we have chosen the upper and lower limits of simultaneous users, we want to figure out how long the tests should run. This is rather simple—all we need to do is perform a test run that will execute for a longer period of time than the 2.5 minutes we chose earlier. Our experience with this kind of test tells us that about 7 minutes is typically a good choice. The test run will be performed with the upper limit, which is 100 users.

Once we have concluded the test run, we take the data file generated by The Grinder that contains the individual response times for every simulated user for every test. This file can be found in the log directory with a file name that starts with the word data. Next, using the pivot table feature of Excel, we plot a curve that presents the AART over the time period of the test. The results of this test run are presented in Figure 9-11. Here, we can see that the response time curve stabilizes at about 75 seconds into the test run. Building in some buffer time, we can conclude that it is fairly safe to exclude the first 90 seconds of the test runs.

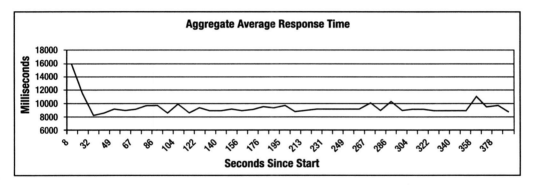

Figure 9-11. *Sample size analysis chart*

We can also see that the curve remains fairly stable after the 75-second mark. Our compromise (of divergent interests) is that we will use 150 seconds of data. Thus, the test runs will last 240 seconds (4 minutes—nice and short), of which we will ignore the first 90 seconds.

Calibration

Now we proceed to find out the accuracy of our performance test. Since this will be done based on three test runs using the upper limit, we only have to do two additional runs. We can use the appropriate data from the previous run to determine the sample size.

■**Tip** It has been our experience that typical margins of error using this method are between 5 and 10 percent. They tend to increase when there are think times in the test scripts—in these cases, it's not unusual to find numbers as high as 30 percent.

Tables 9-2 and 9-3 show the results collected from the test runs.

Table 9-2. *Margin of Error (AART)*

AART	Run 1	Run 2	Run 3
Run 1		101 percent	100 percent
Run 2	99 percent		100 percent
Run 3	98 percent	100 percent	

Table 9-3. *Margin of Error (TTR)*

TTR	Run 1	Run 2	Run 3
Run 1		99 percent	98 percent
Run 2	101 percent		99 percent
Run 3	102 percent	101 percent	

The biggest differences in these tables are 102 percent (run 3 vs. run 1 in the TTR table), and 98 percent (run 3 vs. run 1 in the AART table, and run 1 vs. run 3 in the TTR table). Thus, the official margin of error of this performance test is 2 percent, which is a rather good number.

The Actual Test Runs

Now that we have completed all the preparations, we are ready to start running the formal tests that will give us a picture as to which inheritance model behaves best under extremely stressful conditions.

This part of the performance tests is mechanical and rather boring. The initial step is to start the Grinder console and make sure that the parameters for our tests are set correctly. First, we verify that the sample interval is set to 5,000 milliseconds. Next, we check that we ignore 18 samples (of 5 seconds each, totaling the 90 seconds we chose earlier).

Then we choose to stop collecting data after 30 samples (of 5 seconds each, totaling the 150 seconds we chose earlier).

The steps to follow for each test run are as follows:

1. Stop the GlassFish server.

2. Reset the database.

3. Start the GlassFish server.

4. Edit the `grinder.properties` file and modify the number of users.

5. Start the Grinder computer, which starts the simulated users.

6. Click the "Start to capture statistics" button on the Grinder console. This will clear out all the results of the previous run.

7. Click the "Start processes" button on the Grinder console.

8. Wait for the data collection to complete. A good indicator is when the line on the center of the left panel goes from stating "Collecting samples: XX" in green to stating "Ignoring samples: XX" in red.

9. Click the "Stop processes" button on the Grinder console. This step actually stops the execution of the simulated users.

10. Click the "Save results" button. Provide a descriptive file name and save the results displayed on the console for later analysis.

11. Start over again at the beginning of this list.

Once you have finished with all the test runs for the JOINED table inheritance strategy, you can proceed to do all the preparations for the set of test runs for the SINGLE_TABLE inheritance scheme.

As explained in the earlier sections, the differences between our two tests are O/R mapping annotations and the database schema. Before running the second test using the SINGLE_TABLE inheritance strategy, we need to run the SQL scripts that will create a new schema in the Oracle database. We provide a set of scripts that will create and reset the tables and associated data required for the second performance test. These scripts can be found in the download package as a zipped file under the sqlscripts directory. We installed these scripts on the Oracle machine on the D: drive under the ejb3book\ sqlscripts\test2-st directory. From there, we need to start SQL*Plus and then execute the reset script.

Once the application is ready for the next set of test runs, just repeat the steps you did for the previous set of test runs.

Analyzing the Results

We have to start by stating that the results presented in this chapter are not meant to endorse one inheritance method over another. This is only for illustrating how to apply the methodology and use the Grinder toolkit. At the moment of this writing, the Glass-Fish server is a beta product, and as such the focus is on product stability and not performance. You will see some results that are questionable and for which we have no explanations. We are sure that they are caused by the nature of a beta product. Just out of curiosity, we did a few quick test runs with later versions of the GlassFish server, and noticed that performance in general had improved significantly. On the same token, we also found some later versions to simply crash at any attempt to run these tests.

Because of this, we have gone into this performance test with no expectations of which inheritance model will be better.

We start our analysis by reviewing the results of the test run of the multiple-table inheritance with 100 users. These are shown in Table 9-4.

Table 9-4. *Multiple-Table, 100-User Results*

100 Users	ART	TPS
Request 1	5720	11.11
Request 2	1124	11.17
Request 3	1131	11.20
Request 4	979	11.16
Total	2238	44.64

Two things quickly come to our attention. The first is that the time required to obtain the home page of the application was long—almost 6 seconds—especially when compared to all the other response times in the test script. This is one of those questionable results that we mentioned earlier. The next is that the checkout process lasts less than 1 second. While this is an ideal time for a process that verifies inventory and performs other actions associated with a checkout, it is curious in that it is considerably shorter than the previous two requests, which consist only of the selection of a product and its placement in the shopping cart. As mentioned earlier, even though the results are questionable, it is of interest to analyze them as we are doing now. If this were a production system, we would immediately begin focusing on understanding the reason for such a poor performance produced by the home page JavaServer Pages (JSP) code.

Looking at the results from the test run of the single-table inheritance model with 100 users (shown in Table 9-5), you can see a similar pattern of behavior, so at least it's consistent—except for the fact that the checkout process takes slightly longer that the selection requests.

Table 9-5. *Single-Table, 100-User Results*

100 Users	ART	TPS
Request 1	5917	10.33
Request 2	1251	10.22
Request 3	1276	10.23
Request 4	1313	10.31
Total	2439	41.09

This part of the analysis is limited to reviewing every individual request, and is usually done with the results collected from the test run with the upper limit of users. The next step is to analyze the AART and TTR for all the user loads that we selected. We start with the results from using the multiple-table inheritance model, which is shown in Table 9-6.

Table 9-6. *Multiple-Table, All-User Results*

Users	AART	TTR
40	1444	27.78
60	1674	35.78
80	1915	41.82
100	2238	44.64
120	2780	43.18
140	4045	34.22

From this table, it can be seen clearly that the saturation point is reached with 100 users. It's interesting to see that the AART increases at an average of 15 percent as the user load is increased. However, once the saturation point is reached, the AART grows rapidly, following an exponential pattern.

Let's review the results for the single-table inheritance model so that we can do some comparisons. They are presented in Table 9-7.

Table 9-7. *Single-Table, All-User Results*

Users	AART	TTR
40	1414	28.29
60	1522	39.50
80	1934	41.30
100	2439	41.09
120	3407	34.92
140	5807	24.19

The first thing we can see is that the single-table inheritance model has better overall performance with 40 and 60 users—particularly with the AART, as the times are lower and the difference is greater than the official performance test margin of error of 2 percent. Once we reach 80 users, things change in favor of the multiple-table inheritance model. Not only that, but the saturation point for the single-table inheritance model is at 80 users.

This comparison can be seen more clearly in the charts presented in Figure 9-12, which contains a comparison of both sets of results for the AART, and Figure 9-13, which contains the comparison for the TTR.

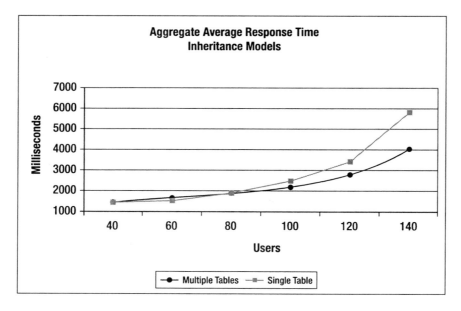

Figure 9-12. *AART comparison*

In Figure 9-12, the response time increases at a quicker rate for the single-table inheritance model than the multiple-table model.

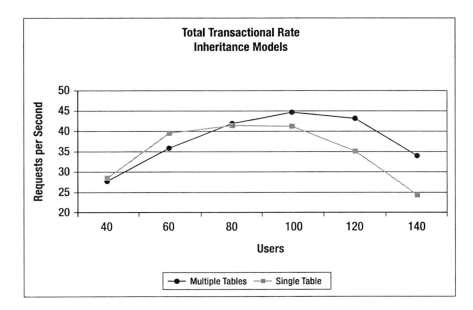

Figure 9-13. *TTR comparison*

In Figure 9-13, not only does the single-table model reach the saturation point faster than the multiple-table model, but saturation happens earlier than we would expect from looking at the data in the tables. With 60 users, the single-table model is only 5 percent away from saturation. The increase in TTR from 40 to 60 users is great; when looking only at this piece of data, one could conclude that it's working very well. However, since the increase takes the TTR to a point so close to saturation, it becomes obvious that it is deceiving.

Based on the data collected, we can conclude that the JOINED table inheritance model presents better performance under highly stressful conditions.

■**Note** The download package contains the spreadsheets with the collected data, chart, and pivot tables, which you can use as a template for you own performance tests.

Conclusion

In this chapter, we have presented The Grinder, a methodology to conduct performance tests, and a toolkit to generate the load for the performance tests. We went through an example of a performance test that used the methodology and the toolkit. In particular, we discussed performance criteria, with a review of the two performance indicators: response time and throughput. We covered the simulation of application usage, with a discussion about test scripts and think times. We also covered the defining of test metrics—such as number of users, sample size, and exclusion of data—as well as how to determine the accuracy of the performance test.

To illustrate the use of this methodology, we presented a detailed case study using the application we created in the previous chapters and compared two inheritance strategies.

In the next chapter, we will look into how you can migrate existing EJB applications that were developed with earlier versions of the specification to EJB 3.

CHAPTER 10

■■■

Migrating EJB 2.x Applications to EJB 3

Each new release of EJB has provided backward compatibility with EJBs written for earlier versions of the spec. Despite the many source-level changes introduced in EJB 3, this latest release is no exception. Your existing EJB 1.x or 2.x applications will run, unmodified, inside an EJB 3–compliant server. Even if you are not planning on modifying your existing EJB application, though, you may wish to migrate it to EJB 3 anyway to take advantage of the performance improvements offered by the new persistence framework. And if you do plan to modify your application, you can leverage the following new features as well:

- New ease-of-development programming model, which includes the following:

  - JDK 5.0 annotations may be used instead of, or in combination with, XML deployment descriptors.

  - The configuration-by-default model provides intelligent default values and reduces code clutter.

  - Home interfaces are no longer required.

  - EJB-specific component interfaces have been replaced by ordinary Java interfaces.

- Execution of entities in a pure Java SE environment, which simplifies unit testing.

- Interceptor method support, providing greater control during component life cycle events.

- Container injection of resources.

- Numerous improvements, simplifications, and wholly new features in the new Java Persistence API (JPA) entity model.

If you are introducing new EJBs into your existing application, note that there are some limitations on how legacy entity beans interact with JPA entities, so writing new EJBs to interact with legacy EJBs can present problems.

The changes introduced in EJB 3 greatly reduce application maintenance costs—and for a living, evolving application, it is likely that savings in source code maintenance, reliability, and even performance will overshadow the costs of the migration process itself. In any case, understanding the details of the transformation process is a requirement of evaluating the costs and benefits of an application migration project.

This chapter is all about how to transform your legacy source code into EJB 3 source so that you can take advantage of the benefits just outlined. While we will suggest options for you to consider once you have migrated your code to EJB 3, in general we will not delve into discussions of the many new features in EJB 3 that are not present in EJB 2.1, unless they are directly relevant to the migration process. Features that are wholly new to EJB 3 are covered elsewhere in the book. Since EJB 2.1 is, on the whole, a superset of EJB 2.x and 1.x, we will indirectly cover migration from these earlier EJB releases as well.

■**Note** At the time of writing, no known tools are available to assist in the process of migrating legacy 2.x source to EJB 3. Look for tools to assist in this process in the near future. Even so, it is unlikely that any tool will provide 100-percent migration automation free of user intervention, so it is good to familiarize yourself with the decisions that you'll have to make to manually migrate the more complicated pieces of your code. This chapter attempts to identify these sticky areas and help you through the process of migrating them manually.

Getting Started

To approach a migration task, we recommend that you iterate through your EJB modules and migrate them one EJB at a time. This process involves creating a new EJB 3 bean class to correspond with the EJB 2.1 one, and then transferring the metadata defined on both the EJB 2.1 bean class and the parts of the `ejb-jar.xml` file dedicated to that bean onto the EJB 3 bean or entity class. The sections that follow will guide you to migrate each of your EJB 2.1 beans according to their EJB type. A client migration section also covers migration of your client EJB usage code.

The final migration section in this chapter provides a sample migration scenario, showing a simple EJB 2.1 application consisting of the following:

- Two entity beans and their corresponding data transfer object (DTO) classes

- A session bean that serves as a façade over the entity beans and communicates their data to clients using the DTO classes

- A simple Java SE client that instantiates the session bean and performs some method calls that interact with the entity beans through their DTO classes

In addition, after migrating the application to EJB 3, we show the minimal steps that can then be applied to transform the migrated EJB 3 application so that it can run purely inside a Java SE environment. The session bean class is modified slightly to use an application-managed EntityManager instead of an injected container-managed EntityManager, and a new <persistence-unit> is defined, but the JPA entity classes remain unchanged.

Session Bean Migration

We begin with the basics of migrating an existing EJB 2.1 session bean to EJB 3, and then provide tables that explain how to map each EJB 2.1 metadata artifact onto its new location in an EJB 3 session bean class.

An EJB 2.1 session bean consists of a bean class, component and home interfaces, and an ejb-jar.xml file that captures its metadata. The EJB 2.1 bean class is required to implement the javax.ejb.SessionBean interface, providing concrete implementations of a number of methods that it may or may not ever use. Its component and home interfaces are required to extend EJB-specific interfaces. At a minimum, an EJB 2.1 session bean is spread out over these four source files, and you can have an additional component and home interface (if the session bean supports both local and remote usage), along with a platform-specific ejb-jar.xml file.

In EJB 3, resources can optionally be injected directly into the bean class by the EJB container, whereas in EJB 2.1, all resources have to be requested explicitly through a Java Naming and Directory Interface (JNDI) lookup.

Let's start by looking at just the session bean class.

EJB 2.1 Session Bean

As an example, we present in Listing 10-1 a minimal "Hello World" stateless session bean and its corresponding sections in the ejb-jar.xml file. In EJB 2.1, a session bean holds no significance without a corresponding section in its ejb-jar.xml file.

In the EJB 2.1 implementation, we can see that five EJB-specific methods must be implemented in an EJB 2.1 session bean class before it is ready to implement a single sayHello(String name) business method.

Listing 10-1. *HelloBean.java, EJB 2.1 Stateless Session Bean Class*

```
/**
 * HelloBean.java:  EJB 2.1 bean class for the Hello session bean
 */
public class HelloBean
  implements SessionBean
{
  private SessionContext _context;

  public void ejbCreate() { }
  public void setSessionContext(SessionContext context)
    throws EJBException { _context = context; }
  public void ejbRemove() throws EJBException { }
  public void ejbActivate() throws EJBException { }
  public void ejbPassivate() throws EJBException { }

  // Our 'sayHello()' business method
  public String sayHello(String name) { return "Hello " + name; }
}
```

EJB 2.1 ejb-jar.xml File

The ejb-jar.xml file shown in Listing 10-2 has two main sections that correspond to our Hello session bean: the <session> element that defines its basic metadata and a <container-transaction> element, inside <assembly-descriptor>, that declares the bean's transaction attribute properties. Other elements, like the <method-permission> properties, are not shown in this example, but their transformation process follows the same guidelines.

Listing 10-2. *ejb-jar.xml: Sections of the EJB 2.1 Deployment Descriptor Corresponding to the Hello Session Bean*

```
<enterprise-beans>
  ...
  <session>
    <description>Session Bean ( Stateless )</description>
    <display-name>Hello</display-name>
    <ejb-name>Hello</ejb-name>
    <home>com.apress.ejb3.ch10.ejb21.hello.HelloHome</home>
    <remote>com.apress.ejb3.ch10.ejb21.hello.Hello</remote>
```

```
      <ejb-class>com.apress.ejb3.ch10.ejb21.hello.HelloBean</ejb-class>
      <session-type>Stateless</session-type>
      <transaction-type>Container</transaction-type>
    </session>
    ...
  </enterprise-beans>
  ...
  <assembly-descriptor>
    ...
    <container-transaction>
      <method>
        <ejb-name>Hello</ejb-name>
        <method-name>*</method-name>
      </method>
      <trans-attribute>Required</trans-attribute>
    </container-transaction>
    ...
  </assembly-descriptor>
</ejb-jar>
```

As you can see, quite a bit of code is needed to capture the required metadata for our simple Hello session bean. Let's now take a look at our Hello session bean reimplemented in EJB 3.

EJB 3 Session Bean Class

The EJB 3 architects noted that much of this metadata can be derived by default, and following the configuration-by-exception philosophy, their work takes a sharp ax to this code. The result, shown in Listing 10-3, is consolidated into a single mean, lean bean class.

Listing 10-3. *HelloBean.java, EJB 3 Stateless Session Bean Class*

```
@Stateless(name = "Hello")
public class HelloBean
  implements Hello
{
  public String sayHello(String name) {
    return "Hello " + name;
  }
}
```

The minimum requirement for an EJB 3 session bean is a bean class that has been annotated `@Stateful` or `@Stateless`, depending on its session type. The remaining metadata in our example is either assumed by intelligent defaults, or, as in the case of the business interfaces, implicitly captured in the Java code itself. Of course, it is unlikely that your existing session beans are this simplistic, but this example gives you the flavor of a conversion.

We will now explore how the artifacts in an EJB 2.1 session bean class, and the properties in its `ejb-jar.xml` file, map to corresponding constructs in an EJB 3 session bean class. We start with the EJB 2.1 session bean class.

Migrating the EJB 2.1 Session Bean Class

Table 10-1 can be used to map EJB 2.1 session bean class artifacts onto EJB 3 session beans. When converting from EJB 2.1 to EJB 3, you can either update the EJB 2.1 source files in place or piece together new files.

Table 10-1. *Mapping EJB 2.1 Session Bean Class Artifacts onto EJB 3 Session Beans*

EJB 2.1 Session Bean Class Artifact	Corresponding EJB 3 Session Bean Construct
`implements javax.ejb.SessionBean`	EJB 3 session beans are not required to implement a special EJB interface. During migration, they must be annotated `@Stateless` or `@Stateful`, based on the `<session>` element's `<session-type>` child in the EJB 2.1 session bean's `ejb-jar.xml` file.
`create()/ejbCreate()` methods	Home and local home interfaces are not required for EJB 3 session beans, so these methods are typically no longer used. A stateless session bean must expose a public constructor that takes no parameters, but you would not typically put initialization code in a constructor. One must assume that the session instance might be pooled, so class-construction time does not necessarily correspond to session bean–creation time. To migrate, you can simply annotate the `ejbCreate()` method with the `@PostConstruct` annotation. This annotation indicates that the method it annotates (`ejbCreate()`, in this case) is to be treated as a life cycle callback interceptor method, and may be used to perform additional work immediately before the session bean instance is handed off to a client.
`ejbActivate()/ejbPassivate()` methods	These are replaced by `@PostActivate` and `@PrePassivate` life cycle callback methods.

EJB 2.1 Session Bean Class Artifact	Corresponding EJB 3 Session Bean Construct
`ejbRemove()` method	An EJB 3 session bean may expose one or more methods, annotated `@Remove`, that may be called by clients to remove the session bean instance. Calling one of these methods will remove the session bean instance once the method completes. To migrate an `ejbRemove()` method, you may be able to simply annotate the method `@Remove`, and change clients to call it directly instead of indirectly through the `EJBHome`. `remove()` method. In addition, one or more `@PreDestroy` life cycle callback interceptor methods may be used to perform any additional processing required prior to removing the session bean instance.
`setSessionContext()` method	In EJB 3, a `SessionContext` instance is injected into the session bean by the container, using `@Resource SessionContext ctx`; alternatively, it may be requested in the session bean code through a JNDI lookup.

Migrating the EJB 2.1 Session Bean Interfaces

EJB 2.1 session beans require separate home and component interfaces for remote and local access. EJB 3 doesn't require a home or local home interface. The `create()` and `remove()` methods that they expose for the `ejbCreate()` and `ejbRemove()` methods are covered in Table 10-1.

Note If you choose to expose a home interface on your EJB 3 stateful session bean, each `createXxx()` method defined on that home interface must be accompanied by a method on the bean class annotated `@Init` and containing the same method arguments as the `createXxx()` method.

To transform a remote component interface, remove the `implements EJBObject` clause and add the `@Remote` annotation to the interface. Also, remove `RemoteException` from the throws clause on each business method, since this usage has been deprecated. In EJB 3, `RemoteException` is reserved for system exceptions. Listing 10-4 shows `Hello.java`, the EJB 2.1 remote interface for our `Hello` session bean.

Listing 10-4. *Hello.java, an EJB 2.1 Remote Interface*

```
public interface Hello
  extends EJBObject
{
  String sayHello(String name)
    throws RemoteException;
}
```

Listing 10-5 shows this interface after transformation to EJB 3.

Listing 10-5. *Hello.java, an EJB 3 Remote Interface*

```
@Remote
public interface Hello
{
  String sayHello(String name);
}
```

To transform a local component interface, remove the `implements EJBLocalObject` clause and add the `@Local` annotation to the interface. Also, you may remove `EJBException` from the throws clause on each business method, unless your code explicitly throws this method. Outside of this case, since `EJBException` is a subclass of `RuntimeException`, it does not need to be declared.

Migrating the EJB 2.1 Session Bean ejb-jar.xml Properties

Now let's look at how the metadata defined in the `<session>` and `<assembly-descriptor>` elements in an EJB 2.1 `ejb-jar.xml` file can be transferred onto the EJB 3 session bean class. Since every piece of metadata on an EJB that can be expressed in JDK 5.0 annotations can also be expressed in an XML deployment descriptor, all of the EJB 2.1 descriptor properties listed in Table 10-2 can be left where they are, and the `ejb-jar.xml` file's XML header can simply be updated to point to the `ejb-jar_3_0.xsd` schema definition file. Nonetheless, should you wish to transfer these properties onto the session bean class, to take advantage of the features listed at the outset of this chapter, Table 10-2 lists the mappings for the `<session>` element.

Table 10-2. *Mapping EJB 2.1 Session Bean ejb-jar.xml session Properties onto EJB 3 Session Beans*

EJB 2.1 Session Bean ejb-jar.xml session Property	Corresponding EJB 3 Session Bean Construct
`<description>`	A session bean's description may alternatively be specified as a property of the `@Session` annotation `@Session(description="...")`.
`<display-name>`	There is no corresponding construct in EJB 3.
`<ejb-class>`	Marking a class `@Stateless` or `@Stateful` indicates that it is a bean class.
`<ejb-name>`	The EJB name may alternatively be expressed through the `@Session(name="...")` annotation property.
`<home>`	Home interfaces are optional in EJB 3, and typically used only to emulate EJB 2.1 behavior.
`<local>`	A session bean may expose one or more Java interfaces that are annotated `@Local` and provide local access to the EJB.
`<local-home>`	Local home interfaces are optional, and typically used only to emulate EJB 2.1 behavior.
`<remote>`	A session bean may expose one or more Java interfaces that are annotated `@Remote` and provide remote access to the EJB.
`<service-endpoint>`	A session bean may expose one or more web service endpoint interfaces, each annotated `@WebService`. It may also annotate the bean class with `@WebService`, bypassing the need to define a new interface for this purpose. As a further refinement, it may declare, using the `@WebMethod` annotation, which of its methods are to be exposed through the web service.
`<session-type>`	This property value determines whether the bean class is annotated `@Stateless` or `@Stateful`.
`<transaction-type>`	An EJB 3 session bean captures this value in the `@TransactionManagement(TransactionManagementType.CONTAINER)` or `@TransactionManagement➥(TransactionManagementType.CONTAINER)` class-level annotation.

Similarly, session bean properties in the `<assembly-descriptor>` section can generally be mapped to EJB 3 annotations. Note that cross-class metadata, such as global container transaction or method permission settings, is an exceptional case. Anything that spans more than one class can only be captured using an EJB 3 `ejb-jar.xml` file. For the majority of properties that do not fall into this category, though, Table 10-3 shows the mappings.

Table 10-3. *Mapping EJB 2.1 Session Bean ejb-jar.xml assembly-descriptor Properties onto EJB 3 Session Beans*

EJB 2.1 Session Bean ejb-jar.xml assembly-descriptor Property	Corresponding EJB 3 Session Bean Construct
`<container-transaction>`	Container transaction attributes are captured using the `TransactionAttribute` annotation (e.g., `@TransactionAttribute(TransactionAttributeType.SUPPORTS)`), either at the bean class level, at the method level, or both. Following the override rules in place for EJB 2.1, a transaction attribute defined on a method will take precedence, for that method, over the transaction attribute specified at the class level, if any is defined. In EJB 3, if no transaction attribute setting is in effect for a given method, its behavior defaults to `REQUIRED`.

Migrating an EJB 2.1 Web Service Endpoint Interface

As described in the `<service-endpoint>` entry in Table 10-2, there are several ways to declare web service support on an EJB 3 session bean. You can use the `@WebMethod` annotation on a bean class method; or you can use the `@WebService` annotation on one or more interfaces implemented by the bean class, or on the bean class itself.

In addition, whereas EJB 2.1 web services used JAX-RPC 1.1 and required `webservices.xml` and JAX-RPC mapping files, EJB 3 supports the new JAX-WS (Java API for XML Web Services) 2.0 standard. The EJB 2.1 web service endpoint interface for our `Hello` session bean is shown in Listing 10-6.

Listing 10-6. *HelloWebService.java, an EJB 2.1 Web Service Endpoint Interface*

```
public interface HelloWebService
  extends Remote
{
  String sayHello(String name)
    throws RemoteException;
}
```

The same interface, after transformation to EJB 3, is shown in Listing 10-7.

Listing 10-7. *HelloWebService.java, an EJB 3 Web Service Endpoint Interface*

```
@WebService
public interface HelloWebService
  extends Remote
{
  String sayHello(String name)
    throws RemoteException;
}
```

Session Bean Migration Wrap-Up

This section has covered the requirements for mapping EJB 2.1 session beans to EJB 3 session beans. The work required to do this is pretty straightforward. Migrating method body code to EJB 3 largely involves reworking the code for looking up entity beans and other session beans, and for changing code that uses find() and create() methods to instead use the EntityManager API, plain old Java object (POJO) constructors, and the like. This process does not fit so neatly into mapping tables; but we will cover this in the "End-toEnd EJB Application Migration Example" section of this chapter. This section will show how to transform an application consisting of a Java SE client talking to a session bean. In this application, the session bean interacts with entity beans through local interfaces and exposes the entity data to the client through DTO wrapper classes.

For now, let's continue exploring the essential migration mappings for message-driven beans (MDBs) and entity beans.

MDB Migration

MDBs are simpler beasts, and since session beans share much of their metadata, we refer you to the mapping subsections of the preceding "Migrating the EJB 2.1 Session Bean ejb-jar.xml Properties" section for their common properties. This section will cover metadata that is specific to MDBs.

As with session bean migration, the biggest differences between MDBs in EJB 2.1 and EJB 3 are dependency injection and the annotations that go with MDBs. You can use dependency injection in the MDB class to inject resources, instead of using JNDI lookup code. In EJB 3, MDBs do not have to implement the javax.ejb.MessageDrivenBean interface; they can instead be annotated with @MessageDriven. Resources and EJB references can be injected into MDBs in the same way as session beans. Similarly, you can inject the context (MessageDrivenContext for an MDB) into the MDB.

Table 10-4 illustrates the transformation of EJB 2.1 MDB metadata onto the EJB 3 MDB bean class. For more information on MDB properties, please see Chapter 5.

Table 10-4. *Mapping EJB 2.1 MDB Class Artifacts onto EJB 3 MDBs*

EJB 2.1 MDB Artifact	Corresponding EJB 3 MDB Construct
implements javax.ejb.MessageDrivenBean	EJB 3 MDBs are not required to implement a special EJB interface. During migration, they must be annotated @MessageDriven.
<activation-config>	This child element of <message-driven> maps to the activationConfig property of the @MessageDriven annotation.
<activation-config-property>	Each occurrence of this descriptor element maps to an @ActivationConfigProperty annotation property nested in the @MessageDriven annotation's activationConfig property.
<message-destination-name>	This element maps to an @Activation➥ConfigProperty instance whose propertyName property value is "destinationName".
<message-destination-type>	This element maps to an @Activation➥ConfigProperty instance whose propertyName property value is "destinationType".
<message-driven>	An alternative to using this descriptor element to identify an MDB is to use the @MessageDriven annotation on the MDB class.
<resource-ref>	Resources like EJBs and mail sessions have to be specified in the deployment descriptor. These resources may then be injected by the container, using an @Resource annotation, into the MDB.
setMessageDrivenContext() method	This method is used to assign a MessageDrivenContext. In EJB 3, the MessageDrivenContext may be acquired through dependency injection.

Entity Bean Migration

When migrating an EJB 2.x application to EJB 3, your entity bean migration will probably require the most work. One reason is that entity beans typically account for the majority of the metadata properties in the `ejb-jar.xml` file. Another is that in EJB 2.x, some of the most complex metadata required by entity beans—the object/relational (O/R) mapping metadata—has to be defined in platform-specific mapping files, since prior to EJB 3, O/R mapping details lay outside the realm of the EJB specification. We cannot cover in this chapter how to convert all the platform-specific O/R mapping formats into EJB 3 O/R annotations, but we will give you a taste of what is involved. Fortunately, from our experience, the mapping formats required by EJB 2.x entity bean vendors map pretty well onto JPA entity annotations—so once you've gotten the hang of it, you should find that things move pretty smoothly.

In Table 10-5, we provide mappings from EJB 2.x metadata captured in an entity bean class and its `ejb-jar.xml` file onto a JPA/EJB 3 entity class. Mappings that were covered in the session bean mapping tables have been omitted, since they apply equally to both entities and session beans. Note that in the "End-toEnd EJB Application Migration Example" section of this chapter, we will examine a simple application migration example that illustrates many of these mappings.

Table 10-5. *Mapping EJB 2.1 Entity Bean Class Artifacts onto EJB 3 Entities*

EJB 2.1 Entity Bean Artifact	Corresponding JPA/EJB 3 Entity Construct
`implements javax.ejb.EntityBean`	An entity class is annotated `@javax.persistence.Entity`.
EJB 2.1 entity bean (must be abstract)	An EJB 3 entity can be either abstract or concrete.
`<abstract-schema-name>` and `<ejb-name>`	In EJB 3, these collapse onto the same property, specified in the `@Entity(name="...")` annotation.
`<cmp-field>`	After transforming an EJB 2.1 entity bean class into a JPA entity class by adding the `@Entity` annotation, all public fields (exposed through public get/set methods) are assumed to be part of the persistent state of the entity. In EJB 2.1, container-managed persistence—including CMR (container-managed relationship)—fields are abstract, while in EJB 3 they are concrete, so you will need to add a default implementation for each one. Any public field that should be excluded from the entity's persistent state must be marked `@Transient`.

Continued

Table 10-5. *Continued*

EJB 2.1 Entity Bean Artifact	Corresponding JPA/EJB 3 Entity Construct
ejbCreate() methods	These initializer methods require corresponding ejbPostCreate() methods. Custom behavior surrounding these life cycle events are now handled through the @PrePersist and @PostPersist interceptor methods.
ejbLoad() and ejbStore() methods	In EJB 2.1, ejbLoad() and ejbStore() methods could be called to ensure cache consistency, as in preparation for query operations or prior to flushing an entity bean out to the database. In EJB 3, there is no direct correlation, but clients who call these methods should call EntityManager.refresh() and EntityManager.flush() instead. If the bean provider added custom code to these methods, they may also be annotated with one of the entity life cycle interceptor methods, depending on the specific behavior desired.
<ejb-relation>	Persistent relationship fields are identified in EJB 3 entities using the @OneToMany, @ManyToOne, @OneToOne, and @ManyToMany annotations. The new annotations for relationship fields are far more succinct, and are covered in Chapters 3 and 4.
<persistence-type> and <cmp-version>	In EJB 3, all entities use container-managed persistence, so these properties become obsolete. To emulate bean-managed persistence, you can simply use an ordinary POJO that manages its own data interaction with the database, using JDBC, for example.
<prim-key-class> and <primkey-field>	An entity may have either a simple primary key or a composite primary key. If simple, it is identified using the @Id annotation on the primary key field. This identifies both the primary key class type (the field's type) and the primary key field. If the entity has a composite key, the key class type is identified by the @IdClass annotation on the entity class. If the composite key is embedded, it is identified by the @EmbeddedId annotation. If the composite key is not embedded, then each of the fields that comprise the composite key is defined on the entity class, and each one is annotated @Id.

EJB 2.1 Entity Bean Artifact	Corresponding JPA/EJB 3 Entity Construct
`<query>`	Static queries in the JPA can now be defined using the `@NamedQuery` annotation on the entity itself (or any entity in the same persistence unit). Query parameters are embedded in the query statement, and so the `<method-params>` properties can be discarded.
`<reentrant>`	This has no direct correlate in EJB 3.

Once these transformations have been applied, you will need to annotate your entity classes with O/R mapping information. This metadata is captured in platform-specific metadata files, but typically specifies each entity's table and column mappings. Many of these mappings will follow default naming, which means that no annotation is required. Relationship fields are specified in JPA entities with `@JoinColumn` annotations, and collection relationship fields leverage JDK 5.0 generic collection types to specify the entity type at the other end of the relationship.

EJB 2.1 entity beans require local and/or remote interfaces; in EJB 3, this requirement is gone. JPA entities may implement interfaces, but the entity class itself is the principal object used in queries, relationships, and other contexts.

Finally, for EJB 2.1 container-managed persistence providers that support their own inheritance strategies, see Chapter 4 for details on how entity inheritance hierarchies may be mapped in EJB 3.

EJB Client Migration

In EJB 2.1, all EJBs were obtained through a two-stage process that involved acquiring an `InitialContext`, and then performing a JNDI lookup to obtain the EJB's home or local home interface, from which the client could obtain actual EJB instances. Let's look at how EJB 2.1 session bean clients typically operate.

Migrating an EJB 2.1 Session Bean Client

The client of an EJB 2.1 session bean typically takes one of two forms:

- A POJO class running in a Java SE environment, looking up a session bean through its remote interface

- A JSF-managed bean or another EJB, running in a Java EE environment, obtaining a session bean through a local interface

Either way, the client of an EJB 2.1 session bean must use JNDI to look up the EJB's home or local home interface, and create or query instances of that EJB using methods on that interface. Clients running outside the Java EE container must specify the details of the application server connection, by using either a `jndi.properties` file or by directly populating a `Hashtable` that is passed to the `InitialContext` through a constructor argument. The actual lookup of the EJB 2.1 session bean's home or local home interface may rely on an `<ejb-ref>` or `<ejb-local-ref>` definition, specified in a J2EE descriptor such as an `ejb-jar.xml` file, an `application-client.xml` file, or a `web.xml` file, to specify the session bean details.

Migrating an EJB 2.1 Java SE Client

In EJB 3, a session bean client running outside of a Java EE container will still need to acquire an `InitialContext` and use JNDI to look up the session bean, but it can look it up directly, without going through the intermediate step of obtaining the session bean's home interface. The result from the JNDI lookup is the EJB 3 session bean class itself, so it may be used directly, or cast to one of its implemented interfaces. In EJB 3, you may still use an `<ejb-ref>` element, except that the `<home>` property need not be specified.

Migrating an EJB 2.1 Java EE Client

For session bean clients running inside the container, EJB 3 now offers the option of using container injection to directly acquire a session bean instance using the `@EJB` annotation. The container is able to resolve the EJB from the type of variable being annotated.

Migrating an EJB 2.1 Entity Bean Client

New entities in EJB 3 may only be obtained through their constructors, instead of through home or local home `create()` methods. Existing instances are retrieved through the `EntityManager`, by issuing a query or invoking the `find()` method. Listing 10-16, in the end-to-end migration example, illustrates the use of a named query, in the `queryDepartmentFindAll()` method, to look up entity instances using the `EntityManager`.

End-to-End EJB Application Migration Example

Now that we have covered the individual transformations required for each of your EJBs, let's look at a simple end-to-end migration example. The application contains two entity beans and their associated DTO classes, a session bean that acts as a façade for these entities and provides CRUD (create, retrieve, update, delete) methods, and a Java SE client that instantiates the session bean and performs some operations on the entities using their DTO proxies.

EJB 2.1 Application Source

Figure 10-1 illustrates our EJB 2.1 session façade and entity beans.

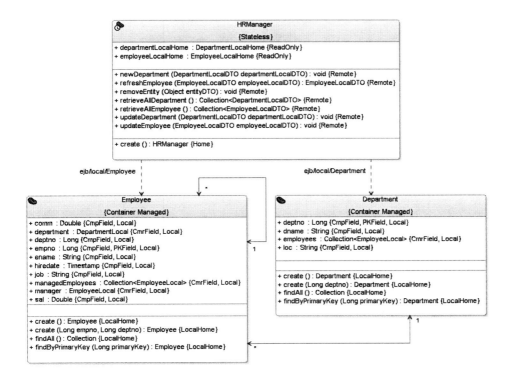

Figure 10-1. *EJB 2.1 HRManager stateless session bean serving as a façade for the Department and Employee entity beans*

Our sample application uses DTO classes because they have grown to become a popular vehicle for allowing clients (especially remote clients) to interact with persistent data without incurring the costs associated with reading/writing property data directly to the entity beans. DTO usage is just one example of the kind of strategy developers employed in earlier releases of EJB, but the concept should be applicable to related entity bean–abstraction strategies as well.

EJB 2.1 Example Entity Bean Source

The bean class for the Department entity bean is shown in Listing 10-8. This class implements two home create() methods, represented by the ejbCreate() and ejbPostCreate() methods, including one that takes a Long deptno argument. This second method, create(Long deptno), must be used when the entity bean is mapped to a table that has a

NOT NULL constraint on the column mapped to the deptno field, since typically an SQL
INSERT statement is issued at the time the create() method is called.

This Department entity bean holds a one-to-many relationship with the Employee entity
bean, represented on the Department bean by its getEmployees()/setEmployees() methods.

Listing 10-8. *DepartmentBean, Bean Class for the EJB 2.1 Department Entity Bean*

```java
public abstract class DepartmentBean implements EntityBean
{
  private EntityContext _context;

  public Long ejbCreate() { return null; }
  public void ejbPostCreate() { }

  public Long ejbCreate(Long deptno) {
    setDeptno(deptno);
    return deptno;
  }
  public void ejbPostCreate(Long deptno) { }

  public void setEntityContext(EntityContext context) throws EJBException {
    _context = context;
  }
  public void unsetEntityContext() throws EJBException { _context = null; }
  public void ejbRemove() throws EJBException, RemoveException { }
  public void ejbActivate() throws EJBException { }
  public void ejbPassivate() throws EJBException { }
  public void ejbLoad() throws EJBException { }
  public void ejbStore() throws EJBException { }

  public abstract Long getDeptno();
  public abstract void setDeptno(Long deptno);

  public abstract String getDname();
  public abstract void setDname(String dname);

  public abstract String getLoc();
  public abstract void setLoc(String loc);

  public abstract Collection<EmployeeLocal> getEmployees();
  public abstract void setEmployees(Collection<EmployeeLocal> employees);
}
```

The bean class for the second entity bean in our example, Employee, is shown in Listing 10-9. This entity bean implements a create(Long empno, Long deptno) method, which is similar in purpose to the create(Long depno) method implemented by the Department bean. EmployeeBean also implements getDepartment()/setDepartment() methods to represent its end of the relationship with Department.

Listing 10-9. *EmployeeBean, Bean Class for the EJB 2.1 Employee Entity Bean*

```
public abstract class EmployeeBean implements EntityBean
{
  private EntityContext _context;

  public Long ejbCreate() { return null; }
  public void ejbPostCreate() { }

  public Long ejbCreate(Long empno, Long deptno) {
    setEmpno(empno);
    setDeptno(deptno);
    return empno;
  }
  public void ejbPostCreate(Long empno, Long deptno) { }

  public void setEntityContext(EntityContext context) throws EJBException {
    _context = context;
  }
  public void unsetEntityContext() throws EJBException { _context = null; }

  public void ejbRemove() throws EJBException, RemoveException { }
  public void ejbActivate() throws EJBException { }
  public void ejbPassivate() throws EJBException { }
  public void ejbLoad() throws EJBException { }
  public void ejbStore() throws EJBException { }

  public abstract Long getEmpno();
  public abstract void setEmpno(Long empno);

>>> Ordinary CMP field get/set methods not shown (getEname(), setEname(), etc.)

  public abstract EmployeeLocal getManager();
  public abstract void setManager(EmployeeLocal manager);
```

```
  public abstract Collection<EmployeeLocal> getManagedEmployees();
  public abstract void setManagedEmployees(Collection<EmployeeLocal>
                                                     managedEmployees);

  public abstract DepartmentLocal getDepartment();
  public abstract void setDepartment(DepartmentLocal department);
}
```

EJB 2.1 Example Session Façade Bean Source

The session bean shown in Listing 10-10 serves as a façade for the Department and
Employee entity beans, providing methods to perform CRUD operations on these entity
beans. Note that this façade exposes these CRUD methods to the client using DTO
classes. This is done for several reasons, not the least of which is that Java SE clients
cannot talk directly to entity beans through their local interfaces, yet CMR methods are
only supported using an entity bean's local interface.

Listing 10-10. *HRManagerBean, Bean Class for the EJB 2.1 HRManager Session Bean,
Serving As a Façade for the Department and Employee Entity Beans*

```
public class HRManagerBean
  implements SessionBean
{
  private SessionContext _context;

  public void ejbCreate() { }
  public void setSessionContext(SessionContext context) throws EJBException {
    _context = context;
  }
  public void ejbRemove() throws EJBException { }
  public void ejbActivate() throws EJBException { }
  public void ejbPassivate() throws EJBException { }

  public void newDepartment(DepartmentLocalDTO departmentLocalDTO)
    throws CreateException, FinderException, NamingException {
    final DepartmentLocal departmentLocal =
      getDepartmentLocalHome().create(departmentLocalDTO.getDeptno());
    departmentLocalDTO.copyToEntity(departmentLocal);
  }
```

```
public Collection<DepartmentLocalDTO> retrieveAllDepartment()
  throws FinderException, NamingException {
  final Collection departmentLocalCollection = new ArrayList();
  final Iterator iter = getDepartmentLocalHome().findAll().iterator();
  while (iter.hasNext()) {
    departmentLocalCollection.add(
        new DepartmentLocalDTO((DepartmentLocal)iter.next()));
  }
  return departmentLocalCollection;
}

public void updateDepartment(DepartmentLocalDTO departmentLocalDTO)
  throws FinderException, NamingException {
  final DepartmentLocal departmentLocal =
    retrieveDepartmentLocalByDTO(departmentLocalDTO);
  departmentLocalDTO.copyToEntity(departmentLocal);
}

public DepartmentLocalDTO refreshDepartment(DepartmentLocalDTO
                                            departmentLocalDTO)
  throws FinderException, NamingException {
  final DepartmentLocal departmentLocal =
    retrieveDepartmentLocalByDTO(departmentLocalDTO);
  departmentLocalDTO.copyFromEntity(departmentLocal);
  return departmentLocalDTO;
}

private DepartmentLocalHome getDepartmentLocalHome()
  throws NamingException {
  final InitialContext context = new InitialContext();
  return (DepartmentLocalHome)context.lookup(
          "java:comp/env/ejb/local/Department");
}

private DepartmentLocal retrieveDepartmentLocalByDTO(DepartmentLocalDTO
                                                     departmentLocalDTO)
  throws FinderException, NamingException {
  return
    getDepartmentLocalHome().findByPrimaryKey(departmentLocalDTO.getDeptno());
}
```

```
public void newEmployee(EmployeeLocalDTO employeeLocalDTO)
  throws CreateException, FinderException, NamingException {
  final EmployeeLocal employeeLocal =
    getEmployeeLocalHome().create(employeeLocalDTO.getEmpno(),
                                  employeeLocalDTO.getDeptno());
  employeeLocalDTO.copyToEntity(employeeLocal);
  if (employeeLocalDTO.getDepartmentDTO() != null) {
    final DepartmentLocal department =
      retrieveDepartmentLocalByDTO(employeeLocalDTO.getDepartmentDTO());
    employeeLocal.setDepartment(department);
  }
  if (employeeLocalDTO.getManagerDTO() != null) {
    final EmployeeLocal manager =
      retrieveEmployeeLocalByDTO(employeeLocalDTO.getManagerDTO());
    employeeLocal.setManager(manager);
  }
}

public Collection<EmployeeLocalDTO> retrieveAllEmployee()
  throws FinderException, NamingException {
  final Collection employeeLocalCollection = new ArrayList();
  final Iterator iter = getEmployeeLocalHome().findAll().iterator();
  while (iter.hasNext()) {
    employeeLocalCollection.add(
        new EmployeeLocalDTO((EmployeeLocal)iter.next()));
  }
  return employeeLocalCollection;
}

public void updateEmployee(EmployeeLocalDTO employeeLocalDTO)
  throws FinderException, NamingException {
  final EmployeeLocal employeeLocal =
    retrieveEmployeeLocalByDTO(employeeLocalDTO);
  employeeLocalDTO.copyToEntity(employeeLocal);
}

public EmployeeLocalDTO refreshEmployee(EmployeeLocalDTO employeeLocalDTO)
  throws FinderException, NamingException {
  final EmployeeLocal employeeLocal =
    retrieveEmployeeLocalByDTO(employeeLocalDTO);
  employeeLocalDTO.copyFromEntity(employeeLocal);
  return employeeLocalDTO;
}
```

```java
private EmployeeLocalHome getEmployeeLocalHome()
  throws NamingException {
  final InitialContext context = new InitialContext();
  return (EmployeeLocalHome)context.lookup("java:comp/env/ejb/local/Employee");
}


private EmployeeLocal retrieveEmployeeLocalByDTO(EmployeeLocalDTO
                                                      employeeLocalDTO)
  throws FinderException, NamingException {
  return getEmployeeLocalHome().findByPrimaryKey(employeeLocalDTO.getEmpno());
}

public void removeEntity(Object entityDTO)
  throws RemoteException, FinderException, RemoveException, NamingException {
  final Object obj = getEntityByDTO(entityDTO);
  if (obj instanceof EJBLocalObject) {
    ((EJBLocalObject)obj).remove();
  }
  else if (obj instanceof EJBObject) {
    ((EJBObject)obj).remove();
  }
}


private Object getEntityByDTO(Object entityDTO)
  throws FinderException, NamingException {
  if (entityDTO instanceof DepartmentLocalDTO) {
    return retrieveDepartmentLocalByDTO((DepartmentLocalDTO)entityDTO);
  }
  if (entityDTO instanceof EmployeeLocalDTO) {
    return retrieveEmployeeLocalByDTO((EmployeeLocalDTO)entityDTO);
  }
  return null;
}
}
```

EJB 2.1 ejb-jar.xml File

The bulk of the metadata for these entities lies in the ejb-jar.xml file, shown in
Listing 10-11.

Listing 10-11. *The ejb-jar.xml file for the Three EJBs Just Listed*

```xml
<?xml version = '1.0' encoding = 'windows-1252'?>
<ejb-jar xmlns:xsi=http://www.w3.org/2001/XMLSchema-instance
 xsi:schemaLocation="http://java.sun.com/xml/ns/j2ee
 http://java.sun.com/xml/ns/j2ee/ejb-jar_2_1.xsd" version="2.1"
 xmlns="http://java.sun.com/xml/ns/j2ee">
  <enterprise-beans>
    <session>
      <description>Session Bean ( Stateless )</description>
      <display-name>HRManager</display-name>
      <ejb-name>HRManager</ejb-name>
      <home>com.apress.ejb3.ch10.ejb21.hr.HRManagerHome</home>
      <remote>com.apress.ejb3.ch10.ejb21.hr.HRManager</remote>
      <ejb-class>com.apress.ejb3.ch10.ejb21.hr.HRManagerBean</ejb-class>
      <session-type>Stateless</session-type>
      <transaction-type>Container</transaction-type>
      <ejb-local-ref>
        <ejb-ref-name>ejb/local/Department</ejb-ref-name>
        <ejb-ref-type>Entity</ejb-ref-type>
        <local-home>
          com.apress.ejb3.ch10.ejb21.entities.DepartmentLocalHome
        </local-home>
        <local>com.apress.ejb3.ch10.ejb21.entities.DepartmentLocal</local>
        <ejb-link>Department</ejb-link>
      </ejb-local-ref>
      <ejb-local-ref>
        <ejb-ref-name>ejb/local/Employee</ejb-ref-name>
        <ejb-ref-type>Entity</ejb-ref-type>
        <local-home>
          com.apress.ejb3.ch10.ejb21.entities.EmployeeLocalHome
        </local-home>
        <local>com.apress.ejb3.ch10.ejb21.entities.EmployeeLocal</local>
        <ejb-link>Employee</ejb-link>
      </ejb-local-ref>
    </session>
    <entity>
      <description>Entity Bean ( CMP )</description>
      <display-name>Department</display-name>
      <ejb-name>Department</ejb-name>
      <local-home>
        com.apress.ejb3.ch10.ejb21.entities.DepartmentLocalHome
```

```
    </local-home>
    <local>com.apress.ejb3.ch10.ejb21.entities.DepartmentLocal</local>
    <ejb-class>com.apress.ejb3.ch10.ejb21.entities.DepartmentBean</ejb-class>
    <persistence-type>Container</persistence-type>
    <prim-key-class>java.lang.Long</prim-key-class>
    <reentrant>false</reentrant>
    <cmp-version>2.x</cmp-version>
    <abstract-schema-name>Department</abstract-schema-name>
    <cmp-field>
      <field-name>deptno</field-name>
    </cmp-field>
    <cmp-field>
      <field-name>dname</field-name>
    </cmp-field>
    <cmp-field>
      <field-name>loc</field-name>
    </cmp-field>
    <primkey-field>deptno</primkey-field>
    <query>
      <query-method>
        <method-name>findAll</method-name>
        <method-params/>
      </query-method>
      <ejb-ql>select object(o) from Department o</ejb-ql>
    </query>
  </entity>
  <entity>
    <description>Entity Bean ( CMP )</description>
    <display-name>Employee</display-name>
    <ejb-name>Employee</ejb-name>

>>> XML properties not shown

  </entity>
</enterprise-beans>
<relationships>
  <ejb-relation>
    <ejb-relation-name>Employee - Department</ejb-relation-name>
    <ejb-relationship-role>
      <ejb-relationship-role-name>
        Employee has one Department
      </ejb-relationship-role-name>
```

```
        <multiplicity>Many</multiplicity>
        <relationship-role-source>
          <ejb-name>Employee</ejb-name>
        </relationship-role-source>
        <cmr-field>
          <cmr-field-name>department</cmr-field-name>
        </cmr-field>
      </ejb-relationship-role>
      <ejb-relationship-role>
        <ejb-relationship-role-name>
          Department may have many Employee
        </ejb-relationship-role-name>
        <multiplicity>One</multiplicity>
        <relationship-role-source>
          <ejb-name>Department</ejb-name>
        </relationship-role-source>
        <cmr-field>
          <cmr-field-name>employees</cmr-field-name>
          <cmr-field-type>java.util.Collection</cmr-field-type>
        </cmr-field>
      </ejb-relationship-role>
    </ejb-relation>
    <ejb-relation>
      <ejb-relation-name>Employee - Employee</ejb-relation-name>
      <ejb-relationship-role>
        <ejb-relationship-role-name>
          Employee may have one Employee
        </ejb-relationship-role-name>
        <multiplicity>Many</multiplicity>
        <relationship-role-source>
          <ejb-name>Employee</ejb-name>
        </relationship-role-source>
        <cmr-field>
          <cmr-field-name>manager</cmr-field-name>
        </cmr-field>
      </ejb-relationship-role>
      <ejb-relationship-role>
        <ejb-relationship-role-name>
          Employee may have many Employee
        </ejb-relationship-role-name>
```

```
        <multiplicity>One</multiplicity>
        <relationship-role-source>
          <ejb-name>Employee</ejb-name>
        </relationship-role-source>
        <cmr-field>
          <cmr-field-name>managedEmployees</cmr-field-name>
          <cmr-field-type>java.util.Collection</cmr-field-type>
        </cmr-field>
      </ejb-relationship-role>
    </ejb-relation>
  </relationships>
  <assembly-descriptor>
    <container-transaction>
      <method>
        <ejb-name>HRManager</ejb-name>
        <method-name>*</method-name>
      </method>
      <trans-attribute>Required</trans-attribute>
    </container-transaction>
  </assembly-descriptor>
</ejb-jar>
```

▓Note To avoid totally overwhelming you with source, we have omitted the component and home interfaces for these EJBs, along with the DTO classes. Please refer to the example code (available from http://www.apress.com) if you want to see the complete source and/or run these examples locally.

EJB 2.1 Example Java SE Client

The simple Java SE client shown in Listing 10-12 creates a new InitialContext instance to provide access to resources in the application server. It then uses this InitialContext instance to perform a JNDI lookup of the home (factory) interface for our HRManager session bean. The HRManagerHome.create() method is called to obtain a remote interface onto an HRManager session bean. The test client asks this session bean to retrieve all instances of the Department entity bean, wrapped in DTO proxies. For each Department DTO instance, the client prints out the department name (dname), obtains all employees in the department (again, using EmployeeDTO), and prints out the employee names (ename).

Listing 10-12. *HRManagerClient.java, Our POJO Session Bean Client*

```java
public class HRManagerClient
{
  public static void main(String[] args) {
    try {
      final Context context = getInitialContext();
      final HRManagerHome hRManagerHome =
        (HRManagerHome)PortableRemoteObject.narrow(context.lookup("HRManager"),
                                                  HRManagerHome.class);
      HRManager hRManager;
      hRManager = hRManagerHome.create();
      for (DepartmentLocalDTO dept : hRManager.retrieveAllDepartment()) {
        System.out.println(dept.getDname());
        for (EmployeeLocalDTO emp : dept.getEmployeesDTO()) {
          System.out.println(' ' + emp.getEname());
        }
      }
    }
    catch (Exception ex) {
      ex.printStackTrace();
    }
  }

  private static Context getInitialContext()
    throws NamingException {
    Hashtable env = new Hashtable();
    // Populate Hashtable with application server-specific connection properties,
    // or rely on a jdbc.properties file to supply the InitialContext with these
    // settings.
    return new InitialContext(env);
  }
}
```

OK, so that's our EJB 2.1 application. Now let's see what this same application looks like after it has been migrated to EJB 3.

EJB 3 Application Source

Our goal is to migrate this application to EJB 3, preserving all existing behavior while opening it up to the new features and other benefits of EJB 3. Our client will perform the same logical operations, but the session bean lookup code can be simplified, and it will talk directly to the entities instead of the DTO proxies.

The postmigration EJB 3 source files are presented following, in the order in which the EJB 2.1 source was presented.

EJB 3 Example Entity Source

Listing 10-13 shows our EJB 2.1 Department entity bean transformed into an EJB 3 JPA entity. The entity bean's component and home interfaces are gone, and the metadata from the home interface, the ejb-jar.xml file, and the platform-specific mapping file has been migrated straight onto the new entity POJO. Specifically, the <query> element named findAll on the Department <entity> has been migrated to a Department.findAll ➡ @NamedQuery annotation; and all O/R mapping data is now represented explicitly, through annotations, or implicitly, through default values. The persistence manager does not manage bidirectional relationships (the client now controls this, with the aid of the addEmployee() and removeEmployee() methods shown following), but relationship information is now indicated through annotations. Also, the related entities are exposed implicitly through property return types, including the generic collection type information, as shown in the Collection<Employee> employeeCollection property.

■ **Note** Several of the listings are shown in an abbreviated form of the sample source file. The actual sample provided for this chapter (available for download from the Apress web site at http://www.apress.com) contains the full, compilable source files.

Listing 10-13. *Department.java, Our Department Bean Class Migrated to an EJB 3 Entity*

```
@Entity
@NamedQuery(name = "Department.findAll", query = "select o from Department o")
@Table(name = "DEPT")
public class Department
  implements Serializable
{
  @Id
  @Column(nullable = false)
  protected Long deptno;
  protected String dname;
  protected String loc;
  @OneToMany(mappedBy = "department", fetch = FetchType.EAGER)
  protected Collection<Employee> employeeCollection;
```

```java
  public Department() {
  }

  public Long getDeptno() { return deptno; }
  public void setDeptno(Long deptno) { this.deptno = deptno; }

>>> Ordinary persistent property accessors (get/set methods) not shown
>>> (getDeptno(), getDname() etc.)

  public Collection<Employee> getEmployeeCollection() {
    return employeeCollection;
  }

  public void setEmployeeCollection(Collection<Employee> employeeCollection) {
    this.employeeCollection = employeeCollection;
  }

  public Employee addEmployee(Employee employee) {
    getEmployeeCollection().add(employee);
    employee.setDepartment(this);
    return employee;
  }

  public Employee removeEmployee(Employee employee) {
    getEmployeeCollection().remove(employee);
    employee.setDepartment(null);
    return employee;
  }
}
```

The EJB 2.1 Employee entity bean, shown in Listing 10-14, has been similarly migrated.

Listing 10-14. *Employee.java, Our Employee Bean Class Migrated to an EJB 3 Entity*

```java
@Entity
@NamedQuery(name = "Employee.findAll", query = "select o from Employee o")
@Table(name = "EMP")
public class Employee
  implements Serializable
```

```
{
  protected Double comm;
  @Id
  @Column(nullable = false)
  protected Long empno;
  protected String ename;
  protected Timestamp hiredate;
  protected String job;
  protected Double sal;
  @ManyToOne
  @JoinColumn(name = "MGR", referencedColumnName = "EMPNO")
  protected Employee employee;
  @OneToMany(mappedBy = "employee")
  protected Collection<Employee> employeeCollection;
  @ManyToOne
  @JoinColumn(name = "DEPTNO", referencedColumnName = "DEPTNO")
  protected Department department;

  public Employee() {
  }

>>> Ordinary persistent property accessors (get/set methods) not shown
>>> (getEmpno(), getEname() etc.)

  public Employee getEmployee() { return employee; }
  public void setEmployee(Employee employee) { this.employee = employee; }

  public Collection<Employee> getEmployeeCollection() {
    return employeeCollection;
  }
  public void setEmployeeCollection(Collection<Employee> employeeCollection) {
    this.employeeCollection = employeeCollection;
  }

  public Employee addEmployee(Employee employee) {
    getEmployeeCollection().add(employee);
    employee.setEmployee(this);
    return employee;
  }
```

```
  public Employee removeEmployee(Employee employee) {
    getEmployeeCollection().remove(employee);
    employee.setEmployee(null);
    return employee;
  }

  public Department getDepartment() { return department; }
  public void setDepartment(Department department) {
    this.department = department;
  }
}
```

EJB 3 persistence.xml JPA Deployment Descriptor

The EJB 3 JPA introduces the `persistence.xml` deployment descriptor, shown in
Listing 10-15, to represent groups of entities called persistence units. A persistence unit
has a few properties that we need to define. The list of entities that are within the scope of
a persistence unit may be specified explicitly, or this information may be left unspecified.
In the latter case, all entities defined in the persistence archive (JAR file) or on the class-
path are included in the persistence unit by default.

Note For more information on persistence units and entity packaging options, please refer to Chapter 11.

Listing 10-15. *persistence.xml, a JPA Deployment Descriptor*

```
<?xml version="1.0" encoding="windows-1252" ?>
<persistence xmlns:xsi="http://www.w3.org/2001/XMLSchema-instance"
             xsi:schemaLocation="http://java.sun.com/xml/ns/persistence
             http://java.sun.com/xml/ns/persistence/persistence_1_0.xsd"
             version="1.0" xmlns="http://java.sun.com/xml/ns/persistence">
  <persistence-unit name="Ch10_EJB30_MigrationExamples">
    <jta-data-source>jdbc/ejb3bookDS</jta-data-source>
  </persistence-unit>
</persistence>
```

The descriptor specifies a name for the `<persistence-unit>` ("Ch10_EJB30_Migration➥
Examples") and an associated `<jta-data-source>`. The data source specifies the details of
the database connection required by the entities in this persistence unit. This database
connection must be defined as a resource in your application server. This task may be

performed through your application server's administration console, or it may be defined during deployment using platform-specific deployment descriptors.

EJB 3 Session Bean Class

The EJB 3 HRManager session bean in Listing 10-16 shows the same logical API as the original EJB 2.1 HRManager bean. However, we can eliminate the use of DTO proxies and cut the number of code lines roughly in half. Note the injection of the EntityManager, using the @PersistenceContext annotation, which identifies the named persistence unit.

Listing 10-16. *HRManagerBean.java, Our HRManager Bean Class Migrated to an EJB 3 Session Bean*

```java
@Stateless(name = "HRManager")
public class HRManagerBean
  implements HRManager
{
  @PersistenceContext(unitName = "Ch10_EJB30_MigrationExamples")
  private EntityManager em;

  private EntityManager getEntityManager() { return em; }

  public Object mergeEntity(Object entity) {
    return getEntityManager().merge(entity);
  }

  public Object persistEntity(Object entity) {
    getEntityManager().persist(entity);
    return entity;
  }

  /** <code>select o from Department o</code> */
  public List<Department> queryDepartmentFindAll() {
    return getEntityManager().
        createNamedQuery("Department.findAll").getResultList();
  }

  public void removeDepartment(Department department) {
    department = getEntityManager().
            find(Department.class, department.getDeptno());
    getEntityManager().remove(department);
  }
```

```
    /** <code>select o from Employee o</code> */
    public List<Employee> queryEmployeeFindAll() {
      return getEntityManager().
          createNamedQuery("Employee.findAll").getResultList();
    }

    public void removeEmployee(Employee employee) {
      employee = getEntityManager().find(Employee.class, employee.getEmpno());
      getEntityManager().remove(employee);
    }
}
```

CRUD operations for our Department and Employee entities are exposed through this session façade, although their implementations differ significantly. The new methods rely heavily on our EntityManager instance as the single interface into the JPA to retrieve and update the entity instances. In EJB 2.1 and earlier, each EJB required its own home interface methods to perform these operations.

The CRUD methods map to these new methods on our EJB 3 session façade as follows:

- *Create*: The entities are now created through their constructors, but the act of creating the persistent instance is performed by the persistEntity() call.

- *Retrieve*: The EJB 3 HRManager session bean provides instance retrieval through the entity-specific query() methods.

- *Update*: A single mergeEntity() method handles the task of updating an entity's row in the database.

- *Delete*: This operation is performed by the entity-specific remove() methods.

EJB 3 Example Java SE Client

As with the EJB 2.1 client, the EJB 3 client (shown in Listing 10-17) creates a new InitialContext instance to provide access to resources in the application server. It then uses this InitialContext instance to perform a direct JNDI lookup of the remote interface onto an HRManager session bean. Note that we no longer need to look up the home interface, and can go straight to the session bean. From that point on, the client test code is similar to the EJB 2.1 client code, except that it works directly with the entities, and no DTO proxies are required.

Listing 10-17. *HRManagerJEEClient.java, Our POJO Session Bean Client Migrated to EJB 3*

```
public class HRManagerJEEClient
{
  public static void main(String[] args) {
    try {
      final Context context = getInitialContext();
      HRManager hRManager = (HRManager)context.lookup("HRManager");
      for (Department dept : hRManager.queryDepartmentFindAll()) {
        System.out.println(dept.getDname());
        for (Employee emp : dept.getEmployeeCollection()) {
          System.out.println(' ' + emp.getEname());
        }
      }
    }
    catch (Exception ex) {
      ex.printStackTrace();
    }
  }

  private static Context getInitialContext()
    throws NamingException {
    Hashtable env = new Hashtable();
    //  Populate Hashtable with application server-specific connection properties,
    //  or rely on a jdbc.properties to supply the InitialContext with these
    //  settings
    return new InitialContext(env);
  }
}
```

Migrating Our Application to Run Outside a Java EE Container

One of the neat things about the new development model is that with a few small tweaks, we can take this newly migrated application and run it outside the Java EE container. The entities require no changes whatsoever, since they rely entirely on persistence services; and the JPA persistence manager is capable of being hosted either inside a Java EE container or in an ordinary Java SE environment. To run this application outside the container, we make changes to the session bean class, the persistence.xml file, and the Java SE client.

EJB 3 Session Bean Class Running Outside the EJB Container

Container-injection services are not available when running outside the Java EE container, so we need to use an alternate means to obtain the `EntityManager` instance. Fortunately, the `javax.persistence.Persistence` class provides a factory method for obtaining an application-managed `EntityManagerFactory` tied to a persistence unit, from which we can acquire an `EntityManager`. The code snippet shown in Listing 10-18, applied to our migrated EJB 3 `HRManagerBean.java` class from Listing 10-16, lazily acquires the `EntityManager` instance so that it can be used by façade methods on our `HRManagerBean` class.

Listing 10-18. *HRManagerBean.java, Our EJB 3 HRManager Bean Class Using an Application-Managed EntityManager*

```
private EntityManager getEntityManager() {
  //  The following code is only used when using this class directly from
  //  a Java SE client.  In this case, we are repurposing this session bean as
  //  an ordinary Java SE service bean.
  if (em == null) {
    //  Create an EntityManagerFactory using a persistence-unit that is
    //  targeted for outside-the-container (Java SE) usage
    final EntityManagerFactory emf =
      Persistence.createEntityManagerFactory(
          "Ch10_EJB30_MigrationExamples-JSE");
    em = emf.createEntityManager();
  }
  return em;
}
```

When running this class outside of a Java EE container, the annotations will be ignored, and so the `em` will not be populated through container injection. Instead, we lazily assign its value the first time `getEntityManager()` is called. Note that we have changed the persistence unit name to `"Ch10_EJB30_MigrationExamples-JSE"`. Application- and container-managed `EntityManagers` typically require persistence units with different properties; in our outside-the-container example, we will add a new `<persistence-unit>` to the existing `META-INF/persistence.xml` file.

To emulate the default (`REQUIRED`) transaction behavior of a session bean method, you will need to add the code that is interposed on business methods by the EJB container to create a transaction context for the duration of the method. The `EntityManager.getTransaction()` method returns a resource-local `EntityTransaction` instance for this purpose. All façade methods that modify entities should manage the transaction explicitly, as shown in the `persistEntityTX()` method in Listing 10-19.

Listing 10-19. *HRManagerBean.java (The persistEntityTX Method, a Modified Form of the persistEntity Method, Which Demonstrates How to Manage Transaction State Explicitly)*

```java
public Object persistEntityTX(Object entity) {
    final EntityManager em = getEntityManager();
    EntityTransaction tx = em.getTransaction();
    if (tx != null) {
        try {
            tx.begin();
            em.persist(entity);
            tx.commit();
            tx = null;
            return entity;
        }
        finally {
            if (tx != null && tx.isActive()) {
                tx.rollback();
            }
        }
    }
    return null;
}
```

A `mergeEntityTX()` method, and any other methods that update the persistence context, would need to be similarly defined to properly emulate the default transactional state of a session bean method.

Alternatively, transaction state could be managed by the client, possibly in conjunction with `beginTrans()`, `commitTrans()`, and `rollbackTrans()` methods defined on the `HRManagerBean` class, which simply redirect to the corresponding methods on its `EntityManager` instance. This approach would alleviate the need for the `persistEntityTX()` and other methods, but would transfer the responsibility for transaction management to the client.

EJB 3 persistence.xml File with an Outside-the-Container Persistence Unit

Listing 10-20 shows how we have modified our `META-INF/persistence.xml` file to add the `<persistence-unit>` element.

Listing 10-20. *persistence-unit Element for an Application-Managed EntityManager*

```
<persistence-unit name="Ch10_EJB30_MigrationExamples-JSE">
  <class>com.apress.ejb3.ch10.ejb30.entities.Department</class>
  <class>com.apress.ejb3.ch10.ejb30.entities.Employee</class>
  <properties>
    <property name="toplink.jdbc.driver" value="oracle.jdbc.OracleDriver"/>
    <property name="toplink.jdbc.url"
              value="jdbc:oracle:thin:@adt-scaler1.us.oracle.com:1521:adt1010"/>
    <property name="toplink.jdbc.user" value="jwetherb"/>
    <property name="toplink.jdbc.password" value="jwetherb"/>
    <property name="toplink.platform.class.name"
              value=
       "oracle.toplink.essentials.platform.database.oracle.OraclePlatform"/>
    <property name="toplink.logging.level" value="FINER"/>
  </properties>
</persistence-unit>
```

To support an application-managed `EntityManager`, we need to explicitly define the JDBC connection details, using properties that are specific to our persistence manager (TopLink Essentials, in this case). We also explicitly list the entity classes to satisfy a requirement with the outside-the-container persistence provider.

EJB 3 Application-Managed EntityManager Client

The only remaining change to our migrated EJB 3 code is to the client itself. The EJB 3 client shown in Listing 10-21 simply instantiates the `HRManager` session bean class as an ordinary POJO, through its constructor, and then calls its methods as before.

Listing 10-21. *HRManagerJSEClient.java, a JSE Client for Our HRManager Session Bean Masquerading As a POJO*

```java
public class HRManagerJSEClient
{
  public static void main(String[] args) {
    // Repurpose our HRManagerBean class as a POJO service class--its
    // injection code is ignored, and it relies instead on an
    // EntityManagerFactory to create its EntityManager instance.
    final HRManagerBean svc = new HRManagerBean();
    for (Department dept : svc.queryDepartmentFindAll()) {
      System.out.println(dept.getDname());
      for (Employee emp : dept.getEmployeeCollection()) {
```

```
            System.out.println(' ' + emp.getEname());
        }
    }
  }
}
```

It doesn't get much more succinct than that. The client code doesn't have to perform any JNDI lookups or have any special knowledge about the framework it's working with.

Conclusion

This chapter provided guidance on how to migrate your EJB 2.1 applications to EJB 3. Recognizing that the migration task largely involves transferring metadata from one location onto another, we recommended partitioning the task by migrating the EJB Java source, the ejb-jar.xml deployment descriptor, and the EJB client individually.

For each of these three areas, we provided transformation tables for migrating the metadata properties from where they were defined in EJB 2.1 onto the enterprise bean or entity class in EJB 3.

We wrapped this up by presenting an example EJB 2.1 application consisting of two related entity beans, a session bean, and a simple Java SE client. The session bean served as a façade for the entity beans, exposing CRUD methods for manipulating them by way of a DTO design pattern. This pattern presents a way to bring local entity bean data into the client, by way of POJO proxies defined for each entity, and was commonly used to work around the limitation that local entity beans could not be accessed directly from outside the EJB container.

The client was a simple Java SE class that instantiated the session bean and used it to retrieve the entity data by way of DTO proxies. We then presented the same application after it had been transformed into EJB 3 source files—to provide a working example and to further illustrate how the DTO pattern translates into (and becomes greatly simplified in) the JPA entity world.

In the next chapter, we explore the topic of EJB 3 deployment. Java EE applications can comprise any number of Java EE application components, and the process of assembling and deploying these modules ranges from trivial to complex. We will define the relevant Java EE roles and terminology as we guide you through the various steps in the deployment process.

CHAPTER 11

■■■

EJB 3 Deployment

Until now, this book has focused on how to build EJBs, Java Persistence API (JPA) entities, and their clients, for exploiting the surrounding enterprise services offered by the EJB container. In Java EE parlance, these tasks fall under the role of Application Component Provider, which is referred to here simply as the Provider. In this chapter, we explore the topics that surround the process of packaging your components into modules and library components, binding external references declared in your Java EE components to actual resources in your server environment, and sending it all off to an application server so that the components can be executed at run time by an application. These responsibilities are handled by the Java EE roles of the Application Assembler (the Assembler) and the Application Deployer (the Deployer). While in practice it is common for a single individual to perform one or more of these roles, or for many people to perform any single role, for the purpose of explaining these topics we will partition the deployment tasks into stages that correspond to these designated roles.

We will emphasize EJB and JPA entity components, but also touch on deployment of the other Java EE module types: web application modules, application clients, and resource adapters. We will also look at the relationship between the Java EE server and the four Java EE containers that it supports, and explore some of the services that are provided by a Java EE server.

Following a brief overview of the deployment tasks, in which we introduce much of the deployment terminology, we offer a look at the Java EE infrastructure components—the Java EE server and containers—that support deployment. We explore the different types of Java EE modules and how they fit together, and how you specify the deployment descriptors—metadata files—that define each module. A section on library components explains how to declare classpath dependencies between Java EE modules and library components. We then provide a more detailed examination of the Assembler and Deployer roles, and conclude with the deployment requirements that are specific to EJB modules and JPA persistence units.

After reading this chapter, you should have a good understanding of how to do the following:

- Group your EJB, JPA, and other application components into Java EE modules and library components

- Resolve naming collisions and redundancies found in external references

- Package a Java EE application consisting of one or more Java EE modules and library components

- Declare classpath dependencies between modules and libraries

- Bind external references to physical resources in the application server environment

A Note on Deployment Tools

This chapter provides some examples of how to structure your application archives, but it is assumed that you have access to software tools, typically offered through an integrated development environment (IDE), to assist you in the assembly and deployment of your Java EE applications. There have been efforts in the Java Community Process (JCP) to standardize in this area (see JSR 88, the Java EE Application Deployment API), but deployment inevitably requires application server–specific configuration tasks. Fortunately, application servers generally provide Ant tasks to invoke their own deployment utilities, and you may also use Ant to create the deployable archives. The use of Ant is prevalent in many development environments, and is nearly ubiquitous in production environments in which automated scripts are required to deploy the same Java EE applications to multiple Java EE server instances. Many of the customization steps that are described in this chapter require the use of interactive editors, mainly for updating Java EE generic and platform-specific XML deployment descriptors. For these tasks, an IDE can prove invaluable, and many IDEs provide platform-specific deployment support that guides you in packaging, configuring, and deploying your Java EE applications.

▓**Note** The Apress Wines Online application covered in Chapter 7, and several other sample applications that accompany this book (provided at www.apress.com), demonstrate the use of Ant scripts to perform many of the deployment tasks described in this chapter.

Overview of the Deployment Process

Deployment is the process of installing Java EE components in an application server so that they can be found and executed when you run your application. This process involves multiple tasks that must be performed roughly in sequence. These tasks are summarized in the following sections, and each is described in greater detail and applied specifically to EJB and JPA deployment later in this chapter. Some steps will only need to be performed under special circumstances, so actual deployment may involve only a subset of these tasks.

The Provider

Generally speaking, the Provider (there may be many for a given project) produces the Java EE application components as a precursor to deployment. The tasks associated with the Provider, along with the files delivered by this role, are shown in Figure 11-1.

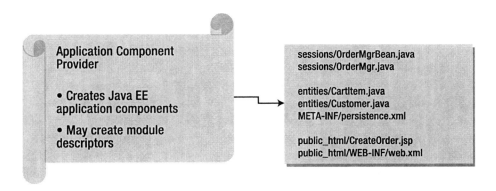

Figure 11-1. *Tasks and deliverables of the Application Component Provider*

The deliverables from the Provider are application components and possibly module descriptors, either as files on disk or packaged into Java Archive (JAR) files.

The Assembler

The Assembler takes the output from the Provider, and with it performs the tasks and produces the deliverables illustrated in Figure 11-2.

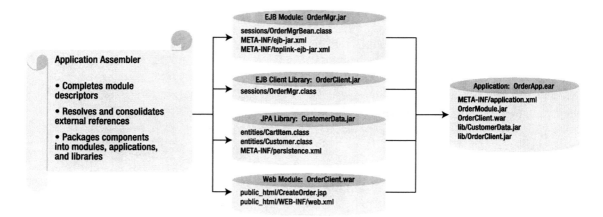

Figure 11-2. *Deployment tasks and deliverables of the Application Assembler*

Grouping Components by Container Type to Produce Java EE Modules

The output of the Provider is a set of Java EE components, such as EJBs, JPA entities, JSF (JavaServer Faces) pages, application client classes, and possibly others. The Provider may also produce non–Java EE components, like ordinary Java classes. The Assembler groups the Java EE components together such that each group contains components of only one Java EE component type. Whenever the Provider has defined a module-level deployment descriptor (XML) file, the Assembler may follow any directives in that file to compose the groups, or the Assembler may choose to either merge or split descriptors to increase or decrease the number of Java EE components in each group. At the end of this process, each resulting group will become a Java EE module. The non–Java EE classes and resources that are left over may be bundled into the Java EE modules, or isolated into their own groups to become sharable library components.

Defining Module-Level Deployment Descriptors (Optional)

For each Java EE module that is formed, the Assembler may locate and assign a deployment descriptor to represent that module. In Java EE 5, this step is optional, since annotations now make it possible to identify the module type by analyzing its file contents. For instance, you (in the role of either the Provider or the Assembler) are free to define an `ejb-jar.xml` deployment descriptor; but unless you are overriding information that is captured in Java annotations, or you have chosen to not use annotations, it is no longer necessary. In Java EE 5, an EJB module is defined simply by the presence of a class in a file group that is annotated `@Stateless`, `@Stateful`, or `@MessageDriven`.

Packaging Components (with Optional Descriptors) into JAR Files

In this stage, the component groups identified in the first stage are packaged, together with their module-level deployment descriptors, if defined, into files using the JAR format. EJB modules are archived into EJB JAR files with a `.jar` extension, web application modules are archived into Web Archive (WAR) files with a `.war` extension, application clients are archived into JAR files with a `.jar` extension, and so on. JPA persistence units may be archived into their own JAR files (with `.jar` extensions) or archived directly into EJB JAR or WAR files. We'll cover this detail in the "Assembling a Persistence Unit" section later in the chapter.

In addition, non–Java EE components, such as ordinary Java classes, may be added to these Java EE module archives; or the Assembler may archive them into their own JAR files to be deployed as library components.

Creating an Enterprise Archive (EAR) File (Optional)

If you (as the Assembler) have created multiple archives that you want to deploy together as a logical group, you will need to bundle these archives together inside a wrapper JAR file known as an EAR file, which uses the suffix `.ear`. This EAR file is referred to as a Java EE application. If you have created only a single EJB JAR or WAR archive, no further packaging is required. You can skip the step of creating a wrapper EAR file, and deploy the EJB JAR or WAR file as a stand-alone module.

An application acts as a packaging boundary, ensuring that the Java EE components in all modules are able to communicate with each other within a single naming context. A Java EE application does not necessarily correspond to an actual end-user application—it may be used by many different client applications—but it allows client applications to connect to the Java EE application once and access the Java EE components in that application from a single context.

An EAR file may contain an application-level deployment descriptor, `application.xml`, in its `META-INF` directory. This file is optional in Java EE 5, since it is now possible to rely on default rules to provide default names and properties for each module. By default, each module name defaults to the short name of its archive file, minus the file suffix (`.jar`, `.war`, etc.). Defining an `application.xml` descriptor allows you to refine the default names and properties, and to selectively choose which modules in the EAR file to include in the application for a particular deployment.

Assembler-Specific Tasks

Depending on the completeness, and the complexity, of the deployment descriptors for each module, the Assembler may be required to complete or refine some of the external references declared by the Provider. In many cases, the modules are sufficiently self-contained and complete that there is no further work for the Assembler to perform, even when a deployment descriptor is not supplied by the Provider. In more complex deployment scenarios, when Provider-supplied documentation (possibly communicated through description properties on either the annotations or in the deployment descriptor) is used, the Assembler may need to consolidate semantically equivalent but disparately named resources into a minimal, distinct set. Conversely, the Assembler may need to avoid resource name collisions by renaming resource references that share the same name but hold different semantics.

For example, if the Assembler is bundling two Java EE modules produced by different providers into a single Java EE application, both providers may reference the same logical EJB but use different names, or reference them with the names not yet bound. It is the responsibility of the Assembler to detect cases such as this, using the documentation provided by the Provider(s), and update the EJB references to bind to a single name. This name may be chosen by the Assembler and assigned to the EJB in that application context.

Any changes made by the Assembler are applied only to the module and application deployment descriptor files, and not to the Java source. This process works because of the rules of precedence dictated by Java EE—that in the case of conflicting metadata properties defined both in the Java annotation source and the XML deployment descriptors, the deployment descriptors prevail. The Assembler is able to resolve inconsistencies in the Java source by working only with the deployment descriptor files.

The Deployer

The tasks and deliverables of the Deployer are depicted in Figure 11-3.

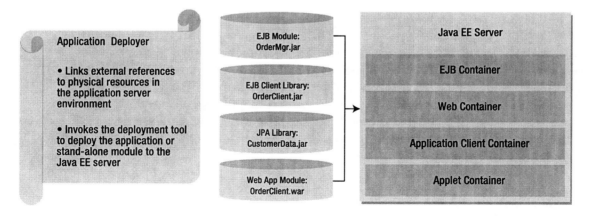

Figure 11-3. *Tasks and deliverables of the Application Deployer*

Deployer-Specific Tasks

Using instructions from the Assembler (and Provider)—again, typically communicated through description properties in the deployment descriptors or source annotations— the Deployer is required to bind all external references onto concrete resources (EJB references, resource references, persistence unit references, etc.) in the target application server environment. Only the Deployer can presume to know about the target server environment, and Java EE has deliberately added a layer of indirection to all resource usage to allow this binding to occur without affecting the work of either the Provider or the Assembler. This is why all resources used by the Java EE components are referred to via indirect references.

As was the case with the Assembler, Java EE policy dictates that the Deployer is allowed to make changes only to the XML deployment descriptor files, and not to annotations in the Java source.

Invoking the Application Server–Specific Deployment Tool

Finally, your Java EE module or your Java EE application is ready to be submitted to the application server. Your application server will provide a deployment tool that lets you complete the deployment and install the Java EE components in the app server, ready to be executed by end-user applications. During this stage, the deployment tool will validate the module(s) being submitted for internal integrity, and ensure that all resources can be bound to actual objects that reside in the application server environment. If any required resources cannot be located at deploy time, or if referenced library components are not found, the deployment will fail.

Summary of Overview

Java EE deployment lets you deploy individual modules, library components, or complete applications. In many cases, a deployment may simply involve packaging the compiled source, together with the descriptors (a persistence.xml file is mandatory for persistence units, but an ejb-jar.xml file is optional for EJB JAR files), and submitting to a deployment tool. When assembling applications from multiple modules that may have been built by different component providers and may be of differing versions, the Assembler role takes on greater importance.

Java EE Deployment Infrastructure

Now that we have summarized the deployment process, let us explore some areas of the Java EE infrastructure that are central to deployment. An understanding of this topic is useful when it comes time to make your own decisions about how to package your code into modules, and resolve and bind external references.

The Java EE Server

The Java EE server is the program running inside your application server that provides enterprise services to your Java EE components when they are run. The Java EE server is also responsible for handling deployment requests and redirecting them to the Java EE containers that it hosts.

The Java EE spec defines the list of core services that must be supported by a Java EE server. These include messaging, database, security, transaction, persistence, and many other services. The Java EE server may also be extended to provide additional services, or alternative implementations of existing services, beyond those mandated by the spec. Java EE defines how a server may be extended to provide its containers with access to remote and external services, by adapting them into the Java EE environment using resource adapters through the Java EE Connector API.

The Java EE Containers

The primary purpose of the Java EE server is to support Java EE containers, which provide the environments in which Java EE components are run. Java EE 5 specifies support for four Java EE containers: EJB, web, application client, and applet. While the EJB and web containers execute in the application server running in the middle tier, the application client container typically executes in a Java SE environment on the client tier, and the applet container typically runs inside a web browser. Nonetheless, they all rely on their underlying Java EE server for the many enterprise services that they in turn provide, through APIs, to the components that execute inside their container environment. For instance, a Java EE server provides native messaging services to a Java EE container, and the container exposes messaging services to its components through the JMS (Java Message Service) API. Similarly, the container exposes database services through Java Database Connectivity (JDBC), transaction services through Java Transaction API (JTA), and so on. The Java EE containers also interpose on all communication between Java EE application components executing in Java EE containers, to provide component and resource injection.

In addition to the many built-in services offered to Java EE components by the Java EE containers, Java EE allows for the integration of third-party services—through resource adapters and the Connector API—that are exposed to Java EE components through their containers using the Java EE Service Provider Interface (SPI).

Java EE Deployment Components

The principal building block components of a Java EE deployment are the Java EE application and the Java EE modules. Let's take a look at what defines these components.

The Java EE Application

Java EE lets you deploy both individual Java EE modules and entire Java EE applications to the server. As mentioned in the preceding "Overview of the Deployment Process" section, when deploying an application, you package the individual Java EE modules, together with any associated deployment descriptors and dependent library components, into a wrapper archive JAR file known as an EAR file, which has the suffix .ear. Deploying an individual Java EE module is essentially a shortcut to avoid wrapping one JAR file around another single JAR file.

Apart from its packaging structure, a Java EE application operates, at run time, as a context in which one or more associated Java EE components—like EJBs, servlets, and application clients—can operate and communicate with one another using a shared class loader and namespace. It may be useful to think of a Java EE application as a loosely coupled group of Java EE modules that are able to see each other and share resources.

Java EE Module Types

Java EE defines the following Java EE module types: EJB, web application, application client, and resource adapter. The first three correspond to their eponymous containers, and their deployment is delegated to these containers. Deploying a resource adapter module installs the resources in the Java EE server and registers these resources for use by Java EE components. Ordinary Java classes and other resources referenced by your Java EE modules may also be included as library components within an EAR file, either packaged as JAR files or stored as directories, and deployed with your Java EE application.

Note that a JPA persistence unit, comprising a set of JPA entities, is not a Java EE module but a library component. We describe some of the reasons for this in the "Persistence Unit" section, which follows.

Let's take a closer look at each of the Java EE module types.

EJB Module

An EJB module is comprised of one or more session and/or message-driven beans (MDBs). It is packaged into an EJB JAR file, and if it includes an ejb-jar.xml deployment descriptor (this is now optional in Java EE 5), it must be located in the META-INF directory in the JAR file. Platform-specific descriptors may be added to this META-INF directory as well. If the EJB JAR file doesn't contain an ejb-jar.xml file, the EJB bean classes must identify themselves as EJBs using @Stateless, @Stateful, or @MessageDriven annotations.

In many cases, it is desirable to isolate the client's view of an EJB module into its own archive. When the client communicates only with a session bean's interfaces, it does not need access to the session bean class. In this case, it is good practice to package only the interfaces of the session bean(s), along with any other dependent classes, into a separate EJB client JAR library. This JAR file can be handed to the client, but it can also be referenced from the EJB JAR file so that these interfaces do not need to be duplicately packaged inside the EJB JAR file. To reference the EJB client JAR file, or any other JAR file or directory in the EAR file, the Assembler adds a `Class-Path` entry to the `META-INF/MANIFEST.MF` file in the JAR file that points to these locations:

```
Class-Path: MyEjb-Client.jar
```

Note For further information on the `MANIFEST.MF` file, including usage of the `Class-Path` and `Extension-List` entries referred to in this chapter, please see `http://java.sun.com/j2se/1.3/docs/guide/jar/jar.html`.

More than one JAR file or directory can be referenced in this way, by separating the `.jar` and directory entries with a space character. The path of referenced JAR files is relative to the EJB JAR file itself, which must be located in the root directory of the EAR file. In the preceding example, the `MyEjb-Client.jar` file is also located in the root directory of the EAR file.

An EJB module may also include a persistence unit (defined in the following section). A persistence unit may only exist in the EJB JAR in expanded form; JAR files may not be nested inside the EJB JAR file. A persistence unit is defined by the presence of a `META-INF/persistence.xml` file in the contents of the EJB JAR file.

An EJB module may be assigned a name using a module declaration inside a `META-INF/application.xml` file. When no `META-INF/application.xml` file is present during deployment, as when the EJB JAR file is deployed stand-alone or within an EAR file that does not include this descriptor, it is assigned a default name. This name is derived from the name of the EJB JAR archive, minus any directory information or the `.jar` suffix. For example, an EJB JAR file may be bundled in an EAR file in the following location:

```
./OrderManagerEJBModule.jar
```

In this case, its default module name would be `OrderManagerEJBModule`.

Persistence Unit

A group of JPA entities, known as a persistence unit, is not strictly a module type, nor does it have its own dedicated container. Instead, the Java EE server supports persistence directly, as one of the core services it offers to the Java EE containers. This allows JPA entities to behave as persistent objects and interact with Java EE components while executing in the other Java EE container environments. By not being constrained to their own container, JPA entities are also free to execute and demonstrate persistent behavior outside the Java EE environment.

▓Note In a deployment context, the term *persistence unit* refers to a group of colocated JPA entities and a corresponding (and mandatory) `META-INF/persistence.xml` file. This group of files may be packaged into its own JAR file, or the files may be bundled directly inside an EJB JAR or WAR file. The `persistence.xml` file in turn defines one or more `<persistence-unit>` entries that may further partition the entities in the persistence unit packaging structure. In this chapter, we differentiate these two concepts that share similar names by always using the hyphen (persistence-unit) when describing the `<persistence-unit>` XML element. So, any reference to a persistent unit can be assumed to refer to the group of entities colocated with a `persistence.xml` file.

As mentioned in the preceding note, the packaging of persistence units is different from the packaging of other module types. When packaged in a Java EE application EAR file, a persistence unit is treated as a library component (see the "Library Components" section, which follows). It can be packaged into a JAR file, or its classes can be packaged directly inside an EJB JAR or WAR file. Either way, a `META-INF/persistence.xml` file serves to identify the entities contained in the persistence unit. We will discuss the packaging details in the "Assembling a Persistence Unit" section later in the chapter.

Web Application Module

A web application module comprises servlets, HTML pages, JSF documents, and any other web-based files. Its deployment descriptor is the `WEB-INF/web.xml` file, and as with the EJB module, the presence of this file is now optional in Java EE 5 since its contents can be derived using default rules. When archived, the contents of a web application module are packaged into a JAR file with the suffix `.war`. This is commonly referred to as a WAR file.

The contents of a WAR file follow a special structure to better suit application partitioning in web browsers. Of particular relevance when bundling persistence units into a WAR file, Java `.class` files are placed in the `WEB-INF/classes` directory, and dependent JAR files may be added directly to the `WEB-INF/lib` directory.

Similar to an EJB module, a web module may be assigned a name using a module declaration inside a `META-INF/application.xml` file. When no `META-INF/application.xml` file is present during deployment, as when the WAR file is deployed stand-alone or within an EAR file that does not include this descriptor, it is assigned a default name. This name is derived from the name of the WAR archive, minus any directory information or the `.war` suffix. For example, a WAR file may be bundled in an EAR file in the following location:

`./OrderManagerWebApp.war`

In this case, its default module name would be `OrderManagerWebApp`.

Resource Adapter Module

Resource adapters offer a mechanism for extending a Java EE server. They allow resources and services managed by external systems to be integrated into the Java EE server for use by components executing in the Java EE containers. A resource adapter module contains a set of resource adapters and an optional `META-INF/ra.xml` deployment descriptor.

During deployment, a resource adapter is packaged into a Resource Archive (RAR) file—a JAR file with the suffix `.rar`.

Application Client Module

An application client module contains Java classes that can be executed in a Java SE environment on the client tier. The application client container is a lightweight Java EE container that supports injection and provides persistence, security, and messaging services, among others. It does not provide many of the services that are available from the middle-tier Java EE containers.

The deployment descriptor for an application client module resides in `META-INF/application-client.xml`, and, like the other Java EE module deployment descriptors, is optional in Java EE 5.

Library Components

Shared classes or other resources that your modules require at run time can be packaged into library components. Libraries may either be installed in the application server (the process of installing a library is not described here) or bundled inside your EAR or WAR file. Any JAR-format file embedded inside an EAR—whether a Java EE module or a bundled library archive—may reference a bundled library component, using the `Class-Path` property in the `META-INF/MANIFEST.MF` file.

■**Note** Whenever a JAR file is referenced through a `Class-Path` entry, only the classes in the referenced JAR file are recognized by the deployment tool. In particular, any descriptor files found in the referenced JAR file will be ignored.

Bundled Libraries

Listing 11-1 shows the file contents of a sample EAR file to demonstrate how the Class-Path property references a bundled library. Here we use a shorthand notation to show the Class-Path: myEjb-Client.jar entries that reside in the META-INF/MANIFEST.MF files for their associated JAR and WAR files.

Listing 11-1. *Example EAR File Contents, Showing Explicit Module Dependencies on a Bundled Library Component*

```
myApp.ear:
 META-INF/application.xml
 myEjb.jar Class-Path: myEjb-Client.jar
 myWebApp.war Class-Path: myEjb-Client.jar
 myEjb-Client.jar
```

In this example, the client-side interfaces (remote, local, and web service endpoint interfaces) have been deliberately stripped from the myEjb.jar EJB module and packaged into the bundled myEjb-Client.jar library component. The META-INF/ejb-jar.xml descriptor in myEjb.jar contains the following entry:

```
<ejb-client-jar>myEjb-Client.jar</ejb-client-jar>
```

This identifies myEjb-Client.jar as the JAR file holding its client-side interfaces. The myEjb.jar EJB module depends upon these EJB interfaces, and declares its dependence through its Class-Path entry referencing the myEjb-Client.jar library. The myWebApp.war web module references these EJB interfaces, too, and declares its dependence on myEjb-Client.jar in the same way. The myEjb-Client.jar library is an ordinary JAR file, and sits alongside the EJB and WAR files in the EAR file.

An alternative to explicitly declaring dependence on a bundled library component is to use the EAR file's built-in library directory, lib, as shown in Listing 11-2. All JAR files found in the lib directory are automatically added to the classpath of the Java EE modules in the EAR file.

Listing 11-2. *Example EAR File Contents, Showing Implicit Module Dependencies on a Shared, Bundled Library Component*

```
myApp.ear:
 META-INF/application.xml
 myEjb.jar
 myWebApp.war
 lib/myEjb-Client.jar
```

This achieves the same result as in Listing 11-1. Assuming application.xml does not specify a <library-directory> element that overrides the default lib directory, the Java EE server will automatically add the myEjb-Client.jar file to the classpaths of the myEjb.jar and myWebApp.war modules.

Libraries may also be bundled in the WEB-INF/lib directory for the JAR files of a WAR file, and in the WEB-INF/classes directory for the unpackaged classes of a WAR file.

Installed Libraries

It is also possible to install libraries in your application server environment and then reference them from the JAR-format files in your EAR file, using the Extension-List property in the JAR file's META-INF/MANIFEST.MF file. This is an efficient means of sharing libraries across Java EE applications, since it avoids having to redundantly bundle the libraries in multiple EAR files. The installed libraries are stored on disk by the application server instance, and typically a shared library entry in one of the application server's configuration files links the name of the installed library with its JAR file or files. Java EE applications may then refer to this installed library by name, without having to know about the JAR file contents of the library.

An example of using an installed library is shown in Listing 11-3.

Listing 11-3. *Example EAR File Contents, Showing Usage of an Installed Library*

```
myApp.ear:
 META-INF/MANIFEST.MF:
   Extension-List: commonUtils
   commonUtils-Extension-Name: com/apress/ejb3/ch11/commonUtils
   commonUtils-Extension-Specification-Version: 1.4
 META-INF/application.xml
 myEjb.jar
```

In this example, the EAR file's META-INF/MANIFEST.MF file is used to declare a reference to an installed library named commonUtils, version 1.4. This gives all the JAR files inside the EAR file access to the contents of the commonUtils library, satisfying the myEjb.jar module's dependence on the contents of this library. The reference could have been defined on myEjb.jar instead, in which case only myEjb.jar would be given access to this library. Either way, the installed library must have been installed prior to deployment of myEjb.jar.

The META-INF/MANIFEST.MF file for the JAR file contained in our commonUtils library is shown in Listing 11-4.

Listing 11-4. *Contents of an Installed Library's JAR File*

```
commonUtils.jar:
 META-INF/MANIFEST.MF:
  Extension-Name: com/apress/ejb3/ch11/commonUtils
  Specification-Title: Utils for implementing common patterns
  Specification-Version: 1.4
```

Versioning of Libraries

Although it is not mandated by the Java EE spec in this release, many application servers support Java EE application isolation levels that allow each Java EE application to have its own class loader. This allows multiple applications running simultaneously in the same Java EE server to reference different versions of the same bundled or installed library component. An example in which this is useful is when you wish to migrate a subset of your applications to use a new library version. You can install the new library version in the server, and then selectively update the Specification-Version property for any applications that you wish to use the new library version.

Alternatively, Java EE servers with this level of isolation support will allow you to deploy a Java EE application that bundles its own version of a dependent library. The rules of precedence in the Java EE spec dictate that in case of conflict between a bundled library and an installed library with the same Extension-Name, the bundled library will be used. This guarantees that the application will always use its bundled library, regardless of which versions of that library are available in the server's installed library base.

Application Servers and Platform Independence

Java EE has always held a keen eye to portability, although in practice this has often been difficult to achieve. Ideally, all Java EE servers implement the spec as far as it goes, and then differentiate themselves on both performance and features like support for configurable isolation levels and advanced object/relational (O/R) mapping options that are recommended (or hinted at, but not mandated) by the spec.

Application servers are expected to define their own platform-specific descriptors to be used to augment the core requirements of the Java EE spec—and indeed, virtually all application server implementations offer such descriptors. Over time (and we have seen this most notably in the area of JPA mapping metadata), features that are found to be lacking in the spec, and are solved by vendor implementations, get rolled into the spec and are made generic. EJB 2.1 offered no support or regulations on how to define O/R mappings for entity beans, nor on how to implement an entity inheritance hierarchy. In EJB 3, the JPA has taken many of the best ideas coming out of TopLink, Hibernate, and JDO, and rolled them straight into the orm.xml file to offer these features, as well as others.

Deployment Tools

Application server vendors have virtually all standardized on JSR 88, which specifies the use of managed JavaBeans—called MBeans—to manage the deployment process. MBeans are self-describing and follow design patterns defined by the Java Management Extensions (JMX) spec to provide an interface between the Java EE server and the application server's deployment tool. The actual interfaces exposed by the Java EE–deployment MBeans vary from one application server to another; but the fact that all deployment tools now use them, to one degree or another, offers some consistency between vendor deployment tools.

Typically, a vendor's deployment tools will guide the Assembler not only through the process of packaging the Java EE modules, libraries, and application archives, but also through specifying some amount of metadata for populating both the Java EE generic and platform-specific deployment descriptors. The tools will also accept EJB, WAR, or EAR files, and actually perform the installation and validation deployment tasks in the server itself.

Note At the time of this writing, an open source product called Cargo is preparing to reach production status. Cargo aims to provide an abstraction API to many of the popular Java EE containers, through the medium of Ant tasks and IDE plug-ins. For more information on Cargo, see `http://cargo.codehaus.org`.

The Deployment Plan

Some vendors' application server tools record the Deployer's choices in a document called a deployment plan. Since deployment is often an iterative process, especially during the development and testing stages, it is convenient to capture the Deployer's choices so that the Deployer does not have to specify the same information repeatedly.

Currently, there is no standard format for a deployment plan specified in JSR 88 or elsewhere, so it is not a document that can be reused across application server implementations. If you find this inconvenient, get involved in the JCP and form or join a JSR to promote a standard in this area.

Deployment Roles

Any encompassing enterprise service platform is, by its very nature, complex. Recognizing this reality, the architects of Java EE have partitioned the Java EE services into well-defined APIs. Similarly, they have partitioned the tasks associated with the various stages of developing and configuring Java EE applications into well-defined roles. We mentioned that the tasks associated with building the various application components—such as

EJBs, entities, servlets, JSF JSPs, and many others—fall under the Java EE role of Application Component Provider. There are other roles as well, such as the System Component Provider, who is responsible for installing resources in the application server that are required by the application components. Among these are database resources, authorization policies, security roles, and many others, including services brought in through resource adapters.

We have already introduced the roles of Application Assembler and Application Deployer, but in this section we will explore these roles in greater depth.

The Application Assembler

So you want to be an application assembler, or at least pretend to be one to impress a date. Here is what you need to know.

Defining and Describing External Dependencies

The Provider identifies the external requirements held by its components, either in annotations, deployment descriptors, or both. These dependencies may be on other EJBs, persistence-units, environment property values, database connections, or any other object external to that application component. It is the responsibility of the Assembler to further describe these external dependencies such that the Deployer can figure out how to map them to concrete resources in a specific application server environment. External dependencies are defined through `<ejb-ref>`, `<ejb-local-ref>`, `<resource-ref>`, `<resource-env-ref>`, `<security-role-ref>`, and `<message-destination-ref>` entries in annotations or deployment descriptors. The Assembler's job is to analyze these external references and patch them up. This process involves the following steps.

Ensuring That All References Are Complete

It is legal, and common, for the Provider to only partially complete the definition of external references. The Provider may not know, or attempt to guess, the actual names of the resources being referenced. In such cases, the Provider will spell out the details of the reference—its object type, its internally used name, and a description of the logical behavior of the referenced object. The Assembler takes this information and then links it to a name of a resource that is internally consistent within the application. An example of this is an EJB reference. A `web.xml`, `ejb-jar.xml`, or `application-client.xml` descriptor is allowed to declare EJB references using an `<ejb-ref>` element. An `<ejb-ref>` has an `ejb-ref-name` property that is used by the referencing component (whether a web form, another EJB, or an application client), and links it to the actual name assigned to the EJB during deployment by assigning a value to the `<ejb-ref>`'s `ejb-link` property. Listing 11-5 illustrates an `<ejb-ref>` that has been fully defined by the Assembler.

Listing 11-5. *An ejb-ref Descriptor Element That Has Been Properly Linked to a Named EJB*

```
<ejb-ref>
 <description>
  Some description that defines this EJB to the Assembler
 </description>
 <ejb-ref-name>ejb/MyAccountManager</ejb-ref-name>
 <ejb-ref-type>Session</ejb-ref-type>
 <remote>com.apress.ejb3.ch11.MyAccountManager</remote>
 <ejb-link>SalesAccountManager</ejb-link>
</ejb-ref>
```

■**Note** Note that, as you would expect, the `<home>` and `<local-home>` properties are optional in EJB 3.

It is also possible to resolve a reference to an EJB that is packaged in a different EJB JAR file in the same application. Listing 11-6 illustrates how you would use a special path notation in the `ejb-link` value to do this. The `ejb-link` property value may refer to any EJB found in an EJB JAR file in the application EAR file.

Listing 11-6. *An ejb-ref Descriptor Element That Links to an EJB Residing in a Different EJB JAR in the Application*

```
<ejb-ref>
 <description>
  Some description that defines this EJB to the Assembler
 </description>
 <ejb-ref-name>ejb/MyAccountManager</ejb-ref-name>
 <ejb-ref-type>Session</ejb-ref-type>
 <remote>com.apress.ejb3.ch11.MyAccountManager</remote>
 <ejb-link>../salesEjbModule.jar#SalesAccountManager</ejb-link>
</ejb-ref>
```

This example shows how the link would appear if the `SalesAccountManager` EJB were moved into a peer EJB module, `salesEjbModule.jar`.

Finally, the Assembler may need to resolve EJB references that have been partially declared using `@EJB` annotations in the Java source, as shown in Listing 11-7.

Listing 11-7. *A Partial @EJB Annotation in a Java Source File*

```
@EJB(name="AccountManager",
    beanInterface=AccountManager.class,
    description="The Department Account Manager")
private AccountManager acctMgr;
```

The Assembler would add an `<ejb-ref>` element to complete this reference, but would leave the properties that have already been defined intact, as shown in Listing 11-8.

Listing 11-8. *An ejb-ref Descriptor Element That Fills In the Missing Properties of an @EJB Annotation*

```
<ejb-ref>
 <ejb-ref-name>ejb/MyAccountManager</ejb-ref-name>
 <ejb-link>SalesAccountManager</ejb-link>
</ejb-ref>
```

■**Note** While it is possible to use JNDI (Java Naming and Directory Interface) to look up EJBs deployed outside the context application, `<ejb-ref>`, `<ejb-local-ref>`, and the corresponding `@EJB` annotation may only be used to access EJBs deployed in the context application.

This process continues until the Assembler has linked all the EJB, resource, resource environment, and any other references that were found dangling.

Resolving Conflicting and Redundant References

The modules presented to the Assembler for assembly into an application may have been built by different Providers, or at different times. In such cases, it is common to find references to the same logical resources, but using different names. It is the responsibility of the Assembler to scan both the source annotations and any XML deployment descriptors, and rename any redundant references to a common name.

Similarly, the same internal name may be used by application components to refer to logically distinct resources. Using the description properties of these references, found both on annotations and in deployment descriptors, along with any other documentation supplied by the Provider, the Assembler must detect such conflicts and rename these references appropriately.

The Assembler may choose to fully populate each module descriptor by merging Java annotations found in the module source files into the descriptor, whenever it is not in conflict. If the Assembler chooses to perform this task, the descriptor's `metadata-complete` property may be set to `true`. This signals to the Deployer that this descriptor, and the Java annotations, need not be further analyzed, leading to a speedier deployment.

Packaging

The Assembler performs the packaging stage to bundle application components into container-specific JAR files and component libraries. This packaging process was outlined in the preceding "Overview of the Deployment Process" section. You can use Ant or ZIP utilities to perform these steps of grouping the Java EE components into modules and packaging them into JAR files—but this is an area that benefits from the use of a visual packaging tool, typically available through an IDE. The Assembler packages EJB and application client modules into JAR files, web application modules into WAR files, and resource adapters into RAR files.

When assembling a stand-alone Java EE module with no bundled libraries, no further packaging is needed. The module's JAR file is ready to be deployed.

If multiple modules are involved, or if libraries need to be bundled as well, the Assembler creates an EAR file and adds the modules and libraries to this archive. The Assembler may add the modules using an internal directory structure, provided that the `lib` directory, or the directory specified by `<library-directory>` in the `application.xml` file, is honored as the location for implicitly shared libraries.

An optional `application.xml` file in the EAR file's `META-INF` directory may be used to explicitly identify the modules that are included in the application. If for some reason the EAR bundles additional modules that are not meant to be part of the application, this is a way of telling the deployment tool to ignore those modules.

The Application Deployer

The module or package produced by the Assembler is then handed off to the Deployer. The Deployer has intimate knowledge of the target application server environment, including information about all the resources that are currently deployed in that environment.

The Deployer's actual experience differs, due to the varying toolsets offered by vendors to accompany their application servers—but the logical processes of the deployment state are outlined in the following sections.

Unpackaging the Archive

The EAR file, or stand-alone module JAR file, is unpackaged and its contents are analyzed.

Deriving the Module Descriptors

The Deployer processes the descriptor for each Java EE module. If a descriptor was provided, and if its metadata-complete property is set to true, then the Deployer can send the module off to the appropriate container. If the descriptor is not supplied, or if metadata-complete is not set to true, then the Java source contents of that module must be scanned to detect annotations. All metadata properties found by scanning the annotations are coalesced with properties found in the descriptor. During this reconciliation step, Java EE precedence rules dictate that whenever both an annotation and the descriptor provide a value for a given property, the value in the descriptor prevails. The result of this reconciliation state is a completed descriptor for that module.

Binding External References

All external references found are checked for completeness, ensuring that the work of the Assembler was performed. These references are then matched to actual resources in the application server environment. If any resources cannot be bound, an error is reported back to the Deployer so that it can be resolved. As you can imagine, this process benefits greatly from a robust deployment toolset provided by the application server.

Deploying to the Containers

Each completed module can be sent to its corresponding container to be installed and registered. Once complete, the Java EE components in these modules are ready to be accessed by clients.

Assembling an EJB JAR Module

An EJB JAR file is a pretty straightforward archive. The .class files are laid out in the JAR file in directories corresponding to their packages, rooted at the top-level directory of the JAR. The ejb-jar.xml deployment descriptor, if present, goes in the META-INF directory, typically accompanied by any other platform-specific descriptors.

Libraries may not be bundled inside the EJB JAR file as JAR files, but arbitrary classes may be included alongside the EJB classes and interfaces. Libraries bundled in the surrounding EAR file may be referenced using the Class-Path property of the EJB JAR file's META-INF/MANIFEST.MF file, as described in the preceding "Library Components" section. Similarly, you may reference installed libraries previously deployed but outside the context application by listing them in the Extension-List property in the META-INF/MANIFEST.MF file.

When it comes to specifying the metadata for an EJB, the ejb-jar.xml descriptor and the Java source annotations are mutually redundant. The decision to use one approach over another is largely a matter of Provider preference, though this decision is also impacted by how the application will be edited, assembled, and deployed. However, the top-level settings, (such as <ejb-client-jar>) have no corresponding annotations and must be assigned through this descriptor.

▓Note New to Java EE 5 is the ability to deploy EJB and WAR modules directly, without packaging them as a Java EE application. This is only appropriate if these modules hold no external dependencies on classes in other JAR files that are not already deployed to the target application server environment.

Naming Scope

Within a Java EE application, no two EJBs may have the same name. It is the Assembler's responsibility to detect this case and rename EJBs appropriately to resolve the conflict.

Assembling a Persistence Unit

A persistence unit is a set of JPA entity, mapped superclass, and embeddable classes coupled with a mandatory META-INF/persistence.xml file. Java EE offers a fixed set of ways to bundle a persistence unit during deployment. You can either package the persistence unit into its own JAR file, with the suffix .jar, or you can add the persistence unit's class and META-INF/persistence.xml files directly to another Java EE module's JAR file. Persistence units packaged into their own JAR files, with the suffix .jar, may be added to the following:

- The root of an EAR file

- The library directory (by default, lib) of an EAR file

- The WEB-INF/lib directory of a WAR file

Alternatively, you can add the persistence unit's class and `META-INF/persistence.xml` files directly to the following:

- An EJB JAR file

- The `WEB-INF/classes` directory of a WAR file

- An application client JAR file

The decision of where you bundle your persistence unit determines which modules will have visibility to it. For instance, adding it to the EAR file's library directory gives access to all other modules in the application. Placing it in the EJB, web application, or application client JAR limits its scope to that module.

The JAR file or directory where its `META-INF/persistence.xml` file is located is called the root of the persistence unit, and defines the root directory for the classes that comprise the persistence unit.

In addition to the `persistence.xml` file, one or more O/R mapping files may be added to the `META-INF` directory to augment or override any annotations that may have been specified in the managed JPA classes. The JPA specifies the default file name to be `META-INF/orm.xml`, but each `<persistence-unit>` defined in the `persistence.xml` file may specify its own mapping files, using `<mapping-file>` elements.

Naming Scope

Within a Java EE application, it is possible for two JPA entities to have the same name, but only if they are in separate contexts. For instance, two web application modules may bundle separate persistence units inside their `WEB-INF/lib` or `WEB-INF/classes` directories. In this case, the persistence units are private to each web application module, and duplicate names between these persistence units will not cause a conflict.

It is the Assembler's responsibility to detect conflicts within the same naming scope, and rename entity `name` properties appropriately to resolve the conflict.

Conclusion

This chapter introduced the topic of Java EE deployment, and covered both general deployment issues and areas of deployment that are specific to EJBs and JPA entities. We began the discussion with an overview of the tasks that are performed during deployment, noting that—depending on the complexity of the Java EE modules being deployed—some steps may not be required. This overview section also explained the roles of the Assembler and Deployer, and explained the deployment tasks in the context of these two roles.

To provide some background into the deployment infrastructure (knowledge that will assist you when choosing how to partition your applications and resolve external references), we explored the Java EE server and the four Java EE containers: EJB, web, application client, and applet. This led to a discussion of the corresponding Java EE module types, and the definition of a Java EE application. We also explained how to use library components to package your JPA persistence units and non–Java EE components.

The remainder of the chapter provided a more in-depth look at the roles of the Assembler and Deployer, and concluded with further specifics on how to deploy EJB modules and JPA persistence units.

In the next chapter, we explore how to build clients that are capable of interacting with EJB components in a multiuser, distributed environment.

■ ■ ■

## CHAPTER 12

EJB 3 Client Applications

So far in our journey, we have covered in detail session beans, entities using the Java Persistence API (JPA), message-driven beans (MDBs), publishing stateless session beans as web services, and integrating all these components. On top of this, we have covered specific details on transactions and performance. While we have so far been developing simple command-line Java programs as our client applications simply to illustrate how the components work, we haven't thoroughly discussed the different types of EJB 3 client applications and how to develop them. In this chapter, we will discuss different application architectures in which client applications can be involved, and focus on building the common ones.

Application Architecture

The Java EE platform provides flexibility on how components can be distributed across different tiers and architectures. You can choose the right architecture and programming model based on the application or configuration requirements. In this section, we will look at the different possible architectures and programming models that you can use.

Figure 12-1 shows the architectural layout for web-based applications. This architecture is typically front-ended by a web application running in the browser of a desktop or laptop machine. These days, other types of client devices (such as PDAs, cell phones, and telnet devices) are also being used to run these applications. The web application running in a browser or mobile device renders the user interface (data entry screen, Submit button, etc.) using web technologies such as JavaServer Pages (JSP), JavaServer Faces (JSF), or Java Servlets. Typical user actions, such as entering search criteria or adding items to a shopping cart, will invoke/call session beans running in an EJB container via one of the aforementioned web technologies. Once the session beans get invoked, they process the requests, and responses are sent back.

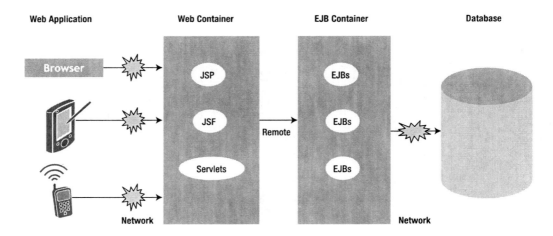

Figure 12-1. *A web-based application architecture*

This architecture allows you to leverage all the benefits of session beans—such as encapsulating interactions with entities, managing transactions and security, and so on. The downside is that you need an EJB container or application server to deploy and run the session beans. Another thing to note in this architecture is that you can run the web and EJB containers on two different physical machines, or two separate Java Virtual Machines (JVMs) on the same machine. The pros and cons of this approach are discussed in Chapter 2.

A slight modification of this architecture is shown in Figure 12-2, in which the web and EJB containers are colocated in the same JVM. In this architecture, web components interact with EJB components in local mode. The pros and cons of this approach are also discussed in Chapter 2.

The JPA specification, which is currently part of EJB 3, provides a lightweight persistence object model with plain old Java objects (POJOs) and annotations for object/relational (O/R) mapping. This is drastically different from what the earlier EJB specifications were doing for persistence. The lightweight nature of this persistence model makes possible application architectures that allow web applications to directly interact with persistence object models or JPA entities. Figure 12-3 shows the architectural layout for this kind of programming model. In this architecture, the web components will interact with entities using the `EntityManager` to perform CRUD (create, retrieve, update, delete) operations and queries to retrieve data.

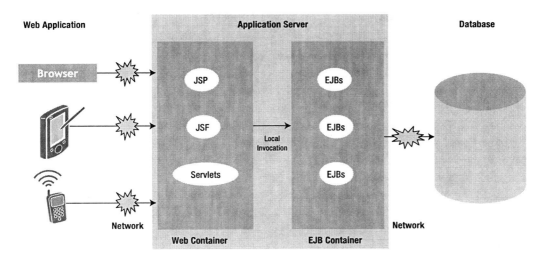

Figure 12-2. *A web-based application architecture with local invocation*

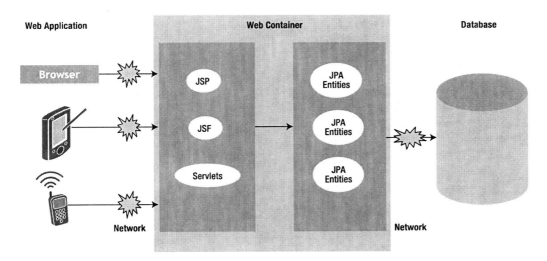

Figure 12-3. *A web-based application architecture using JPA entities*

The upside of this programming model is that you can run your web applications on any standard lightweight web container (such as Tomcat). You don't need any EJB containers or application servers, as you aren't using session beans or MDBs. This architecture is widely used with other O/R frameworks—such as Oracle TopLink and Hibernate—on which the JPA specification is based. The downside is that you lose some of the services provided by EJB containers (such as transactions and security).

The preceding three architectures are most commonly used when building web applications with EJBs or entities. Other variants of these architectures are possible, but we will not be drilling down on all the options.

The next two architectures are programming models in which the client applications are desktop applications that provide rich UI functionality for data entry purposes.

Figure 12-4 shows an architecture in which the client application running on the desktop invokes a remote session. The client application running on the desktop has data entry screens used by end users (such as customer service representatives and bank tellers). These client applications can be developed using Java Swing technology in Java SE, or using plain Java classes (POJOs) that are run from the command line. Generally, the end user launches the client application from her desktop, enters some data, and triggers an event by pressing some onscreen UI component (such as a Submit button).

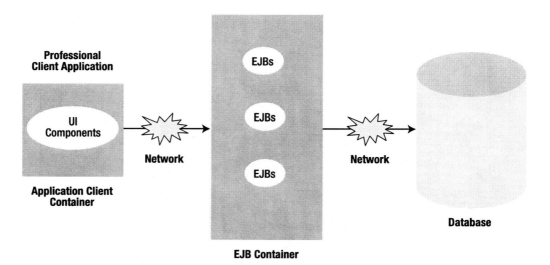

Figure 12-4. *A professional desktop client application architecture*

Client applications can either be installed on the desktop machine or downloaded from a server using technologies like Java Web Start. In this architecture, there will always be a remote invocation of the session beans from the client applications, as the session beans will be running on a remote server. This architecture is able to leverage the benefits of session beans, as is the case with web applications.

Figure 12-5 shows this architecture, which uses JPA entities directly, instead of going through the session beans. In this programming model, the client application and entities packaged in a persistence unit are colocated and assembled as a single application unit. The client application makes use of the EntityManager to perform CRUD operations and queries to retrieve the data.

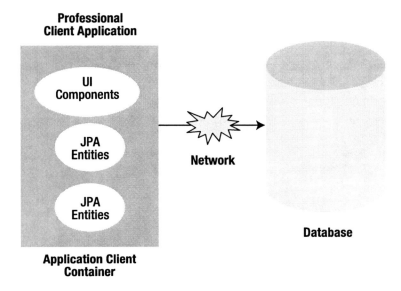

Figure 12-5. *A professional client application architecture using JPA entities*

The upside of this programming model is that you can run your applications in a standard Java SE environment without using an EJB container, but the obvious downside is that you will lose the services provided by the EJB container.

As described Chapter 6, stateless session beans can be published as web services. Once a stateless session bean is published as a web service, any web service client application that can assemble and send a Simple Object Access Protocol (SOAP) message can invoke the published web service. Figure 12-6 shows this architecture.

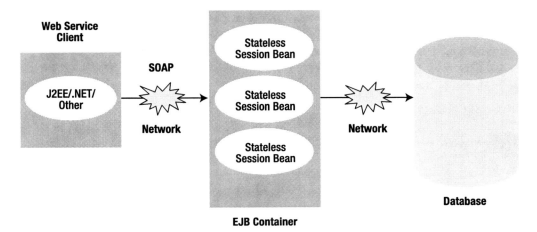

Figure 12-6. *A web service client application architecture*

Enterprises typically have several business processes that interact with heterogeneous back-end systems or services. Business Process Execution Language (BPEL) is a standard markup language that allows you to assemble discrete web services as a single business process. BPEL-based business processes use standard Web Services architecture and infrastructure to invoke one or more web services. Figure 12-7 shows an architecture in which a BPEL-based business process invokes a stateless session bean published as a web service. For example, Chapter 6 demonstrated how to create and publish a credit service that checks the validity of a credit card. In the context of an order-processing business process, this credit service may be one of the several services with which the business process interacts to fulfill the order process.

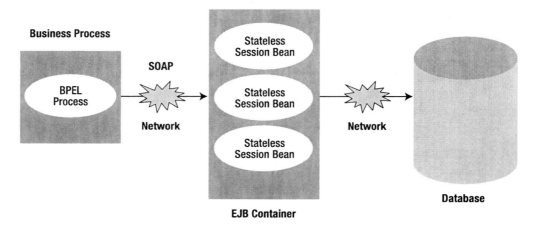

Figure 12-7. *A business process as a client application*

So far, we have looked at the possible architectures and programming models that involve EJB or JPA components. In the next sections, we will drill down into the web-based application architecture shown in Figure 12-2, and demonstrate how you can expand on the integrated back-end application developed for the Wines Online application in Chapter 7. We chose this architecture because it is commonly used and helps us illustrate the usage of container services.

JSF

In this section, we will look at developing a web application that uses JavaServer Faces (JSF) to talk to an integrated EJB back-end application using the architecture shown in Figure 12-2. We will start with a brief introduction to several concepts of JSF to prepare you to develop a full-fledged web application.

> **Note** This section by no means provides a comprehensive discussion on JSF. As with any other Java EE technology, detailed information on JSF can be found at `http://java.sun.com/javaee/javaserverfaces`.

Evolution of Java EE Web Technologies

Over the last several years, Java EE technologies have evolved to deliver a mature, reliable, and stable platform that allows developers to build enterprise-scale applications. The platform has evolved significantly in the web technologies space as well. Figure 12-8 shows the evolution of web technologies in the Java EE platform.

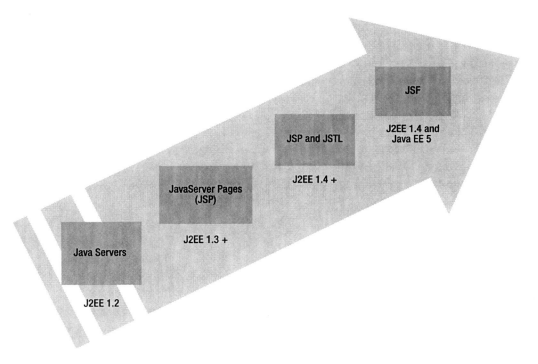

Figure 12-8. *The evolution of Java EE web technologies*

Prior to the arrival of Java Servlets, CGI scripts were used to generate dynamic web content. CGI scripts had their own limitations, including the scripts being run as individual processes, which led to scalability issues.

After CGI scripts, Java Servlets became the basis of all web technologies in the Java EE platform. Java Servlets provided a great start for developing standards-based web components and applications that are portable across web containers. One of the disadvantages of Java Servlets was they were code intensive—all the HTML was printed out using `println()` methods. Servlets did not provide any bridge between the graphic designers who created the design of the pages and the Java programmers who created the dynamic content.

JSP was next in the evolution of web technologies; it bridged the gap between graphic designers and Java programmers. Based on Java Servlets technology, JSP pages are HTML pages with embedded Java code. This model allowed graphic designers to create JSP pages, which programmers could then make dynamic by adding Java code or scriplets. When compiled, JSP pages become Java servlets.

While the advent of JSP pages was nice, many developers now had to deal with mundane tasks like iterating over collections of data. This led to the creation of the JSP Standard Tag Library (JSTL), which automated some of these tasks.

While all these advances in technologies provided more simplicity in building web applications, there was no standard component model for developing web applications. On top of this, development of web applications with reusable components in fourth-generation languages (4GLs) like Visual Basic, Oracle Forms, and PowerBuilder weren't available yet either.

JSF is the latest Java EE web technology—with the component model, it addresses the issues of reusable components and ease of building web applications. The reusable component model is not the only thing that JSF provides, though—we will look into some of the other features and benefits of JSF in the following sections.

The Model-View-Controller Pattern

During the early phases of Java EE web technology development, most of the web applications were built using the so-called Model-I approach. The basic idea of Model-I is that the web technology that renders the dynamic web content is closely intertwined with the business logic of the back-end systems. There was no separation of concerns in this approach—which led to application maintenance issues. The Model-II approach (also known as the Model-View-Controller [MVC] pattern) was a follow-up to the Model-I approach. The key to this approach is the clean separation between the view layer and the model layer that supplies the data and business logic.

The MVC pattern isn't specific to the Java language as such; it dates back to languages like Smalltalk. In this approach, the model layer is used for the business logic and data, the view is used to render the user interfaces, and the controller is used for application flow and event handling. While the Java EE platform had been evolving with respect to the model- and view-side technologies, it didn't include a built-in framework that could be used on the controller side. Instead, many developers built home-grown controllers using Java Servlets technology. Many others turned to Apache Struts, which provided an alternative to writing home-grown controllers. Apache Struts is a widely used open source framework that has become the de facto controller framework for web applications.

Finally, JSF technology standardized the controller aspect of the MVC pattern by providing a controller as part of the framework.

JSF Architecture

Figure 12-9 shows the simplified JSF architecture. JSF has a front controller servlet called `FacesServlet`. `FacesServlet` performs the role of brokering the incoming requests from clients to the right places. As mentioned earlier, JSF comes with reusable web components that can be used to develop user interfaces. These UI components can be associated with objects called managed beans. These managed beans handle the logic for the application and interact with back-end systems or components like EJBs. Each UI component in JSF can be associated with a different render kit that can generate different markup such as HTML or WML (Wireless Markup Language) onto different types of devices.

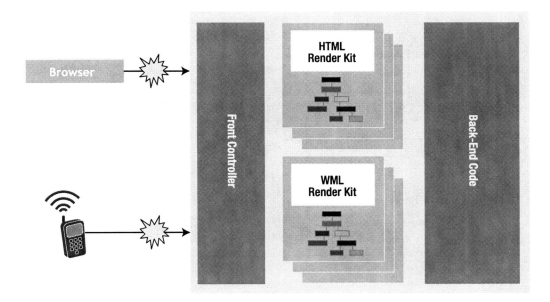

Figure 12-9. *JSF architecture*

The JSF Life Cycle

Figure 12-10 shows the JSF life cycle that handles the initial requests, as well as the post-backs from the client application or user interface. The following list describes the life cycle phases:

- *Restore view*: If the incoming request is an initial request, the JSF implementation creates the view. During the view creation, the UI objects for each UI component are created and stored in a component tree. The state of the UI view is then saved for subsequent requests. If the incoming request is a postback, the JSF implementation restores the saved UI to process the current request.

- *Render response*: In this phase of the life cycle, the UI components are rendered and the response is sent back to the client.

- *Apply request values*: In this phase, the data that was sent as part of the request is used to update the UI objects that are part of the view.

- *Process validation*: In this phase, the data that has been submitted is validated.

- *Update model*: In this phase, the back-end objects are updated with the validated data from the request. Conversion of received data also happens in this phase.

- *Invoke application*: In this phase, the back-end application is invoked to complete the processing of the request, and the response is rendered back to the client.

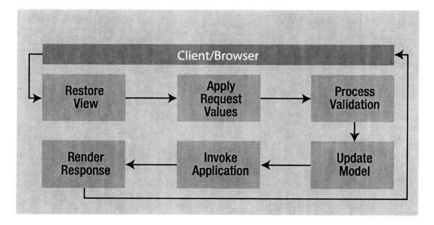

Figure 12-10. *The JSF life cycle*

The JSF Application

A typical JSF application consists of the following:

JSP pages: The JSP pages in the application contain the JSF UI components that are encapsulated in the JSP tags. Each JSF component is a building block that is markup agnostic. It contains three major pieces: a `UIComponent`, a renderer, and a tag handler. The `UIComponent` defines the behavior of the component (e.g., the behavior of a UI component like a radio group or a menu). It is also associated with a specific renderer at run time. The renderer is in charge of what markup is being rendered to the client. A tag handler is a JSP tag that allows for usage of JSF UI components in JSP.

Navigation model: The information about how the control flows through the application is defined in an XML deployment descriptor called `faces-config.xml`. This file can hold several other types of information, such as validators, converters, and lists of managed beans. Each JSF application can contain more than one `faces-config.xml` file.

Managed beans: These are plain Java classes that facilitate the application logic. They can be used as bindings to the data coming from a back-end component, or to invoke a business method in the back-end application.

JSF Tools and Components

Having a standard doesn't always help. Support from developer communities and vendors is what makes a technology successful. While the goal of JSF is to drastically simplify web application development, this goal cannot be reached with standardization alone. We need the full range of available UI components for developers to build applications, as well as the full range of development tools to assist in the application-building process. In the last couple of years, development tools such as Oracle JDeveloper, Java Studio Creator, and Eclipse have provided support for building JSF applications. Apache MyFaces, an open source implementation of the JSF framework, offers components that provide more functionality than those from the JSF reference implementation. Oracle has also released more than 100 standard Faces components under the umbrella of ADF Faces. These ADF Faces components have been donated to the Apache Software Foundation, and are now part of the MyFaces project, a.k.a. Trinidad. All these factors have significantly contributed to the success of the JSF technology and its adoption by developers.

■**Note** Further information on JSF support in Oracle JDeveloper can be found at `http://otn.oracle.com/jsf`. Information about the MyFaces project can be found at `http://myfaces.apache.org`.

Developing Web Applications Using JSF and EJB

In Chapter 7, a significant amount of work was done to integrate different types of EJBs (session beans, MDBs, entities, and web services) to develop a full-fledged EJB back-end infrastructure for the Wines Online application. In this section, we will develop a JSF client application that will work on top of the EJB back-end application (shown in Figure 12-11).

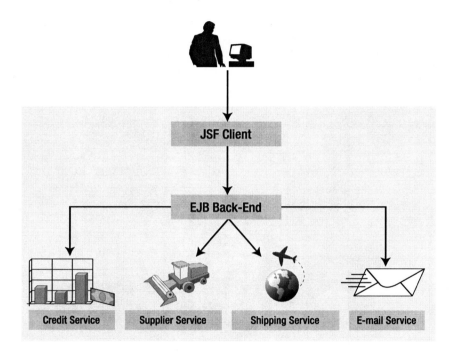

Figure 12-11. *Sample application architecture*

The main goal of this section is to show how to develop a set of JSF pages and wire them to EJB components in the back-end application, including the techniques you can use to do this. With this in mind, we'll start with the ways in which the user would navigate through a set of web pages to perform the following operations:

- Register as a new customer

- Log in

- Search wines based on different criteria

- Add wines to the shopping cart

- View the contents of the shopping cart

- Submit orders

Figure 12-12 shows the application flow and illustrates a set of JSF pages that allow the user to perform the aforementioned actions. We will build one page at a time, wire each page to the EJB back-end application as needed, and complete the application.

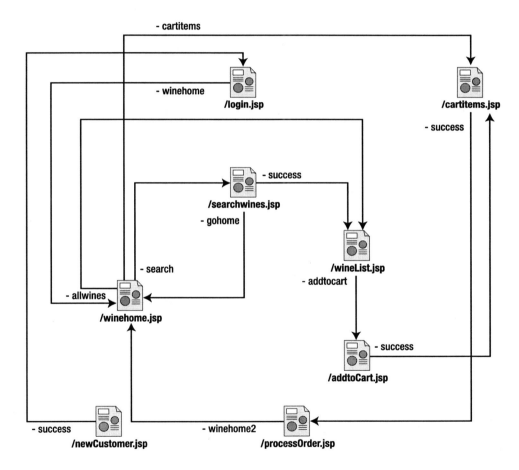

Figure 12-12. *JSF application page flow*

We'll start with a simple login page.

The Login Page

To simplify the login process, we will just use the e-mail address of the customer to authenticate and authorize the order process. email is one of the mapped fields in the Customer entity of the persistence unit used in Chapter 7. Listing 12-1 shows the code for login.jsp. To start with, there are two tag library directives, some standard HTML tags, and some tags to render the JSF UI components. Any page that includes JSF elements must have the f:view tag as the outermost JSF tag. The h:form tag creates an HTML form, the h:inputText tag creates an input text field, and the h:commandButton tag creates a Submit button in the form. As you may notice, the value attributes for h:inputText have a different syntax from the ones used in HTML. We are using #{}, which is Expression Language (EL) syntax. The expression #{Login.email} means that the JSP page wants to access a property e-mail from the Login object. The Login object is a managed bean—it will be discussed shortly. Similar to the HTML form, there is an action attribute for h:commandButton. The EL syntax used for action is #{Login.processLogin}, which means that when the user hits the Submit button, a POST operation will trigger the processLogin method in the Login managed bean.

Listing 12-1. *login.jsp*

```
<!DOCTYPE HTML PUBLIC "-//W3C//DTD HTML 4.01 Transitional//EN"
"http://www.w3.org/TR/html4/loose.dtd">
<%@ page contentType="text/html;charset=windows-1252"%>
<%@ taglib uri="http://java.sun.com/jsf/html" prefix="h"%>
<%@ taglib uri="http://java.sun.com/jsf/core" prefix="f"%>
<f:view>
  <html>
    <head>
      <meta http-equiv="Content-Type"
            content="text/html; charset=windows-1252"/>
      <title>login</title>
    </head>
    <body><h:form>
        <h3>
          Beginning EJB 3 Wine Store Application
        </h3>
        <h5>
          Enter Email address
        </h5>
        <p>
```

```
        <h:inputText value="#{Login.email}"/>
      </p>
      <p>
        <h:commandButton value="Login" action="#{Login.processLogin}"/>
      </p>
    </h:form></body>
  </html>
</f:view>
```

Figure 12-15, shown in the "Packaging, Deploying, and Testing the Application" section later in the chapter, shows the login.jsp page rendered in the browser.

The next step is to create a Login managed bean to use in login.jsp. Managed beans are JavaBeans that are used by JSF applications. These objects are managed by the JSF implementation, and the properties and methods in these objects can be referenced from JSP pages using value-binding and method-binding expressions. Listing 12-2 shows the Login managed bean. Login has three property fields, email, customer, and shoppingCart, which have getter and setter methods. As you will notice, we have an @EJB annotation on top of the setShoppingCart() method. We are using setter injection to inject the ShoppingCart stateful session bean developed in Chapter 7. We have one additional method, processLogin(), in our bean, which calls the findCustomerEmail() business method using the injected shoppingCart stateful session bean. This business method returns a customer object (which is of Individual entity type) if the e-mail exists in our customer database. Additional logic is incorporated to return a string value stored in the faces-config.xml file, for use in our navigation model. We will discuss this shortly.

Listing 12-2. *Login.java*

```
package com.apress.ejb3.ch12.view.managed;
import com.apress.ejb3.ch07.ShoppingCartLocal;
import com.apress.ejb3.wineapp.Individual;
import javax.ejb.EJB;
import javax.naming.InitialContext;
import javax.naming.NamingException;

public class Login {
    public Login() {
    }
    String email;
    Individual customer;
    ShoppingCartLocal shoppingCart;

    public void setEmail(String email) {
```

```java
        this.email = email;
    }

    public String getEmail() {
        return email;
    }

    public String processLogin(){
        String navigation = null;
        customer = shoppingCart.findCustomer(email);


         if (customer != null)
         {
            navigation = "winehome";
         }
         else
         {
            //add some message and show the same login page.
            navigation = "home";
         }
        return navigation;

    }

    public void setCustomer(Individual customer) {
        this.customer = customer;
    }

    public Individual getCustomer() {
        return customer;
    }

    @EJB
    public void setShoppingCart(ShoppingCartLocal shoppingCart) {
        this.shoppingCart = shoppingCart;
    }

    public ShoppingCartLocal getShoppingCart() {
        return shoppingCart;
    }
}
```

faces-config.xml is the deployment descriptor file that has information on page navigation, managed beans, and so on. Listing 12-3 shows faces-config.xml with the flow of control to and from login.jsp, and the Login class being registered as a managed bean. We have set the scope of the Login managed bean to session. This allows us to store information about the customer and shopping cart through the session, so that we don't have to query our back-end application again for the same information. This also facilitates the usage of this information across other pages and invokes other business methods on the ShoppingCart stateful session bean without having to look up the bean again. Additionally, we have created three navigation rules:

- *From* login.jsp *to* winehome.jsp, *with the value* winehome: This will be used if the login is successful.

- *From* login.jsp *to* newCustomer.jsp, *with the value* register: This will be used if the login fails and the customer wants to register as a new customer.

- *From* newCustomer.jsp *to* login.jsp, *with the value* success: This will be used to navigate the customer back to the login page after successful registration.

Listing 12-3. *faces-config.xml*

```xml
<?xml version="1.0" encoding="windows-1252"?>
<!DOCTYPE faces-config PUBLIC
  "-//Sun Microsystems, Inc.//DTD JavaServer Faces Config 1.1//EN"
  "http://java.sun.com/dtd/web-facesconfig_1_1.dtd">
<faces-config xmlns="http://java.sun.com/JSF/Configuration">

  <managed-bean>
    <managed-bean-name>Login</managed-bean-name>
    <managed-bean-class>com.apress.ejb3.ch12.view.managed.Login➥
</managed-bean-class>
    <managed-bean-scope>session</managed-bean-scope>
  </managed-bean>
  <navigation-rule>
    <from-view-id>/login.jsp</from-view-id>
    <navigation-case>
      <from-outcome>winehome</from-outcome>
      <to-view-id>/winehome.jsp</to-view-id>
    </navigation-case>
  </navigation-rule>
  <navigation-rule>
    <from-view-id>/newCustomer.jsp</from-view-id>
    <navigation-case>
```

```
      <from-outcome>success</from-outcome>
      <to-view-id>/login.jsp</to-view-id>
    </navigation-case>
    <navigation-case>
      <from-outcome>register</from-outcome>
      <to-view-id>/newCustomer.jsp</to-view-id>
    </navigation-case>
  </navigation-rule>
</faces-config>
```

So far, we have shown how to get started with a JSF application with a simple login page that can look up EJBs and invoke business methods. In the next sections, we will continue on our venture to complete the remaining wine store JSF application pages.

The New Customer Registration Page

Listing 12-4 shows the code for the newCustomer.jsp JSF page. This page is very similar to the login.jsp page created earlier, except that it has more input fields that capture the customer information. All input fields in the JSP page (First Name, Last Name, Phone, Email, Street 1, Street 2, City, State, Zip Code, Credit Card, and Credit Card Expiry date) have value-binding expressions, which map to properties in the NewCustomer managed bean. There is also a Submit button whose action is mapped to the AddNewCustomer() method in the managed bean using the expression #{NewCustomer.AddNewCustomer}.

Listing 12-4. *newCustomer.jsp*

```
<!DOCTYPE HTML PUBLIC "-//W3C//DTD HTML 4.01 Transitional//EN"
"http://www.w3.org/TR/html4/loose.dtd">
<%@ page contentType="text/html;charset=windows-1252"%>
<%@ taglib uri="http://java.sun.com/jsf/html" prefix="h"%>
<%@ taglib uri="http://java.sun.com/jsf/core" prefix="f"%>
<f:view>
  <html>
    <head>
      <meta http-equiv="Content-Type"
            content="text/html; charset=windows-1252"/>
      <title>newCustomer</title>
    </head>
    <body><h:form>
        <h1>
          Beginning EJB 3 : Wine Store Application
        </h1>
```

Enter the following information to register as a new customer

```html
<table cellspacing="2" cellpadding="3" border="1" width="100%">
  <tr>
    <td width="33%">First Name</td>
    <td width="67%">
      <h:inputText value="#{NewCustomer.firstName}"/>
    </td>
  </tr>
  <tr>
    <td width="33%">Last Name</td>
    <td width="67%">
      <h:inputText value="#{NewCustomer.lastName}"/>
    </td>
  </tr>
  <tr>
    <td width="33%">Phone</td>
    <td width="67%">
      <h:inputText
                 value="#{NewCustomer.phone}"/>
    </td>
  </tr>
  <tr>
    <td width="33%">Email</td>
    <td width="67%">
      <h:inputText
                 value="#{NewCustomer.email}"/>
    </td>
  </tr>
  <tr>
    <td width="33%">Street 1</td>
    <td width="67%">
      <h:inputText value="#{NewCustomer.streetOne}"/>
    </td>
  </tr>
  <tr>
    <td width="33%">Street 2</td>
    <td width="67%">
      <h:inputText value="#{NewCustomer.streetTwo}"/>
    </td>
  </tr>
  <tr>
    <td width="33%">City</td>
```

```
                <td width="67%">
                  <h:inputText value="#{NewCustomer.city}"/>
                </td>
              </tr>
              <tr>
                <td width="33%">State</td>
                <td width="67%">
                  <h:inputText value="#{NewCustomer.state}"/>
                </td>
              </tr>
              <tr>
                <td width="33%">Zip Code</td>
                <td width="67%">
                  <h:inputText value="#{NewCustomer.zipCode}"/>
                </td>
              </tr>
              <tr>
                <td width="33%">Credit Card </td>
                <td width="67%">
                  <h:inputText value="#{NewCustomer.ccnum}"/>
                </td>
              </tr>
              <tr>
                <td width="33%">Credit Card Expiry date</td>
                <td width="67%">
                  <h:inputText value="#{NewCustomer.ccexpDate}"/>
                </td>
              </tr>
            </table>
            <h1>
              <h:commandButton value="Submit"
                            action="#{NewCustomer.AddNewCustomer}"/>
            </h1>
          </h:form></body>
      </html>
  </f:view>
```

Figure 12-16 (in the "Packaging, Deploying, and Testing the Application" section later in the chapter) shows the newCustomer.jsp page being rendered in the browser.

Once the newCustomer.jsp page is created, the next step is to come up with the NewCustomer managed bean. Listing 12-5 shows the code for this managed bean, which has getter and setter methods for all the properties referred by the newCustomer.jsp page. In addition, the class injects the CustomerFacade stateless session bean using the @EJB annotation. Finally, the AddNewCustomer() method creates a new Individual entity instance using the getter methods of the properties, and calls the AddCustomer() business method in CustomerFacade. On successful execution, this method returns a success string that navigates the user back to the login page.

Listing 12-5. *NewCustomer.java*

```
package com.apress.ejb3.ch12.view.managed;
import com.apress.ejb3.ch07.CustomerFacadeLocal;
import com.apress.ejb3.wineapp.Address;
import com.apress.ejb3.wineapp.Individual;
import javax.ejb.EJB;
public class NewCustomer {
    private String firstName;
    private String lastName;
    private String phone;
    private String email;
    private String streetOne;
    private String streetTwo;
    private String city;
    private String state;
    private String zipCode;
    private String ccnum;
    private String ccexpDate;

    @EJB
    CustomerFacadeLocal customerFacade;

    public NewCustomer() {
    }

    public void setFirstName(String firstName) {
        this.firstName = firstName;
    }

    public String getFirstName() {
        return firstName;
    }
```

```java
    public void setLastName(String lastName) {
        this.lastName = lastName;
    }

    public String getLastName() {
        return lastName;
    }

    public void setPhone(String phone) {
        this.phone = phone;
    }

    public String getPhone() {
        return phone;
    }

    public void setEmail(String email) {
        this.email = email;
    }

    public String getEmail() {
        return email;
    }

    public void setStreetOne(String streetOne) {
        this.streetOne = streetOne;
    }

    public String getStreetOne() {
        return streetOne;
    }

    public void setStreetTwo(String streetTwo) {
        this.streetTwo = streetTwo;
    }

    public String getStreetTwo() {
        return streetTwo;
    }
```

```java
public void setCity(String city) {
    this.city = city;
}

public String getCity() {
    return city;
}

public void setState(String state) {
    this.state = state;
}

public String getState() {
    return state;
}

public void setZipCode(String zipCode) {
    this.zipCode = zipCode;
}

public String getZipCode() {
    return zipCode;
}

public void setCcnum(String ccnum) {
    this.ccnum = ccnum;
}

public String getCcnum() {
    return ccnum;
}

public void setCcexpDate(String ccexpDate) {
    this.ccexpDate = ccexpDate;
}

public String getCcexpDate() {
    return ccexpDate;
}
```

```
public String AddNewCustomer() {
    // Add event code here...
    Individual customer = new Individual();
    customer.setFirstName(firstName);
    customer.setLastName(lastName);
    customer.setPhone(phone);
    customer.setEmail(email);

    Address address = new Address();
    address.setStreet1(streetOne);
    address.setStreet2(streetTwo);
    address.setState(state);
    address.setCity(city);
    address.setZipCode(new Long(zipCode));

    customer.setBillingAddress(address);
    customer.setCcNum(new Long(ccnum));
    customer.setCcExpDate(ccexpDate);

    customerFacade.AddCustomer(customer);
    return "success";
    }
}
```

Note Chapter 7 provides all the details on the EJBs used and the business methods available for the clients.

One last thing that we need to do is update the faces-config.xml file shown in Listing 12-3. We need to add NewCustomer as a managed bean. Listing 12-6 shows the snippet of XML that needs to be added. Unlike the Login managed bean, we are going to set the scope of this bean to request, as we don't need to store the customer registration information across the session.

Listing 12-6. *faces-config.xml, with the NewCustomer Managed Bean*

```
<managed-bean>
  <managed-bean-name>NewCustomer</managed-bean-name>
  <managed-bean-class>com.apress.ejb3.ch12.view.managed.NewCustomer➥
</managed-bean-class>
  <managed-bean-scope>request</managed-bean-scope>
</managed-bean>
```

Note We have already added the navigation case from `newCustomer.jsp` to `login.jsp` in Listing 12-3.

We have finished the login and new customer registration tasks. We will assume that the user can successfully log into the application. The next step is to allow the user to search for wines based on different criteria. We will start by creating a simple JSF page that will provide the links to different options available to the user.

The Links Page

Listing 12-7 shows the code for the `winehome.jsp` JSF page. This page uses an `h:commandLink` JSF UI component, which allows you to embed output text to be displayed when the page is rendered. It includes a live link that the user can click to navigate to the next page. This page provides three options to the user:

- A complete list of available wines

- The ability to search wines by year, country, or varietal

- The ability to view the shopping cart and submit orders

We can specify the `action` attribute with the `h:commandLink` component, which can be an expression based on a method or property in a managed bean. Alternatively, the `action` attribute can be the name of the navigation case that is defined in `faces-config.xml`. We are going to use the method-binding expression `#{WineList.findAllWines}` as an `action` property value for the "Complete List of Wines" option, and we will use the names of the navigation case for the remaining two options.

Listing 12-7. *winehome.jsp*

```jsp
<!DOCTYPE HTML PUBLIC "-//W3C//DTD HTML 4.01 Transitional//EN"
"http://www.w3.org/TR/html4/loose.dtd">
<%@ page contentType="text/html;charset=windows-1252"%>
<%@ taglib uri="http://java.sun.com/jsf/html" prefix="h"%>
<%@ taglib uri="http://java.sun.com/jsf/core" prefix="f"%>
<f:view>
  <html>
    <head>
      <meta http-equiv="Content-Type"
            content="text/html; charset=windows-1252"/>
      <title>winehome</title>
    </head>
    <body><h:form>
      <h1>
        Beginning EJB 3 : Wine Store Application
      </h1>
      <p>
         
      </p>
      <p>
        <h:commandLink action="#{WineList.findAllWines}">
          <h:outputText value="Complete List of Wines"/>
        </h:commandLink>
      </p>
      <p>
        <h:commandLink action="search">
          <h:outputText value="Search by Year or Country or Varietal"/>
        </h:commandLink>
      </p>
      <p>
              <h:commandLink action="cartitems">
          <h:outputText value="View shopping cart and submit order"/>
        </h:commandLink>

      </p>
      <p>
         
      </p>
    </h:form></body>
  </html>
</f:view>
```

Figure 12-17 (shown later in the chapter) shows the winehome.jsp page rendered in the browser.

The next step is to define the WineList managed bean that will talk to the back-end EJB to get the list of all wines. Listing 12-8 shows the code for the WineList bean. We start off by injecting the SearchFacade EJB using the @EJB annotation. The findAllWines() method in the bean class makes use of the injected SearchFacade stateless session bean and calls the findAllWines() business method that returns the list of available wines. The returned list of wines is stored in the winesList property of the managed bean, and the allwines string is returned as the navigation case.

Listing 12-8. *WineList.java*

```java
package com.apress.ejb3.wineapp.view.managed;
import com.apress.ejb3.ch07.SearchFacade;
import com.apress.ejb3.ch07.SearchFacadeLocal;
import com.apress.ejb3.wineapp.Wine;
import java.util.ArrayList;
import java.util.List;
import javax.ejb.EJB;
import javax.naming.InitialContext;
import javax.naming.NamingException;
import javax.persistence.EntityManager;
import javax.persistence.EntityManagerFactory;
import javax.persistence.PersistenceContext;

public class WineList {
    public WineList() {
    }

    @EJB
    private SearchFacade searchFacade;
    private List<Wine> winesList  = new ArrayList();

    public String findAllWines(){
        // winesList = searchFacade.findAllWine();
        InitialContext ic;
        try {
            ic = new InitialContext();
            SearchFacade searchFacade = (SearchFacade)ic.lookup➥
("com.apress.ejb3.ch07.SearchFacade");
            if(searchFacade == null) {
                System.out.println("print it is null");
```

```
                    return "gohome";
            }
            else {
             winesList = searchFacade.findAllWine();
                    return "allwines";
            }
        } catch (NamingException e) {
            e.printStackTrace();
        }
        return "allwines";
    }


    public void setWinesList(List<Wine> winesList) {
        this.winesList = winesList;
    }

    public List<Wine> getWinesList() {
        return winesList;
    }
}
```

To finish the work for this page, we will extend the faces-config.xml file with the details shown in Listing 12-9. We have defined WineList as a managed bean and added three more navigation rules that create the following links:

- From winehome.jsp to searchwines.jsp, to take the user to the search page

- From winehome.jsp to wineList.jsp, after executing the findAllWines() method provided in the managed bean

- From winehome.jsp to cartItems.jsp, to show the list of all items in the shopping cart

We will work on the three pages we are navigating to in the next sections.

Listing 12-9. *faces-config.xml, with the WineList Managed Bean*

```
  <managed-bean>
    <managed-bean-name>WineList</managed-bean-name>
    <managed-bean-class>com.apress.ejb3.wineapp.view.managed.WineList➥
</managed-bean-class>
    <managed-bean-scope>session</managed-bean-scope>
  </managed-bean>
```

```
<navigation-rule>
    <from-view-id>/winehome.jsp</from-view-id>
    <navigation-case>
      <from-outcome>search</from-outcome>
      <to-view-id>/searchwines.jsp</to-view-id>
    </navigation-case>
    <navigation-case>
      <from-outcome>allwines</from-outcome>
      <to-view-id>/wineList.jsp</to-view-id>
    </navigation-case>
    <navigation-case>
      <from-outcome>cartitems</from-outcome>
      <to-view-id>/cartItems.jsp</to-view-id>
    </navigation-case>
  </navigation-rule>
```

The Search Page

Listing 12-10 shows the code for the searchwines.jsp JSF page. This page allows the user to search for wines by year, country, or varietal. We are using h:selectOneListBox compo-nents, which are populated with a static list of values for each of the search criteria. The value selected from the list box is stored in the properties of the SearchWines managed bean using the value-binding expressions specified in the "value attribute" of the h:selectOneListBox component. We have also provided three Submit buttons whose action attributes have method-binding expressions, such as #{WineList.searchByYear}, to trigger a method in the WineList managed bean to retrieve the results from the EJB back-end application.

Listing 12-10. *searchwines.jsp*

```
<!DOCTYPE HTML PUBLIC "-//W3C//DTD HTML 4.01 Transitional//EN"
"http://www.w3.org/TR/html4/loose.dtd">
<%@ page contentType="text/html;charset=windows-1252"%>
<%@ taglib uri="http://java.sun.com/jsf/html" prefix="h"%>
<%@ taglib uri="http://java.sun.com/jsf/core" prefix="f"%>
<f:view>
  <html>
    <head>
      <meta http-equiv="Content-Type"
            content="text/html; charset=windows-1252"/>
```

```
    <title>searchwines</title>
</head>
<body><h:form>
    <h2>
        Beginning EJB 3 : Wine Store Application
    </h2>
    <h4>
        Search Wines
    </h4>
    <h4/>
    <table cellspacing="2" cellpadding="3" border="1" width="100%">
        <tr>
            <td><h:outputText value="Year"/></td>
            <td>
            <h:selectOneListbox value="#{SearchWines.year}">
                <f:selectItem itemLabel="1991" itemValue="1991"/>
                <f:selectItem itemLabel="1992" itemValue="1992"/>
                <f:selectItem itemLabel="1993" itemValue="1993"/>
                <f:selectItem itemLabel="1994" itemValue="1994"/>
                <f:selectItem itemLabel="1995" itemValue="1995"/>
                <f:selectItem itemLabel="1996" itemValue="1996"/>
            </h:selectOneListbox></td>
            <td>   <h:commandButton value="Go"
                               action="#{WineList.searchByYear}"/></td>
        </tr>
        <tr>
            <td><h:outputLabel value="Country"/></td>
            <td>
            <h:selectOneListbox value="#{SearchWines.country}">
                <f:selectItem itemLabel="USA" itemValue="USA"/>
                <f:selectItem itemLabel="France" itemValue="France"/>
                <f:selectItem itemLabel="Italy" itemValue="Italy"/>
                <f:selectItem itemLabel="Australia" itemValue="Australia"/>
            </h:selectOneListbox></td>
            <td>
            <h:commandButton value="Go" action="#{WineList.searchByCountry}"/></td>
        </tr>
        <tr>
            <td><h:outputLabel value="Varietal"/></td>
            <td>          <h:selectOneListbox value="#{SearchWines.varietal}">
                <f:selectItem itemLabel="Zinfandel" itemValue="Zinfandel"/>
            </h:selectOneListbox></td>
```

```
                <td><h:commandButton value="Go"
                                action="#{WineList.searchByVarietal}"/></td>
            </tr>
        </table>

    </h:form></body>
  </html>
</f:view>
```

Figure 12-19 (shown later in the chapter) shows the searchwines.jsp page rendered in the browser.

The next step is to add new methods to the WineList managed bean and define a new managed bean called SearchWines. Listing 12-11 shows the SearchWines managed bean, which has three properties (year, varietal, and country) with associated getter and setter methods. User-selected values in the searchwines.jsp page are stored in these properties, which can be retrieved by the WineList managed bean.

Listing 12-11. *SearchWines.java*

```
package com.apress.ejb3.wineapp.view.managed;
public class SearchWines {
    public SearchWines() {
    }

    public String year;
    public String varietal;
    public String country;

    public void setYear(String year) {
        this.year = year;
    }

    public String getYear() {
        return year;
    }

    public void setVarietal(String varietal) {
        this.varietal = varietal;
    }

    public String getVarietal() {
        return varietal;
    }
```

```
    public void setCountry(String country) {
        this.country = country;
    }

    public String getCountry() {
        return country;
    }
}
```

We have to add new functionality to the WineList managed bean created earlier
(Listing 12-8) by adding three more methods that are named in the method-binding
expressions of the searchwines.jsp JSF page. Listing 12-12 shows the three methods:
searchByYear(), searchByCountry(), and searchByVarietal(). Each of these methods needs
the value of the properties from the SearchWines managed bean. JSF provides access to
the requested data, and data from other objects, through the FacesContext object. Once
we have the reference to FacesContext, we can get access to the application and the managed beans. All methods use the technique of getting the Application from FacesContext
and calling the createValueBinding() method with the value-binding expression to
retrieve the value of the relevant property from the SearchWines managed bean. Once the
value of the property is retrieved from SearchWines, the method calls the business methods in the SearchFacade EJB by passing in the parameters that match the search criteria to
retrieve the list of wines. The retrieved list of wines is stored in the winesList property,
which is of java.util.List type.

Listing 12-12. *WineList.java, with Search Methods*

```
    public String searchByYear(){
        FacesContext ctx = FacesContext.getCurrentInstance();
        Application app = ctx.getApplication();
        ValueBinding wineyear = app.createValueBinding("#{SearchWines.year}");
        String year = wineyear.getValue(ctx).toString();
            InitialContext ic;
        try {
            ic = new InitialContext();
            SearchFacade searchFacade = (SearchFacade)ic.lookup➥
("com.apress.ejb3.ch07.SearchFacade");
            if(searchFacade == null) {
                System.out.println("print it is null");
                return "gohome";
            }
            else {
             winesList = searchFacade.findWineByYear(new Long(year));
```

```
                return "success";
            }
        } catch (NamingException e) {
            e.printStackTrace();
        }


    return "success";


    }


    public String searchByCountry(){
        FacesContext ctx = FacesContext.getCurrentInstance();
        Application app = ctx.getApplication();
        ValueBinding wineyear = app.createValueBinding("#{SearchWines.country}");
        String country = wineyear.getValue(ctx).toString();

        InitialContext ic;
        try {
            ic = new InitialContext();
            SearchFacade searchFacade = (SearchFacade)ic.lookup➥
("com.apress.ejb3.ch07.SearchFacade");
            if(searchFacade == null) {
                System.out.println("print it is null");
                return "gohome";
            }
            else {
             winesList = searchFacade.findWineByCountry(country);
                return "success";
            }
        } catch (NamingException e) {
            e.printStackTrace();
        }
        return "success";

    }


    public String searchByVarietal(){
        FacesContext ctx = FacesContext.getCurrentInstance();
        Application app = ctx.getApplication();
        ValueBinding wineyear = app.createValueBinding("#{SearchWines.varietal}");
        String varietal  = wineyear.getValue(ctx).toString();
        InitialContext ic;
```

```
        try {
            ic = new InitialContext();
            SearchFacade searchFacade = (SearchFacade)ic.lookup➥
("com.apress.ejb3.ch07.SearchFacade");
            if(searchFacade == null) {
                System.out.println("print it is null");
                return "gohome";
            }
            else {
              winesList = searchFacade.findWineByVarietal(varietal);
                return "success";
            }
        } catch (NamingException e) {
            e.printStackTrace();
        }
        return "success";


    }
```

All the methods return a value of success that will be used as a navigation case. We need to add this navigation case into faces-config.xml and also register SearchWines as a managed bean. Listing 12-13 shows the snippets of XML that need to be added to faces-config.xml. A success value returned by the methods will take the user to wineList.jsp, which will display the list of wines. Notice that we have set the scope of the SearchWines managed bean to session, as we are accessing the properties from other managed beans as well.

Listing 12-13. *faces-config.xml, with the SearchWines Managed Bean*

```
<navigation-rule>
  <from-view-id>/searchwines.jsp</from-view-id>
  <navigation-case>
    <from-outcome>gohome</from-outcome>
    <to-view-id>/winehome.jsp</to-view-id>
  </navigation-case>
  <navigation-case>
    <from-outcome>success</from-outcome>
    <to-view-id>/wineList.jsp</to-view-id>
  </navigation-case>
</navigation-rule>
```

```
<managed-bean>
  <managed-bean-name>SearchWines</managed-bean-name>
  <managed-bean-class>com.apress.ejb3.wineapp.view.managed.SearchWines➥
</managed-bean-class>
  <managed-bean-scope>session</managed-bean-scope>
</managed-bean>
```

So, far we have completed the following tasks:

- Creating the login page

- Creating the registration page

- Creating the home page with a list of options

- Creating the search page

We will work on showing the wine list to the user in the wineList.jsp page.

The Wine List Page

Listing 12-14 shows the code for the wineList.jsp JSF page. In this page, we are using a new UI component: h:dataTable. This component allows collections of data to be rendered from managed bean properties that are of type java.util.List. In the previous sections, we have been storing the retrieved wines in the winesList property. The #{WinesList.winesList} expression is used for the value attribute of h:dataTable to display the list of wines in table format. Once the list of wines is displayed to the user, the user can select one of the wines displayed in the data table component so that he can see the details of the wine in a different page and add it to the shopping cart if he wants to buy it. In order to keep track of the selected wine in the data table component, we have added the binding attribute to h:dataTable. One last thing we need to do is provide a hyperlink for each row in the data table that the user can click to select the wine. To achieve this, we will wrap the column displaying the wine ID with the h:commandLink component. The value of the h:commandLink action attribute is set to the #{WinesList.invokeAddToCart} expression, which means that we need to extend the WinesList managed bean with a new method: invokeAddToCart().

Listing 12-14. *wineList.jsp*

```
<!DOCTYPE HTML PUBLIC "-//W3C//DTD HTML 4.01 Transitional//EN"
"http://www.w3.org/TR/html4/loose.dtd">
<%@ page contentType="text/html;charset=windows-1252"%>
<%@ taglib uri="http://java.sun.com/jsf/html" prefix="h"%>
```

```
<%@ taglib uri="http://java.sun.com/jsf/core" prefix="f"%>
<f:view>
  <html>
    <head>
      <meta http-equiv="Content-Type"
            content="text/html; charset=windows-1252"/>
      <title>wineList</title>
    </head>
    <body><h:form>
        <h2>
          Beginning EJB 3 : Wine Store Application
        </h2>
        <h:dataTable value="#{WineList.winesList}" var="wines"  binding=➥
"#{WineList.dataTable1}" id="dataTable1">
          <h:column>
            <f:facet name="header">
              <h:outputText value="Id"/>
            </f:facet>
            <h:commandLink action="#{WineList.invokeAddToCart}">
                <h:outputText value="#{wines.id}"/>
            </h:commandLink>

          </h:column>
          <h:column>
            <f:facet name="header">
              <h:outputText value="Name"/>
            </f:facet>
            <h:outputText value="#{wines.name}"/>
          </h:column>
          <h:column>
            <f:facet name="header">
              <h:outputText value="Varietal"/>
            </f:facet>
            <h:outputText value="#{wines.varietal}"/>
          </h:column>
          <h:column>
            <f:facet name="header">
              <h:outputText value="Country"/>
            </f:facet>
            <h:outputText value="#{wines.country}"/>
          </h:column>
          <h:column>
```

```
            <f:facet name="header">
              <h:outputText value="Year"/>
            </f:facet>
            <h:outputText value="#{wines.year}"/>
          </h:column>
          <h:column>
            <f:facet name="header">
              <h:outputText value="Region"/>
            </f:facet>
            <h:outputText value="#{wines.region}"/>
          </h:column>
          <h:column>
            <f:facet name="header">
              <h:outputText value="Rating"/>
            </f:facet>
            <h:outputText value="#{wines.rating}"/>
          </h:column>
          <h:column>
            <f:facet name="header">
              <h:outputText value="Retail Price"/>
            </f:facet>
            <h:outputText value="#{wines.retailPrice}"/>
          </h:column>
          <h:column>
            <f:facet name="header">
              <h:outputText value="Description"/>
            </f:facet>
            <h:outputText value="#{wines.description}"/>
          </h:column>
          <h:column>
            <h:commandButton value="Add to Cart"
                             action="#{WineList.invokeAddToCart}"/>
          </h:column>
        </h:dataTable>
      </h:form></body>
  </html>
</f:view>
```

Figure 12-20 (shown later in the chapter) shows the wineList.jsp page rendered in the browser.

Listing 12-15 shows the new code that we need to add to the WinesList managed bean. We will add a new property, dataTable1, with respective accessor methods and a brand new method, invokeAddToCart(). The new dataTable1 property is used to set the value of the binding attribute in the h:dataTable1 component in wineList.jsp, as shown in Listing 12-14. In the invokeAddToCart() method, we are retrieving the selected row using the getRowData() method of the dataTable1 property, and setting it as the value of the selectedWine property in a new managed bean: JSFShoppingCart. We have used the technique of getting the application from FacesContext and setting the value of the property, instead of retrieving the value, as we did in the earlier use case. The invokeAddToCart() method returns addtocart on successful execution, which we will use as a navigation case.

Listing 12-15. *WineList.java, with the invokeAddToCart Method*

```
private HtmlDataTable dataTable1;
 public void setDataTable1(HtmlDataTable dataTable1) {
        this.dataTable1 = dataTable1;
    }

    public HtmlDataTable getDataTable1() {
        return dataTable1;
    }
public String invokeAddToCart(){
        Wine addWine = (Wine)this.getDataTable1().getRowData();
        FacesContext ctx = FacesContext.getCurrentInstance();
        Application app = ctx.getApplication();
        ValueBinding binding = app.createValueBinding➡
("#{JSFShoppingCart.selectedWine}");
        binding.setValue(ctx,addWine);
        return "addtocart";
    }
```

Before we update faces-config.xml, we need to create a new managed bean, JSFShoppingCart. Listing 12-16 shows the code for this managed bean. We will start with a simple property, selectedWine, with associated accessor methods, and then extend the bean to meet the new requirements (these requirements will be discussed in later sections of the chapter).

Listing 12-16. *JSFShoppingCart.java*

```
package com.apress.ejb3.ch12.view.managed;
import com.apress.ejb3.wineapp.Wine;
public class JSFShoppingCart {
    public JSFShoppingCart() {
    }
```

```
    Wine selectedWine;
  public void setSelectedWine(Wine selectedWine) {
      this.selectedWine = selectedWine;
  }

  public Wine getSelectedWine() {
      return selectedWine;
  }
}
```

We need to update faces-config.xml by registering JSFShoppingCart as a managed bean, and add a new navigation case from wineList.jsp. Listing 12-17 shows the XML snippets that will go into the faces-config.xml file.

Listing 12-17. *faces-config.xml, with the JSFShoppingCart Managed Bean*

```
  <managed-bean>
    <managed-bean-name>JSFShoppingCart</managed-bean-name>
    <managed-bean-class>com.apress.ejb3.ch12.view.managed.JSFShoppingCart➥
</managed-bean-class>
    <managed-bean-scope>session</managed-bean-scope>
  </managed-bean>

  <navigation-rule>
    <from-view-id>/wineList.jsp</from-view-id>
    <navigation-case>
      <from-outcome>addtocart</from-outcome>
      <to-view-id>/addtoCart.jsp</to-view-id>
    </navigation-case>
  </navigation-rule>
```

In this particular task, we have displayed the list of wines in a data table component and provided the user with the ability to select one of the wines. The selected wine is stored in the JSFShoppingCart managed bean.

The Display Selected Wine Details Page

Listing 12-18 shows the code for the addtoCart.jsp JSF page. In this particular page, we are going to use the h:outputText component to display the wine information and the h:inputText component to let the user enter the quantity for the selected wine. The value attribute of h:outputText is populated from the selectedWine property in the JSFShoppingCart managed bean developed in the preceding section. The value of h:inputText is set with the expression #{JSFShoppingCart.quantity}; this will be a new property that we need to add to JSFShoppingCart. One last thing to notice in this page is the h:commandButton component, which users will use as a Submit button to add wines to the shopping cart. The value of the action attribute for h:commandButton is set to the #{JSFShoppingCart.addToCart} expression. addToCart() is a new method that we will have to add to the JSFShoppingCart bean.

Listing 12-18. *addtoCart.jsp*

```
<!DOCTYPE HTML PUBLIC "-//W3C//DTD HTML 4.01 Transitional//EN"
"http://www.w3.org/TR/html4/loose.dtd">
<%@ page contentType="text/html;charset=windows-1252"%>
<%@ taglib uri="http://java.sun.com/jsf/html" prefix="h"%>
<%@ taglib uri="http://java.sun.com/jsf/core" prefix="f"%>
<f:view>
  <html>
    <head>
      <meta http-equiv="Content-Type"
            content="text/html; charset=windows-1252"/>
      <title>addtoCart</title>
    </head>
    <body><h:form>
        <p>
           
        </p>
        <p>
           
        </p>
        <h3>
          Beginning EJB 3 : Wine Store Application
        </h3>
        <h5>
          Selected Wine - Enter Quantity and hit AddtoCart button
        </h5>
        <h3/>
        <table cellspacing="3" cellpadding="2" border="1" width="100%">
          <tr>
            <td>Wine ID</td>
            <td>
              <h:outputText value="#{JSFShoppingCart.selectedWine.id}"/>
            </td>
          </tr>
```

```
<tr>
  <td>Name</td>
  <td>
    <h:outputText value="#{JSFShoppingCart.selectedWine.name}"/>
  </td>
</tr>
<tr>
  <td>Description</td>
  <td>
    <h:outputText value="#{JSFShoppingCart.selectedWine.description}"/>
  </td>
</tr>
<tr>
  <td>Country</td>
  <td>
    <h:outputText value="#{JSFShoppingCart.selectedWine.country}"/>
  </td>
</tr>
<tr>
  <td>Rating</td>
  <td>
    <h:outputText value="#{JSFShoppingCart.selectedWine.rating}"/>
  </td>
</tr>
<tr>
  <td>Region</td>
  <td>
    <h:outputText value="#{JSFShoppingCart.selectedWine.region}"/>
  </td>
</tr>
<tr>
  <td>Retail Price</td>
  <td>
    <h:outputText value="#{JSFShoppingCart.selectedWine.retailPrice}"/>
  </td>
</tr>
<tr>
  <td>Varietal</td>
  <td>
    <h:outputText value="#{JSFShoppingCart.selectedWine.varietal}"/>
  </td>
</tr>
```

```
        <tr>
          <td>Year</td>
          <td>
            <h:outputText value="#{JSFShoppingCart.selectedWine.year}"/>
          </td>
        </tr>
                    <tr>
          <td>Quantity</td>
          <td>
            <h:inputText value="#{JSFShoppingCart.quantity}"/>
          </td>
        </tr>
      </table>
      <p>
        <h:commandButton value="Add to cart"
                         action="#{JSFShoppingCart.addToCart}"/>
      </p>
    </h:form></body>
  </html>
</f:view>
```

Figure 12-21 (shown later in the chapter) shows the addtoCart.jsp page rendered in the browser.

We will update the JSFShoppingCart managed bean with a new Quantity property and an addToCart() method. Listing 12-19 shows the code snippets for these two things. The Quantity property has the accessor methods, and the addToCart() method uses the technique of getting the application from FacesContext and retrieving the instance of the ShoppingCart stateful EJB from the Login managed bean. Once that is done, the addWineItem() business method is invoked to add the selected wine and quantity to the list of cart items in the ShoppingCart EJB. The addToCart() method returns a value of success, which will be used as a navigation case.

Listing 12-19. *JSFShoppingCart.java, with the addToCart Method*

```
String Quantity;

public void setQuantity(String quantity) {
        this.Quantity = quantity;
    }

    public String getQuantity() {
        return Quantity;
    }
```

```
    public String addToCart(){

            Long qty = new Long(Quantity);
            FacesContext ctx = FacesContext.getCurrentInstance();
            Application app = ctx.getApplication();

            //check whether customer has already logged in.
             ValueBinding customerBinding = app.createValueBinding➡
("#{Login.customer}");
                if (customerBinding.getValue(ctx) == null){
                    return "success";
                }
                else {

                    ValueBinding shoppingCartBinding = app.createValueBinding➡
("#{Login.shoppingCart}");
                    shoppingCart = (ShoppingCartLocal)➡
shoppingCartBinding.getValue(ctx);
                    shoppingCart.addWineItem(selectedWine, qty);
                    return "success";
                }
    }
```

To complete this task, we need to add one navigation case to faces-config.xml.
Listing 12-20 shows the XML snippet. When a wine is successfully added to the shopping
cart, the user is taken to a new page, cartItems.jsp, which displays the list of all items in
the cart.

Listing 12-20. *faces-config.xml, with the addtoCart Navigation Rule*

```
  <navigation-rule>
    <from-view-id>/addtoCart.jsp</from-view-id>
    <navigation-case>
      <from-outcome>success</from-outcome>
      <to-view-id>/cartItems.jsp</to-view-id>
    </navigation-case>
  </navigation-rule>
```

The Display Cart Items Page

Listing 12-21 shows the cartItems.jsp JSF page. In this page, we want to display all the items in the shopping cart using a data table component. The #{JSFShoppingCart. cartItems} expression is used as the value-binding expression for the h:dataTable1 component. This means that we have to, again, update our JSFShoppingCart managed bean with code that will populate the cartItems property. Finally, the JSF page has an h:commandButton component that the user will use as a Submit button to complete the order. #{JSFShoppingCart.ProcessOrder} is a method-binding expression used for the Submit button.

Listing 12-21. *cartItems.jsp*

```
<!DOCTYPE HTML PUBLIC "-//W3C//DTD HTML 4.01 Transitional//EN"
"http://www.w3.org/TR/html4/loose.dtd">
<%@ page contentType="text/html;charset=windows-1252"%>
<%@ taglib uri="http://java.sun.com/jsf/html" prefix="h"%>
<%@ taglib uri="http://java.sun.com/jsf/core" prefix="f"%>
<f:view>
  <html>
    <head>
      <meta http-equiv="Content-Type"
            content="text/html; charset=windows-1252"/>
      <title>cartItems</title>
    </head>
    <body><h:form>
        <p>
           
        </p>
        <h3>
          Beginning EJB 3  Wine Store Application
        </h3>
        <h5>
          Shopping Cart
        </h5>
        <h5/>
        <h3>
          <h:dataTable value="#{JSFShoppingCart.cartItems}" var="cartItems">
            <h:column>
              <f:facet name="header">
```

```
                <h:outputText value="Id"/>
              </f:facet>
              <h:outputText value="#{cartItems.id}"/>
            </h:column>
            <h:column>
              <f:facet name="header">
                <h:outputText value="Created Date"/>
              </f:facet>
              <h:outputText value="#{cartItems.createdDate}"/>
            </h:column>
            <h:column>
              <f:facet name="header">
                <h:outputText value="Wine"/>
              </f:facet>
              <h:outputText value="#{cartItems.wine.name}"/>
            </h:column>
            <h:column>
              <f:facet name="header">
                <h:outputText value="Quantity"/>
              </f:facet>
              <h:outputText value="#{cartItems.quantity}"/>
            </h:column>
          </h:dataTable>
          <h:commandButton value="Submit Order"
                           action="#{JSFShoppingCart.ProcessOrder}"/>
        </h3>
      </h:form></body>
  </html>
</f:view>
```

Figure 12-22 (shown later in the chapter) shows the cartItems.jsp page rendered in the browser.

Take a look at Listing 12-22, which has the code snippets that are used to update the JSFShoppingCart managed bean. We have a property, cartItems, of java.util.List type, with accessor methods. In the getter method, we are retrieving the Customer object and the instance of the ShoppingCart stateful EJB from the Login managed bean and calling the business method getAllCartItems(), which returns the list of items in the cart. The second method, ProcessOrder(), also retrieves the instance of the ShoppingCart stateful EJB from the Login managed bean and invokes the ProcessOrder business method on the back-end application to complete the order on the JSF application side. Upon successful execution, the ProcessOrder() method in JSFShoppingCart returns success as a value, which is used for navigation back to the home page of the application.

Listing 12-22. *JSFShoppingCart.java, with the getCartItems and ProcessOrder Methods*

```
List<CartItem> cartItems = new ArrayList();
 public void setCartItems(List<CartItem> cartItems) {
        this.cartItems = cartItems;
    }


    public List<CartItem> getCartItems() {
        FacesContext ctx = FacesContext.getCurrentInstance();
        Application app = ctx.getApplication();
        ValueBinding customerBinding = app.createValueBinding("#{Login.customer}");
        Individual customer = (Individual)customerBinding.getValue(ctx);
        ValueBinding shoppingCartBinding = app.createValueBinding➥
("#{Login.shoppingCart}");
        shoppingCart = (ShoppingCartLocal)shoppingCartBinding.getValue(ctx);
        return shoppingCart.getAllCartItems(customer);
    }


    public String ProcessOrder() {
        // Add event code here...
         FacesContext ctx = FacesContext.getCurrentInstance();
         Application app = ctx.getApplication();
         ValueBinding shoppingCartBinding = app.createValueBinding➥
("#{Login.shoppingCart}");
        shoppingCart = (ShoppingCartLocal)shoppingCartBinding.getValue(ctx);
        shoppingCart.ProcessOrder();

        return "success";
    }
```

One last thing that we need to do is add a navigation case to faces-config.xml that will route the user back to the notification page (processOrder.jsp). Listing 12-23 shows the XML snippet.

Listing 12-23. *faces-config.xml, with the cartItems Navigation Rule*

```
  <navigation-rule>
    <from-view-id>/cartItems.jsp</from-view-id>
    <navigation-case>
      <from-outcome>success</from-outcome>
      <to-view-id>/processOrder.jsp</to-view-id>
    </navigation-case>
  </navigation-rule>
```

The Notification Page

We're almost there! We will add one final JSF page, processOrder.jsp, that will display an order submission message to the user and provide a link to navigate back to the home page. Listing 12-24 shows the code for processOrder.jsp. As you can see, the page is pretty static—it prints out notification text and uses an h:commandLink component to route the user back to the winehome.jsp page, which shows the list of options for searching wines, viewing the contents of the shopping cart, and so on.

Listing 12-24. *processOrder.jsp*

```
<!DOCTYPE HTML PUBLIC "-//W3C//DTD HTML 4.01 Transitional//EN"
"http://www.w3.org/TR/html4/loose.dtd">
<%@ page contentType="text/html;charset=windows-1252"%>
<%@ taglib uri="http://java.sun.com/jsf/html" prefix="h"%>
<%@ taglib uri="http://java.sun.com/jsf/core" prefix="f"%>
<f:view>
  <html>
    <head>
      <meta http-equiv="Content-Type"
            content="text/html; charset=windows-1252"/>
      <title>processOrder</title>
    </head>
    <body><h:form>
        <p/>
        <p>
          <strong>Beginning EJB 3  Wine Store Application </strong>
        </p>
        <p>
          <strong>Your order has been submitted, you will receive an email with➡
 order id and details.</strong>
        </p>
        <p>
          <h:commandLink value="Back to Home" action="winehome2">
            <h:outputText value="Back to wine search"/>
          </h:commandLink>
        </p>
      </h:form></body>
  </html>
</f:view>
```

Figure 12-23 (shown later in the chapter) shows the processOrder.jsp page being rendered in the browser.

To complete the process, we will add one final navigation case into `faces-config.xml`, as shown in Listing 12-25.

Listing 12-25. *faces-config.xml, with the processOrder Navigation Rule*

```
<navigation-rule>
  <from-view-id>/processOrder.jsp</from-view-id>
  <navigation-case>
    <from-outcome>winehome2</from-outcome>
    <to-view-id>/winehome.jsp</to-view-id>
  </navigation-case>
</navigation-rule>
```

With that, we have completed the JSF application with the control flow shown previously in Figure 12-12. Now we will look at packaging and deploying the completed application and walk through the screens we have developed that access the EJB back-end application.

Packaging, Deploying, and Testing the Application

JSF applications need to be packaged into Web Archive (WAR) files before they're assembled into Enterprise Archive (EAR) files, which hold all the required modules and libraries for the application. Most application servers provide deployment utilities or Ant tasks to facilitate deployment of EJBs to their containers. Java integrated development environments (IDEs) like Oracle JDeveloper, NetBeans, and Eclipse also provide deployment features that allow developers to package, assemble, and deploy applications to application servers.

Packaging, assembly, and deployment aspects are covered in detail in Chapter 11. In this chapter, we have developed a JSF application that accesses the back-end application built in Chapter 7. We will perform the following steps to package, assemble, deploy, and test the JSF application.

Prerequisites

Before performing any of the steps detailed in the next sections, complete the "Getting Started" section of Chapter 1, which will walk you through the installation and environment setup required for the samples in this chapter. Since we have built our JSF application on top of the work we have done in Chapter 7, you will need to make sure that you have completed the following steps:

- Successfully complete the "Creating Data Sources, JMS Resources, and Mail Resources" section of Chapter 7.

- Successfully deploy the credit service detailed in the "Packaging, Deploying, and Testing the Application" section of Chapter 7.

Instead of repeating the work we have done for packaging the EJBs in Chapter 7, we have made the packaged Java Archive (JAR) files for the persistence unit and wine store EJBs available with the source code of this chapter (available from `http://www.apress.com`) so that we can focus on packaging the JSF application and assembling it with the remaining JAR files.

■**Note** We will assume that the source code for this chapter's samples is located in the `z:` drive. Substitute this with the location of the directory into which you have downloaded the source.

Compiling and Packaging the JSF Application

Unlike the chapters in which we provided command-line syntax for executing the individual compilation and packaging steps along with Ant tasks, here we will use a single Ant task, `CreateJSFApplication`, that will compile our JSF application and package it into a WAR file.

From the DOS console, execute the following Ant task:

```
Z:\>%ANT_HOME%/bin/ant CreateJSFWAR
```

Figure 12-13 shows the successful packing of the JSF application.

Figure 12-13. *Compiling and packaging the JSF application*

■**Note** The `build.xml` file is available with the downloadable source code. Make appropriate changes to the `build.properties` file to reflect the settings for the GlassFish application server you have installed.

Assembling the Wine Store Application

Once you have the JSF application packaged as a WAR file, the next step is to assemble the back-end wine store EJB application archives, along with the JSF application, into an EAR file. From the DOS console, execute the following Ant task:

```
Z:\>%ANT_HOME%/bin/ant AssembleWineStoreApplication
```

Figure 12-14 shows the successful assembly of the wine store application.

Figure 12-14. *Assembling the wine store application*

■**Note** The `archive` directory in the downloadable samples comes with the wine store EJBs and persistence unit JAR files.

Deploying the Wine Store Application

Now you can deploy the generated JAR file (`winestore.ear`) to the GlassFish application server. You can deploy the JAR file from GlassFish administration console—but for all practical purposes, you'll want to automate these tasks as much as possible, so you'll use the following command-line tools and Ant task to deploy.

From the DOS console, execute the following command:

```
Z:\archive>%GLASSFISH_HOME%/bin/asadmin.bat deploy --host localhost --port 4848 --➡
user admin --passwordfile %GLASSFISH_HOME%\asadminpass --upload=true -target➡
 server winestore.ear
```

Alternatively, you can use the following Ant task to deploy:

```
Z:\>%ANT_HOME%/bin/ant DeployWineStoreApplication
```

■**Note** If you are running the GlassFish application server on a different machine, replace `localhost` with that machine name in the command-line arguments. Similarly, if you are running on a different port, replace 4848 with the number of the port on which you are running. If you are using the Ant task to deploy, make appropriate changes to the `build.properties` file to reflect the settings for the GlassFish application server you have installed.

Running the Wine Store Application

Now you are ready to run the wine store application with the JSF user interface. Launch the browser, and type in the following URL:

```
http://<hostname>:<port#>/winestoreapp/faces/login.jsp
```

■**Note** Replace `<hostname>` with the name of the host on which your GlassFish application server is running, and `<port#>` with the number of the port that you have configured. In our case, it is `http://localhost:8080/winestoreapp/faces/login.jsp`.

This URL will render the login page as shown in Figure 12-15.

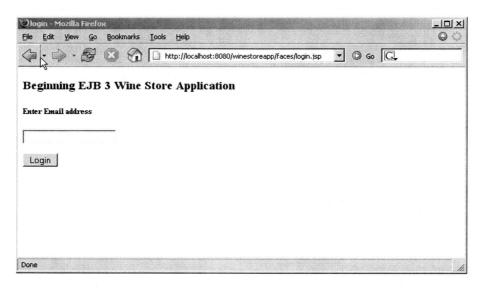

Figure 12-15. *The login page*

Since you haven't registered as a customer yet, click the link on the login page that reads "Register as new user." Figure 12-16 shows the user registration screen. Enter some values into the input fields as shown, and click the Submit button.

On successful registration, you will be routed back to the login page. On the login page, enter the e-mail address you have registered, and click the Login button, as shown in Figure 12-17.

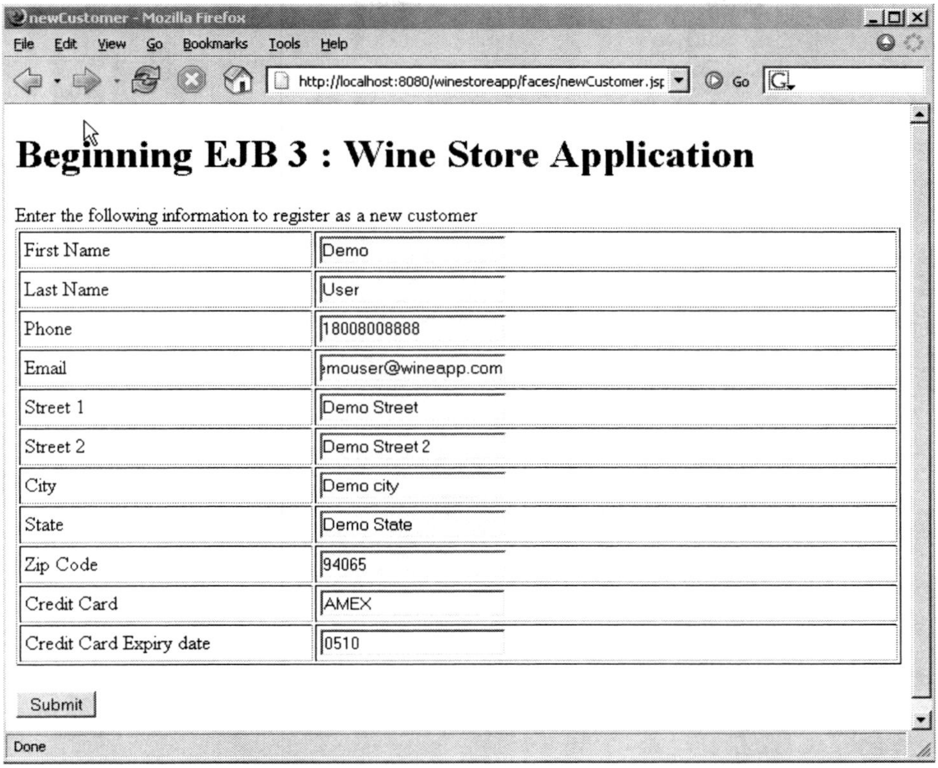

Figure 12-16. *The registration page*

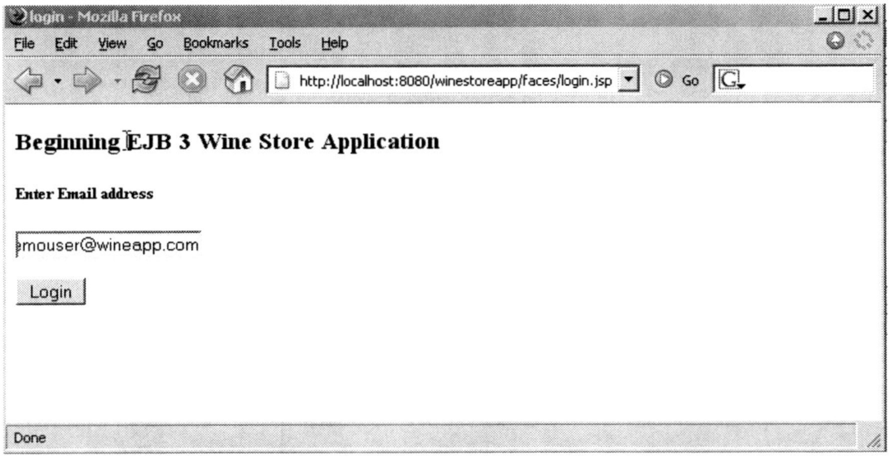

Figure 12-17. *The wine store application login page*

After the e-mail address is validated, you will be routed to the wine store home page, which will show you a list of options (as shown in Figure 12-18).

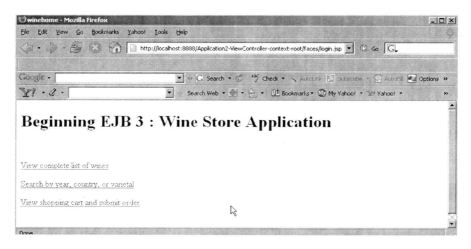

Figure 12-18. *The wine store home page*

To start with, we will walk you through the search use case. Click the link that reads "Search by year, country, or varietal." You will be routed to the search page, as shown in Figure 12-19.

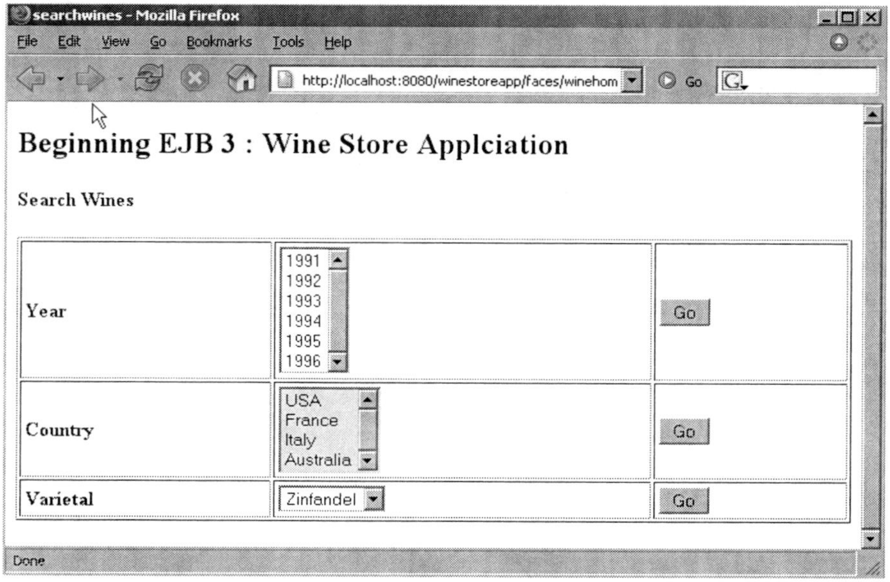

Figure 12-19. *The search page*

Select "Zinfandel" as the varietal, and click the Go button. Figure 12-20 shows the list of wines that satisfy the search criteria.

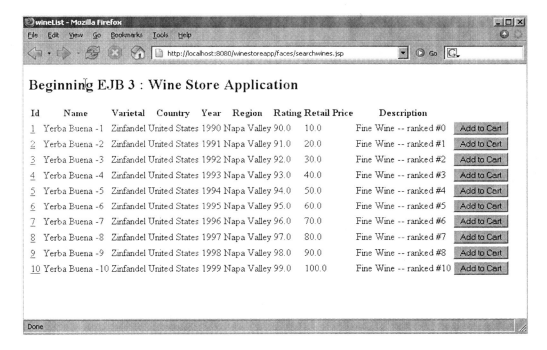

Figure 12-20. *The wine list page*

In the wine list page, click the link in the Id column of the wine that you want to add to the shopping cart. This will bring you to the JSF page, which shows the details of the wines and a text box for entering the quantity, as shown in Figure 12-21.

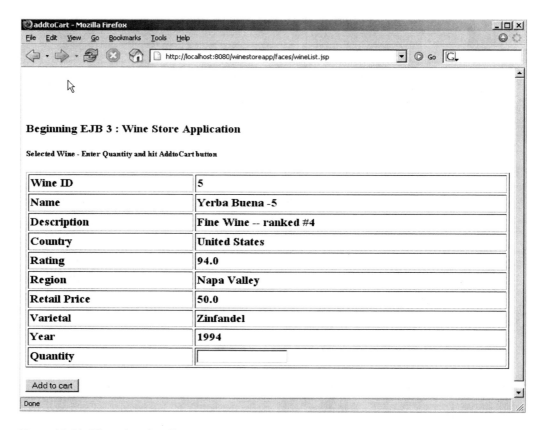

Figure 12-21. *The wine details page*

Enter **10** for the quantity, and click the Add to cart button. You will be routed to the shopping cart page, which shows you all the items in the shopping cart (see Figure 12-22).

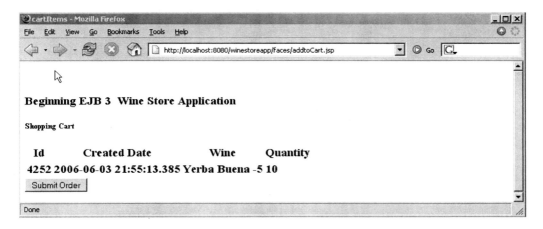

Figure 12-22. *The shopping cart page*

The shopping cart page provides a Submit Order button for submitting the order. Click this button, and the order will be processed on the EJB back-end application. You will then be shown a notification page, as in Figure 12-23.

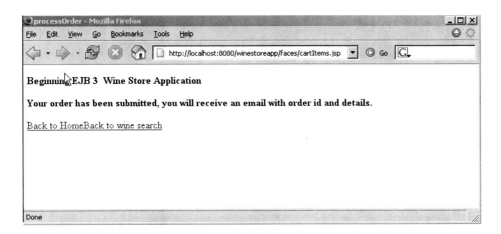

Figure 12-23. *The notification page*

Once the order has been processed, you (the user) will receive an e-mail notification, as shown in Figure 12-24.

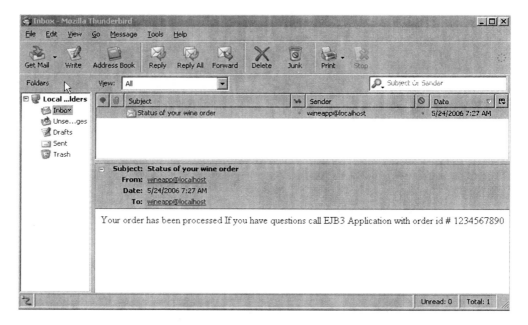

Figure 12-24. *The notification e-mail*

The Application Client Container

We have mentioned and used the application client container in earlier chapters, and we have shown a couple of application architectures in Figures 12-4 and 12-5. Application clients or client programs that are developed using technologies like Java Swing can be run in stand-alone Java SE environments. Application client containers provide additional system services (such as security and deployment) that client programs can make use of during execution.

An application client can leverage authentication services provided by the application client container for authenticating its users. The container's service may be integrated with the native platform's authentication system to provide single sign-on capability to the enterprise users.

Client programs using an application client container can invoke EJBs. Similar to other Java EE components, programs running in a client container can use Java Naming and Directory Interface (JNDI) to look up EJBs or resources like Java Message Service (JMS) and JavaMail. Application client containers provide injection facilities to client programs as well. Since application client containers do not create instances of an application client, static fields and methods should be used for injecting any resources.

Application clients are packaged into JAR files. If an application client container is used to run the client programs, then you will have to bundle or package the application client container along with the application so that you can run it on individual desktop machines.

Conclusion

In this chapter, we introduced different application architectures that you can use to meet different requirements, as well as the programming models that go along with them. We looked at architectures that are useful for web, professional, and desktop applications, and we also looked at web service client applications and business process services that can make use of EJBs published as web services.

We discussed how Java EE–based web technologies have evolved into the latest JSF applications, which has simplified web application development significantly.

We drilled down into JSF architecture, the JSF life cycle, and JSF applications, as well as the current state of tools and UI components for JSF.

Once the stage was set, we built a comprehensive JSF application to communicate with the integrated EJB back-end application developed in Chapter 7. During the development process, we illustrated several programming techniques for sharing the data in the JSF application and looking up and invoking business methods in the back-end application.

We looked at what it takes to package the JSF application and assemble it into a Java EE application that contains persistence units and EJBs.

Finally, we examined the application client container, including the services that it provides to client programs running on desktop machines.

As a follow-up to the performance discussion in Chapter 9, the Appendix will detail the performance tests that we used to compare EJB 2.1 with EJB 3.

APPENDIX

■ ■ ■

Performance: EJB 2 vs. EJB 3

This appendix presents some performance work that was done a few months before the writing of this book. The premise of this work was the idea that since EJB 3 is so powerful and simple, there must be a performance penalty—after all, the simplicity has to come at a price. With this as a motivation, we set out to test the performance of EJB 3 using an early implementation offered by Oracle. This was kind of unfair, since the implementation we used was a developer's preview, for which the focus is typically on product stability instead of performance, so our expectations were that the performance would be below par at best.

The question was how to do a fair comparison using both versions of EJB and still exercise the new features offered in EJB 3. The conclusion was to develop a test application that included the things that developers typically do when using EJB 2.1, and then try the equivalent with EJB 3. This way, we could do a comparative performance study rather than deal with raw numbers that probably don't mean much. We chose to test the Data Transfer Object (DTO) design pattern, the Session Façade design pattern, and container-managed relationship (CMR) functionality of the entity beans.

The application, test harness, and methodology we used are described in the book *J2EE Performance Testing with BEA WebLogic Server,* by Peter Zadrozny (Apress, 2003). The test harness is a simple dispatcher servlet that executes each discrete test case based on the JazzCat application. JazzCat is a catalog of jazz recordings. The database schema includes tables for the bands, musicians, instruments, tracks, and albums. Additionally, the application also handles the notion of recording sessions and takes of a track.

The test environment was based on the Oracle Application Server EJB 3 preview (developer preview 3, June 2005) and the Sun Java HotSpot Client VM (build 1.5.0_03-b07, mixed mode, sharing). The database used was Oracle 10*g* Enterprise Edition, release 10.1.0.2.0. No special tuning was done on any of the software—it was run using the default settings.

The users were simulated using The Grinder 3, Beta 25 (http://grinder.sourceforge.net), with a sample size of 5,000 milliseconds. Each test run lasted 8 minutes, of which we ignored the first 3 minutes to allow the test to stabilize. Each simulated user ran a test script that called the corresponding test case 10 times. The test scripts were executed continuously in a sequential fashion for the duration of the test run. There are two things worth noting: there was a separate HTTP session for each execution of the test scripts, and there was no sleep time between each call to the test case. The latter was done to create a highly stressful situation to better explore the behavior when limits are pushed.

▓Note Chapter 9 provides detailed information on The Grinder and how to set it up.

To get a complete picture of the performance, we used two key indicators: aggregate average response time (AART) to reflect the end-user perspective and total transactional rate (TTR), or throughput, to reflect the load on the systems involved.

The type of computer used was a Dell PowerEdge 2850 with dual Intel Xeon (HT) 3.4 GHz processors, with 4 GB of memory. It used Microsoft Windows Server 2003 Standard Edition as the operating system. A total of three computers were used: one for generating the load with The Grinder, one for running OC4J (Oracle Containers for J2EE), and one for running the database. They were connected on a switched network in which the only traffic present was generated by the tests themselves.

The DTO Design Pattern

Using the JazzCat application to test the DTO design pattern, we created a servlet that lists all the albums in our test database via an entity bean, where each row in the listing shows the field values of the album entity. Since we were in testing mode, we thought that while using EJB 2.1 we would start by testing the case in which this functionality is programmed without using DTO. In this case, which we called DTO Off, our test servlet (shown in Figure A-1) retrieves a list of all the album entities, and then gets the individual field values for each entity via the entity's accessor methods.

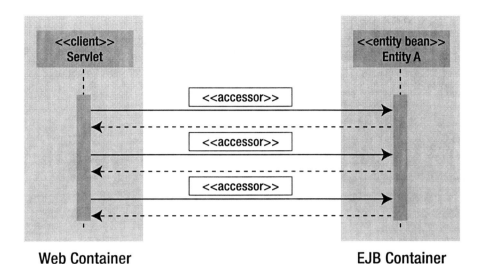

Figure A-1. *EJB 2.1 without DTO*

Using the DTO design pattern, our test servlet, which we called DTO On, makes a single method call (getData()). The entity bean constructs a corresponding DTO, loads it with the entity's field values, and returns the object to the servlet. Now the servlet can access the fields on the local object (as shown in Figure A-2).

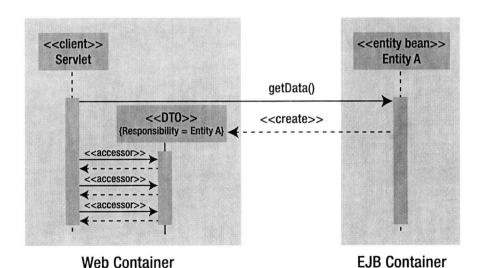

Figure A-2. *EJB 2.1 with DTO*

Note The DTO design pattern is used to encapsulate the data that can be used to send and receive data in a single method call. Typically, the client application requests the data, and the back-end application (which could be an EJB session bean) constructs the transfer object and sends it to the client in a single network trip. More information on the DTO design pattern can be found at `http://java.sun.com/blueprints/corej2eepatterns/Patterns/TransferObject.html`.

With EJB 3, the entity beans are replaced by plain old Java objects (POJOs), and all the traditional CRUD (create, retrieve, update, delete) and query operations are done with the `EntityManager`. The queries can be defined as stand-alone named queries, which are predefined in the bean class, or dynamic queries that can be constructed using the `CreateNamedQuery()` method.

In the JazzCat application, the dispatch servlet of the test harness (shown in Listing A-1) calls the corresponding test servlet, which in turn looks up the `EntityManager` (as shown in Figure A-3). The `EntityManager` then executes the named query that was defined for the `Albums` class.

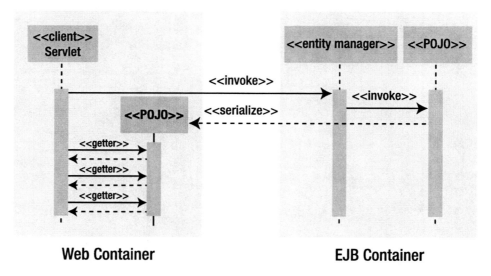

Figure A-3. *An EJB 3 application using the EntityManager*

Listing A-1. *DispatcherServlet.java*

```java
package org.migrate.jazzcat.servlet;
import java.io.*;
import java.util.*;
import javax.servlet.*;
import javax.servlet.http.*;


/**
 * Routes GET requests to JazzCat EJB test drivers
 */
public class DispatcherServlet extends HttpServlet {

    /**
     * Dispatch POST requests to appropriate test script. Test is the
     * servlet name that executes the test (set in request parameter
     * "test").
     */
    public void doPost(HttpServletRequest req,
                       HttpServletResponse res) throws IOException,
                                                       ServletException {

        try {
            res.setContentType("text/html");
            PrintWriter out = res.getWriter();
            String testId = req.getParameter("test_id");
            Test test = null;
            Iterator iter = Test.LIST.iterator();
            while (iter.hasNext()) {
                test = (Test)iter.next();
                if (testId.equals(test.toString())) {
                    req.setAttribute("test", test);
                    break;
                }
            }
```

```
                    // Dispatch to appropriate test servlet
                    RequestDispatcher rd;
                    if (test.toString().startsWith("Dd")) {
                        rd = getServletContext().getNamedDispatcher("DeploymentTest");
                    } else {
                        rd = getServletContext().getNamedDispatcher(test.toString());
                    }
                    out.println("<H1>JazzCat Test Servlet: " + test + "</H1>");
                    out.println("<EM>" + test.LABEL + "</EM>");
                    out.println("<HR>");
                    rd.include(req, res); // print test output "inline"
                    out.println("<HR>");
                    out.println("<A HREF=\"Dispatcher\">Home</A>");
                } catch (Throwable th) {
                    ByteArrayOutputStream buf = new ByteArrayOutputStream();
                    try {
                        PrintWriter ps = new PrintWriter(buf);
                        th.printStackTrace(ps);
                        ps.flush();
                    } catch (Exception e) {
                    }
                }
            }
        }


        /**
         * Show menu of available tests
         */
        public void doGet(HttpServletRequest req,
                          HttpServletResponse res) throws IOException,
                                                          ServletException {
            try {
                res.setContentType("text/html");
                PrintWriter out = res.getWriter();
                out.println("<HTML><HEAD><TITLE>" +
                            "JazzCat Test Dispatcher</TITLE></HEAD><BODY>");

                out.println("<H1>JazzCat Test Dispatcher</H1>");
                out.println("<HR>");
                // Show menu of tests
```

```
                out.println("<FORM ACTION=\"Redirector\" METHOD=\"POST\" " +
                        "ENCTYPE=\"application/x-www-form-urlencoded\">");
            out.println("Select a test:<BR>");
            out.println("<SELECT NAME=\"test_id\" SIZE=\"7\" >");
            Iterator iter = Test.LIST.iterator();
            for (int i = 1; iter.hasNext(); i++) {
                if (i == 1) {
                    out.println("<OPTION SELECTED ");
                } else {
                    out.println("<OPTION ");
                }
                Test t = (Test)iter.next();
                out.println("VALUE=\"" + t + "\">" + i + ") " + t.LABEL +
                        "</OPTION>");
            }
            out.println("</SELECT><BR>");
            // Input box for tests that do title searches
            out.println("Search for:<BR><INPUT TYPE=\"TEXT\" NAME=\➡
"search_string\" " +"SIZE=\"20\" MAXLENGTH=\"256\">");
            // Input boxes for Deployment tests (all add new Musicians)
            out.println("<HR>");
            out.println("<INPUT TYPE=\"CHECKBOX\" CHECKED NAME=\"query\" " +
                    "VALUE=\"true\">");
            out.println("Add <I>and</I> query for musicians with same " +
                    "primary instrument");
            out.println("<HR>");
            out.println("<INPUT TYPE=\"SUBMIT\" NAME=\"Search\" VALUE=\"Run\">");
            out.println("<INPUT TYPE=\"RESET\">");
            out.println("</FORM>");
        } catch (Throwable th) {
            ByteArrayOutputStream buf = new ByteArrayOutputStream();
            try {
                PrintWriter ps = new PrintWriter(buf);
                th.printStackTrace(ps);
                ps.flush();
            } catch (Exception e) {
            }
        }
    }
}
```

The definition of this class and the named query that returns the albums are shown in Listing A-2.

Listing A-2. *Albums.java*

```
package org.migrate.entity;
import java.io.Serializable;
import java.util.List;
import javax.persistence.Column;
import javax.persistence.Entity;
import javax.persistence.Id;
import javax.persistence.JoinColumn;
import javax.persistence.ManyToOne;
import javax.persistence.OneToMany;
import javax.persistence.Table;
import javax.persistence.NamedQuery;

@Entity
@Table(name = "ALBUMS")
@NamedQuery(name = "findAll", queryString = "Select object(a) from Albums a")
public class Albums implements Serializable {
    public Albums() {
    }

    @Column(name = "CAT_NO", nullable = false)
    public String getCatNo() {
        return catNo;
    }

    public void setCatNo(String catNo) {
        this.catNo = catNo;
    }

    private String catNo;
    private Long id;
    private String label;
    private String media;
    private Long rating;
    private String title;
    private List<Tracks> tracksList;
```

```java
private Musicians musicians;

@Id
@Column(name = "ID", primaryKey = true, nullable = false)
public Long getId() {
    return id;
}

protected void setId(Long id) {
    this.id = id;
}

@Column(name = "LABEL", nullable = false)
public String getLabel() {
    return label;
}

public void setLabel(String label) {
    this.label = label;
}

@Column(name = "MEDIA", nullable = false)
public String getMedia() {
    return media;
}

public void setMedia(String media) {
    this.media = media;
}


@Column(name = "RATING", nullable = false)
public Long getRating() {
    return rating;
}

public void setRating(Long rating) {
    this.rating = rating;
}
```

```java
@Column(name = "TITLE", nullable = false)
public String getTitle() {
    return title;
}

public void setTitle(String title) {
    this.title = title;
}

public Albums(String catNo, Long id, String label, String media,
              Long rating, String title) {
    this.catNo = catNo;
    this.id = id;
    this.label = label;
    this.media = media;
    this.rating = rating;
    this.title = title;
}

@OneToMany(targetEntity = "org.migrate.entity.Tracks")
@JoinColumn(name = "TRACKS.ALBUM_ID", referencedColumnName = "ALBUMS.ID")
public List<Tracks> getTracksList() {
    return tracksList;
}

public void setTracksList(List<Tracks> tracksList) {
    this.tracksList = tracksList;
}

public Tracks addToTracksList(Tracks tracks) {
    getTracksList().add(tracks);
    tracks.setAlbums(this);
    return tracks;
}

public Tracks removeFromTracksList(Tracks tracks) {
    getTracksList().remove(tracks);
    tracks.setAlbums(null);
    return tracks;
}
```

```
@ManyToOne(targetEntity = "org.migrate.entity.Musicians")
@JoinColumn(name = "ALBUMS.MUS_ID", referencedColumnName = "MUSICIANS.ID")
public Musicians getMusicians() {
    return musicians;
}

public void setMusicians(Musicians musicians) {
    this.musicians = musicians;
}
}
```

Once the named query returns the list of all the albums, it is printed out as an HTML table using the getter methods of the Albums POJO.

The tests were run with 15, 25, 50, 100, 150, 200, and 250 simultaneous users. In both cases, we found that the differences in response time and throughput between EJB 2.1 using DTO and EJB 3 were within 4 percent, which is within the margin of error of 5 percent. So, for all practical purposes, the performance is similar. To give you an idea of the actual performance, with 250 simultaneous users, the AART was 1,100 milliseconds, and the throughput was an average 225 requests per second. That was quite impressive—more so considering that there is no sleep time in the test scripts.

The DTO Off test case produced an AART that was 28 percent higher than DTO On using EJB 3, and a TTR that was 19 percent lower. The reason for this is that each call to an accessor method on the entity bean is a transaction by itself, whereas there is only one transaction when DTO and EJB 3 are used. So, remember to demarcate your transactions correctly to obtain better performance.

It is interesting to note the throughput curves for each case in Figure A-4. Remember that the TTR, or throughput, is a measure of the capacity of the system as a whole (application, Java Virtual Machine [JVM], database, OS, and hardware). In this particular chart, you can see that in all cases the saturation point is reached at 100 users; however, in the DTO Off case, things go downhill quite faster than in the others. EJB 3 and DTO On hold longer before going down. Interestingly enough, EJB 3 holds a little longer by presenting 12-percent-better throughput than DTO On with 250 users. This happens similarly with the response time, for which EJB 3 does 13-percent better than DTO On with 250 users. So, under heavy loads, EJB 3 tends to perform better than EJB 2.1—at least for this particular test case.

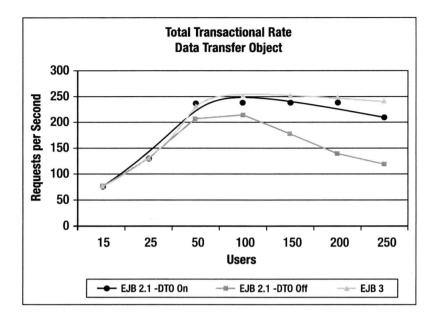

Figure A-4. *DTO TTR*

The Session Façade Design Pattern

To test this design pattern, we searched the JazzCat catalog for albums containing a particular song title or substring of it. This was an interesting case, as we had to call a few entities to provide this listing: Album (the thing we are searching for), Take (which holds the song title), Track (which identifies occurrences of Takes on Albums), and Musician (which identifies the artist name for an Album).

Note The Session Façade pattern provides a coarse-grained access layer to the client applications. The client applications make calls to methods in the façade that coordinate a set of tasks with one or more objects, and send the response back to the client applications. This results in fewer network trips from the client, and also shields the client from changes that happen in the domain model. More information about the Session Façade design pattern can be found at http://java.sun.com/blueprints/ corej2eepatterns/Patterns/SessionFacade.html.

Using EJB 2.1, this is straightforward. The dispatcher servlet of the test harness calls the FacadeOn servlet, which in turn calls the stateless session bean that acts as the façade and calls all the necessary entities to obtain the required information. This is later sent back to the FacadeOn servlet in the form of a data transfer hash map and presented to the user.

With EJB 3, things are pretty much the same until the point at which the entity beans are called. Instead, we call the EntityManager and, using named queries, we load the information from the POJOs into the data transfer hash map. The main difference is that with EJB 2.1, we look up the entity beans using ejb-local-refs and then work on these entity beans to get the required information. Listing A-3 shows the session façade used in the EJB 3 application.

Listing A-3. *SearchFacadeBean.java*

```java
package org.migrate.session;
import java.util.ArrayList;
import java.util.Collection;
import java.util.HashMap;
import java.util.Iterator;
import javax.ejb.Inject;
import javax.ejb.Stateless;
import javax.persistence.EntityManager;
import org.migrate.entity.Albums;
import org.migrate.entity.Musicians;
import org.migrate.entity.Takes;
import org.migrate.entity.Tracks;

@Stateless(name = "SearchFacade")
public class SearchFacadeBean implements SearchFacadeLocal {
    public SearchFacadeBean() {
    }

    private EntityManager _entityManager;

    public EntityManager getEntityManager() {
        return _entityManager;
    }

    @Inject
    public void setEntityManager(EntityManager entityManager) {
        _entityManager = entityManager;
    }
```

```
    public Collection forTuneUsingLocal(String title) {
        Takes take;
        Tracks track;
        Albums album;
        Musicians musician;
        ArrayList trackList = new ArrayList();
        HashMap trackInfo;

        try {
            Iterator takeIterator = ➡
                this.getEntityManager().createNamedQuery("findByTitle")➡
.setParameter("title",title).getResultList().iterator();
            if (!takeIterator.hasNext()) {
                return trackList;
            }
            while (takeIterator.hasNext()) {
                take = (Takes)takeIterator.next();

                // Find album on which track appears
                Long tid = take.getId();
                Iterator trackIterator =➡
                    this.getEntityManager().createNamedQuery("findByTakeId")➡
.setParameter(0, tid).getResultList().iterator();
                if (!trackIterator.hasNext()) {
                    throw new Exception("trackIterator has no elements for takeId ➡
" +take.getId() + "!");
                }
                while (trackIterator.hasNext()) {
                    trackInfo = new HashMap();
                    track = (Tracks)trackIterator.next();
                    album = track.getAlbums();
                    musician = album.getMusicians();
                    trackInfo.put("lname", musician.getLname());
                    trackInfo.put("fname", musician.getFname());
                    trackInfo.put("atitle", album.getTitle());
                    trackInfo.put("label", album.getLabel());
                    trackInfo.put("catno", album.getCatNo());
                    trackInfo.put("media", album.getMedia());
                    trackInfo.put("seq", track.getTrackSeq());
                    trackInfo.put("ttitle", take.getTitle());
                    trackInfo.put("length", track.getRecTime());
                    trackList.add(trackInfo);
```

```
            } // next track
          } // next take
          return trackList;
      } catch (Exception e) {
          e.printStackTrace();
      }
      return trackList;
  }
}
```

■Note The EJB 3 application we developed used an early draft version of the EJB 3 specification. You will see differences in annotations used in the bean class.

The tests were conducted with 15, 25, 50, 75, and 100 simultaneous users. The test script did ten different searches, starting with the letter *a* and ending with the letter *j*. To our surprise, we found that EJB 3 had roughly double the performance than EJB 2.1. Take a look at the response time in Figure A-5. Notice that as the load increases, the difference in response time increases dramatically, from 18 percent for 15 users up to 58 percent for 100 users, giving an overall average of 46 percent.

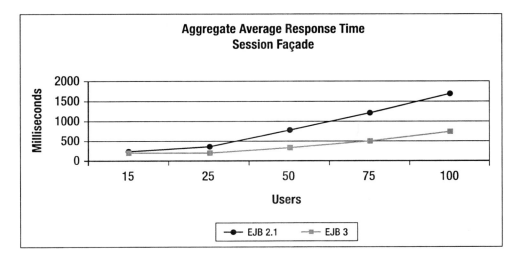

Figure A-5. *AART for the Session Façade pattern*

Even more interesting is the TTR chart in Figure A-6, which clearly shows the throughput for the EJB 2.1 Session Façade pattern more or less stable for all user loads, but going down very slowly at 25 users. In the case of EJB 3, there is a clear peak at 50 users and then a slow descent. However, the average throughput of EJB 3 is roughly double that of EJB 2.1.

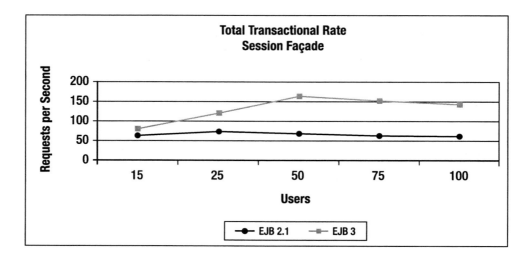

Figure A-6. *TTR for the Session Façade pattern*

Just to provide some numbers, with 100 users, the AART of EJB 3 is 716 milliseconds and the throughput is 140 requests per second. This wonderful performance of EJB 3 for such a popular design pattern is a welcome surprise, which only attracts us even more to EJB 3.

Container-Managed Relationships

Although entity beans in general and CMRs in particular have bad reputations, there are various EJB containers that actually have high-performance implementations. Because of this, our expectations were that the results of the performance comparison would be basically the same.

This test case is based on a search that exercises the relationships between the tables of the JazzCat application. Given a song title to search for (or substring of it), the test servlet displays a list of takes matching the title, along with the band members playing on each particular take of that title. Among the many relationships and navigations that exist in this application and this particular search, there are a couple that we can point out: there is a one-to-many relationship between Takes and Bands (a take has many band members), and there is a many-to-one relationship between Bands and Musicians (several different bands can have the same musician as a member).

Compared to programming this search using bean-managed persistence entity beans, using container-managed persistence is easy. However, we still have to deal with the deployment descriptor, for which we have to declare all the relationships of each entity.

In contrast, using the annotations of EJB 3, we can quickly and easily define the relationships (for example, the one between Takes and Bands, as shown in Listing A-4).

Listing A-4. *Takes.java*

```java
package org.migrate.entity;
import java.io.Serializable;
import java.util.List;
import javax.persistence.Column;
import javax.persistence.Entity;
import javax.persistence.Id;
import javax.persistence.JoinColumn;
import javax.persistence.ManyToOne;
import javax.persistence.OneToMany;
import javax.persistence.Table;
import javax.persistence.NamedQuery;

@Entity
@Table(name = "TAKES")
@NamedQuery(name = "findByTitle",queryString = "Select object ➥
 (t) from Takes t where t.title LIKE :title")
public class Takes implements Serializable {
    public Takes() {
    }

    @Id
    @Column(name = "ID", primaryKey = true, nullable = false)
    public Long getId() {
        return id;
    }
}
```

```java
    protected void setId(Long id) {
        this.id = id;
    }

    private Long id;
    private String title;
    private Sessions sessions;
    private List<Bands> bandsList;
    @Column(name = "TITLE", nullable = false)
    public String getTitle() {
        return title;
    }

    public void setTitle(String title) {
        this.title = title;
    }

    public Takes(Long id, Sessions sessions, String title) {
        this.id = id;
        this.sessions = sessions;
        this.title = title;
    }

    @ManyToOne(targetEntity = "org.migrate.entity.Sessions")
    @JoinColumn(name = "TAKES.SESSION_ID",
                referencedColumnName = "SESSIONS.ID")
    public Sessions getSessions() {
        return sessions;
    }

    public void setSessions(Sessions sessions) {
        this.sessions = sessions;
    }

    @OneToMany(targetEntity = "org.migrate.entity.Bands")
    @JoinColumn(name = "BANDS.TAKE_ID", referencedColumnName = "TAKES.ID")
    public List<Bands> getBandsList() {
        return bandsList;
    }
```

```
    public void setBandsList(List<Bands> bandsList) {
        this.bandsList = bandsList;
    }

    public Bands addToBandsList(Bands bands) {
        getBandsList().add(bands);
        bands.setTakes(this);
        return bands;
    }

    public Bands removeFromBandsList(Bands bands) {
        getBandsList().remove(bands);
        bands.setTakes(null);
        return bands;
    }
}
```

The EJB 3 test code is very similar to that of EJB 2.1 until the point at which the session façade bean calls the EntityManager. Using the EntityManager, we navigate through the POJO relationships using getter methods, and assemble the information for the test servlet to present to the user.

The test scripts for this test case were basically the same as those used for the Session Façade test case: ten searches, starting with the letter *a* and ending with the letter *j*. The user load started with 5, and we increased it to 15, 25, 50, 75, and 100 users. The reason we had to add the case of 5 users was that the throughput of EJB 2.1 peaked at 15 users.

The results again were pleasantly surprising, as the performance of EJB 3 was roughly double that of EJB 2.1. The chart for the response time looks very similar to that of the Session Façade test case. The difference started with 20 percent for 5 users, and pretty much jumped to 55 percent for the rest of the user load.

The results from the TTR standpoint are shown in Figure A-7. As shown, the throughput starts with a 25 percent difference and quickly grows to 140 percent, presenting an average of 111-percent-better throughput.

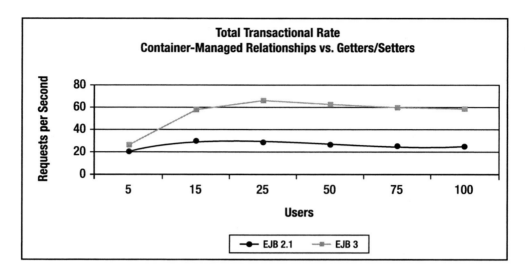

Figure A-7. *CMRs vs. getters/setters TTR*

Conclusion

Considering that we used only a developer's preview of EJB 3, we're very impressed with this specification—at least Oracle's implementation of it. As mentioned previously, we're very attracted to the simplicity and power of EJB 3. The wonderful work done with annotations and persistence, the ability to use POJOs, and the ability to test outside of the container are very attractive all by themselves. But now, with an implementation that equals or doubles the performance of EJB 2.1 (at least for our test cases), we are very confident that applications developed with EJB 3 will be considerably easier to maintain.

If you are interested in doing your own test cases using the JazzCat application, test harness, and methodology that we used, you can download a package that contains everything you need from http://www.jroller.com/resources/r/raghukodali/jazzcat.jar.

Index

Printed in the United States
132274LV00007B/12/P

9 781590 596715